Praise for
Corporate Governance Matters

"No board of directors ought to be without Larcker and Tayan's *Corporate Governance Matters*. In today's increasingly regulated environment, this comprehensive book is not only an important reference manual, but also an interesting read and a valuable roadmap."

—**Joel Peterson**, Chairman, JetBlue Airways,
and former Lead Director, Franklin Covey

"An outstanding work of unique breadth and depth providing practical advice supported by detailed research. This should be required reading for all board members and everyone who serves as an advisor to boards."

—**Alan Crain, Jr.**, Senior Vice President and General Counsel,
Baker Hughes Incorporated

"*Corporate Governance Matters* is by far and away the most useful, fact-based book on corporate governance available. It is essential reading for all current and prospective board members, anyone interested in how boards work, and for students of corporate governance. Its chapters on executive and equity pay, in particular, shine a bright light on a topic too often discussed without substance and context."

—**Mark H. Edwards**, Chairman and CEO, Compensia

"The complexity of corporate governance often lies in its propensity to become highly subjective. David and Brian's objective and unbiased approach to this important subject is very refreshing. This book reflects the meticulous and thorough manner in which the authors have approached corporate governance systems. They have an eye for detail and present every statement and observation with a firm factual foundation. Extensively researched, with highly relevant insights, this book serves as an ideal and practical reference for corporate executives and students of business administration."

—**Narayana N.R. Murthy**, Infosys Technologies Limited

"*Corporate Governance Matters* should be on the reading list for any public or private company director. The authors present comprehensive coverage of current topics using both research and real-world examples to drive home the issues and uncover the best practices. I found their survey of foreign practices and cultural differences to be particularly fascinating and helpful as I work with one of my companies on an offshore partnership. Fascinating, engaging, and full of useful information—a must-read!"

—**Heidi Roizen**, Founder, CEO and Chief Lyrical Officer, Skinny Songs

"David Larcker and Brian Tayan are the premier students and among the most thoughtful authorities on corporate governance. They have written extensively on the subject with keen insight into the problems and possible solutions, and this book is the culmination of those efforts. It should be read by anyone interested in how corporations can be better governed."

—**Arthur Rock**, Principal of Arthur Rock & Co., former Chairman Intel and former Board Member Apple

"Corporate Governance Matters is a comprehensive, objective, and insightful analysis of academic and professional research on corporate governance. In contrast to legal treatments, these authors take an organizational perspective and present a fact-based, business-oriented, and long overdue reconsideration of how certain corporate governance features actually function."

—**Professor Katherine Schipper**, Thomas Keller Professor of Business Administration, Duke University, and former member of the Financial Accounting Standards Board

"They did it! Larcker and Tayan have cracked the code on the connections between corporate governance and corporate performance. Debunking lots of myths along the way, they give practical advice on what works and what doesn't. Their chapters on board composition and executive pay capture the challenge to directors to manage corporations in the best interests of shareholders. This is a must-read for anyone who is interested in improving the performance of corporations."

—**Ira Kay**, Managing Partner, Pay Governance

"When it comes to corporate governance, it seems that everyone has an opinion. David Larcker and Brian Tayan, however, have the facts. This refreshing, hard-headed review describes what we do and don't know about corporate governance. It lays bare assumptions about governance that simply aren't correct and is destined to become a central reference for anyone interested in how corporate America governs itself."

—**Professor Joseph A. Grundfest**, The William A. Franke Professor of Law and Business, Senior Faculty, Rock Center on Corporate Governance, Stanford Law School

Corporate Governance Matters

Corporate Governance Matters

A Closer Look at Organizational Choices and Their Consequences

David Larcker
Brian Tayan

Vice President, Publisher: Tim Moore
Associate Publisher and Director of Marketing: Amy Neidlinger
Executive Editor: Jeanne Glasser
Editorial Assistant: Pamela Boland
Operations Manager: Gina Kanouse
Senior Marketing Manager: Julie Phifer
Publicity Manager: Laura Czaja
Assistant Marketing Manager: Megan Colvin
Cover Designer: Chuti Prasertsith
Managing Editor: Kristy Hart
Senior Project Editor: Lori Lyons
Copy Editor: Krista Hansing Editorial Services, Inc.
Proofreader: Language Logistics, LLC
Indexer: Angie Martin
Senior Compositor: Gloria Schurick
Manufacturing Buyer: Dan Uhrig

© 2011 by Pearson Education, Inc.
Publishing as FT Press
Upper Saddle River, New Jersey 07458

FT Press offers excellent discounts on this book when ordered in quantity for bulk purchases or special sales. For more information, please contact U.S. Corporate and Government Sales, 1-800-382-3419, corpsales@pearsontechgroup.com. For sales outside the U.S., please contact International Sales at international@pearson.com.

Company and product names mentioned herein are the trademarks or registered trademarks of their respective owners.

Printed in the United States of America

Second Printing September 2011

ISBN-10: 0-13-218026-X
ISBN-13: 978-0-13-218026-9

Pearson Education LTD.
Pearson Education Australia PTY, Limited.
Pearson Education Singapore, Pte. Ltd.
Pearson Education Asia, Ltd.
Pearson Education Canada, Ltd.
Pearson Educatio[ac]n de Mexico, S.A. de C.V.
Pearson Education—Japan
Pearson Education Malaysia, Pte. Ltd.

Library of Congress Cataloging-in-Publication Data

Larcker, David F.
  Corporate governance matters : a closer look at organizational choices and their consequences / David F. Larcker, Brian Tayan.
      p. cm.
  ISBN 978-0-13-218026-9 (hardback : alk. paper)
  1. Corporate governance. I. Tayan, Brian, 1975- II. Title.
  HD2741.L3153 2012
  658.4—dc22
                              2011002152

To Sally, Sarah, and Daniel,
Jack, Louise, and Brad

Contents

Acknowledgments

First and foremost, we would like to thank Michelle E. Gutman of the Stanford Graduate School of Business, without whom this book would not have been possible. Michelle provided incredible support throughout this project and was instrumental at each step of the way, from concept and outline, to research, editing, and production. Her incredible work ethic and positive attitude are a model that researchers should strive to emulate, and our work and lives have been greatly enhanced because of her.

We would also like to thank the many experts who provided insight, commentary, and feedback to this work. In particular, we would like to thank Michael Klausner (Stanford Law School), who was invaluable in clarifying legal constructs—particularly those described in Chapter 3, "Board of Directors: Duties and Liability," and Chapter 11, "The Market for Corporate Control." Priya Cherian Huskins (Woodruff-Sawyer & Co) was similarly invaluable in clarifying indemnifications and D&O insurance. Stephen Miles and Thomas Friel (Heidrick & Struggles), H. Ross Brown (Egon Zehnder), and David Lord (Executive Search Information Services) provided real-world insight into CEO succession planning, the executive recruitment process, and the labor market for directors. Alan Jagolinzer (University of Colorado), Brendan Sheehan (Cross Border USA), and Lois Cartwright (Merrill Lynch) assisted in our understanding of executive hedging and pledging and the behavioral implications of executive equity ownership. Jack Zwingli (GovernanceMetrics International) explained professional models to detect financial manipulation through the combination of accounting and corporate governance data. Abe Friedman (BlackRock) helped us understand proxy voting from an institutional investor perspective.

The factual depth of this book would not have been possible without the generous resources made available to us by Stanford University. We would like to extend a special thank you to Arthur and Toni Rembi Rock for their generous funding of governance research through the Rock Center for Corporate Governance at Stanford University. We have been greatly enriched through the collaboration this center has allowed, particularly with our colleagues Robert Daines, Joseph Grundfest, Daniel Siciliano, and Evan Epstein. Thank you also to Dean Garth Saloner of the Stanford Graduate School of Business for his support of the Corporate Governance Research Program. We would also like to thank David Chun (Equilar) and Thomas Quinn (FactSet TrueCourse) for providing some of the data used in the book.

We are grateful to Christopher Armstrong, Maria Correia, Ian Gow, Allan McCall, Gaizka Ormazabal, Daniel Taylor, and Anastasia Zakolyukina for their excellent assistance and thoughtful conversations about corporate governance. They also tolerated the idiosyncrasies of the lead author, for which he is particularly thankful.

Thank you to Sally Larcker for her rigorous and methodical editing of this work as we approached publication, and to Jeannine Williams for her diligent assistance throughout this project.

Finally, we are grateful to the high-quality support provided by Jeanne Glasser, Lori Lyons, Krista Hansing, and others at Pearson. We would like to thank Stephen Kobrin for encouraging us to write this book.

About the Authors

David Larcker is James Irvin Miller Professor of Accounting at the Graduate School of Business of Stanford University; Director of the Corporate Governance Research Program; Senior Faculty, Arthur and Toni Rembe Rock Center for Corporate Governance. David's research focuses on executive compensation, corporate governance, and managerial accounting. He has published many research papers and is frequently quoted in both the popular and business press.

He received his BS and MS in engineering from the University of Missouri-Rolla and his PhD in business from the University of Kansas. He previously was on the faculty of the Kellogg Graduate School of Management at Northwestern University and The Wharton School at the University of Pennsylvania. Professor Larcker presently serves on the Board of Trustees for the Wells Fargo Advantage Funds.

Brian Tayan is a member of the Corporate Governance Research Program at the Stanford Graduate School of Business. He has written broadly on the subject of corporate governance, including case studies and other materials on boards of directors, succession planning, executive compensation, financial accounting, and shareholder relations.

Previously, Brian worked as a financial analyst at Stanford University's Office of the CEO and as an investment associate at UBS Private Wealth Management. He received his MBA from the Stanford Graduate School of Business and his BA from Princeton University.

Additional resources and supporting material for this book are available at:

> Stanford Graduate School of Business
> The Corporate Governance Research Program
> www.gsb.stanford.edu/cgrp/

Preface

This is a book about corporate governance, written from an organizational perspective. It is intended for practitioners and aspiring practitioners who are interested in improving governance systems in their organizations. Unlike many books on governance, this book is *not* written primarily from a legal perspective. Although we describe the legal obligations of selected organizational participants, our objective is not to rehash legal constructs. Books written by trained lawyers are much better for that purpose, and many fine works explain these obligations for the practitioner. Instead, our purpose is to examine the choices that organizations can make in designing governance systems and the impact those choices have on executive decision-making and the organization's performance. This book is therefore relevant to corporate directors, executives, institutional investors, lawyers, and regulators who make organizational decisions.

Corporate governance is a topic that suffers from considerable rhetoric. In writing this book, we have attempted to correct many misconceptions. Rather than write a book that is based on opinion, we use the knowledge contained in the extensive body of professional and scholarly research to guide our discussion and justify our conclusions. This approach does not always lead to simple recommendations, but it has the advantage of being grounded in factual evidence. As you will see, not every governance question has been the subject of rigorous empirical study, nor is every question amenable to a simple solution. There are gaps in our knowledge that will need to be addressed by further study. Still, we hope this book provides a framework that enables practitioners to make sound decisions that are well supported by careful research.

In each chapter, we focus on a particular governance feature, describe its potential benefits and costs, review the research evidence, and then draw conclusions. Although the book is written so that it can be read from cover to cover, each chapter also stands on its own; readers can select the chapters that are most relevant to their interests, (strategic oversight and risk management, CEO succession planning, executive compensation, and so on). This book—along with our set of associated case studies and teaching materials—is also suitable for undergraduate and graduate university courses and executive education programs.

We believe it is important for organizations to take a deliberate approach in designing governance systems. We believe this book provides the information that allows them to do so.

1

Introduction to Corporate Governance

Corporate governance has become a well-discussed and controversial topic in both the popular and business press. Newspapers produce detailed accounts of corporate fraud, accounting scandals, insider trading, excessive compensation, and other perceived organizational failures—many of which culminate in lawsuits, resignations, and bankruptcy. The stories have run the gamut from the shocking and instructive (epitomized by Enron and the elaborate use of special-purpose entities and aggressive accounting to distort its financial condition) to the shocking and outrageous (epitomized by Tyco partially funding a $2.1 million birthday party in 2002 for the wife of Chief Executive Officer [CEO] Dennis Kozlowski that included a vodka-dispensing replica of the statue *David*). Central to these stories is the assumption that somehow *corporate governance* is to blame—that is, the system of checks and balances meant to prevent abuse by executives failed (see the following sidebar).[1]

A Breakdown in Corporate Governance: HealthSouth

Consider HealthSouth Corp., the once high-flying healthcare service provider based in Birmingham, Alabama.[2]

- CEO Richard Scrushy and other corporate officers were accused of overstating earnings by at least $1.4 billion between 1999 and 2002 to meet analyst expectations.[3]

- The CEO was paid a salary of $4.0 million, awarded a cash bonus of $6.5 million, and granted 1.2 million stock options during fiscal 2001, the year before the manipulation was uncovered.[4]

- The CEO sold back 2.5 million shares to the company—94 percent of his total holdings—just weeks before the firm revealed that regulatory changes would significantly hurt earnings, causing the company's share price to plummet.[5]

- Former Chief Financial Officer (CFO) Weston L. Smith and other senior executives pleaded guilty to a scheme to artificially inflate financial results.[6]

- The CEO was found guilty of civil charges brought by shareholders in a derivative lawsuit and ordered to pay the company $2.88 billion in restitution.[7]

What was the board of directors doing during this period?

- The compensation committee met only *once* during 2001.[8]

- *Forbes* wrote that the CEO has "provided subpar returns to shareholders while earning huge sums for [himself]. Still, the board doesn't toss [him] out."[9]

What was the external auditor (Ernst & Young) doing?

- The audit committee met only *once* during 2001.[10]

- The president and CFO both previously were employed as auditors for Ernst & Young.

- The company paid Ernst & Young $2.5 million in consulting and other fees while also paying $1.2 million for auditing services.[11]

What were the analysts doing?

- A UBS analyst had a "strong buy" recommendation on HealthSouth.

- UBS earned $7 million in investment banking fees for services provided to the company.[12]

Perhaps not surprisingly, the CEO also received backdated stock options during his tenure—stock options whose grant dates were retroactively changed to coincide with low points in the company's stock price (see Figure 1.1).

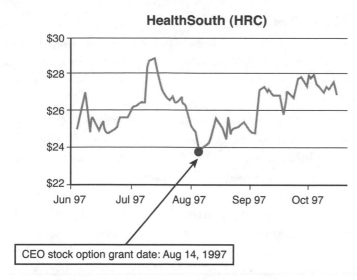

Source: Chart prepared by David F. Larcker and Brian Tayan (2010).

Figure 1.1   HealthSouth: CEO stock option grant date.

Interestingly, Scrushy was not convicted of accounting manipulations in a criminal trial brought by the U.S. Justice Department. However, he was ordered to pay $2.9 billion in a civil suit and, separately, was sentenced to seven years in prison for bribing a former Alabama governor.

As the case of HealthSouth illustrates, the system of checks and balances meant to prevent abuse by senior executives does not always function properly. Unfortunately, governance failures are not isolated instances. In recent years, several corporations have collapsed in prominent fashion, including American International Group, Adelphia, Bear Stearns, Enron, Global Crossing, Lehman Brothers, Tyco, and WorldCom. This list does not even include the dozens of lesser-known companies that did not make the front page of the *Wall Street Journal* or *Financial Times,* but whose owners also suffered. Furthermore, this problem is not limited to U.S. corporations. Major international companies such as Ahold, Parmalat, Royal Dutch/Shell, Satyam, and Siemens were all plagued by scandal that involved a breakdown of management oversight. Foreign companies listed on U.S. exchanges are as likely to restate their financial results as domestic companies, indicating that governance is a global issue.

Self-Interested Executives

What is the root cause of these failures? Reports suggest that these companies suffered from a "breakdown in corporate governance." What does that mean? What is corporate governance, and what is it expected to prevent?

In theory, the need for corporate governance rests on the idea that when separation exists between the ownership of a company and its management, self-interested executives have the opportunity to take actions that benefit themselves, with shareholders and stakeholders bearing the cost of these actions.[13] This scenario is typically referred to as the **agency problem**, with the costs resulting from this problem described as **agency costs**. Executives make investment, financing, and operating decisions that better themselves at the expense of other parties related to the firm.[14] To lessen agency costs, some type of control or monitoring system is put in place in the organization. That system of checks and balances is called **corporate governance**.

Behavioral psychology and other social sciences have provided evidence that individuals are self-interested. In *The Economic Approach to Human Behavior,* Gary Becker (1976) applies a theory of "rational self-interest" to economics to explain human tendencies, including one to commit crime or fraud.[15] He demonstrates that, in a wide variety of settings, individuals can take actions to benefit themselves without detection and, therefore, avoid the cost of punishment. Control mechanisms are put in place in society to deter such behavior by increasing the probability of detection and shifting the risk–reward balance so that the expected payoff from crime is decreased.

Before we rely on this theory too heavily, it is important to highlight that individuals are not always uniformly and completely self-interested. Many people exhibit self-restraint on moral grounds that have little to do with economic rewards. Not all employees who are unobserved in front of an open cash box will steal from it, and not all executives knowingly make decisions that better themselves at the expense of shareholders. This is known as **moral salience**, the knowledge that certain actions are inherently wrong even if they are undetected and left unpunished. Individuals exhibit varying degrees of moral salience, depending on their personality, religious convictions, and personal and financial circumstances. Moral salience also depends on the company involved, the country of business, and the cultural norms.[16]

The need for a governance control mechanism to discourage costly, self-interested behavior therefore depends on the size of the potential agency costs, the ability of the control mechanism to mitigate agency costs, and the cost of implementing the control mechanism (see the following sidebar).

Evidence of Self-Interested Behavior

How prevalent are agency problems? Are they outlier events or an epidemic affecting the broad population? How severe are agency costs? Are they chronic and frictional or terminal and catastrophic?

To gain some insight into these questions, it is useful to consider the frequency of negative corporate events that, in whole or in part, are correlated with agency problems. However, before looking at the statistics, we also need to highlight that not all bad outcomes are caused by self-seeking behavior. A bad outcome might well occur even though the managerial decision was appropriate (that is, other management might have made the same decision when provided with the same information). With that important caveat, consider the following descriptive statistics:

- **Bankruptcy**—Between 2000 and 2005, 1,009 publicly traded companies filed for Chapter 11 bankruptcy protection in the United States.[17] Of these, approximately 10 percent were subject to a Securities and Exchange Commission (SEC) enforcement action for violating SEC or federal rules, implying that some form of fraud played a part in the bankruptcy.[18] Bankruptcies linked to fraud are a severe case of agency problems, usually resulting in a complete loss of capital for shareholders and a significant loss for creditors.

- **Financial restatement**—Between 2004 and 2008, approximately 8 percent of publicly traded companies in the United States had to restate their financial results.[19] Although some financial restatements result from honest procedural errors in applying accounting standards, financial restatements also can occur when senior management manipulates reported earnings for personal gain. According to Glass Lewis, the average market-adjusted two-day return for companies announcing a restatement was approximately –0.5 percent. In the case of "severe restatements" (classified as those affecting revenue recognition, core earnings, or involving fraud), share losses were –1.5 percent to –2.0 percent. Losses persist well beyond the announcement period, suggesting a material long-term impairment of shareholder value (see Figure 1.2).

Number of U.S.-listed companies that restated, restatements and restatement rate

Source: Mark Grothe and Poonam Goyal (2009).

Figure 1.2   Restatements in the United States

- **Class action lawsuits**—Between 1996 and 2008, almost 200 class-action lawsuits were filed annually against corporate officers and directors for securities fraud. No doubt, some of this litigation was frivolous. However, market capitalization losses for defendant firms totaled approximately $130 billion each year (measured as the change in market capitalization during the class period). Although this is a somewhat crude approximation, this averages $677 million per company (see Figure 1.3).

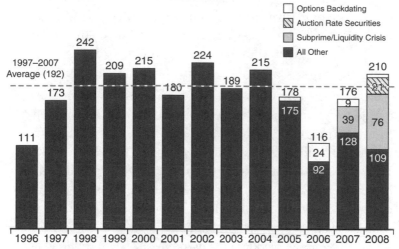

Source: *Securities Class Action Filings 2008: A Year in Review,* Cornerstone Research.

Figure 1.3   Annual number of class action filings (1996–2008)

- **Foreign Corrupt Practices Act violations**—The Foreign Corrupt Practices Act (FCPA) of 1977 makes it illegal for a company to offer payments to foreign officials for the purpose of obtaining or retaining business, to fail to keep accurate records of transactions, or to fail to maintain effective controls to detect potential violations of the FCPA. Between 2004 and 2008, the SEC and the U.S. Department of Justice filed approximately 20 enforcement actions per year against U.S. listed corporations for alleged FCPA violations. Notably, this figure has trended upward. Violations are settled through a disgorgement of profits and other penalties. In 2008, the SEC enforced more than $380 million in disgorgements, a record amount.[20]

- **Stock option backdating**—Backdated stock options are those whose grant dates have been retroactively changed to coincide with a relative low in the company's share price. This practice reduces the strike price of the option and increases the potential payoff to its recipient. The *Wall Street Journal* has identified 167 companies that have engaged in backdating.[21] Research suggests that the practice might have been even more pervasive.[22] Bernile and Jarrell (2009) found that the average abnormal stock market return for the first announcement that a company engaged in backdating is –7 percent.[23]

- **"Massaging" earnings**—Senior executives are under considerable pressure from the investment community to forecast future earnings and then to deliver on those targets. In a survey of senior financial executives, Graham, Harvey, and Rajgopal (2006) found that a majority are willing to massage the company's earnings to meet quarterly forecasts.[24] For example, 55 percent state that they would delay starting a new project, even if the project is expected to create long-term value. Separately, respondents were given a scenario in which initiating a new project would cause earnings per share in the current quarter to come in $0.10 lower. The respondents reported an 80 percent probability that they would accept the project if doing so enabled them to still meet their earnings target, but only a 60 percent probability if the project caused them to miss their earnings target.

These statistics suggest that agency problems caused by self-interested executives are likely to be quite prevalent, and the cost of managerial self-interest can be substantial.

Defining Corporate Governance

We define **corporate governance** as the collection of control mechanisms that an organization adopts to prevent or dissuade potentially self-interested managers from engaging in activities detrimental to the welfare of shareholders and stakeholders. At a minimum, the monitoring system consists of a board of directors to oversee management and an external auditor to express an opinion on the reliability of financial statements. In most cases, however, governance systems are influenced by a much broader group of constituents, including owners of the firm, creditors, labor unions, customers, suppliers, investment analysts, the media, and regulators (see Figure 1.4).

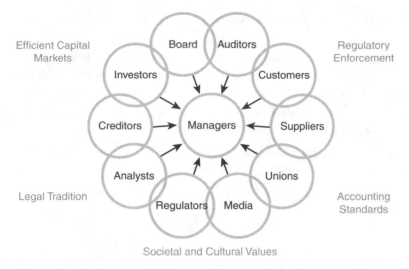

Source: Chart prepared by David F. Larcker and Brian Tayan (2011).

Figure 1.4   Selected determinants and participants in corporate governance systems.

For a governance system to be economically efficient, it should decrease agency costs more than the costs of implementation. However, because implementation costs arc greater than zero, even the best corporate governance system will not make the cost of the agency problem disappear completely.

The structure of the governance system also depends on the fundamental orientation of the firm and the role that the firm plays in society. From a **shareholder perspective** (the viewpoint that the primary obligation of the organization is to maximize shareholder value), effective corporate governance should increase the value of equity holders by better aligning incentives between management and shareholders. From a **stakeholder perspective** (the viewpoint that the organization has a societal obligation beyond increasing shareholder value), effective governance should support policies that produce stable and safe employment, provide an acceptable standard of living to workers, mitigate risk for debt holders, and improve the community and environment.[25] Obviously, the governance system that maximizes shareholder value might not be the same as the one that maximizes stakeholder value.

A broad set of external forces that vary across nations also influence the structure of the governance system. These include the efficiency of local capital markets, legal tradition, reliability of accounting standards, regulatory enforcement, and societal and cultural values. These forces serve as an external disciplining mechanism on managerial behavior. Their relative effectiveness determines the extent to which additional monitoring mechanisms are required.

Finally, any system of corporate governance involves third parties that are linked with the company but do not have a direct ownership stake. These include regulators (such as the SEC), politicians, the external auditor, security analysts, external legal counsel, employees and unions, proxy advisory firms, customers, suppliers, and other similar participants. Third parties might be subject to their own agency issues that compromise their ability to work solely in the interest of the company. For example, the external auditor is employed by an accounting firm that seeks to improve its own financial condition; when the accounting firm also provides non-audit services, the auditor *might* be confronted with conflicting objectives. Likewise, security analysts are employed by investment firms that serve both institutional and retail clients; when the analyst covers a company that is also a client of the investment firm, the analyst might face added pressure by his firm to publish positive comments about the company that are misleading to shareholders. These types of conflicts can contribute to a breakdown in oversight of management activity.

Corporate Governance Standards

There are no universally agreed-upon standards that determine good governance. Still, this has not stopped blue-ribbon panels from recommending uniform standards to market participants. For example, in December 1992, the Cadbury Committee—commissioned by the British government "to help raise the standards of corporate governance and the level of confidence in financial reporting and auditing"—issued a *Code of Best Practices* that, in many ways, provided a benchmark set of recommendations on governance.[26] Key recommendations included separating the chairman and chief executive officer titles, appointing independent directors, reducing conflicts of interest at the board level because of business or other relationships, convening an independent audit committee, and reviewing the effectiveness of the company's internal controls. These standards set the basis for listing requirements on the London Stock Exchange and were largely adopted by the New York Stock Exchange (NYSE). However, compliance with these standards has not always translated into effective governance. For example, Enron was compliant with NYSE requirements, including requirements to have a majority of independent directors and fully independent audit and compensation committees, yet it still failed along many legal and ethical dimensions.

Over time, a series of formal regulations and informal guidelines has been proposed to address perceived shortcomings in governance systems as they are exposed. One of the most important pieces of formal legislation relating to governance is the Sarbanes–Oxley Act of 2002 (SOX). Primarily a reaction to the failures of Enron and others, SOX mandated a series of requirements to improve corporate controls and reduce conflicts of interest. Importantly, CEOs and CFOs found to have made material misrepresentations in the financial statements are now subject to criminal penalties. Despite these efforts, corporate failures stemming from deficient governance systems continue. In 2005, Refco, a large U.S. based foreign exchange and commodity broker, filed for bankruptcy after revealing that it had hidden $430 million in loans made to its CEO.[27] The disclosure came just two months after the firm raised $583 million in an initial public offering. That same year, mortgage guarantor Fannie Mae announced that it had overstated earnings by $6.3 billion because it had misapplied more than 20 accounting standards relating to loans, investment securities, and derivatives. Insufficient capital levels eventually led the company to seek conservatorship by the U.S. government.[28]

In 2009, Sen. Charles Schumer of New York proposed new legislation to stem the tide of governance collapses. Known as the Shareholder's Bill of Rights, the legislation stipulated that companies adopt procedural changes designed to give shareholders greater influence over director elections and compensation. Requirements included a shift toward annual elections for all directors (thereby disallowing staggered or classified boards), a standard of majority voting for director elections (instead of plurality voting) in which directors in uncontested elections must resign if they do not receive a majority vote, the right for certain institutional shareholders to directly nominate board candidates on the company proxy (proxy access), the separation of the chairman and CEO roles, and the right for shareholders to have an advisory vote on executive compensation (say-on-pay). The 2010 Dodd–Frank Wall Street Reform and Consumer Protection Act subsequently adopted several of these recommendations, including proxy access and say-on-pay. The interesting question is whether this legislation is a product of political expediency or actually is based on rigorous theory and empirical research.[29]

Several third-party organizations, such as The Corporate Library and Risk Metrics Group/Institutional Shareholder Services (ISS), attempt to protect investors from inadequate corporate governance by publishing governance ratings on individual companies. These rating agencies use alphanumeric or numeric systems that rank companies according to a set of criteria that they believe measure governance effectiveness. Companies with high ratings are considered less risky and most likely to grow shareholder value. Companies with low ratings are considered more risky and have the highest potential for failure or fraud. However, the accuracy and predictive power of these ratings has not been clearly demonstrated. Critics allege that ratings encourage a "check-the-box" approach to governance that overlooks important context. The potential shortcomings of these ratings were spotlighted in the case of HealthSouth. Before evidence of earnings manipulation was brought to light, the company had a RiskMetrics/ISS rating that placed it in the top 35 percent of Standard & Poor's 500 companies and the top 8 percent of its industry peers.[30]

Changes in the business environment further complicate attempts to identify uniform standards of governance. Some recent trends include the increased prominence of private equity, activist investors, and proxy advisory firms in the governance space.

- **Private equity**—Private equity firms implement governance systems that are considerably different from those at most public companies. Publicly owned companies must demonstrate independence at the board level, but private equity–owned companies operate with very low levels of independence (almost everyone on the board has a relationship to the company and has a vested interest in its operations). Private equity companies also offer extremely high compensation to senior executives, a practice that is criticized among public companies but one that is strictly tied to the creation of economic value. Should public companies adopt certain aspects from the private equity model of governance? Would this produce more or less shareholder value?

- **Activist investors**—Institutional investors, hedge funds, and pension funds have become considerably more active in attempting to influence management and the board through the annual proxy voting process. Are the interests of these parties consistent with those of individual shareholders? Does public debate between these parties reflect a movement toward improved dialogue about corporate objectives and strategy? Or does it constitute an unnecessary intrusion by activists who have their own self-interested agendas?

- **Proxy advisory firms**—Recent SEC rules require that mutual funds disclose how they vote their annual proxies.[31] These rules have coincided with increased media attention on the voting process, which was previously considered a formality of little interest. Has the disclosure of voting improved corporate governance? At the same time, these rules have stimulated demand for commercial firms—such as RiskMetrics/ISS and Glass Lewis—to provide recommendations on how to vote on proxy proposals. What is the impact of shareholders relying on third parties to inform their voting decisions? Are the recommendations of these firms consistent with good governance?

Best Practice or Best Practices? Does "One Size Fit All?"

It is highly unlikely that a single set of best practices exists for all firms, despite the attempts of some to impose uniform standards. Governance is a complex and dynamic system that involves the interaction of a diverse set of constituents, all of whom play a role in monitoring executive behavior. Because of this complexity, it is difficult to assess the impact of a single component. Focusing an analysis on one or two mechanisms without considering the broader context can be a prescription for failure. For example, is it sufficient to insist that a

company separate the chairman and CEO positions without considering who the CEO is and other structural, cultural, and governance
features of the company?

Applying a "one-size-fits-all" approach to governance can lead to
incorrect conclusions and is unlikely to substantially improve corporate performance. The standards most often associated with good
governance might appear to be good ideas, but when applied universally, they can result in failure as often as success. For example, consider the idea of board independence. Is a board consisting primarily
of independent directors superior to a board comprised entirely of
internal directors? How should individual attributes such as their
business acumen, professional background, ethical standards of
responsibility, level of engagement, relationship with the CEO, and
reliance on director fees to maintain their standard of living factor
into our analysis?[32] Personal attributes might influence independence
of perspective more than predetermined standards.[33] However, these
elements are rarely captured in regulatory requirements.[34]

In governance, context matters. A set of governance mechanisms
that works well in one setting might prove disastrous in another. This
situation becomes apparent when considering international governance systems. For example, Germany requires labor union representation on many corporate boards. How effective would such a system
be in the United States? Japanese boards have few outside directors,
and many of those who are outside directors come from banks that
provide capital to the firm or key customers and suppliers. What
would be the impact on Japanese companies if they were required to
adopt the independence standards of the United States? These are
difficult questions, but ones that investors must consider when deciding where to allocate their investment dollars.

Relationship between Corporate Governance and Firm Performance

According to a 2002 survey by McKinsey & Company, nearly 80 percent of institutional investors responded that they would pay a premium for a well-governed company. The size of the premium varied

by market, ranging from 11 percent for a company in Canada to around 40 percent for a company in Morocco, Egypt, or Russia (see Figure 1.5).[35] These results imply that investors perceive well-governed companies to be better investments than poorly governed companies.[36] They are also consistent with the idea that governance systems are more important in certain countries than in others.

Premium in 2002

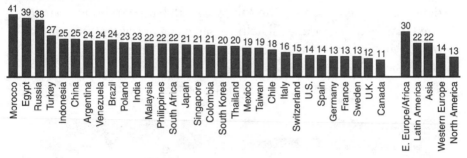

Source: Paul Coombes and Mark Watson (2002). "Global Investor Opinion Survey 2002: Key Findings." McKinsey & Company.

Figure 1.5   Indicated premiums for good corporate governance, by country.

As we will see throughout this book, many studies link measures of corporate governance with firm operating and stock price performance. Perhaps the most widely cited study was done by Gompers, Ishii, and Metrick (2003).[37] They found that companies that employ "shareholder-friendly" governance features significantly outperform companies that employ "shareholder unfriendly" governance features. This is an important research study, but as we will see in Chapter 13, these results are not completely definitive. Currently, researchers have not produced a reliable litmus test that measures overall governance quality.

The purpose of this book is to provide the basis for constructive debate among executives, directors, investors, regulators, and other constituents that have an important stake in the success of corporations. This book focuses on corporate governance from an *organizational* instead of purely *legal* perspective, with an emphasis on exploring the relationships between control mechanisms and their impact on mitigating agency costs and improving shareholder and stakeholder outcomes.

Each chapter examines a specific component of corporate governance and summarizes what is known and what remains unknown about the topic. We have taken an agnostic approach, with no agenda other than to "get the story straight." In each chapter, we provide an overview of the specific topic, a synthesis of the relevant research, and concrete examples that illustrate key points.[38] Sometimes the evidence is inconclusive (see the following sidebar). We hope that the combination of materials will help you arrive at intelligent insights. In particular, we hope to benefit the individuals who participate in corporate governance processes so that they can make informed decisions that benefit the organizations they serve.

Interpreting Empirical Research

Oliver Williamson, winner of the 2009 Nobel Prize in Economics, observed the following:

"I have no doubt that the economics of governance is influential in significant measure because it does speak to real-world phenomena and invites *empirical testing* .... All feasible forms of organizations are flawed, and ... we need to understand the trade-offs that are going on, the factors that are responsible for using one form of governance rather than another, and the strengths and weaknesses that are associated with each of them."[39]

Still, the interpretation of empirical tests (academic, consulting, or other) requires some understanding of their limitations:

1. The results cited in **empirical tests** are typically average results generated from the statistical analysis of large samples of firms. Large samples enable a researcher to identify trends that are generally prevalent across companies. However, they do not tell us what we can expect to find at a specific company. Case or field studies can help answer firm-specific questions, but their results are difficult to generalize because they are based on only a handful of firms that may not be typical of the general population of firms.

2. Empirical tests can identify associations between variables, but they do not demonstrate causality. This is a recurring problem in nonexperimental social science. If we observe a negative stock price return when a company adopts a governance change, it does not tell us that the change caused the stock price decline. It is possible that another (exogenous) factor might have been the cause. Ideally, we would control for this by observing what would have happened had another action been taken (the counterfactual outcome); however, this is impossible to observe. In corporate governance, we do not have the luxury of controlled samples. Still, empirical results are superior to guesswork or intuition.

3. The performance metrics that governance researchers typically use fall into two broad categories: operating metrics and stock price metrics. Operating metrics (such as return on assets and operating cash flow) are somewhat backward looking but are generally considered to provide insight into value changes within the firm. Stock price metrics are typically based on **abnormal** or **excess** returns (the so-called **alpha**, calculated as observed returns minus the expected returns, given the risk of the stock). Assuming reasonably efficient markets, excess returns provide a measure of change in economic value for shareholders. The researcher must determine which metric is better for evaluating the question at hand. The choice will depend on whether the market should be able to anticipate the impact of interest.

4. Another metric that is commonly used in governance research is the ratio of market-to-book value (sometimes referred to as **Tobin's Q** or simply **Q**). Q is based on the theory that a firm with superior performance will trade in the market at a valuation that is higher than the accounting value of its net assets. While this may be true, we view Q to be an ambiguous measure of firm performance and inferior to traditional operating metrics and excess stock price returns.

5. We sometimes refer to **event studies**. Event studies measure the stock market's reaction to news or events. These studies have validity only to the extent that the reader believes that markets are at least partly efficient. Even if so, event studies cannot easily control for confounding events (such as other news released by the company during the measurement period). Moreover, event studies require the researcher to make important risk adjustments when computing excess stock returns. Although several risk adjustments have become "accepted," their computation is complex, and it is difficult to know whether the researcher made them properly.

Endnotes

1. Some material in this chapter is adapted from David F. Larcker and Brian Tayan, "Models of Corporate Governance: Who's the Fairest of Them All?" Stanford GSB Case No. CG 11, January 15, 2008. See https://gsbapps.stanford.edu/cases/detail1.asp?Document_ID=3054. Copyright 2008 by the Board of Trustees of the Leland Stanford Junior University. All rights reserved. Used with permission from the Stanford University Graduate School of Business.

2. See Aaron Beam and Chris Warner, *HealthSouth: The Wagon to Disaster* (Fairhope, AL: Wagon Publishing, 2009).

3. Lisa Fingeret Roth, "HealthSouth CFO Admits Fraud Charges," FT.com (March 26, 2003). See http://proquest.umi.com/pqdweb?did=318664941&sid=1&Fmt=3&clientId=12498&RQT=309&VName=PQD.

4. HealthSouth Corporation, Form DEF14-A, filed with the Securities and Exchange Commission, May 16, 2002.

5. In re: HealthSouth Corporation Bondholder Litigation. United States District Court Northern District of Alabama Southern Division. Master File No. CV-03-BE-1500-S.

6. Chad Terhune and Carrick Mollenkamp, "HealthSouth Officials May Sign Plea Agreements—Moves by Finance Executives Would Likely Help Build Criminal Case Against CEO," *Wall Street Journal* (March 26, 2003, Eastern edition): A.14.

7. Carrick Mollenkamp, "Some of Scrushy's Lawyers Ask Others on Team for Money Back," *Wall Street Journal* (December 17, 2003, Eastern edition): A.16.

8. HealthSouth Corporation, Form DEF14-A.

9. Dan Ackman, "CEO Compensation for Life?" Forbes.com (April 25, 2002). Accessed November 16, 2010. www.forbes.com/2002/04/25/0425ceotenure. html.

10. HealthSouth Corporation, Form DEF14-A. See also Jonathan Weil and Cassell Bryan-Low, "Questioning the Books: Audit Committee Met Only Once During 2001," *Wall Street Journal* (March 21, 2003, Eastern edition): A.2.

11. HealthSouth Corporation, Form DEF14-A.

12. Ken Brown and Robert Frank, "Analyst's Bullishness on HealthSouth's Stock Didn't Waver," *Wall Street Journal* (April 4, 2003, Eastern edition): C.1.

13. This issue was the basis of the classic discussion in Adolph Berle and Gardiner Means, *The Modern Corporation and Private Property* (New York: Harcourt, Brace, and World, 1932).

14. The phrase *rent extraction* is another commonly used term for agency costs and refers to economic costs taken out of the system without any corresponding contribution in productivity.

15. Gary Becker, *The Economic Approach to Human Behavior* (Chicago: University of Chicago Press, 1976).

16. For example, a study by Boivie, Lange, McDonald, and Westphal found that CEOs who strongly identify with their company are less likely to accept expensive perquisites or make other decisions that are at odds with shareholder interests. Source: Steven Boivie, Donald Lange, Michael L. McDonald, and James D. Westphal, "Me or We: The Effects of CEO Organizational Identification of Agency Costs," *Academy of Management Proceedings* (2009): 1-6.

17. Deloitte, "Ten Things about Bankruptcy and Fraud: A Review of Bankruptcy Filings," Deloitte Forensic Center (2008). See www.deloitte.com/view/ en_US/us/Services/Financial-Advisory-Services/Forensic-Center/ 1d42a68c4d101210VgnVCM100000ba42f00aRCRD.htm.

18. Enforcement actions are measured as the number of Accounting and Auditing Enforcement Releases (AAER) by the SEC. The SEC issues an AAER for alleged violations of SEC and federal rules. Academic researchers have used AAER as a proxy for severe fraud because most companies that commit financial statement fraud receive SEC enforcement actions.

19. Mark Grothe, "The Errors of Their Ways," Yellow Card Trend Report, Glass Lewis & Co. (February 27, 2007).

20. David C. Weiss, "The Foreign Corrupt Practices Act, SEC Disgorgement of Profits, and the Evolving International Bribery Regime: Weighing Proportionality, Retribution, and Deterrence," *Michigan Journal of International Law* 30 (2009): 147. See www.heinonline.org/HOL/Page?handle=hein.journals/ mjil30&id=1&size=2&collection=journals&index=journals/mjil.

21. Anonymous, "Perfect Payday: Options Scorecard," Wall Street Journal Online (2007). See http://online.wsj.com/public/resources/documents/info-optionsscore06-full.html.

22. Erik Lie, "On the Timing of CEO Stock Option Awards," *Management Science* 51 (2005): 802–812. Lucian A. Bebchuk, Yaniv Grinstein, and Urs C. Peyer. "Lucky CEOs and Lucky Directors," *Journal of Finance* 65 (2010): 2,363–2,401.

23. Gennaro Bernile and Gregg A. Jarrell, "The Impact of the Options Backdating Scandal on Shareholders," *Journal of Accounting and Economics* 47 (2009): 1–2. Also Accounting Research on Issues of Contemporary Interest (March 2009): 2-26.

24. John Graham, Campbell Harvey, and Shiva Rajgopal, "Value Destruction and Financial Reporting Decisions," *Financial Analysts Journal* 62 (2006): 27–39.

25. The cost–benefit assessment of a governance system also depends on whether the company operates under a shareholder-centric or stakeholder-centric model. The fundamentally different orientation of these models makes it difficult for an outside observer to compare their effectiveness. For example, a decision to maximize shareholder value might come at the cost of the employee and environmental objectives of stakeholders, but comparing these costs is not easy. We discuss this more in Chapter 2, "International Corporate Governance."

26. Cadbury Committee, *Report of the Committee on the Financial Aspects of Corporate Governance* (London: Gee, 1992).

27. Deborah Solomon, Carrick Mollenkamp, Peter A. McKay, and Jonathan Weil, "Refco's Debts Started with Several Clients; Bennett Secretly Intervened to Assume Some Obligations; Return of Victor Niederhoffer," *Wall Street Journal* (October 21, 2005, Eastern edition): C1.

28. James R. Hagerty, "Politics & Economics: Fannie Mae Moves Toward Resolution with Restatement," *Wall Street Journal* (December 7, 2006, Eastern edition) A.4. Damian Paletta, "Fannie Sues KPMG for $2 Billion Over Costs of Accounting Issues," *Wall Street Journal* (December 13, 2006, Eastern edition): A.16.

29. A forthcoming study by Larcker, Ormazabal, and Taylor found that the legislative provisions in Schumer and Dodd–Frank are associated with negative stock price returns for affected companies. These results seemed to have little impact on the congressional debate. Similarly, the legislators who drafted the Sarbanes–Oxley Act of 2002 did not take into account research literature. See David F. Larcker, Gaizka Ormazabal, and Daniel J. Taylor, "The Market Reaction to Corporate Governance Regulation," *Journal of Financial Economics* (forthcoming); and Roberta Romano, "The Sarbanes–Oxley Act and the Making of Quack Corporate Governance," *Yale Law Review* 114 (2005): 1,521–1,612.

30. Cited in Jeffrey Sonnenfeld, "Good Governance and the Misleading Myths of Bad Metrics," *Academy of Management Executive* 18 (2001): 108–113.

31. Securities Lawyer's Deskbook. "Investment Company Act of 1940. Rule 30b1-4," *The University of Cincinnati College of Law*. See www.law.uc.edu/CCL/InvCoRls/rule30b1-4.html. See also "Report of Proxy Voting, Record Disclosure of Proxy Voting Policies, and Proxy Voting Records by Registered Management Investment Companies," Securities and Exchange Commission: 17 CFR Parts 239, 249, 270, and 274 Release Nos. 33-8188, 34-47304, IC-25922; File No. S7-36-02. www.sec.gov/rules/final/33-8188.htm.

32. The NYSE acknowledges this risk. See Chapters 3, "Board of Directors: Duties and Liability," and 5, "Board of Directors: Structure and Consequences," for a more detailed discussion of board independence.

33. Sonnenfeld has written, "At least as important are the human dynamics of boards as social systems where leadership character, individual values, decision-making processes, conflict management, and strategic thinking will truly differentiate a firm's governance." Jeffrey Sonnenfeld, "Good Governance and the Misleading Myths of Bad Metrics," *Academy of Management Executive* 18 (2004): 108–113.

34. Milton Harris and Artur Ravi, "A Theory of Board Control and Size," *Review of Financial Studies* 21 (2008): 1,797–1,831.

35. Paul Coombes and Mark Watson, "Global Investor Opinion Survey 2002: Key Findings," McKinsey & Co. (2002). Accessed November 1, 2010. See www.mckinsey.com/clientservice/organizationleadership/service/corpgovernance/pdf/globalinvestoropinionsurvey2002.pdf.

36. This is what investors say they would do when asked in a formal survey. However, this study does not provide evidence that investors actually take governance into account when making investment decisions.

37. Paul Gompers, Joy Ishii, and Andrew Metrick, "Corporate Governance and Equity Prices," *Quarterly Journal of Economics* 118 (2003): 107–155.

38. We are not attempting to provide a complete and comprehensive review of the research literature. Our goal is to select specific papers that provide a fair reflection of general research results.

39. Emphasis added. Nobel Prize Organization, "Oliver E. Williamson—Interview" (2009). See http://nobelprize.org/nobel_prizes/economics/laureates/2009/williamson-telephone.html.

2

International Corporate Governance

In Chapter 1, "Introduction to Corporate Governance," we defined corporate governance as the collection of control mechanisms that an organization adopts to prevent or dissuade potentially self-interested managers from engaging in activities detrimental to the welfare of shareholders and stakeholders. The governance system that a company adopts is not independent of its environment. A variety of factors inherent to the business setting shape the governance system. Some of these factors include the following:

- Efficiency of local capital markets
- Extent to which the legal system provides protection to all shareholders
- Reliability of accounting standards
- Enforcement of regulations
- Societal and cultural values

Differences in these factors have important implications for the prevalence and severity of agency problems and the type of governance mechanisms required to monitor and control managerial self-interested behavior.

In this chapter, we evaluate the research evidence on these factors and consider how they give rise to the governance systems observed in different countries. We then illustrate these principles by providing an overview of governance systems in selected countries. You will see that although globalization has tended to standardize certain features (such as an independence standard for the board of directors), international governance systems as a whole remain broadly diverse. This diversity reflects the unique combination of economic, legal, cultural, and other forces that have developed over time. Therefore, the national context is important to understand how governance systems work to shape managerial behavior.

Capital Market Efficiency

Markets set the prices for labor, natural resources, and capital. When **capital markets** are efficient, these prices are expected to be correct based on the information available to both parties in a transaction. Accurate pricing is necessary for firms to make rational decisions about allocating capital to its most efficient uses. Owners of the firm are rewarded for rational decision making through an increase in shareholder value. When capital markets are inefficient, prices are subject to distortion and corporate decision making suffers.

Efficient capital markets also act as a disciplining mechanism on corporations. Companies are held to a "market standard" of performance, and those that fail to meet these standards are punished with a decrease in share price. Companies that do not perform well over time risk going out of business or becoming an acquisition target. (We discuss this more in Chapter 11, "The Market for Corporate Control.") If the market is not reasonably efficient, shareholders cannot rely on the market for corporate control to punish management for making poor capital allocation decisions that decrease shareholder value.

Rajan and Zingales (1998) demonstrated the importance of capital markets by measuring the relationship between capital market efficiency and economic growth across countries. They found that industries that require external financing grow faster in countries with efficient capital markets. They concluded that a well-developed financial market is a source of competitive advantage for firms that rely on external capital for growth.[1]

If a country does not have efficient capital markets, its companies must instead rely on alternative sources of financing for growth, such as influential wealthy families, large banking institutions, other companies, or governments. As providers of capital, these parties also discipline corporate behavior because they actively monitor their investments. However, because their objectives might differ from the pure financial returns that the investing public seeks, their capacity to act as a disciplining mechanism might not coincide with the interests of shareholders or stakeholders. For example, a wealthy family might be satisfied with below-market returns if it can use a position of control over the organization to extract other benefits—such as corporate perquisites, social prestige, or political influence.

Morck (2010) examined the role that family-controlled business groups play in selected economies. He found that family-controlled business groups dominate the national economy in countries such as Hong Kong, Sweden, Canada, and the Philippines. For example, Investor AB (controlled by the Wallenberg family) holds majority and minority ownership positions in companies that constitute half of the total market capitalization of the Swedish stock market (see Figure 2.1).[2]

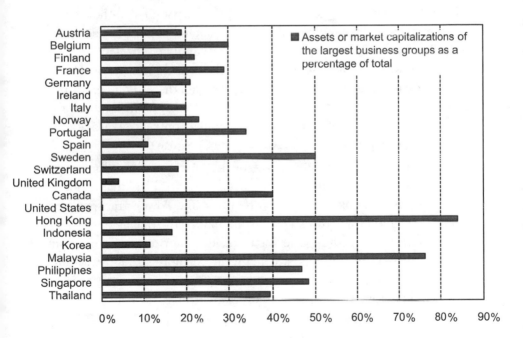

Source: Adapted by David F. Larcker and Brian Tayan. Data from: Morck (2010).

Figure 2.1   Family-controlled business groups in selected countries.

However, the influence of these firms varies, depending on the degree of local economic development. Morck cited as an example the important role that family-controlled business groups played in both Korea and Japan to encourage the rapid economic development of those nations following the Korean War and World War II, respectively. These groups successfully allocated resources from profitable group businesses to subsidize unprofitable group businesses that were deemed nationally important. As such, they coordinated large-scale domestic development that otherwise would have been difficult to achieve. This type of internal capital allocation can be an effective substitute for weak capital markets if the managers have the objective of increasing economic value. The influence of these groups in developed markets such as Sweden is strong but less extensive.

Family-controlled business groups bring greater risk to the economy when they operate with minimal external oversight and when their objectives are to extract rents at the expense of shareholders or stakeholders. For example, Black (2001) concluded that poor accounting disclosure and weak oversight enabled family-controlled business groups in Korea to mask operating problems and prop up weak subsidiaries with financial guarantees that were not disclosed to creditors. Such practices were not sustainable and eventually contributed to the Asian financial crisis of 1997.[3] As such, family control can also lead to serious agency problems that retard economic growth.[4]

To this end, Leuz, Lins, and Warnock (2009) found that foreigners invest less money in companies that insiders control and that reside in countries with weak investor protections and lower transparency. They concluded that "firms with problematic governance structures, particularly those with high levels of insider control and from countries with weak institutions, are likely to be more taxing to foreign investors in terms of their information and monitoring costs, which in turn could explain why foreigners shy away from these firms."[5]

Finally, efficient capital markets can also serve as a disciplining mechanism on managerial behavior when they are appropriately used in compensation contracts. By offering equity-based incentives such as stock options, the firm can align the interests of management and shareholders. This discourages management from taking self-interested actions that reduce firm value. The absence of an efficient market essentially limits the effectiveness of these types of incentives. In such a setting, agency problems might be best addressed by requiring managers to hold direct and substantial equity positions, by active regulation, or by other governance features that do not rely on efficient capital markets. (We discuss equity incentives in greater detail in Chapters 8, "Executive Compensation and Incentives," and 9, "Executive Equity Ownership.")

Legal Tradition

A country's legal tradition has important implications on the rights afforded to business owners and minority shareholders. Business owners are particularly concerned with the protection of their property against expropriation, the predictability of how claims will be resolved under the law, the enforceability of contracts, and the efficiency and honesty of the judiciary. Minority shareholders are concerned with how the legal system protects their ownership rights and discourages abuse by controlling owners. A system that provides strong protection can be an important factor in mitigating the prevalence and severity of agency problems because penalties can be imposed on self-interested managers or insiders. However, if the legal system is corrupt or cannot be relied upon to provide appropriate protections, this disciplining device will not constrain agency problems.

La Porta, Lopez-de-Silanes, Shleifer, and Vishny (1998) found that countries whose legal systems are based on a tradition of common law afford more rights to shareholders than countries whose legal systems are based on civil law (or code law).[6] The authors also found that creditors are afforded greater protection in common-law countries. They concluded that governance systems are more effective in countries that combine common-law tradition with a reliable enforcement mechanism (discussed in the later section "Enforcement of Regulations"). In a separate study, La Porta, Lopez-de-Silanes, Shleifer, and Vishny (2002) found that companies operating in countries whose legal systems protect minority interests have higher stock market valuations than companies operating in countries with lesser protections.[7]

Similarly, studies have shown that political corruption has a negative impact on economic development. According to the World Bank, corruption "undermines development by distorting the rule of law and weakening the institutional foundation on which economic growth depends."[8] Mauro (1995) found that higher levels of corruption are associated with lower economic growth and lower private investment.[9] He explained that a corrupt government provides worse protection of property rights and that bureaucratic delay in granting licenses can deter investment in technological advancement. Finally, Pantzalis, Park, and Sutton (2008) found that political corruption is associated with lower corporate valuations.[10]

If the legal system is corrupt or ineffective, alternative disciplining mechanisms are necessary in the governance process. For example, if contracts are not enforced through traditional legal channels, they could be "enforced" by the threat of not engaging in future business with the other party. Firms could place directors on the boards of companies that are important suppliers or customers, to monitor management and to ensure that contracts are honored. These mechanisms would enable the firms to bypass the legal system and to ensure that shareholder and stakeholder interests are protected.

Accounting Standards

Reliable and sensible accounting standards are critical in ensuring that financial statements convey accurate information to shareholders. Investors rely on this information to evaluate investment risk and reward. Inaccurate information and low levels of transparency can lead to poor decision making and reduce the efficiency of capital markets. The practice of hiring an external auditor to review the application of accounting principles improves investor confidence in financial reporting.

Reliable accounting standards also are critical in ensuring the proper oversight of management. Shareholders and stakeholders use this information to measure performance and detect agency problems. The board of directors uses this information to structure appropriate compensation incentives and to award bonuses. If accounting standards lack transparency or if management manipulates their application, financial reporting will suffer, compensation incentives will be distorted, and shareholders and stakeholders will be less effective in providing oversight.

To improve the integrity of financial reporting, regulators have devised standards that are based on the expert opinions of economists, academics, auditors, and practitioners. In some countries, such as the United States and Japan, accounting systems are **rules-based**—that is, they prescribe detailed rules for how accounting standards should be applied to various business activities. In other countries, such as many European nations, accounting systems are **principles-based**—they outline general accounting concepts but do not always dictate the specific application of these concepts to business activities (see the following sidebar).

Harmonization of Accounting Standards

Country-specific accounting standards make it difficult for investors to compare corporate performance across nations. To improve this situation, the **International Accounting Standards Board (IASB)** was formed in 2001. The organization, which superseded the International Accounting Standards Committee, was established to develop reliable accounting standards that could be used worldwide. The IASB expects that a single set of accounting standards will support the efficiency of global capital markets through improved disclosure and transparency.

The IASB issued its first International Financial Reporting Standard (IFRS) in 2003. By 2008, more than 100 countries worldwide were either required or allowed to use IFRSs. These countries included the European Union members, the United Kingdom, Australia, New Zealand, and South Africa, among others. In the United States, regulators have signaled an intention to convert from U.S. Generally Accepted Accounting Principles (GAAP) to IFRS by the middle of the decade 2010. However, many practical considerations will make harmonization a challenge in the United States, including differences in the treatment of certain principles; political pressure on the cost of compliance; and investor, managerial, and auditor education.

Despite the move toward harmonization, considerable differences in accounting quality will likely remain. This is because the board of directors and management still retain discretion over the application of accounting principles and the level of transparency in reporting. Furthermore, external audit quality also varies across countries in the extent to which accounting problems are detected and enforcement is applied. (We discuss issues of accounting and audit quality in Chapter 10, "Financial Reporting and External Audit.")

Academic research demonstrates the importance of reliable accounting standards. Ernstberger and Vogler (2008) found that German companies that adopted international accounting standards had a lower cost of capital.[11] They determined that companies that adopted either IFRS or U.S. GAAP received an "accounting premium" from investors for improved earnings quality and disclosure. Similarly, Francis, Huang, Khurana, and Pereira (2009) found that transparency in financial disclosure contributed to higher national economic growth rates through the facilitation of efficient resource allocation.[12]

However, the adoption of reliable accounting standards does not guarantee the integrity of financial reporting. Benston, Bromwich, and Wagenhofer (2006) warned that principles-based accounting systems have potential shortcomings because they provide less-strict guidance and are subject to management interpretation. They cited a 2002 review by accounting regulators in the United States that questioned whether the adoption of a concept-based system "could lead to situations in which professional judgments, made in good faith, result in different interpretations for similar transactions and events, raising concerns about comparability."[13] Price, Román, and Rountree (2011) found that compliance with accounting codes does not necessarily lead to increased transparency or better corporate performance. They concluded that institutional features of the business environment—including ownership characteristics, board attributes, and protection of minority rights by the legal system—are also important contributors to effective governance.[14]

If accounting rules are unreliable or external auditors cannot be trusted to verify their proper application, countries will require a substitute mechanism to discourage agency problems. These might include severe legal penalties for abuse and a vigilant enforcement mechanism.

Enforcement of Regulations

Legal and regulatory mechanisms alone cannot protect the interests of minority shareholders. Government officials must be willing to enforce the rules in a fair and consistent manner. Regulatory enforcement mitigates agency problems by dissuading executives from engaging in behaviors such as insider trading, misleading disclosure, self-dealing, and fraud because they acknowledge a real risk of punishment.

Hail and Leuz (2006) found that countries with developed securities regulations and legal enforcement mechanisms have a lower cost of capital than those that lack these characteristics. Controlling for macroeconomic and firm-specific factors, the authors found that differences in securities regulation and legal systems explain about 60 percent of country-level differences in implied equity cost of capital. The importance of regulatory enforcement is greater in countries whose economies are not integrated into international capital markets (such as Brazil, India, and the Philippines) than in those whose economies are integrated (such as Belgium, Hong Kong, and the United Kingdom). When a country's economy is integrated into international capital markets, the efficiency of those markets can partially make up for deficiencies in the country-specific securities regulation and legal system.[15]

Regulatory enforcement also contributes to investor confidence that management will be monitored and property rights will be protected. Bushman and Piotroski (2006) found that companies apply more conservative accounting in countries where public enforcement of securities regulation is strong. Because regulators are more likely to be penalized if the companies they monitor overstate accounting results, they will be more rigorous in their enforcement. Knowing this, companies recognize bad news in their financial reports more quickly to avoid regulatory infractions.[16] Similarly, researchers have found that participation in equity markets increases when countries adopt insider

trading laws because the laws put outside investors on more even foot-
ing with insiders who have access to nonpublic information.[17]

If regulatory enforcement is weak or inconsistent, shareholders
cannot expect to have their interests protected by official channels.
Therefore, they have to take a more direct role in governance oversight, either through greater rights afforded through the bylaws and
charters, or through direct representation on the board. Without
these tools, they will demand higher returns on capital to compensate
for the greater risk of investing their money.

Societal and Cultural Values

The society in which a company operates also strongly influences managerial behavior. Activities that might be deemed acceptable in some
societies are considered inappropriate in others (such as conspicuous
personal consumption). This impacts the types of activities that executives are willing to participate in and the likelihood of self-serving
behavior. Cultural values also influence the relationship between the
company and its shareholders and stakeholders. Although complex
and difficult to quantify, these forces play a significant role in shaping
governance systems.

For example, corporations in Korea have a responsibility to society as a whole, beyond maximizing shareholder profits. Executives
who take actions that benefit themselves at the expense of others are
seen as betraying the social trust and bringing disgrace on the corporation and its employees. This cultural norm—the concept of shame
or "lost face"—becomes a disciplining mechanism that deters self-
interested behavior, similar to the threat of legal penalties in other
nations. By contrast, in Russia, personal displays of wealth are tolerated, and corruption is widely seen as an inevitable aspect of the
business process. Executives there might be more likely to take self-
interested actions because they do not risk the same level of scorn as
executives in Korea. In this case, cultural norms do not act as a successful deterrent, and explicit government regulation and enforcement are likely (see the following sidebar).

The Hofstede Model of Cultural Dimensions

Many systems categorize cultural values. One that has received considerable attention is a model developed by Geert Hofstede. The Hofstede model is based on survey data of employee values in more than 70 countries. It consolidates these values into five indices that are broadly used to characterize cultural attributes:

- **Power distance**—The extent to which members of society accept that power is distributed unequally.

- **Individualism**—The extent to which members of society feel a responsibility to look after only themselves and their families rather than others in society.

- **Masculinity**—The extent to which members of society are assertive or competitive.

- **Uncertainty avoidance**—The extent to which members of society feel uncomfortable in unstructured situations.

- **Long-term orientation**—The extent to which members of society tend toward thrift and perseverance.[18]

Although these measures are perhaps crude or stereotypical, they are indicative of a system that attempts to quantify differences across cultures. If properly developed, such a system might serve as an indicator of the likelihood that executives will engage in self-interested behavior and the extent to which a country's governance system requires rigorous controls. For example, the Hofstede system gives Korea a low score (18) for individualism and a high score (85) for uncertainty avoidance. This suggests that Korea has a cooperative business culture built around structured processes and is not subject to a high degree of agency risk.[19]

Although countries vary on many levels, one of the most important social attitudes that shapes governance systems is the role of the corporation in society. As mentioned in Chapter 1, some countries tend toward a **shareholder-centric** view, which holds that the primary responsibility of the corporation is to maximize shareholder wealth. Actions such as improving labor conditions, reducing environmental impact, and treating suppliers fairly are seen as desirable only to the extent that they are consistent with improving the long-term financial performance of the firm. Other countries tend toward a **stakeholder-centric** view, which holds that obligations toward constituents such as employees, suppliers, customers, and local communities should be held in equal importance to shareholder returns.

The United States and the United Kingdom are two countries that predominantly embrace the shareholder-centric view. The laws of these countries stipulate that boards and executives have a fiduciary responsibility to protect the interest of shareholders. If the board of directors of a U.S. company were to reject an unsolicited takeover bid on the premise that it would lead to widespread layoffs, it would likely face a lawsuit filed by its investors for not maximizing shareholder value. However, all members of society in these countries might not uniformly adopt the shareholder-centric view. For example, union pension funds advocate stakeholder-friendly objectives, such as fair labor laws, and environmental groups encourage corporations to embrace sustainability goals even if they might increase the company's cost of production. Many corporations embrace these objectives as well, even as their primary focus remains on long-term value creation.

In other societies, the stakeholder-centric view dominates. For example, German law is based on a philosophy of **codetermination**, in which the interests of shareholders and employees are expected to be balanced in strategic considerations. Germanic legal code enforces this approach by mandating that employees have either one-third or one-half representation on the supervisory board of German companies (depending on the size of the company). In this way, labor is given a real vote on corporate direction. (We consider the impact of employee board representation in Chapter 5, "Board of Directors: Structure and Consequence.") The Swedish government encourages full employment through Consequences that make it difficult to carry out large-scale layoffs, even though such a policy runs the risk of decreasing firm profitability. In Asia, the Japanese are known for job protection and rewarding employees for tenure. In one survey of international executives, only 3 percent of respondents from Japan agreed that a company should lay off workers to maintain its dividend during difficult economic times. In the United States and the United

Kingdom, 89 percent of respondents believed that maintaining the dividend was more important.[20]

Individual National Governance Structures

To get a better sense of how economic, legal, and cultural realities contribute to the governance systems in specific markets, we will consider the United States, the United Kingdom, Germany, Japan, South Korea, China, India, Brazil, and Russia.

United States

The United States has the largest and most liquid capital markets in the world. U.S. publicly listed companies had an aggregate market value of $15 trillion, representing approximately 35 percent of the total value of equity worldwide in 2009.[21] The U.S. market is the largest by trading volume, by value of public equity offerings, and by corporate and securitized debt outstanding.[22]

The most important regulatory body in the United States is the **Securities and Exchange Commission (SEC)**. Congress created the SEC through the Securities and Exchange Act of 1934 to oversee the proper functioning of primary and secondary financial markets, with an emphasis on the protection of security holder rights and the prevention of corporate fraud. Among its various powers, the SEC has the authority to regulate securities exchanges (such as the New York Stock Exchange [NYSE], the NASDAQ, and the Chicago Mercantile Exchange), bring civil enforcement actions against companies or executives who violate securities laws (through false disclosures, insider trading, or fraud), ensure the quality of accounting standards and financial reporting, and oversee the proxy solicitation and annual voting process.

Although the SEC bears ultimate responsibility for the quality of accounting standards, it has delegated the process of drafting them to the **Financial Accounting Standards Board (FASB)**. Founded in 1973, FASB is a nonprofit organization comprised of accounting experts from academia, industry, audit firms, and the investing public. These individuals draft accounting provisions based on accounting and economic principles, taking into consideration the perspective of practitioners. Then they release draft rules for public comment and update the rules as necessary before adoption. After these rules are adopted, they become part of U.S. GAAP. As mentioned earlier, U.S. regulators have signaled an intention to transition from U.S. GAAP to IFRS by the middle of the decade 2010, to increase comparability of financial reporting between the United States and other countries.

Approximately 27 percent of all publicly traded companies in the United States are incorporated in their state of origin, 63 percent in the state of Delaware, and 10 percent in a state other than these.[23] Delaware has the most developed body of case law, which gives companies clarity on how corporate matters might be decided if they come to trial. Furthermore, trials over corporate matters in Delaware are heard by a judge instead of a jury, a process that some companies prefer because they believe it reduces their liability risk.[24]

Companies are required to comply with the listing requirements of the exchanges on which their securities trade. The largest exchange in the United States is the **New York Stock Exchange (NYSE)**. The NYSE requires that a listed company have at least 400 shareholders, maintain a minimum market value and trading volume in its securities, and demonstrate compliance with the following governance standards:

- The listed company's board is required to have a majority of independent directors.
- Nonexecutive directors must meet independently from executive directors on a scheduled basis.
- The compensation committee of the board must consist entirely of independent directors.
- The audit committee must have a minimum of three members, all of whom are "financially literate" and at least one of whom is a "financial expert."
- The company must have an internal audit function.
- The chief executive officer (CEO) must certify annually that the company is in compliance with NYSE requirements.

The NYSE Corporate Governance Rules provide a detailed definition of board member independence, which the NYSE defines as the director having "no material relationship with the listed company."[25] However, each company is allowed a degree of discretion in determining whether a board member meets certain of these criteria. Likewise, the NYSE affords flexibility to companies in establishing guidelines for director qualifications, director responsibilities, access to management and independent advisors, compensation, management succession, and self-review. (Legal and regulatory issues are discussed more fully in Chapter 3.)

One important piece of federal legislation related to U.S. governance is the **Sarbanes–Oxley Act of 2002**. Important provisions of Sarbanes-Oxley include the following:

- The requirement that the CEO and chief financial officer (CFO) certify financial results (with misrepresentations subject to criminal penalties)
- An attestation by executives and auditors to the sufficiency of internal controls
- Independence of the audit committee of the board of directors (as incorporated in the listing standards of the NYSE)
- A limitation of the types of nonaudit work an auditor can perform for a company
- A ban on most personal loans to executives or directors

A second important piece of legislation relating to U.S. governance is the **Dodd–Frank Financial Reform Act of 2010**. Some of the important provisions include the following:

- **Proxy access**—Shareholders or groups of shareholders who own 3 percent or more of a company's securities for at least three years are eligible to nominate directors on the company proxy (up to 25 percent of the board).
- **Say-on-pay**—Shareholders are given a nonbinding vote on executive compensation.
- **Disclosure**—Companies must provide expanded disclosure on executive compensation, hedging of company equity by executives and directors, the independence of compensation committee members, and the decision of whether to have an independent chairman.[26]

The U.S. governance system is shareholder-centric. Directors have a legal obligation to act "in the interest of the corporation," which the courts have defined to mean "in the interest of shareholders." With rare exceptions, employees are not represented on boards of directors. Although shareholders have submitted proxy proposals to further goals of social responsibility—such as environmentalism, fair labor practices, and internal pay equity—few have succeeded. An active market for corporate control and the threat of litigation for companies that do not satisfy shareholder demands serve as an effective control on company behavior. (The market for corporate control and shareholder activism are discussed in Chapters 11 and 12, "Institutional Shareholders" and "Activist Investors," respectively.)

Executive compensation is higher in the United States than in most other countries. Fernandes, Ferreira, Matos, and Murphy (2010) found that average total compensation for CEOs in the United States is more than twice what CEOs outside the United States earn ($5.5 million versus $2.3 million).[27] Most cross-country differences are explained by pay structure: CEOs who are more highly paid receive a larger percentage of their pay in the form of equity incentives, with U.S. CEOs falling at the high end of the spectrum. It is unknown why CEOs in the United States are paid higher than global averages, but cultural, tax, accounting, political, and other determinants likely are all contributing factors. (Compensation issues are discussed more fully in Chapters 8 and 9.)

United Kingdom

The British model of governance shares many similarities with that of the U.S. model. This likely results from the commonalities between these two countries in terms of capital markets structure, legal tradition, regulatory approach, and societal values. As in the U.S., the British model is shareholder-centric, with a single board of directors, management participation on the board (particularly for the CEO), and an emphasis on transparency and disclosure through audited financial reports. This model is generally referred to as the **Anglo-Saxon model**.

Instead of legislative bodies passing detailed statutes, the British model relies on market mechanisms to determine governance standards. Historically, British Parliament has taken a hands-off approach to regulation. For example, the Companies Act 1985, which consolidates seven Companies Acts passed by Parliament between 1948 and 1983, imposes few governance requirements on companies. The Companies Act 1985 states quite simply that companies are required to have a board (with at least two directors for publicly traded companies) and that the board is responsible for certain administrative functions, including the production of annual financial reports. The act does not specify a required structure for boards, nor does it mandate procedures for conducting business. The company's shareholders determine such rules through the articles of association. As a result, U.K. tradition provides flexibility to the corporate body in developing governance standards.

Despite this hands-off approach to regulation, the U.K. has been a leader in governance reform, promoting the following standards of best practices based on the recommendation of expert panels:

- **The Cadbury Report (1992)**—Parliament commissioned the Cadbury Committee in the early 1990s to provide a benchmark set of recommendations on governance. The committee recommended a set of voluntary guidelines known as the Code of Best Practices. These included the separation of the chairman and chief executive officer titles, the appointment of independent directors to the board, reduced conflicts of interest at the board level because of business or other relationships, the creation of an independent audit committee, and a review of the effectiveness of the company's internal controls. The recommendations of the Cadbury Committee set the basis for the standards for the London Stock Exchange and have influenced governance standards in the U.S. and several other countries (see the sidebar that follows).[28]

- **The Greenbury Report (1995)**—The Greenbury Committee was commissioned to review the executive compensation package process. The committee recommended establishing an independent remuneration committee entirely comprised of nonexecutive directors.[29]

- **The Hampel Report (1998)**—The Hampel Committee was established to review the effectiveness of the Cadbury and Greenbury reports. The committee recommended no substantive changes and consolidated the Cadbury and Greenbury

reports into the Combined Code of Best Practices, which the
London Stock Exchange subsequently adopted.[30]

- **The Turnbull Report (1999)**—The Turnbull Committee was
commissioned to provide recommendations on ways to
improve corporate internal controls. The committee recommended that companies review the nature of risks facing their
organization, establish processes by which these risks are identified and remedied, and perform an annual review of internal
controls to assess their effectiveness.[31]

- **The Higgs Report (2003)**—The British government asked Sir
Derek Higgs to evaluate the role, quality, and effectiveness of
nonexecutive directors.[32] Higgs recommended that at least half
of the board be nonexecutive directors, that the board appoint a
lead independent director to serve as a liaison with shareholders,
that the nomination committee be headed by a nonexecutive
director, and that executive directors not serve more than six
years on the board. The Higgs Report also advised boards to
"undertake a formal and rigorous annual evaluation of its own
performance and that of its committees and individual directors."[33] The recommendations of the Higgs Report were combined with those of the Turnbull Report and the Combined
Code to create the Revised Combined Code of Best Practices.
Higgs believed that the elevated status of nonexecutive directors
on the board would be "pivotal in creating conditions for board
effectiveness."[34]

Cadbury Committee on Corporate Governance: Code of Best Practices (1992)

The Cadbury Committee provided these original recommendations in 1992:

Relating to the board of directors:

- The board should meet regularly, retain full and effective control over the company, and monitor the executive management.

- A clearly accepted division of responsibilities should exist at
the head of a company, to ensure a balance of power and
authority so that no individual has unfettered decision-making

powers. Companies in which the chairman is also the chief executive should have a strong and independent board with a recognized senior member.

- The board should include nonexecutive directors whose views carry significant weight in the board's decisions.
- The board should meet according to a formal schedule, to ensure that the direction and control of the company rests firmly in its hands.
- Directors should follow an agreed-upon procedure in performing their duties and should consult independent professional advice, if necessary, at the company's expense.
- All directors should have access to the advice and services of the company secretary, who is responsible for ensuring that board procedures are followed and that applicable rules and regulations are complied with. The entire board must address the issue of removing the company secretary.

Relating to nonexecutive directors:

- Nonexecutive directors should pass an independent judgment on issues of strategy, performance, and resources, including key appointments and standards of conduct.
- The majority of nonexecutive directors should not have any business or other relationship that could prevent them from exercising independent judgment, apart from their fees and shareholding. Their fees should reflect the time they commit to the company.
- Nonexecutive directors should be appointed for specified terms, without automatic reappointment.
- The board should select nonexecutive directors through a formal process.

For the executive directors:

- Directors' service contracts should not exceed three years without shareholders' approval.

- Total compensation of the executive directors, the chairman, and the highest-paid U.K. directors should be disclosed, including pension contributions and stock options. Separate figures should be given for salary and performance-related elements, and documentation should explain the basis on which performance is measured.

- The executive directors' pay should be subject to the recommendations of a remunerations committee made up of nonexecutive directors.

On reporting and controls:

- The board should present a balanced and understandable assessment of the company's position.

- The board should maintain an objective and professional relationship with the auditors.

- The board should establish an audit committee of at least three nonexecutive directors, with clearly written terms regarding its authority and duties.

- The directors should explain their responsibility for preparing the accounts, and the auditors should prepare a statement about their reporting responsibilities.

- The directors should report on the effectiveness of the company's system of internal control.

- The directors should report that the business is a "going concern."

Together, these reports have shaped the board of directors into a monitoring and control body in addition to a strategy-setting body.[35]

Publicly traded companies in the United Kingdom are not legally required to adopt the standards of the Revised Combined Code. Instead, the London Stock Exchange requires that they issue an annual statement to shareholders explaining whether they are in compliance with the Code and, if not, stating their reasons for noncompliance. This practice, known as **comply or explain**, puts the burden on public shareholders to monitor whether the company's explanation for noncompliance is acceptable. As a result, the Code advocates a flexible standard that grants a company, its board, and its shareholders discretion in devising appropriate governance processes.

It is widely accepted that the Code has improved governance standards in the U.K. and the countries that have adopted its key provisions. Still, sparse academic evidence supports this claim. Padgett and Shabbir (2005) found only weak evidence that compliance with Code provisions is correlated with stock price performance, and they found no evidence that compliance is correlated with operating performance. This is not to say that the Code has not contributed to governance quality, but simply that any improvements are difficult to detect. (We examine the evidence for specific provisions, such as independence, lead directors, and the separation of the chairman and CEO positions, in Chapter 5.)

Economics aside, the comply-or-explain system enables us to observe which governance provisions are deemed useful from the board's perspective. Surprisingly, a recent study by accounting firm Grant Thornton found that two-thirds of the largest 350 companies on the London Stock Exchange were not fully compliant. The most frequent areas of noncompliance were failure to disclose the terms and conditions by which nonexecutive directors were appointed (45 percent), an audit committee without at least one member with relevant financial experience (21 percent), and an audit committee that did not review the effectiveness of internal auditors (21 percent).[36] Such information might help explain why studies have not found a correlation between compliance levels and operating performance: Perhaps companies are prudently rejecting recommended best practices that are inappropriate for their specific situation.

The U.K. has also been a leader in compensation reform. In 2002, Parliament passed the Directors' Remuneration Report Regulations, which requires that shareholders be granted an advisory vote on director and executive compensation (say-on-pay). Say-on-pay policies have subsequently been adopted in varying form by Australia, the Netherlands, Sweden, Norway, India, and, recently, the United States. Because the shareholder vote is advisory in the U.K., a company is not considered in breach of the act if it ignores the outcome of the vote and implements the defeated policy anyway. As such, say-on-pay in the U.K. is consistent with the country's general comply-or-explain approach to governance standards. However, as we discuss in Chapter 8, say-on-pay has had a mixed impact on the rate of compensation increases in countries that have adopted this practice.

Germany

Legal tradition in Germany is based on civil code instead of the common-law tradition of the United Kingdom and the United States. A civil-code tradition means that legislation mandates more aspects of governance and German corporations are afforded less discretion to determine their own structures and processes. For example, German law stipulates that corporations have a two-tiered board structure (instead of the unitary structure practiced in the Anglo-Saxon model). One board is the **management board** *(Vorstand)*, which is responsible for making decisions on such matters as strategy, product development, manufacturing, finance, marketing, distribution, and supply chain. The second board is the **supervisory board** *(Aufischtsrat)*, which oversees the management board. The supervisory board is responsible for appointing members to the management board; approving financial statements; and making decisions regarding major capital investment, mergers and acquisitions, and the payment of dividends. No managers are allowed to sit on the supervisory board. Members of the supervisory board are elected annually by shareholders at the general meeting.[37]

The law requires the supervisory board to have employee representation. Under the German Corporate Governance Code, a company that has at least 500 employees must allocate one-third of its supervisory board seats to labor representatives; a company with at least 2,000 employees must allocate half to labor. These representation requirements are legal obligations that cannot be amended through bylaw changes. As a result, the German system implicitly places greater emphasis on the preservation of jobs, in contrast to the Anglo-Saxon emphasis on shareholder returns. As mentioned earlier, a system that balances employee and shareholder interest is commonly referred to as codetermination. (Employee board representation is discussed in more detail in Chapter 5.)

German supervisory boards also have representation from founding family members and German national banks or insurance companies. Historically, German corporations have relied heavily on banks instead of capital markets for financing. These relationships grew out of the post–World War II era in which German finance organizations provided loans to hard-hit businesses and received portions of the companies' ownership as collateral. In return, bank officials were given a seat on the supervisory board. This structure gave German corporations stability through the rebuilding process by ensuring a reliable source of capital for expansion and a major investor with a long-term outlook.[38] For example, Deutsche Bank owned a 12.1 percent stake in DaimlerChrysler in 2001, a 7.5 percent share of Munich Re, and a 4.2 percent share of Allianz. Likewise, Allianz/Dresdner Holdings owned 1.6 percent of DaimlerChrysler, 29.8 percent of Munich Re, and 4.6 percent of Deutsche Bank.[39]

Given the large representation by labor and financial institutions, German shareholders traditionally have had far less influence over board matters than shareholders in the U.K. and U.S. This structure poses a risk to minority shareholders because they have to rely on other stakeholders to protect their interests. However, increased liberalization of capital markets in recent years and a gradual shift from bank financing to financing through securities markets are beginning to undo some features of the German governance system.

German corporations have moved toward the adoption of global accounting standards. Historically, German financial statements were published according to German GAAP. The German parliament issues the standards of German GAAP instead of private standards-setting bodies such as the FASB or the IASB. German GAAP is also more closely related to tax accounting, so it is more likely to reflect historical instead of fair-market valuations. As a result, international standards might provide more transparent disclosure regarding a company's financial position than has been the case historically. As mentioned earlier, Ernstberger and Vogler (2008) found that companies that adopt international accounting standards realize a lower cost of capital than companies that use German GAAP.

The German corporate governance system confronts several serious challenges from globalization. Although German citizens might prefer a system of codetermination, the international investment community demands financial returns. This has created conflicts as German corporations balance the needs of employees and shareholders. A second challenge is dealing with a rising level of executive compensation. As corporations grow in size and compete with foreign multinationals for executive talent, compensation levels have risen. For example, politicians and the media fiercely criticized Porsche CEO Wendelin Wiedeking in 2007 for accepting €68 million in compensation after the company's net income nearly tripled compared to 2006 levels (€4.2 billion versus €1.4 billion). Although a payment of this magnitude is more common in the United States, it is considered unacceptable by the cultural standards of Europe, which place greater emphasis on social equality. Conflicts over the role of the corporation and executive compensation levels will likely continue in future years.

Japan

As in Germany, the Japanese system of governance has its roots in post–World War II reconstruction. At the end of the war, Allied forces banned the Japanese *zaibatsu,* the powerful industrial and financial conglomerates that accounted for much of the country's pre-war economic strength. The Japanese responded by developing a loose system of interrelations between companies, called the **keiretsu**. Under the *keiretsu,* companies maintain small but not insignificant ownership positions among suppliers, customers, and other business affiliates. These ownership positions cement business relations along the supply chain and encourage firms to work together toward an objective of shared financial success. As in Germany, bank financiers own minority stakes in industrial firms and are key partners in the *keiretsu.* Their investments indicate that capital for financing is available as needed.

The culture in Japan is highly stakeholder-centric, and companies view themselves as having a responsibility to contribute to the prosperity of the nation. One of the most important objectives of Japanese management is to encourage the success of the entire supply chain, including industrial and financial partners. Another objective is to maintain healthy levels of employment and preserve wages and benefits. Proponents believe that the Japanese system, unlike Western styles of capitalism, encourages a long-term perspective, builds

internal commitment to organizational success, and shares the benefits of success more equitably among constituents. Critics of the
Japanese system believe it to be insular and overly resistant to change
(see the following sidebar).

Toyota Board of Directors

Japanese boards have few outside directors, and those that are
nonexecutive directors often include representatives from the lead
bank or a major supplier or customer. For example, Toyota Motor
Corp had a 30-member board of directors in 2007, all of whom
were executives and insiders. Each board member had extensive
experience working within the company. Toyota explained its
rationale for appointing only insiders to the board:

"With respect to our system regarding directors, we believe that it
is important to elect individuals that comprehend and engage in
Toyota's strengths, including commitment to manufacturing, with
an emphasis on frontline operations and problem solving based on
the actual situation on the site (*genchi genbutsu*). Toyota will consider the appointment of outside directors should there be suitable
individuals."[40]

To protect against insider abuse, Toyota developed a system of
adjunct committees that provide advisory or monitoring services to
the board.[41] Toyota convenes an International Advisory Board
(IAB) that includes ten external advisors with backgrounds in politics, economics, environmental issues, and business. The IAB provides an outside viewpoint on issues that are critical to the
company's long-term strategy. Toyota also relies on the advice of
several other committees, including those on labor, philanthropy,
the environment, ethics, and stock options. Toyota maintains a
seven-member corporate auditor board (comprising three Toyota
executives and four external auditors), which is responsible for
reviewing accounting methods and auditing financial results. As a
result, the Toyota corporate governance system seeks to compensate for potential deficiencies that might come from having a board
of executive directors, without compromising the traditional structure that has contributed to the company's success (see Figure 2.2).

Toyota's Corporate Governance

Emphasizing Frontline Operations + Multidirectional Monitoring

Source: Toyota Motor Corporation (2006).

Figure 2.2   Toyota Corporation's corporate governance structure.

> Not all Japanese companies have retained traditional Japanese
> board structures. In the late 1990s, Sony Corporation reduced the
> size of its board from 38 to 10, added outside board members, and
> created both nominating and compensation committees. It made
> these moves to improve policy and decision making.

In 2002, the Japanese Ministry of Justice modified its laws to
encourage the adoption of Western-style systems of governance. The
revised code enabled Japanese companies to choose between a
keiretsu board structure and one with majority-independent audit,
nomination, and compensation committees. It also granted board
members new authority to delegate broad powers to senior management, including discretion to access public markets for debt and
equity. The code revisions enhanced shareholder rights as well, such
as the right to appoint or dismiss certain directors and the external
auditor. Companies were also allowed more freedom to issue
employee stock options. These revisions were intended to improve

governance quality, facilitate access to global capital markets, and increase transparency and accountability.[42] Some evidence shows that it was successful. Eberhart (2009) found that companies that adopted these governance changes experienced a subsequent increase in their market-to-book ratio. However, he did not find an improvement in operating performance.[43]

In addition, Japanese companies are facing many of the same pressures from globalization as German companies. As Japanese companies access global capital markets, international institutional shareholders have somewhat replaced the influence of major banks.[44] For the first time, Japanese companies find themselves faced with shareholder activists that emphasize operational efficiency and shareholder value over stable employment and conservative management. To shield themselves, companies have adopted defense mechanisms such as "poison pills" (discussed further in Chapter 11). Although shareholder activists are critical of these measures, traditionalists believe that they are necessary to preserve the prevailing culture of respect and cooperation between the company and its stakeholders.

Finally, the Japanese Financial Services Authority proposed new disclosure regulations for Japanese-listed companies in 2010. These include more detailed information about the governance system the firm selects; whether outside directors have been appointed to the board and, if not, the reason for not doing so; expanded disclosure on director compensation; expanded disclosure on the strategic and financial nature of cross-holdings; and the voting results for proxy proposals. The changes are intended to improve transparency.[45]

South Korea

Korean economic activity is dominated by conglomerate organizations known as the **chaebol**. *Chaebol*, which means "financial house," are not single corporations but groups of affiliated companies that operate under the strategic and financial direction of a central headquarters. A powerful group chairman, who holds ultimate decision-making authority on all investments, leads headquarters.

The *chaebol* structure was formed following the Korean War. During reconstruction, business leaders worked with government officials to develop a plan for economic growth. Together they identified industries that were deemed critical for the country's long-term success. These included everything from shipbuilding and construction, to textiles, to financial services. The government offered subsidized loans to business leaders to encourage new investment, and business leaders used these loans to expand aggressively. Although investments were managed as separate enterprises, they shared a common affiliation. The plan was highly successful—the Korean economy grew at an almost unprecedented scale. With economic prosperity came great wealth for the *chaebol*. In 1995, the 30 largest *chaebol* accounted for 41 percent of total domestic sales in South Korea.[46]

However, deficiencies in the *chaebol* structure came to light in the Asian financial crisis of 1997. First, they were overly insulated from the market forces that compel efficiency. Founding families had unequal voting rights in proportion to their economic interest (two-thirds voting interest compared with 25 percent economic rights), so their decision making was unchallenged. Second, *chaebol* did not rely on public capital markets for financing, instead relying on internal sources, bank loans, and government subsidies. Therefore, the *chaebol* were not subject to the disciplining force of institutional shareholders.

Over time, these factors led to deterioration in the financial strength of the *chaebol*. Despite their size, they were not very profitable. By the mid-1990s, most were publicly traded at a market-to-book ratio of less than 1, indicating that the financial value of their assets was less than investment cost. Furthermore, they were highly leveraged. A debt-to-equity ratio of 5 to 1 was not uncommon.[47] In addition, group affiliates were tied together by financial guarantees. This created interconnections that made affiliates more vulnerable to financial distress than was initially apparent. Because the groups were not required under accounting rules to disclose these obligations, their true financial condition was unknown to regulators, investors, and creditors. However, the Asian financial crisis brought these troubles to a head. When the Korean currency collapsed, the *chaebol* were unable to repay their debts, many of which were denominated in U.S. dollars. Eight *chaebol* went bankrupt in 1997 alone.

To bring stability to the Korean economy and boost investor confidence, the government issued a series of reforms. First, the practice of transferring funds between *chaebol* affiliates was eliminated. Group companies were forced to become financially self-sufficient, although they could still operate under the strategic direction of group headquarters. Regulators also passed governance reforms that boosted board independence, eliminated intergroup guarantees, and afforded greater rights to minority shareholders. These standards applied only to large corporations with assets greater than 2 trillion won (approximately $2 billion); small companies were exempted.[48]

Black and Kim (2010) examined the impact of these reforms and found superior stock price performance for the companies that adopted them.[49]

China

The Chinese model of corporate governance reflects a partial transition from a communist regime to a capitalist economic system. The Chinese government owns a full or controlling interest in many of the country's largest corporations. Although the government seeks to improve the efficiency of its enterprises, it balances these objectives against stakeholder concerns. These include maintaining high levels of employment and ensuring that critical industries—such as banking, telecommunications, energy, and real estate— are protected from excessive foreign investment and influence.

Chinese companies issue three types of shares: those held by the state, those held by founders and employees, and those held by the public. Shares held by the public fall into three categories: A-shares, B-shares, and H-shares. **A-shares** trade on the Shanghai Stock Exchange and the Shenzhen Stock Exchange on mainland China. Ownership is restricted to domestic investors, and shares are denominated in renminbi. **B-shares** also trade on the Shanghai and Shenzhen markets but are denominated in foreign currencies. **H-shares** trade on the Hong Kong Stock Exchange and are available to foreign investors. H-shares are denominated in Hong Kong dollars. The ownership restrictions placed on these markets have created vastly different liquidity levels, and it is not uncommon for A-shares and H-shares to trade at divergent valuations (with A-shares trading at a significant premium). For example, Zhao, Ma, and Liu (2005) found that, despite identical ownership rights, a basket of companies with both A-share and H-share listings traded at a 113 percent premium on the Shanghai Exchange relative to the Hong Kong Exchange in 2003.[50] In addition, limited float and ownership restrictions limit the influence of public shareholders in China (see Figure 2.3).

Source: China Securities Regulatory Commission.
Figure 2.3   Distribution of shareholder classes in Chinese publicly listed companies.

The Company Law of the People's Republic of China (revised in 2005) outlines the governance requirements for publicly traded companies.[51] Chinese companies are required to have a two-tiered board structure, consisting of a board of directors and a board of supervisors. The board of directors has between 5 and 19 members and usually includes a significant number of company executives. The board of directors is permitted (but not required) to have employee representation. In contrast, the board of supervisors is required to have three or more members, at least one-third of whom are employee representatives. No members of the board of directors or executives are allowed to serve on the board of supervisors.[52] Companies are not required to have audit or compensation committees unless they choose to list their shares on foreign exchanges that require them (such as the NYSE).

The Chinese government maintains significant influence over publicly traded companies. The government selects the companies that are eligible for public listing. It is also often the majority owner and has representatives serving on the board of supervisors. For example, PetroChina was a publicly traded company with shares listed on the New York Stock Exchange (American depository shares, or ADSs), the Hong Kong Stock Exchange (H-shares), and the

Shanghai Stock Exchange (A-shares) in 2007. However, only 14 percent of the company's shares were freely traded by the public in these three markets; the remaining 86 percent of its shares were held by China National Petroleum Corp. (CNPC), which was itself 100 percent owned by the Chinese government.[53] As a result, individual shareholders who invest in Chinese companies are effectively minority owners in partnership with the Chinese government, and they face uncertain legal remedies if controversies arise.

India

Following India's independence from British rule in 1947, the country pursued a socialist economic agenda. Public policy was intended to encourage economic development in a variety of manufacturing industries, but burdensome regulatory requirements led to low productivity, poor-quality products, and marginal profitability. National banks, which provided financing to private companies, often evaluated loans on the size of capital required and the number of jobs created instead of the companies' return on investment.[54] As a result, private companies had little incentive to deploy capital efficiently, and a weak system of corporate governance evolved.

By 1991, the economic situation in the country had deteriorated to such an extent that the Indian government passed a series of major reforms to liberalize the economy and encourage a competitive financial system. With these reforms came pressure to improve governance standards. As a first step, the Confederation of Indian Industries (CII) created a voluntary Corporate Governance Code in 1998. Large companies were encouraged, although not required, to adopt the standards of the Code. One year later, the Securities and Exchange Board of India (SEBI) commissioned the Kumar Mangalam Birla Committee to propose standards of corporate governance that would apply to companies listed on the Indian stock exchange. These reforms were incorporated in **Clause 49** and applied to all publicly traded companies. In 2004, a second panel chaired by N. R. Narayana Murthy, chairman of Infosys, made additional recommendations to revise and further update Clause 49.

Clause 49 requires a majority of nonexecutive directors on the board. If the chairman is an executive of the company, at least half of the directors must be independent; if the chairman is a nonexecutive, the requirement for independent directors is reduced to one-third. Board members are limited to serving on no more than ten committees across all boards to which they are elected. Companies are required to have an audit committee consisting of at least three members, two of whom must be independent directors. The CEO and CFO must certify financial statements. Clause 49 also includes extensive disclosure requirements for related-party transactions, board of directors' compensation and shareholdings in the company, and any financial relationships that might lead to board member conflicts. Companies are required to include a section in the annual report explaining whether they are in compliance with these standards.[55]

Although India has made significant reforms in recent years, several challenges remain. One is that capital markets are largely inefficient. Foreign individual investors are restricted in their ability to directly invest in companies listed on the Bombay Stock Exchange and the National Stock Exchange of India.[56] These restrictions reduce capital flows and remove an important disciplining mechanism on managerial behavior. The country's bond markets are also relatively undeveloped. In 2007, the corporate bond market in India had notional value of only $16.8 billion, less than 2 percent of gross domestic product (GDP). By comparison, the corporate bond market in the United States was more than $6 trillion notional and 20 percent of GDP.[57] With public financing less available, corporations must turn to private sources, which often come with their own agency problems and are less effective monitors.

Another challenge to governance reform is the outsized role that wealthy Indian families continue to play in most major corporations. Family-run companies continue to dominate the Indian economy. For example, Tata Group—which has subsidiaries in the auto manufacturing, agricultural chemicals, hospitality, telecommunications, and consulting sectors—accounts for almost 6 percent of the country's GDP.[58] In aggregate, company insiders and their families own approximately 45 percent of the equity value of all Indian companies.[59] When insiders own concentrated levels of a company's equity, corporate assets could be diverted for the personal benefits of these individuals (such as through excessive salary and perquisites), with minority shareholders bearing the cost of these abuses. (We discuss the relationship between block ownership and corporate performance in more detail in Chapter 12.)

Brazil

As in many emerging economies, corporate governance in Brazil is characterized by excessive influence by insiders and controlling shareholders, and by low levels of disclosure. Brazilian law dictates that only one-third of board members must be nonexecutive. As a result, Brazilian boards tend to have a majority of executive directors. Furthermore, no independence standards exist for nonexecutive directors. Therefore, nonexecutive directors tend to be representatives of a controlling shareholder group or former executives. According to a survey by Black, de Carvalho, and Gorga (2009), 35 percent of Brazilian companies did not have a single independent director, half had fewer than 20 percent independent directors, and only 11 percent had a majority of independent directors.[60] Disclosure rules provide further disincentive to add independent directors to the board: Brazilian companies are not required to disclose the independence status of board members, nor are they required to disclose biographical information that would enable a shareholder to infer this information.

Brazilian firms issue two classes of shares: common shares with voting rights and preferred shares that carry no voting rights. Preferred shares do not pay a fixed dividend. Almost all Brazilian companies have a controlling shareholder or a group that owns a majority of the voting shares. These shareholders hold considerable influence in nominating and electing directors, so the board essentially represents their interests. Minority common shareholders and preferred shareholders have much less influence over board selection and can elect only one director by majority vote.

Traditionally, Brazil has had highly regulated capital markets. In the early 1900s, the government ran public exchanges and set transaction fees. Brokers were employees of the state and could pass on their positions to their children. Liberalization began in the 1960s, and by the 1970s, brokerages were transitioned from government control to private ownership. By the 1980s, the largest trading market became the São Paulo Stock Exchange (Bovespa). To stimulate demand for listing on its exchange, Bovespa created three markets for listing based on a company's governance features. Nivel 1 has the least stringent governance requirements, Nivel 2 has more stringent requirements, and the Novo Mercado has the most stringent requirements. To satisfy the listing requirements of the **Novo Mercado**, a company must do the following:

- Issue only voting shares
- Maintain a minimum free float equivalent to 25 percent of capital
- Establish a two-year unified mandate for the entire board, which must have at least five members and at least 20 percent independent members
- Publish financial reports in accordance with either U.S. GAAP or IFRS
- Grant minority shareholders the rights to dispose of shares on the same terms as majority shareholders (known as **tag-along rights**)

These requirements are intended to provide the greatest level of protection for minority shareholders against expropriation by insiders.[61]

In 2001, the first year the new system was operational, 18 companies transferred their listing to Nivel 1 from the regular exchange. Novo Mercado did not receive its first listing until the following year and did not gain widespread traction until 2004, when Natura, Brazil's leading cosmetics company, transferred its listing there. Since that point, the number of listed companies on all three of these new exchanges has grown exponentially (see Figure 2.4).

De Carvalho and Pennacchi (2009) found a positive impact on stock prices, trading volume, and liquidity for Brazilian companies that migrate their listing to these new exchanges. They concluded that shareholders positively view the governance changes associated with the new listing requirements.[62]

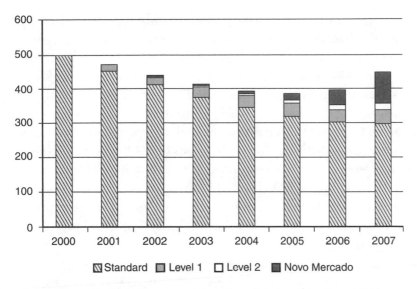

Source: Adapted by David F. Larcker and Brian Tayan. Data from: Érica Gorga (2009).

Figure 2.4   Number of companies listed on the Bovespa.

Russia

Corporate governance in Russia is characterized by concentrated ownership of shares, insider control, weak legal protection for minority shareholders, modest disclosure, inefficient capital markets, and heavy government involvement in private enterprise. Executives are often controlling shareholders or are closely affiliated with the controlling shareholder, whose interests they tend to serve. A disproportionate number of board members are insiders. In an examination of the boards of directors of the largest 75 public Russian companies in 2006, Standard & Poor's found that an average of two-thirds are executive directors.[63] Of the remaining one-third, a significant portion (32 percent) represent a strategic investor. The vast majority of board members do not represent minority investors.

Controlling shareholders use their influence to increase their claim on corporate assets, sometimes using illegal methods to do so. These methods include forcing solvent companies into bankruptcy to seize assets from minority shareholders, bribing the registrar to lose records of ownership by certain shareholders, manipulating transfer pricing to siphon money to an affiliated company that is wholly owned by the controlling shareholder, and forcing dilution of minority shareholders through a private offering to the controlling shareholder.[64] Because legal protections are weak, minority shareholders have limited ability to prevent these actions or seek compensation. For example, BP accused a Russian investor group in 2008 of trying to seize control of joint-venture assets (TNK–BP) by forcing the resignation of the BP-appointed CEO. The chairman of BP stated that the move was "just a return to the corporate raiding activities that were prevalent in Russia in the 1990s [after the fall of the Soviet Union]. Unfortunately, our partners continue to use them and the leaders of the country seem unwilling or unable to step in and stop them."[65] Another international investor agreed: "Corporate governance has improved ... but when someone really wants to break the rules, unfortunately, they can do it. It's a big concern, as it is causing real losses and damaging investor confidence in this country." He cited as an example his firm's investment in a Russian energy company in which "millions of dollars were transferred out of the company in exchange for assets of questionable value."[66]

The Russian government is another source of potential abuse for shareholders. The government has shown a tendency to intervene in business to promote its own interests. A primary method involves making dubious claims of unpaid taxes, which are then used as justification for seizing assets. This method was used in 2006 to transfer the assets from privately held Yukos to Gazprom—Russia's largest oil company, which the Russian government controls. Government corruption also occurs at the regional level as regional governors accept bribes from local employers in exchange for protection from foreign competition. The government also interferes to maintain employment levels and prevent mass layoffs.

Finally, lack of transparency restricts the influence of shareholders. Disclosure requirements are weak, obscuring the nature of interparty transactions. A state-controlled media also contributes to a lack of transparency.

Black, Love, and Rachinsky (2006) examined the relationship between governance quality and share price in Russia. They found some evidence that firms with better governance features trade at higher market valuations than those with lesser protections.[67]

Endnotes

1. Raghuram G. Rajan and Luigi Zingales, "Financial Dependence and Growth," *American Economic Review* 88 (1998): 559–586.

2. Pyramidal business groups are defined as "two or more listed firms under a common controlling shareholder and presumed to be the largest blockholder, voting at least 20 percent or, alternatively, 10 percent." See Randall Morck, "The Riddle of the Great Pyramids," *The Oxford Handbook of Business Groups*, edited by Asli M. Colpan, Takashi Hikino and James R. Lincoln (New York: Oxford University Press, 2010).

3. Bernard Black, "Corporate Governance in Korea at the Millennium: Enhancing International Competitiveness," *Journal of Corporation Law* 26 (2001): 537.

4. That said, Kanna and Palepu (1999) warn that family-controlled business groups cannot be safely dismantled unless a so-called "soft infrastructure" is in place, including well-functioning markets for capital, management, labor, and information technology. Tarun Khanna and Krishna Palepu, "The Right Way to Restructure Conglomerates in Emerging Markets," *Harvard Business Review* 77 (1999): 125–134.

5. Christian Leuz, Karl V. Lins, and Francis E. Warnock, "Do Foreigners Invest Less in Poorly Governed Firms?" *The Review of Financial Studies* 22 (2009): 3,245–3,285.

6. Under common law, judicial precedent shapes the interpretation and application of laws. Judges consider previous court rulings on similar matters and use this information as the basis for settling current claims. By contrast, civil law (or code law) relies on comprehensive legal codes or statutes written by legislative bodies. The judiciary must base its decisions on strict interpretation of the law instead of legal precedent. Rafael La Porta, Florencio Lopez-de-Silanes, Andrei Shleifer, and Robert W. Vishny, "Law and Finance," *Journal of Political Economy* 106 (1998): 1,113–1,155.

7. The results in these two La Porta, Lopez-de-Silanes, Shleifer, and Vishny papers have been examined in subsequent research. For example, Spamann (2010) constructs a new "antidirector rights index" using local lawyers and finds that many of the prior results in these papers become statistically insignificant. Thus, these results might be fragile. See Rafael La Porta, Florencio Lopez-de-Silanes, Andrei Shleifer, and Robert W. Vishny, "Investor Protection and Corporate Valuation," *Journal of Finance* 57 (2002): 1,147–1,170; and Holger Spamann, "The 'Antidirector Rights Index' Revisited," *Review of Financial Studies* 23 (2010): 467–86.

8. Cited in Jacob De Haan and Harry Seldadyo, "The Determinants of Corruption: A Literature Survey and New Evidence," paper presented at the Annual Conference of the European Public Choice Society, Turku (April 24, 2006).

9. Paulo Mauro, "Corruption and Growth," *Quarterly Journal of Economics* 110 (1995): 681–712.

10. Christos Pantzalis, Jung Chul Park, and Ninon Sutton, "Corruption and Valuation of Multinational Corporations," *Journal of Empirical Finance* 15 (2008): 387–417.

11. Jürgen Ernstberger and Oliver Vogler, "Analyzing the German Accounting Triad—'Accounting Premium' for IAS/IFRS and U.S. GAAP vis-á-vis German GAAP?" *International Journal of Accounting* 43 (2008): 339–386.

12. Jere R. Francis, Shawn Huang, Inder K. Khurana, and Raynolde Pereira, "Does Corporate Transparency Contribute to Efficient Resource Allocation?" *Journal of Accounting Research* 47 (2009): 943–989.

13. George J. Benston, Michael Bromwich, and Alfred Wagenhofer, "Principles-Versus Rules-Based Accounting Standards: The FASB's Standard Setting Strategy," *Abacus* 42 (2006): 165–188.

14. Richard Price, Francisco J. Román, and Brian Rountree, "The Impact of Governance Reform on Performance and Transparency," *Journal of Financial Economics* 99 (2011): 76–96.

15. Luzi Hail and Christian Leuz, "International Differences in the Cost of Equity Capital: Do Legal Institutions and Securities Regulation Matter?" *Journal of Accounting Research* 44 (2006): 485–531.

16. Robert M. Bushman and Joseph D. Piotroski, "Financial Reporting Incentives for Conservative Accounting: The Influence of Legal and Political Institutions," *Journal of Accounting and Economics* 42 (2006): 1–2.

17. Victor Brudney, "Insiders, Outsiders, and Informational Advantages under the Federal Securities Laws," *Harvard Law Review* 93 (1979): 322. See Lawrence M. Ausubel, "Insider Trading in a Rational Expectations Economy," *American Economic Review* 80 (1990): 1,022–1,041. Hayne E. Leland, "Insider Trading: Should It Be Prohibited?" *Journal of Political Economy* 100 (1992): 859–887.

18. Geert Hofstede, "Cultural Dimensions," Itim Focus, http://www.itimfocus.org/index.php/frontpage/page/concepts/5d/more. Accessed November 3, 2010.

19. The Hofstede research has been the subject of considerable criticism. We discuss it here as representative of a system for describing cultural attributes without commentary on its accuracy. See Nigel J. Holden, *Cross-Cultural Management: A Knowledge Management Perspective* (London: FT Prentice Hall, 2002). Brendan McSweeney, "Hofstede's Model of National Cultural Differences and Their Consequences: A Triumph of Faith—a Failure of Analysis," *Human Relations* 55 (2002): 89–118.

20. Anonymous, "Whose Company Is It? New Insights on the Debate over Shareholders vs. Stakeholders," Knowledge@Wharton (2008). Accessed July 7, 2008. See http://knowledge.wharton.upenn.edu/article.cfm?articleid=1826.

21. Despite the impression that diffuse ownership of U.S. securities exists, the ownership of U.S. firms is similar to and, by some measures, more concentrated than the ownership of firms in other countries. See World Federation of Exchanges, "WFE 2009 Market Highlights," *WFE Statistics Database*, Accessed February 24, 2011; and Clifford G. Holderness, "The Myth of Diffuse Ownership in the United States," *Review of Financial Studies* 22 (2009): 1,377–1,408.

22. However, U.S. markets have been losing their share in several of these categories during recent years. See Committee On Capital Markets Regulation, "The Competitive Position of the U.S. Public Equity Market" (2007). Accessed December 15, 2010. See www.capmktsreg.org/pdfs/The_Competitive_Position_of_the_US_Public_Equity_Market.pdf.

23. Computed using 2009 data for 3,875 companies covered by SharkRepellent, FactSet Research Systems Inc.

24. Daines (2001) finds that companies incorporated in Delaware are worth approximately 5 percent more than firms incorporated in other states. Debate exists over whether this is because of increased governance quality, greater clarity on shareholder rights, or higher likelihood of receiving a takeover bid from another firm. Source: Robert M. Daines, "Does Delaware Law Improve Firm Value?" *Journal of Financial Economics* 62 (2001): 525–558.

25. See Chapter 5 for a discussion of NYSE independence standards. Source: Anonymous, "Corporate Governance Standards, Listed Company Manual Section 303A.02, Independence Tests," NYSE Euronext (2010). See www.nyse.com/regulation/nyse/1101074746736.html.

26. See Weil, Gotshal & Manges, LLP, "Financial Regulatory Reform: An Overview of The Dodd–Frank Wall Street Reform and Consumer Protection Act" (2010). Accessed November 2, 2010. See www.weil.com/news/pubdetail.aspx?pub=9877.

27. Nuno G. Fernandes, Miguel A. Ferreira, Pedro P. Matos, and Kevin J. Murphy, "The Pay Divide: (Why) Are U.S. Top Executives Paid More?" EFA 2009 Bergen Meetings Paper; AFA 2011 Denver Meetings Paper; ECGI—Finance Working Paper No. 255/2009, *Social Science Research Network* (2010). See http://ssrn.com/abstract=1341639.

28. Adrian Cadbury, "The Financial Aspects of Corporate Governance; Report of the Committee on the Financial Aspects of Corporate Governance" (London: Gee & Co, 1992). Accessed November 3, 2010. See www.ecgi.org/codes/documents/cadbury.pdf.

29. Richard Greenbury, "Directors' Remuneration: Report of a Study Group Chaired by Sir Richard Greenbury," (London: Gee Publishing, 1995). Accessed November 3, 2010. See www.ecgi.org/codes/documents/greenbury.pdf.

30. Ronnie Hampel, "Committee on Corporate Governance: Final Report," (London: Gee Publishing 1998). Accessed November 3, 2010. See www.ecgi. org/codes/documents/hampel.pdf.

31. Nigel Turnbull, et al., "Internal Control: Guidance for Directors on the Combined Code" (1999). Accessed November 1, 2010. See www.icaew.com/ index.cfm/route/120907/icaew_ga/pdf.

32. Dechert, LLP, "The Higgs Report on Non-Executive Directors: Summary Recommendations" (2003). Accessed December 5, 2007. See www.dechert. com/library/Summary%20of%20Recommendations1.pdf.

33. Cited in Rob Goffee, "Feedback Helps Boards to Focus on Their Roles," *Financial Times* (June 10, 2005): 32.

34. Martin Dickson, "Higgs and the History of Corporate Protest," *Financial Times* (February 18, 2003): 25. The Higgs Report was subsequently revised in June 2006 and again in May 2010. See www.ecgi.org/codes/documents/frc_ combined_code_june2006.pdf. Accessed October 30, 2010. Also see www.frc. org.uk/images/uploaded/documents/May%202010%20report%20on% 20Code%20consultation.pdf. Accessed October 30, 2010.

35. Paul L. Davies, "Board Structure in the United Kingdom and Germany: Convergence or Continuing Divergence?" *Social Science Research Network* (2001): 1–24. Accessed October 30, 2010.

36. Grant Thornton UK, LLP, "Fifth FTSE 350 Corporate Governance Review 2007" (2007). Accessed October 30, 2010. See www.grantthornton.co.uk/pdf/ CGR-2007.pdf.

37. Commission of the German Corporate Governance Code, "German Corporate Governance—Code" (May 26, 2010). Accessed June 30, 2010. See www. corporate-governance-code.de/eng/kodex/index.html.

38. Christopher Rhoads and Vanessa Fuhrmans, "Trouble Brewing: Corporate Germany Braces for a Big Shift from Postwar Stability—Layoffs, Predators, Gadflies Loom with Unwinding of Cross-Shareholdings—Dry Times for Beer Workers," *Wall Street Journal* (June 21, 2001, Eastern edition): A1.

39. Deutsche Bank, "2001 List of Shareholdings, Deutsche Bank: Results 2001 Annual Report" (2001). Accessed August 29, 2008. See www.db.com/ir/en/ download/E_Results_01_orig.pdf. Allianz Group, "Allianz Consolidated Financial Statements 2001" (2001). Accessed August 29, 2008. See www. allianz.com/static-resources/migration/images/pdf/saobj_215071_group_ financial_statem_2001.pdf.

40. Toyota Motor Corporation, Form 6-K filed with the Securities and Exchange Commission, June 29, 2007. One of the guiding precepts of the Toyota Production System, *genchi genbutsu,* means "go and see for yourself."

41. Toyota Motor Corporation, "2006 Annual Report." Accessed June 23, 2008. See www.toyota.co.jp/en/pdf/2006/toyota_up_close0611.pdf. Also see Toyota Motor Corporation, "Toyota Governance." Accessed November 2, 2010. See www. toyota-industries.com/corporateinfo/governance/.

42. TMI Associates and Simmons & Simmons, "Amendments to the Japanese Commercial Code." Amendment enacted in May 2002, in force as of April 1, 2003 (2003). Accessed November 1, 2010. See www.tmi.gr.jp/english/ backnumber/pdf/H14-AMENDMENTS_TO_THE_JAPANESE_ COMMERCIAL_CODE.pdf.

43. Robert Eberhart, "Corporate Governance Systems and Firm Value: Empirical Evidence for the Value of Committee Systems with Outside Directors," *Social Science Research Network* (May 1, 2009). See http://ssrn.com/abstract= 1422039.

44. In the late 1980s, Japanese banks owned almost 50 percent of total tradable public equity. By 2006, they held around 20 percent. See Masahiko Aoki, "Conclusion: Whither Japan's Corporate Governance?" *Corporate Governance in Japan: Institutional Change and Organizational Diversity,* edited by Masahiko Aoki, Gregory Jackson, and Hideaki Miyajima (New York: Oxford University Press, 2007).

45. Financial Services Agency, "Outline of Proposal of Disclosure Items concerning Corporate Governance" (2010). Accessed February 19, 2010. See www.fsa. go.jp/en/news/2010/20100219-2/01.pdf.

46. Barry Metzger, Bernard S. Black, Timothy O'Brien, and Young Moo Shin, "Corporate Governance in Korea at the Millennium: Enhancing International Competitiveness," *Journal of Corporation Law* 26 (2001): 537–608.

47. Ibid.

48. Ibid.

49. Bernard S. Black and Woochan Kim, "The Effect of Board Structure on Firm Value: A Multiple Identification Strategies Approach Using Korean Data," *University of Texas Law, Law and Economics Research Paper No. 89* (2010); *McCombs Research Paper No. FIN-02-07; ECGI Finance Working Paper No. 179/2007; KDI School of Pub Policy & Management Paper No. 07-02; EFA 2007 Ljubljana Meetings Paper, Social Science Research Network.* Accessed November 3, 2010. See http://ssrn.com/abstract=968287.

50. Zhijun Zhao, Yue Ma, and Yuhui Liu, "Equity Valuation in Mainland China and Hong Kong: The Chinese A-H Share Premium," *HKIMR Working Paper No. 14/2005, Social Science Research Network* (2005): 1–28. Accessed September 8, 2010. See http://ssrn.com/abstract=1008778/.

51. Sean Liu, "Corporate Governance and Development: The Case of China," *Managerial and Decision Economics* 26 (2005): 445–449.

52. Standing Committee of the NPC, Law Bridge, "The Company Law of the People's Republic of China (Revised in 2005)." See www.law-bridge.net/english/LAW/20064/0221042566163-5.html.

53. PetroChina Company, 2006 Form 20-F filed with the Securities and Exchange Commission (May 11, 2007).

54. Bernard Black and Vikramaditya Khanna, "Can Corporate Governance Reforms Increase Firms' Market Values?: Evidence from India," *American Law & Economics Association Papers* 40 (2007): 1–38.

55. Securities and Exchange Board of India (SEBI), "Corporate Governance in Listed Companies: Clause 49 of the Listing Agreement" (2004). Accessed December 5, 2007. See www.sebi.gov.in/circulars/2004/cfdcir0104.pdf.

56. India Mart, "India Finance and Investment Mart: Foreign Institutional Investor" (2010). Accessed November 3, 2010. See http://finance.indiamart. com/india_business_information/sebi_foreign_institutional_investor.html.

57. Deutsche Bank Research, "India's Capital Markets: Unlocking the Door to Future Growth" (2007). Accessed August 19, 2009. See www.dbresearch.com/ PROD/DBR_INTERNET_EN-PROD/PROD0000000000206002.pdf.

58. Anonymous, "Here Be Dragons," *The Economist* (April 17, 2010). Accessed November 3, 2010. See www.economist.com/node/15879289.

59. Nandini Rajagopalan and Yan Zhang, "Corporate Governance Reforms in China and India: Challenges and Opportunities," *Business Horizons* 51 (2008): 55–64.

60. In the study, independent directors are defined as "persons who are not officers or former officers and are independent of the controlling shareholder, controlling shareholder group, or controlling family." Bernard S. Black, Antonio Gledson De Carvalho, and Érica Gorga, "The Corporate Governance of Privately Controlled Brazilian Firms (A Governança Corporativa Das Empresas Brasileiras Com Controle Privado Nacional)," *Revista Brasileira de Finanças, Social Science Research Network* (2009): 7. Accessed November 3, 2010. See http://ssrn.com/abstract=1528183.

61. Nivel 2 primarily differs from the Novo Mercado in that companies are allowed to issue nonvoting shares. Nivel 1 does not require tag-along rights for minority shareholders and also does not have a 20 percent requirement for board independence. Érica Gorga, "Changing the Paradigm of Stock Ownership from Concentrated Towards Dispersed Ownership? Evidence from Brazil and Consequences for Emerging Countries," *Northwestern Journal of International Law & Business* 29 (2009): 439–554. See search.ebscohost.com/login.aspx?direct =true&db=bth&AN=40100493&site=ehost-live.

62. Antonio Gledson De Carvalho and George G Pennacchi, "Can a Stock Exchange Improve Corporate Behavior? Evidence from Firms' Migration to Premium Listings in Brazil," *Social Science Research Network* (2009): 1–50.

63. See Olga Lazareva, Andrei Rachinsky, and Sergey Stepanov, "A Survey of Corporate Governance in Russia." CEFIR/NES Working Paper series, *Social Science Research Network* (2007). Accessed November 1, 2010. See http://ssrn. com/abstract=997965.

64. Bernard S. Black, Inessa Love, and Andrei Rachinsky, "Corporate Governance Indices and Firms' Market Values: Time Series Evidence from Russia," *Emerging Markets Review* 7 (2006): 361–379.

65. Robert Anderson, Catherine Belton, and Ed Crooks, "BP Accuses Russian Partners in TNK–BP of 'Corporate Raiding,'" *Financial Times* (June 13, 2008): 13.

66. John Bowker, "Russia Held Back by Corporate Governance Weakness: Fund," *Reuters* (September 10, 2010).
See www.reuters.com/article/idUSTRE6893BO20100910.

67. Bernard S. Black, Inessa Love, and Andrei Rachinsky.

Interlude

The board of directors plays a central role in the corporate governance system. All countries require that publicly listed companies have such a board. The attributes of boards vary across nations (in terms of their mandated structure, independence levels, stakeholder representation, and other compositional features), but they universally share two fundamental responsibilities: to advise management and oversee its activities.

In the next few chapters, we take a critical look at the board of directors. We start by examining the basic operations of the board and the duties that come with directorship (in Chapter 3, "Board of Directors: Duties and Liability"). Then we discuss the process by which directors are selected, compensated, and replaced (in Chapter 4, "Board of Directors: Selection, Compensation, and Removal"). Finally, we review the scientific evidence on how the structure of the board does (and does not) impact firm performance and governance quality (in Chapter 5, "Board of Directors: Structure and Consequences").

These chapters are intended to help you think critically about board effectiveness and make concrete decisions about how a board should be structured.

3

Board of Directors: Duties and Liability

In this chapter, we examine the duties and liabilities that come with directorship. We start with an overview of the role of the board and the requirement for independence. We then review the basic operations of the board. This includes evaluating the process by which topics are selected, deliberated, and decided. Next, we review the process by which directors are elected and removed. Finally, we examine the legal responsibilities that come with directorship and consider the potential liability directors face when they fail to uphold their duties. While we focus on boards of U.S. corporations, the broad principles apply to boards in all countries.

Board Responsibilities

In a document called Principles of Corporate Governance, the Organization for Economic Cooperation and Development (OECD) lays out a vision of the responsibilities of the board:

> The corporate governance framework should ensure the strategic guidance of the company, the effective monitoring of management by the board, and the board's accountability to the company and the shareholders.[1]

That is, the board is expected to provide both advisory and oversight functions. Although these responsibilities are linked in many ways, they have fundamentally different focuses. In an **advisory** capacity, the board consults with management regarding the strategic and operational direction of the company. Attention is paid to decisions that balance risk and reward. Board members are selected based on the skill and expertise they offer for this purpose, including previous experience in a relevant industry or function.

In its **oversight** capacity, the board is expected to monitor management and ensure that it is acting diligently in the interests of shareholders. The board hires and fires the chief executive officer, measures corporate performance, evaluates management contribution to performance, and awards compensation. It also oversees legal and regulatory compliance, including the audit process, reporting requirements for publicly traded companies, and industry-specific regulations. In fulfilling these responsibilities, the board often relies on the advice of legal counsel and other paid professionals, such as external auditors, executive recruiters, compensation consultants, investment bankers, and tax advisors. Effective board members are individuals that can capably complete both advisory and oversight responsibilities.

The responsibilities of directors are separate and distinct from those of management. Directors are expected to advise on corporate strategy but do not develop the strategy. They are expected to ensure the integrity of the financial statements but do not prepare the statements themselves. The board is not an extension of management. The board is a governing body elected to represent the interests of shareholders.

Survey data suggests that board members understand the role they are expected to serve. When asked to describe what areas directors should pay most attention to, other than profitability and shareholder value, directors list future growth, risk management, and development of human capital as their top three priorities. Other areas of focus include cultural development, executive compensation, and regulatory compliance.[2] Still, some evidence indicates that directors prefer the advisory function to the monitoring function. When asked what issues they would like to spend more time discussing, directors list strategic planning, competition, and succession planning among their top responses. By contrast, most want to spend the same or less time on executive compensation, monitoring performance, and compliance and regulatory issues.[3]

Board Independence

To be effective in an advisory and oversight capacity, board members are expected to exhibit independence. From a regulatory standpoint, independence is evaluated by the degree to which a director is free from conflicts of interest that might compromise his or her ability to act solely in the interest of the firm. Independence is critical in that it ensures that directors are able to take positions in opposition to those of management when necessary. In the United States, the New York Stock Exchange (NYSE) requires that listed companies have a majority of independent directors. It also requires solely independent audit, compensation, and nominating and governance committees.

However, regulatory standards are not necessarily the same as true independence. Board members who have worked with management over a long period of time may well form ties that will challenge a truly independent perspective. Independence may also be compromised by individual factors, such as the board member's background, education, experience, values, and personal relation to management. There are many examples of boards comprised of highly capable directors who went along with management decisions that later proved disastrous. For example, the board of Enron failed to rein in management actions that were later held to be criminal. Similarly, the board of Disney acquiesced to management in the hiring and firing of Michael Ovitz, which later drew harsh criticism from shareholders.

Anecdotal evidence suggests that board members do not necessarily believe that formal independence standards are correlated with true independence. An informal study conducted by professors at Harvard Business School found that relevant experience is a more important indicator of director quality than regulatory requirements. According to one respondent, "I don't think independence is anywhere near as important as people thought it was. ... It was a red herring."[4] Nevertheless, most directors believe that they are capable of maintaining independence. In a survey by *Corporate Board Member* magazine, 85 percent of directors responded that they and their fellow board members effectively challenged management when necessary.[5] (We discuss independence in more detail in Chapter 5, "Board of Directors: Structure and Consequences.")

The Operations of the Board

A chairman presides over meetings of the board of directors. The chairman is responsible for setting the agenda, scheduling meetings, and coordinating actions of board committees. As such, the chairman holds considerable sway over the governance process by determining the content and timing of matters brought before the board.

Traditionally, the CEO has served as the chairman of the board in most U.S. corporations. In recent years, however, it has become more common for a nonexecutive director to serve as chair. Given the advising and oversight responsibilities of the board, several obvious conflicts could arise from a dual chairman/CEO. Chief among them are the commingling of responsibilities that are afforded separately to management and the board, and the potential for weakened oversight in the areas of performance evaluation, compensation, succession planning, and recruitment of independent directors. At the same time, a dual chairman/CEO offers potential benefits regarding singular leadership within the organization and clear, efficient decision making. (We examine the evidence on independent chairmen in Chapter 5.)

In the debate over the Sarbanes-Oxley Act of 2002 (SOX), Congress considered but ultimately rejected calls to require an independent director to serve as chairman. Instead, SOX required that companies designate an independent director as "lead director" for each board meeting. The lead director may be named to serve on a meeting-by-meeting basis or may be appointed to serve continuously until replaced. The role of the lead director is to represent the independent directors in conversations with the CEO. This structure is intended to fortify an independent review of management among companies with a dual chairman/CEO. (We discuss the role of the lead director in more detail in Chapter 5.)

Board actions take place either at board meetings or by written consent. At a board meeting, resolutions are presented to the board and voted upon. An action is complete when it receives a majority of votes in support. When the board acts by **written consent**, a written resolution is circulated among board members for their signatures. The action is complete when a majority of the directors have signed the document. Because board actions by written consent do not require advance notice, they can occur more quickly than actions taken at board meetings.

In addition to attending meetings of the full board, independent directors meet at least once a year in **executive session**, in which executive directors are not present. This practice was mandated by SOX. While no formal actions are taken at these meetings, executive sessions give outside directors an opportunity to discuss candidly the performance of management, operating results, internal controls, and succession planning. The lead independent director presides over these meetings.

Directors report spending approximately 20 hours per month on board matters. A typical meeting lasts between two and six hours, but some last as long as eight hours. Increased regulatory requirements in recent years have done much to lengthen board meetings. Still, most directors believe that the agenda is structured to make efficient use of their time and that 20 hours per month is sufficient to satisfy their duties.[6]

To inform its decisions, the board relies on materials provided by management. Survey data indicates that the quality of this information might not be adequate. For example, a study by Deloitte Consulting found that although 91 percent of directors reported receiving good or excellent information about their company's financial results, only 61 percent were satisfied with the information they received on operational performance. Additionally, fewer than half believed they were receiving excellent or good information about important areas of the business, including product quality, product innovation, relationships with business partners and suppliers, customer satisfaction, and employee commitment.[7] Nonexecutive directors can address these deficiencies by requesting that management improve reporting on nonfinancial as well as financial strategic performance measures. Directors may also benefit through more direct contact with management. According to one director, "There is no substitute for time spent meeting with management of the different divisions or sectors that are the next level down the corporate ladder, having them present directly to the board, [and] visiting operations."[8] (We examine these issues in greater detail in Chapter 6, "Organizational Strategy, Business Models, and Risk Management.")

Board Committees

Not all corporate matters are deliberated by the full board of directors. Some are delegated to committees. These committees can be standing or *ad hoc*, depending on the nature of the topic. Directors are assigned to committees based on their qualifications. On important matters, such as the design and approval of executive compensation contracts, recommendations of the committee are brought before the full board for a vote.

Historically, the creation of committees was left largely to the discretion of the board. The only committee that the Securities and Exchange Commission (SEC) required was an audit committee, which was mandated for all publicly listed companies in 1977. In 2002, the Sarbanes-Oxley Act required additional committees, including a compensation committee, a governance committee, and a nominating committee. The act stipulated that these committees and the audit committee consist entirely of independent directors.

The **audit committee** is responsible for overseeing the company's external audit and is the primary contact between the auditor and the company. This reporting relationship is intended to prevent management manipulation of the audit. Under SOX, the audit committee must have at least three members, all of whom are financially literate; the chair also must be a financial expert. The audit committee maintains a written charter that outlines its duties to the full board, including these obligations:

1. Overseeing the financial reporting and disclosure process
2. Monitoring the choice of accounting policies and principles
3. Overseeing the hiring, performance, and independence of the external auditor
4. Overseeing regulatory compliance, ethics, and whistleblower hotlines
5. Monitoring internal control processes
6. Overseeing the performance of the internal audit function
7. Discussing risk-management policies and practices with management[9]

According to the NACD, audit committees meet an average of seven times per year for 3.2 hours.[10] Ninety-four percent of directors believe that the audit committee is effective in its oversight of the financial reporting process.[11] (We explore the duties of the audit committee in greater detail in Chapter 10, "Financial Reporting and External Audit.")

The **compensation committee** is responsible for setting the compensation of the CEO and for advising the CEO on the compensation of other senior executives. Sarbanes-Oxley established no minimum committee size. The obligations of the compensation committee include the following:

1. Setting the compensation of the CEO
2. Setting and reviewing performance-related goals for the CEO
3. Determining appropriate compensation structure for the CEO, given these performance expectations
4. Monitoring CEO performance relative to targets
5. Setting or advising the CEO on other officers' compensation
6. Advising the CEO on and overseeing compensation of nonexecutive employees
7. Setting board compensation
8. Hiring consultants to assist in the compensation process, as appropriate[12]

Compensation committees meet an average of five times per year for 2.4 hours.[13] Seventy-six percent of directors believe the compensation committee can properly manage CEO compensation.[14] (We explore compensation in greater detail in Chapters 8, "Executive Compensation and Incentives," and 9, "Executive Equity Ownership.")

The **governance committee** is responsible for evaluating the company's governance structure and processes and recommending improvements, when appropriate. The **nominating committee** is responsible for identifying, evaluating, and nominating new directors when board seats need to be filled. The nominating committee is also typically in charge of leading the CEO succession-planning process.

In most companies, the nominating and governance committees are combined into a single committee with these responsibilities:

1. Identifying qualified individuals to serve on the board
2. Selecting nominees to be put before a shareholder vote at the annual meeting
3. Hiring consultants to assist in the director recruitment process, as appropriate
4. Determining governance standards for the corporation
5. Managing the board evaluation process
6. Managing the CEO evaluation process[15]

The nominating and governance committee meets an average of four times per year for 1.9 hours.[16] Despite the independence of this committee, the CEO often has significant input into the choice of directors nominated to the board. This is true whether or not the CEO holds the dual role of chairman. (We explore director recruitment in Chapter 4, "Board of Directors: Selection, Compensation, and Removal," and CEO succession in Chapter 7, "Labor Market for Executives and CEO Succession Planning.")

Boards are free to establish additional committees beyond those required by listing exchanges. These committees generally monitor functional areas that the board believes to hold strategic importance for the firm, thus meriting additional oversight (**specialized committees**). According to Spencer Stuart, 34 percent of companies have a committee dedicated to finance, 11 percent to corporate social responsibility, 6 percent to science and technology, 4 percent to legal, 4 percent to the environment, and 3 percent to risk.[17] These committees oversee and advise these functions; they do not directly manage them, which is the purview of management (see the following sidebar).

Specialized Board Committees

The board of Merck & Co. convenes a Research Committee to monitor its drug discovery and development process:

"The Research Committee, which is comprised of independent directors, assists the Board in its oversight of matters pertaining to the Company's strategies and operations for the research and development of pharmaceutical products and vaccines. The Research Committee identifies areas and activities that are critical to the success of the Company's drug and vaccine discovery, development, and licensing efforts, as well as evaluates the effectiveness of the Company's drug and vaccine discovery, development, and licensing strategies and operations. The Research Committee also keeps the Board apprised of this evaluation process and findings and makes appropriate recommendations to the President of Merck Research Laboratories and to the Board on modifications of strategies and operations."[18]

Fifth Third Bancorp has a Risk and Compliance Committee that monitors financial, credit, and regulatory risk:

"The Committee oversees management's compliance with all of the Company's regulatory obligations arising under applicable federal and state banking laws, rules, and regulations, including any terms and conditions required from time to time by any action, formal or informal, of any federal or state banking regulatory agency or authority and any responses of management to any inquiries from any applicable banking regulator, and oversees management's implementation and enforcement of the Company's risk management policies and procedures."[19]

The board of Cisco Systems has an Investment and Finance Committee that monitors a broad range of financial activities:

"The Investment/Finance Committee reviews and approves Cisco's global investment policy; reviews minority investments, fixed income assets, insurance risk management policies and programs, and tax programs; oversees Cisco's stock repurchase programs; and also reviews Cisco's currency, interest rate, and equity risk management policies. This committee is also authorized to approve the issuance of debt securities, certain real estate acquisitions and leases, and charitable contributions made on behalf of Cisco."[20]

General Mills has a Public Responsibility Committee that has these functions:

- Reviews public policy and social trends affecting General Mills
- Monitors corporate citizenship activities
- Evaluates policies to ensure that they meet ethical obligations to employees, consumers, and society
- Reviews policies governing political contributions and the company's record of contributions[21]

Duration of Director Terms

Traditionally, directors are elected annually to one-year terms. In some companies, directors are elected to two- or three-year terms, with a subset of directors standing for reelection each year. Companies that follow this protocol are referred to as having **staggered** (or **classified**) boards. Under a typical staggered board, directors are elected to three-year terms, with one-third of the board standing for reelection every three years. As a result, it is not possible for the board to be ousted in a single year; two election cycles are needed for a majority of the board to turn over. As we discuss in Chapter 11, "The Market for Corporate Control," staggered boards can be an effective antitakeover protection.

Largely in response to the increased incidence of hostile takeovers in the 1980s, firms began adopting staggered boards. For example, from 1994 to 1999, the percentage of firms that adopted staggered boards at the time they went public increased from 43 percent to 82 percent in the United States.[22] In recent years, however, the trend has reversed. Companies have come under fire from shareholder activists and proxy advisory firms who believe that staggered board elections insulate directors from shareholder influence.[23] Institutional investors, particularly public pension plans, often have policies of opposing staggered boards. Some public companies have responded to shareholder pressure by destaggering their boards. In

2009, about 50 percent of publicly traded companies had staggered boards, down from 63 percent in 2002.[24]

Director Elections

In most companies, the board of directors is elected by shareholders on a one-share, one-vote basis. For example, if there are nine seats on a board, a shareholder with 100 shares can cast 100 votes for each of the nine people nominated. Shareholders who do not want to vote for one or all of the nominees can withhold votes for selected individuals. Directors win an election by obtaining a **plurality** of votes, meaning that the directors who receive the most votes win, regardless of whether they receive a majority of votes. In an uncontested election, a director is elected as long as he or she receives at least one vote.

Three main alternatives to this system of voting exist: dual-class stock, majority voting, and cumulative voting. A company with **dual-class shares** has more than one class of common stock. In general, each class has equal economic interest in the company but unequal voting rights. For example, Class A shares might be afforded one vote per share, whereas Class B shares might have ten votes per share. Typically, an insider, founding family member, or other shareholder friendly to management holds the class of shares with preferential voting rights, which gives that person significant (if not outright) influence over board elections. Dual-class stock thus tends to weaken the influence of public shareholders. Approximately 9 percent of publicly traded corporations in the United States have some form of dual-class structure.[25] Google, the New York Times Co., and Hershey all have dual-class shares.

The second variation in voting procedures is **majority voting**. Majority voting differs from plurality voting in that a director is required to receive a majority of votes to be elected. This means that even in an uncontested election, a director can fail to win a board seat if over half of all outstanding votes are withheld from him or her. The specific procedures of majority voting systems vary. In some companies, candidates who receive more withhold votes than votes in favor are strictly refused a seat on the board. More commonly, the director is required to submit a letter of resignation, and the rest of the board has discretion over whether to accept it. Other companies require resignation, but only after a replacement director is appointed. Majority voting gives shareholders more power to control the composition of the board, even in the absence of an alternative slate. In 2010, more than two-thirds of companies in the S&P 500 had adopted majority voting for director elections—a percentage that has been increasing in recent years.[26]

The third variation is **cumulative voting**. Cumulative voting allows a shareholder to concentrate votes on a single board candidate instead of requiring one vote for each candidate. A shareholder is given a number of votes equal to the product of the number of shares owned times the number of seats the company has on its board. For example, a shareholder with 100 shares in a company with a board of nine directors has 900 votes. The shareholder can allocate those votes among board candidates as he or she chooses. To increase the chances of electing a specific director, the shareholder might concentrate more votes toward a single candidate or a subset of candidates. Cumulative voting is relatively rare. Fewer than 10 percent of companies in the S&P 500 have adopted cumulative voting (less than 1 percent for the broader university of U.S. corporations; cumulative voting is almost nonexistent in smaller companies).[27]

In the ordinary course, board elections are uncontested. The company puts up a slate of directors for election, and the shareholders are expected to elect the slate. **Contested elections** occur in two circumstances. First, in the case of a hostile takeover battle, the bidding firm puts up a full slate of directors that is sympathetic to the acquisition. If the target shareholders elect the bidder's slate, those directors will remove impediments to the takeover (such as a poison pill) and vote in favor of the deal. The second context in which contested elections take place involves an activist investor who is dissatisfied with management and wants to gain influence over the company. In this situation, the shareholder might put up a "short slate" of directors—a limited number of directors who, if elected, would constitute a minority of the board. These directors would then serve as a vehicle through which the activist investor could participate in board-level decisions. Historically, the cost of nominating a dissident slate was borne entirely by the hostile bidder or activist. For this reason, proxy contests unrelated to takeovers have been quite rare. According to the NACD, only 45 proxy contests occurred in 2008.[28]

The Dodd–Frank Financial Reform Act now stipulates that investors or groups of investors that own at least 3 percent of the company's shares continuously for three years are eligible to nominate up to 25 percent of the board. This right is known as proxy access. Importantly, these board candidates are listed on the proxy, with the cost of the contested election borne by the company. Assuming that the Dodd–Frank Act survives legal challenges, it is not yet clear how proxy access will impact the frequency of contested elections in an activist setting. (We discuss proxy access in greater detail in Chapter 12, "Institutional Shareholders and Activist Investors.")

Removal of Directors

Once elected, directors generally serve their full term—one year for annually elected boards and three years for staggered boards. Shareholders may be able to prevent directors from being reelected at the next election by withholding votes. Their ability to do so, however, depends on the voting procedures in place. They can also replace directors at the next election if a competing slate of nominees is put up for election. Finally, unless a company's certificate of incorporation provides otherwise, shareholders may vote to "remove" a director between meetings. That said, shareholder power to remove a director is generally limited. (We discuss director removal in greater detail in the next chapter.)

Legal Obligations of Directors

In the United States, state corporate law and federal securities law set forth the legal duties of the board. The state law applicable to a corporation is the law of the state in which the company is incorporated. A company may incorporate in any state, regardless of where its headquarters are located or where it does business. As we discussed in the previous chapter, Delaware is by far the most common state of incorporation. Delaware has the most developed body of case law, which gives companies greater clarity on how corporate governance and liability matters might be decided.

Under state corporate law, the primary duties of the board are embodied in the broad principle of **fiduciary duty**. Under federal securities law, the directors' duties stem from the corporation's obligation to disclose material information to the public.

Fiduciary Duty

Under state corporate law, the board of directors has a legal obligation to act in the "interest of the corporation."[29] In legal terminology, this is referred to as a fiduciary duty to the corporation. Although somewhat ambiguous—since a corporation is simply a legal construct that cannot have its own interests—the courts have interpreted this phrase to mean that a director is expected to act in the interest of shareholders. Indeed, court decisions often refer to a fiduciary duty to "the corporation and the shareholders" or even just to the shareholders.

The fiduciary duty of the board includes three components:

- A duty of care
- A duty of loyalty
- A duty of candor

The **duty of care** requires that a director make decisions with due deliberation. In the United States, courts enforce the duty of care through the rubric of the "business judgment rule." This rule provides that the judgment of a board will not be overridden by a court unless a plaintiff can show that the board failed to inform itself regarding the decision at issue or that the board was infected with a conflict of interest, in which case there may have been a violation of the duty of loyalty. Courts have rarely ruled against a board for a violation of the duty of care. Even if a board decision was clearly wrong, if the board can show that it engaged in some consideration of information related to the decision, the courts will adopt a hands-off posture. The business judgment rule is most protective of outside directors. In the absence of "red flags" regarding what management is telling them, they are permitted to rely on what they hear from management to inform their decision. Moreover, companies are permitted to include exculpatory provisions in the charters that protect an outside director from suits for monetary damages for breach of the duty of care, so long as the director has not acted intentionally or in bad faith.

The **duty of loyalty** addresses conflicts of interest. For example, if management is considering a transaction with a company in which a director has a significant financial interest, the duty of loyalty requires that the terms of the transaction promote the interests of the shareholders over those of the director. As another example, if a director discovers a business opportunity in the course of his or her service to the company, the duty of loyalty requires that the director refrain from taking the opportunity before first determining whether the company will take it. The law lays out procedures for a board to follow in situations when a potential conflict of interest may exist.

The **duty of candor** requires that management and the board inform shareholders of all information that is important to their evaluation of the company and its management. The company's management is required in the first instance to provide accurate and timely information to shareholders, and the board is expected to oversee this process. In the absence of direct knowledge of wrongdoing, the board is permitted to rely on management assurances that the information is complete and accurate.

As a practical matter for publicly held companies, disclosure requirements mandated by federal securities law are more relevant than the duty of candor (discussed in the next section, "Disclosure Obligations Under Securities Laws"). Like the duty of candor, federal securities laws require a company and its management to disclose material information to shareholders, and that they do so in great detail. Consequently, public company shareholders are more likely to assert disclosure violations under securities laws than under the duty of candor. The duty of candor is important, however, for nonpublic companies.

Because the courts have interpreted the board's obligation to serve "in the interest of the corporation" to mean "in the interest of shareholders," corporate governance in the United States is said to be shareholder-centric. Survey data indicates that directors accept a shareholder-centric view of their responsibilities. When asked to identify in order of importance the constituents they serve, directors ranked "all shareholders" first, followed by institutional investors, customers, and creditors. They ranked other constituents such as employees and the community lower (see Table 3.1).[30]

Table 3.1 Constituents Directors Serve

Given that directors serve multiple constituencies, which are most important? (*Listed in order, according to director responses*)
All shareholders
Institutional investors
Customers
Creditors
Management
Employees
Analysts and Wall Street
Activist shareholders
The community

Source: Corporate Board Member and PricewaterhouseCoopers, LLP (2007).

In the 1990s, the legislatures of many states enacted statutes that allow the board to consider nonshareholder interests. (Delaware, where the majority of public companies are incorporated, did not adopt such a statute.) These statutes are referred to as "nonshareholder constituency" or "expanded constituency" provisions. They allow the board to consider the impact of their actions on stakeholders such as workers, customers, suppliers, and the surrounding community. The primary application of these statutes is in the evaluation of a takeover bid. These statutes purportedly allow management and the board to reject a takeover offer that is in the interest of shareholders if the takeover would harm other constituents. Still, courts generally have not allowed these statutes to be used to the disadvantage of shareholders.

According to data from SharkRepellent, approximately 10 percent of firms are incorporated in states with such a provision.[31] Ohio and Pennsylvania have gone further and *require* that the board consider nonshareholder interests. In 2010, Maryland became the first state to allow entrepreneurs to incorporate as a "benefit corporation," whereby a for-profit organization is dedicated to a specific public good, such as the environment or community involvement. This allows the company to take nonshareholder concerns into account in making decisions (see the following sidebar).

Statutes that provide for nonshareholder considerations have been litigated only to a limited extent. As a result, their meaning is still uncertain. To date, courts have interpreted them to mean that boards should take into account nonshareholder interests only to the extent that shareholder interests are not compromised. Thus, even the board of a corporation that is governed by one of these statutes has a duty to promote the interests of shareholders.

Stakeholder Interests Outside the United States

In the United Kingdom, the Companies Act 2006 allows for the consideration of nonshareholder interests in boardroom decisions. A director is required to "act in the way he considers, in good faith, would be most likely to promote the success of the company for the benefit of its members as a whole."[32] The act specifies that this includes employees, customers, suppliers, community members, the environment, creditors, and others. As this statute is relatively new in the United Kingdom, the manner in which it will be upheld is not clear.

In South Africa, governance standards are outlined in the King Report (1994), King Report II (2001), and King Report III (2009). These require that the board of directors identify all stakeholders and define the methods according to which the company promises to serve their interests. The company is expected to report financial, environmental, and social results (the so-called **triple-bottom line**), and the board of directors is expected to communicate progress against all three measures in a report to stakeholders.[33]

Disclosure Obligations Under Securities Laws

Directors have legal obligations under federal securities laws as well as state corporate laws. Federal securities laws require companies to disclose information to the public through filings with the SEC. (As we discussed in Chapter 2, "International Corporate Governance," financial transparency improves the efficiency of capital markets by facilitating the flow of information needed for rational decision making.) SEC filings fall into three categories: filings made when a company issues securities; annual and quarterly filings; and filings upon the occurrence of transactions or events, such as a merger, a change in auditor, or the hiring of a CEO. SEC regulations specify in considerable detail the information that each of these filings must disclose. For example, the annual Form 10-K must contain a description of the company's business, risk factors, financial results by management, audited financial statements and footnotes, and compensation practices. In each filing, the company is required to include all **material information**, which is defined as information that an investor would consider important to an investment decision.

A failure to comply with these rules—by misstating material information or by omitting information and thereby making the information provided materially incorrect—exposes the company, its managers, and its directors to liability. Directors are expected to question management regarding the rationale for its disclosure decisions but, absent any red flags, they are not expected to verify information on their own.

Legal Enforcement of State Corporate Law (Fiduciary Duties)

Fiduciary duties under state corporate law are enforced through two types of judicial intervention. First, a court can issue an **injunction**, an order that the company take or refrain from taking a specified action. For example, the injunction might order that the company refrain from consummating a pending merger and allow other parties to bid. A judge might make this ruling if he or she believes that management and the board did not take all steps necessary to obtain the best deal for shareholders. Second, a court can require management and/or the directors to pay **damages** for losses sustained as a result of violating their duties.

When shareholders file suits alleging that directors have taken an action that violated their fiduciary duties, courts use different standards to review the action, depending on the nature of the alleged violation. As explained earlier, when a violation of the duty of care is involved, the courts apply the **business judgment rule**, which is most deferential to the board's decision. Under the business judgment rule, a court will not second guess a board's decision—even if, in retrospect, it was proved to be seriously deficient—if the board followed a reasonable process by which it informed itself of key, relevant facts and then made the decision in good faith. (**Good faith** requires that the board act without conflicting interests and that it not turn a blind eye to issues within its responsibility.) If the board can demonstrate that it satisfied these criteria, the courts will not intervene.

The *Disney* case is a recent high-water (or perhaps *low-water*) mark for nonintervention by the Delaware courts. In 2005, shareholders filed a derivative lawsuit against the Walt Disney Company in which they claimed that the directors did not sufficiently review the appointment of Michael Ovitz as president of the company in 1995 or his no-fault termination 14 months later. They sought to void his original employment agreement or, alternatively, to change his termination to "with cause," which under the agreement would mean the return of nearly $140 million in severance payments. Although the court agreed with the plaintiffs that the board's handling of the matter was seriously deficient, it nonetheless ruled that the business judgment rule protected the board's conduct and declined to intervene.

On the other hand, if a plaintiff successfully shows that a director has violated the duty of loyalty by virtue of a conflict of interest, the courts will not hesitate to intervene. The courts will apply a strict standard of review under which they make their own judgment whether the director has placed his or her own interest above those of shareholders. In such a case, the burden shifts to directors to demonstrate the fairness of their decision.

A board's decision to sell a company also receives a higher level of scrutiny by the courts. Because management self-interest may taint its decision to sell the company and, if so, to whom, the courts spend more time ensuring that the sale and process by which it was conducted were in the best interest of shareholders.

Legal Enforcement of Federal Securities Laws

As stated, a securities law violation stems from a material misstatement or omission of information to the public. Unless a public offering is involved, management or the directors will be held liable only if they acted intentionally or with a degree of recklessness that approaches intentionality. Importantly, the court must find that the misstatement was the cause of the investors' loss. Securities laws are stricter when a misstatement occurs in the context of a public offering. In this context, an individual can be held liable based on negligence.

Securities laws are enforced through both private lawsuits and SEC enforcement actions. Private lawsuits take the form of class actions by investors who bought (or sold) a security during the period in which its price was artificially high (or low) as a result of a material misstatement. Because it is difficult for investors to coordinate their efforts, the law allows lawyers to sue in the name of a class of investors who have suffered from a common alleged violation. Although U.S. Congress enacted reforms to the securities class action system in 1996 to facilitate a degree of oversight by institutional investors and lessen the influence of plaintiff's lawyers, plaintiff's lawyers remain largely in control of these lawsuits.

In a securities class action lawsuit, the plantiff's lawyers typically name the company and its CEO as defendants. In cases involving financial misstatements, the CFO is typically named as well. Outside board members are named much less frequently.

In an SEC enforcement action, the SEC targets members of management who were responsible for a violation. Managers are subject to monetary penalties and can be barred from serving as an officer or director of a public company, either for a specified number of years or permanently. The SEC occasionally imposes monetary penalties on companies as well. It is very unusual, however, for the SEC to target outside directors.

Director Indemnification and D&O Insurance

State corporate law and federal securities laws create some risk of liability for board members, but two mechanisms reduce the actual danger that directors make out-of-pocket payments: indemnification agreements and the purchase of directors' and officers' (D&O) liability insurance.

A company may indemnify directors for costs associated with securities class actions and some fiduciary duty cases. Indemnification generally is available to an individual director for any expense incurred in connection with litigation, including legal fees, settlements, and judgments against the director. Indemnification is only permitted, however, if the director has acted in good faith. Indemnification agreements have been widely adopted by most public companies. According to one study, 98 percent of a sample of Fortune 500 companies have indemnification arrangements for the benefit of their directors.[34]

Corporations also protect directors by purchasing **director and officer liability insurance (or D&O insurance)**. These policies cover litigation expenses, settlement payments, and, in rare cases, amounts paid in damages (up to a limit specified in the policy). A D&O insurance policy has three parts, referred to as Side A, Side B, and Side C. **Side A** protects the directors when indemnification is not available, for example, if the company becomes insolvent. **Side B** reimburses a corporation for its indemnification obligations to its directors. **Side C** insurance reimburses a corporation for its own litigation expenses and amounts it pays in settlement. As the name implies, D&O insurance contracts cover both a company's directors and officers.

D&O insurance contracts are written broadly and are intended to apply when directors are sued in private action for violating securities fraud. However, as with all insurance policies, D&O insurance has limits. First, they contain dollar limits on the coverage they provide. Amounts owed in excess of coverage limits must be paid by the company. Second, they contain exclusions. The most important of these arises when the director has committed "deliberate fraud" or otherwise illegally enriched him or herself. Third, although D&O insurance covers litigation expenses and some costs of responding to an SEC investigation that precedes litigation, it does not cover civil fines levied by the SEC (see the following sidebar).

D&O Claims and Payments

Most public attention is on high-level liabilities, such as securities violations. However, according to data from Towers Watson, a significant number of D&O claims are for other infractions, such as discrimination, wrongful termination, and contract disputes (see Table 3.2).

Table 3.2 D&O Claims and Payments

Source of Claim	Example of Allegations	% of All Claims	Average Payment	Average Defense Cost
Employees	Wrongful termination, discrimination, wage disputes	33%	$146,078	$158,698
Competitors, suppliers, and contractors	Contract disputes, business interference, copyright infringement	8%	$87,000	$420,026
Customers	Contract disputes, false advertising, deceptive trade practices	3%	—	$809,701
Government, agencies, and other third parties	Breach of fiduciary duty, false advertising, dishonesty, antitrust	16%	$13,818,125	$3,768,747
Shareholders	Inadequate disclosure, breach of fiduciary duty, stock offerings	40%	$26,456,948	$3,042,159

Source: Towers Watson, "Directors and Officers Liability: 2007 Survey of Insurance Purchasing and Claim Trends" (2007).

Despite the protections afforded to directors through indemnifications and D&O insurance, most directors believe they are at legal risk by serving on the board. When polled, more than two-thirds believe that the liability risk of serving on boards has increased in recent years. Almost 15 percent have thought seriously about resigning due to concerns about personal liability.[35] Notwithstanding this perception, the actual risk of out-of pocket payment is quite low. Black, Cheffens, and Klausner (2006) found that between 1980 and 2005, outside directors made out-of-pocket payments—meaning unindemnified and uninsured—in only 12 cases.[36] This figure includes cases where directors only incurred out-of-pocket litigation expenses and did not incur settlement costs (see Table 3.3).

Although indemnification and D&O insurance afford directors considerable financial protection, they do not reimburse directors for the emotional cost of the litigation process, the time involved, and the adverse impact the lawsuits might have on their reputations.[37]

Table 3.3 Settlements in Which Outside Directors Made Out-of-Pocket Payments (1980–2005)

	Settlement Payment	Litigation Expenses	Payment and Expenses	Total
Securities Suits under Section 10		2		2
Securities Suits That Included Section 11 Claims	4	1	1	6
SEC Enforcement Actions	1			1
Corporate Lawsuits	3			3
Total	**8**	**3**	**1**	**12**

Source: Black, Cheffens, and Klausner (2006).

Endnotes

1. The Organization for Economic Cooperation and Development, "OECD Principles of Corporate Governance. Directorate for Financial and Enterprise Affairs" (2004). Accessed July 22, 2008. See www.oecd.org/dataoecd/32/18/31557724.pdf.

2. Corporate Board Member and PricewaterhouseCoopers LLP, "What Directors Think 2009: Annual Board of Directors Survey. A Corporate Board Member Magazine/PricewaterhouseCoopers LLP Research Study. Special Supplement," *Corporate Board Member Magazine* (2009): 1-16. Accessed January 21, 2010. See www.boardmember.com/WorkArea/DownloadAsset.aspx?id=4481.

3. Corporate Board Member & PricewaterhouseCoopers LLP, "What Directors Think 2008: The Corporate Board Member/PricewaterhouseCoopers LLP Survey," *Corporate Board Member Magazine* (2008). Accessed January 21, 2010. See www.boardmember.com/Article_Details.aspx?id=1411.

4. Jay W. Lorsch, Joseph L. Bower, Clayton S. Rose, and Suraj Srinivasan, "Perspectives from the Boardroom—2009," *Harvard Business School Working Knowledge* (September 9, 2009): 1-20. Accessed January 21, 2010. See http://hbswk.hbs.edu/item/6281.html.

5. Corporate Board Member and PricewaterhouseCoopers LLP (2009).

6. *Ibid.*

7. Deloitte Touche Tohmatsu, "In the Dark: What Boards and Executives Don't Know About the Health of Their Businesses. A Survey by Deloitte in Cooperation with the Economist Intelligence Unit" (2004). Accessed September 2, 2008. See www.deloitte.com/dtt/article/0,1002,cid%253D157828,00.html.

8. Jay W. Lorsch, Joseph L. Bower, Clayton S. Rose, and Suraj Srinivasan.

9. AICPA, *The AICPA Audit Committee Toolkit* (New York: American Institute of Certified Public Accountants, 2004).

10. National Association of Corporate Directors, *2009 NACD Public Company Governance Survey* (Washington, D.C.: National Association of Corporate Directors, 2009).

11. Corporate Board Member and PricewaterhouseCoopers LLP (2009).

12. New York Stock Exchange, NYSE Listed Company Manual §303A.00, Corporate Governance Standards. See www.nyse.com/Frameset.html ?nyseref=http%3A//www.nyse.com/regulation/listed/1182508124422.html& displayPage=/lcm/lcm_section.html.

13. National Association of Corporate Directors.

14. Corporate Board Member and PricewaterhouseCoopers LLP (2009).

15. New York Stock Exchange.

16. National Association of Corporate Directors.

17. Spencer Stuart "Spencer Stuart U.S. Board Index 2008" (2008). Accessed May 4, 2010. See http://content.spencerstuart.com/sswebsite/pdf/lib/SSBI_08.pdf.

18. Merck & Co., Inc., Form DEF 14A, filed with the Securities and Exchange Commission March 10, 2008.

19. Fifth Third Bancorp, Form DEF 14A, filed with the Securities and Exchange Commission March 6, 2008.

20. Cisco Systems, Inc., Form DEF 14A, filed with the Securities and Exchange Commission September 26, 2007.

21. General Mills, Inc., Form DEF 14A, filed with the Securities and Exchange Commission August 12, 2008.

22. Robert M. Daines and Michael Klausner "Do IPO Charters Maximize Firm Value? Antitakeover Protection in IPOs," *Journal of Law, Economics & Organization* 17 (2001): 83–120; John C. Coates, "Explaining Variation in Takeover Defenses: Blame the Lawyers," *California Law Review* 89 (2001): 1,301.

23. In the first half of 2009, there were 76 proposals to destagger the board. Source: National Association of Corporate Directors.

24. These descriptive statistics were generated from data supplied by SharkRepellent, FactSet Research Systems, Inc. The sample used 3,875 firms in 2009 sample and 2,849 firms in 2002.

25. Scott Smart, Chad Zutter, and Ramabhadran Thirumalai. "Why Dual-Class Shares Don't Add Up," *Directorship* 33 (2007): 14–15.

26. ISS, "Preparing for the Dodd–Frank Act" (2010). Accessed November 5, 2010. See www.issgovernance.com/weekly/20100723DoddFrank.

27. ISS Governance Analytics, *U.S. Proxy Voting Manual,* Chapter 3, "Proxy Contests, Cumulative Voting." Accessed November 5, 2010. See http://governance-analytics.com/content/menutop/content/subscription/usvmfiles/x1616.html. Descriptive statistics were generated from data supplied by SharkRepellent, FactSet Research Systems, Inc. The sample used 3,875 firms in 2009.

28. National Association of Corporate Directors.

29. See Joseph Hinsey IV, "Business Judgment and The American Law Institute's Corporate Governance Project: The Rule, the Doctrine, and the Reality," *George Washington Law Review* 52 (1984): 609–610.

30. Interestingly enough, directors apparently do not view "activist shareholders" as included in the group "all shareholders," given their disparate rankings. This implies that directors do not see themselves as serving all shareholders equally. Corporate Board Member and PricewaterhouseCoopers LLP (2007).

31. Descriptive statistics were generated from data supplied by SharkRepellent, FactSet Research Systems, Inc. The sample used 3,875 firms in 2009.

32. U.K. Companies Act of 2006 (c. 46), Part 10—A company's directors Chapter 2—General duties of directors Section 172 (1).

33. Dr. Janette Minnaar-van Veijeren, "The King II Report on Corporate Governance," i-Value Risk Management (PTY), Ltd. Accessed November 8, 2010. See www.i-value.co.za/king.html.

34. Lawrence A. Hamermesh, "Why I Do Not Teach Van Gorkom," *Georgia Law Review 34* (2000): 477–490.

35. Corporate Board Member and PricewaterhouseCoopers LLP (2009).

36. Three of the cases are quite well known: Enron ($13 million for misleading statements and $1.5 million for violating ERISA), WorldCom ($24.75 million for misleading statements), and Tyco ($22.5 million from an SEC enforcement action). The fact that these high-profile cases resulted in out-of-pocket payments no doubt contributes to the perception that a director's risk of liability has increased. See Bernard S. Black, Brian R. Cheffens, and Michael Klausner, "Outside Director Liability," *Stanford Law Review* 58 (2006): 1,055–1,159.

37. Helland (2006) finds that board member reputation generally does not suffer following allegations of fraud and that the majority of directors named in such lawsuits do not experience a decrease in board seats. An exception arises for directors named in SEC-initiated cases and those named in class actions that end in large settlements. In these cases, director reputation does suffer. Fich and Shivdasani (2007) also found that outside directors named in class-action lawsuits experience a decrease in board seats. See Eric A. Helland, "Reputational Penalties and the Merits of Class Action Securities Litigation," *Journal of Law and Economics* 49 (October 2006): 365–395. Accessed February 24, 2011. Eliezer M. Fich and Anil Shivdasani, "Financial Fraud, Director Reputation, and Shareholder Wealth" *Journal of Financial Economics* 86 (2007): 306–336.

4

Board of Directors: Selection, Compensation, and Removal

In this chapter, we examine how companies select, compensate, and remove board members. We start by examining the size of the market for directors and the qualifications of board members. Next, we discuss how companies identify gaps in the board's capabilities and recruit individuals to fill those gaps. We then evaluate director compensation and equity ownership guidelines. Finally, we consider the resignation and removal of directors.

Market for Directors

The United States has approximately 50,000 directors of large private and publicly traded corporations (see Table 4.1). The average director stays on a corporate board for seven years. Among companies that establish an age limit for serving on a board, the average mandatory retirement age is about 72 years. Although survey data from the National Association of Corporate Directors (NACD) indicates that board members are replaced through a combination of director evaluations and age limits, general observation suggests that board members tend to retire voluntarily.[1] According to Audit Analytics, only about 2 percent of directors who left the board in 2009 were dismissed or not reelected.[2]

Table 4.1 Number of Directors in the United States

Year	2000	2001	2002	2003	2004	2005	2006	2007
#Firms	7,594	7,527	6,998	6,303	6,103	6,100	6,072	6,066
#Directors	56,444	52,673	54,388	51,382	51,103	52,321	52,375	52,265

Source: Data collected by Corporate Board Member Magazine and computations by the authors.

The typical board consists of a mix of professionals with managerial, functional, and other specialized backgrounds. Approximately half of newly elected directors have current or former experience as senior management (CEO, president, COO, chairman, or vice chairman). Twenty percent have experience in an operational or other functional position. The rest come from diverse backgrounds, including finance, consulting, law, academia, and nonprofits (see Figure 4.1).[3]

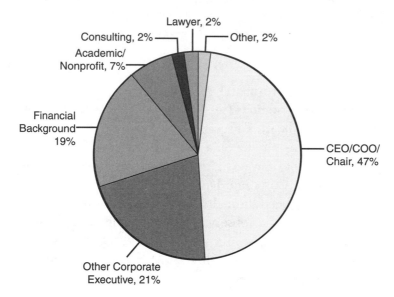

Note: "CEO/COO/Chair" also includes president and vice chair. "Other corporate executive" includes division heads and senior/executive vice presidents. "Financial background" includes CFO and treasurer, bankers, investment managers/investors, and accountants.

Source: Adapted from Spencer Stuart, "Spencer Stuart U.S. Board Index" (2007).

Figure 4.1   Background of new independent directors.

Because of the critical role board members play in the governance process, the quality of individuals who are elected to the board has a direct correlation with the quality of advice and oversight the board provides to management. This raises an important question: How difficult is it to find "qualified" directors? If the number of qualified directors greatly exceeds total demand, competition should increase for board seats and companies should have no trouble finding directors who are informed, engaged, and independent. However, if an insufficient supply of qualified directors exists, board quality will suffer. Furthermore, inadequate supply might not be uniformly distributed; it might be concentrated in only specialized areas or industries.

The answers to these questions are far from clear. Interviews with directors and search consultants indicate that many more people want to serve on boards than positions are available. However, it is not clear how much of this readily available supply is qualified for the role. According to a survey by *Corporate Board Member* magazine, 56 percent of directors believe there is a shortage of qualified directors. Among the qualifications most difficult to fulfill are ethnic and gender diversity (57 percent and 50 percent, respectively), technological expertise (45 percent), and international expertise (42 percent). In addition, directors report that it is difficult to fulfill a broad set of functional expertise, including marketing, finance, corporate turnaround, public policy, government, and legal.[4] (Figure 4.2 illustrates this more completely.)

Criteria for Director Recruitment

CEOs within a company's industry are the most heavily recruited for directorships. These results have remained mostly unchanged since 2006, demonstrating
the importance of a director's industry knowledge and management experience.
Effective Boards followed this trend in importance of professional experience.

Importance of Professional Experience as Criteria for
Recruiting Board Candidates

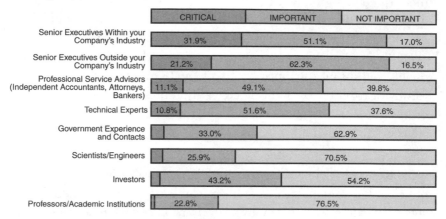

Importance of Functional Experience for Recruiting Board Candidates

National Association of Corporate Directors (NACD) and The Center for Board Leadership, "2009
NACD Public Company Governance Survey" (2009).

Figure 4.2   Criteria for director recruitment.

Active CEOs

Directors with current CEO-level experience offer a useful mix of managerial, industry, and functional knowledge. These individuals can contribute to multiple areas of oversight, including strategy, risk management, succession planning, performance measurement, and shareholder and stakeholder relations. It is expected that active CEOs currently perform these tasks at a high level in their own organizations and that the companies will benefit from their joining the boards. As shown in Figure 4.2, CEO-level experience is the single most important criterion for recruiting a new director.[5] However, to our knowledge, no definitive research study confirms that current or retired CEOs are better board members than directors with other backgrounds.

At the same time, it might be very difficult for active CEOs to monitor and advise a company other than their own. The CEO role is very demanding (which some describe as a "24-hours-a-day, 7-days-a-week" responsibility). If the CEO manages a large, complex organization, can he or she really take the time to serve as director for another corporation and be fully engaged in this process? In addition, serving in an advisory and oversight capacity is very different from having direct managerial responsibility. Directors who are active CEOs might easily be too hands-on or hands-off. They also might be prone to using their own organizations as the primary benchmark for the companies (such as saying, "Let me tell you what works for us") and assuming that this can readily transfer to a company with a different strategy, people, and competitive pressures.

In recent years, the number of active CEOs serving as directors has declined. Spencer Stuart reports a 20 percent decrease between 2002 and 2007.[6] Similarly, *Corporate Board Member* magazine identified 50 active CEOs who resigned outside directorships during 2008, including the CEOs of Raytheon (stepped down from Sprint Nextel), Moody's (stepped down from John Wiley & Sons), and CB Richard Ellis (stepped down from Edison International).[7]

Active CEOs sit on an average of 0.8 external boards, down from 1.2 five years ago and 2.0 in 1998. The reasons cited for this trend are increased workload from active positions, too much time spent traveling for directorships, and limits placed on the number of outside directorships by current employers. More than half of all S&P 500 companies now limit outside directorships for CEOs, a policy that was not widely in effect a few years ago. Boards have responded to this trend by recruiting new directors from levels below "C-level" positions. According to Spencer Stuart, such directors comprise 19 percent of new independent directors, up from only 9 percent ten years ago.[8]

Although some experts laud restrictions on outside board service by current CEOs, this represents a tangible decrease in practical experience at the board level and a likely reduction in governance quality. Research has also shown that network connections between companies at the board level facilitate important information flows that improve corporate performance and increase shareholder value.[9] (We discuss the evidence on the value of information flow through board connections in greater detail in the next chapter, "Board of Directors: Structure and Consequences").

International Experience

As companies expand into international markets, it is important that the board understand how the company might be impacted from a strategic, operating, financial, risk, and regulatory perspective. For this reason, directors with knowledge of local market conditions are highly valued. These directors have contacts with key government decision makers and business executives who can help with supply chain development, manufacturing, customer development, and distribution. This network should help a company enter or expand into a new market by minimizing risk and lowering the cost of executing an international strategy.

Some evidence suggests that the demand for international knowledge exceeds the available supply. Only a quarter of directors in the United States have international work experience, and only 7 percent are of foreign birth. Egon Zehnder compared the percentage of revenues that a company earns outside the United States to the percentage of directors with international experience (the logic being that if a company derives half of its revenue from outside the United States, roughly half of the board should have some international experience). They found that international revenue (32 percent) exceeds international board representation among S&P 500 firms when representation is measured by citizenship (7 percent), work experience (27 percent), and education (9 percent).[10] This suggests that boards might have insufficient international experience, a potential competitive obstacle as U.S. firms expand into new markets.

Special Expertise

Companies also have demand for directors with special expertise that matches the functional or situational needs of the firm. For example, a technological firm needs directors who are experts in the industry to advise on research, development, and production (academics in engineering, computer science, medicine, and natural sciences are commonly used in this capacity). These directors might not have the background to oversee certain business or compliance functions, but their presence is critical for the commercial success of the firm. Similarly, companies in dire financial or operating condition might benefit from directors with experience in a corporate turnaround or financial restructuring. Specialized experience can also help companies that face regulatory or legal challenges, or companies that regularly engage in mergers, acquisitions, or divestitures. For example, Polycom (maker of voice and videoconferencing equipment) has a standing strategy committee whose responsibility, according to one director, "is to regularly review, evaluate, and give input to management on strategic direction and potential partnerships and deals." The director adds, "The strategy committee sets the parameters that management can use to do smaller deals on its own, and it gives us a good on-the-spot mechanism for reviewing bigger ones, including potential offers for the company itself."[11]

In some cases, these individuals are not formally elected to the board but instead participate in board meetings as **observer** or **advisory directors**. This practice appears to be common among financial institutions. These directors do not vote on corporate matters, so they are shielded from the potential liability that comes with being an elected director. However, they are available to advise the corporation on important matters. For example, a venture capital firm might invite a partner to sit on the board and an associate to attend board meetings as a nonvoting observer (see the following sidebar).

Board Observers

In 1997, Excite and Intuit entered into an agreement that, among other things, gave Intuit rights to appoint a boardroom observer:

"For so long as Intuit continues to own at least ten percent (10%) of the outstanding Common Stock of the Company ... and an Intuit Designee is not a member of the Board of Directors, the Company shall invite a representative of Intuit (the 'Representative'), which Representative shall be reasonably acceptable to the Company, to attend all meetings of the Board of Directors and the audit committee thereof in a nonvoting observer capacity and, in this respect, shall give such Representative copies of all notices, minutes, consents, and other Board of Directors' or audit committee members' materials ... provided, however, (i) that the Company reserves the right to withhold any information and to exclude such Representative from any meeting, or any portion thereof, as is reasonably determined by the Chairman of the Board ... to be necessary for purposes of confidentiality, competitive factors, attorney-client privilege, or other reasonable purposes."[12]

In 2010, Napera, maker of cloud–based IT management products, granted observer status to an associate of its investor's firm:

"Mark Ashida (Observer): Mark Ashida joined OVP Venture Partners in 2007, and focuses on investments in infrastructure and enterprise software. Prior to joining OVP, Mark served as General Manager of Windows Enterprise Networking at Microsoft Corp., where he drove all development, testing, and product management for Microsoft's networking infrastructure and authentication servers, representing over $450 million in enterprise sales. [P]rior to Microsoft, Mark was Chief Operating Officer at InterTrust, a public company. Before joining InterTrust, Mark was a General Manager at Intel Corporation, launched three companies, served as a turnaround specialist for troubled technology companies, and spent time as a strategy consultant as a partner at Deloitte and Touche/Braxton Associates. He currently serves on the Board of Directors for Serus, and is a Board Observer to Accelerator, Applied Identity, Collaborative Software Initiative, and Tzero."[13]

The role of the observer is to monitor various decisions of the board and management. The information the observer obtains then is valuable to outside shareholders in making investment decisions.

Diverse Directors

Companies might seek directors of diverse ethnic origin or female directors when they believe diversity of personal perspective contributes to board deliberation or decision making. However, such groups tend to have low representation in the senior ranks of corporations (relative to the general population). For example, only 3.8 percent of the CEOs of Fortune 500 companies are ethnic minorities (African-American, Latino, or Asian), and only 2.4 percent are female.[14] For this reason, a potential imbalance between supply and demand might make recruiting qualified directors difficult. For example, if CEO experience is required background for a new board member, ethnic minorities and females will be slow to obtain director positions.

Furthermore, research by Heidrick & Struggles suggests that practitioners don't agree on the value of diversity on the board. For example, 90 percent of female directors believe that women bring special attributes to the board, whereas only 56 percent of male directors believe this to be true. Similarly, 51 percent of women believe that having three or more female directors on a board make it more effective, whereas only 12 percent of male directors hold this opinion.[15] These are considerable perception gaps that need to be researched.

Despite the difference of opinions, companies have made significant effort toward recruiting diverse board members. Eighty-five percent of companies have at least one female director on the board, and 78 percent have an ethnic minority director.[16] According to the NACD, more than 75 percent of directors believe that ethnic and gender diversity is a critical factor in board recruitment.[17] (We discuss the impact of diversity on corporate performance in Chapter 5.)

Professional Directors

Professional directors are individuals whose full-time careers are serving on boards of directors. They might be retired executives, consultants, lawyers, financiers, or politicians who bring extensive expertise based not only on their professional background, but also on the multitude of current and previous board seats. For example, Vernon Jordan (a former legal advisor to Bill Clinton) is considered by some to be a professional director, having served on more than a dozen corporate boards, including American Express, Ashbury Automotive, J.C. Penney, and Xerox.[18] After a successful career in retailing, Allan Leighton of the United Kingdom retired from executive positions at the age of 47 and decided to pursue a career as a professional director (calling the move "going plural"). Recently, he has been either a board member or advisor at Royal Mail, Lastminute.com, Scottish Power, and BSkyB.[19]

Professional directors might be effective as advisors and monitors, given their extensive experience on boards. They have participated in multiple governance systems and have likely witnessed both successes and failures. They might also have more time to dedicate to their board responsibilities because they do not need to balance them with the demands of a "day job." In addition, professional directors help to alleviate supply imbalances for board seats because they can serve on more boards than active professionals.[20]

However, relying on professional directors can be risky. Because they serve on multiple boards simultaneously, professional directors tend to be "busy." As we see in the next chapter, "busy" directors are associated with lower governance quality. In addition, professional directors might not have the motivation to be effective monitors if they are attracted to the position for its reputational prestige (such as bragging to their social peers) or if they view their directorships as a form of "active retirement." Finally, professional directors might lack independence and be unwilling to stand up to management or fellow directors if they substantially rely on their director fees for income.[21]

Disclosure Requirements for Director Qualifications

In 2010, the Securities and Exchange Commission (SEC) amended Regulation S–K to require expanded disclosure about the qualifications of directors. Companies must now disclose the specific experience, qualifications, and attributes that make the individual qualified to serve as a director. Companies must also disclose directorships that the individual held during the previous five years (instead of only current directorships), legal proceedings involving the director during the previous ten years, and disciplinary sanctions imposed by regulatory bodies. This information is intended to improve shareholder decisions in a director election.

Regulation S–K was also amended to require disclosure of whether the company has a policy regarding boardroom diversity and, if so, how diversity is considered in identifying director nominees. The SEC did not define diversity, but it suggested that the term could be broadly defined to include differences of viewpoint, professional experience, education, and skills, as well as race, gender, and national origin.[22]

Although shareholders might value expanded disclosure of director qualifications, it is not clear what information would be relevant to improving shareholder understanding. Companies might point to information that is readily apparent from the director's resumé or make generic claims about "business knowledge" and "sound judgment" (see the following sidebar). It is unclear how companies can provide an informative summary of the qualifications of their directors.

Director Qualifications—How Informative Are These Disclosures?

SunTrust Banks provides a somewhat humorous view of qualifications, with the following as the last sentences of each director's biographies:

"Mr. Correll's long and varied business career, including service as Chairman and CEO of a large, publicly traded company, well qualifies him to serve on our Board."

"Mr. Hughes's long and varied business career, including service as Chairman and CEO of a large, publicly traded company, well qualifies him to serve on our Board."

"Mr. Ivester's long and varied business career, including service as Chairman and CEO of a large, publicly traded company, well qualifies him to serve on our Board."

"Mr. Beall's executive and management experience well qualify him to serve on our Board."

"Mr. Crowe's executive and management experience well qualify him to serve on our Board."[23]

Analog Devices

Analog Devices provides a detailed explanation of the criteria that the company uses to identify new directors:

"In considering whether to recommend any candidate for inclusion in the Board's slate of recommended director nominees ... the Nominating and Corporate Governance Committee will apply the criteria set forth in Analog Devices' Corporate Governance Guidelines. These criteria include the candidate's integrity, business acumen, age, experience, commitment, diligence, conflicts of interest, and the ability to act in the interests of all shareholders.... The Committee seeks nominees with a broad diversity of experience, professions, skills, geographic representation, and backgrounds. The Committee does not assign specific weights to particular criteria and no particular criterion is necessarily applicable to all prospective nominees. Analog Devices believes that the backgrounds and qualifications of the directors, considered as a group, should provide a significant composite mix of experience, knowledge, and abilities that will allow the Board to fulfill its responsibilities."[24]

Covidien

Covidien explains how a director's biography qualifies him to sit on the board of directors and the audit committee:

"Mr. Brust has been the Chief Financial Officer of Sprint Nextel Corporation, a wireless and wireline communications company, since May 2008. Mr. Brust is an experienced financial leader with the skills necessary to lead our Audit Committee. His service as Chief Financial Officer of Sprint Nextel Corporation, the Eastman Kodak Company, and Unisys Corporation, as well as his 31 years at

General Electric Company, make him a valuable asset, both on our Board of Directors and as the Chairman of our Audit Committee. Mr. Brust's positions have provided him with a wealth of knowledge in dealing with financial and accounting matters. The depth and breadth of his exposure to complex financial issues at such large corporations makes him a skilled advisor."[25]

Director Recruitment Process

As we discussed in Chapter 3, "Board of Directors: Duties and Liability," director recruitment is a key responsibility of the nominating and governance committee. The committee is responsible for identifying qualified candidates to serve on the board, interviewing and selecting candidates to be put before shareholders for a vote, hiring a search firm to assist in the recruitment process (if necessary), and managing the board evaluation process.

The process should begin by evaluating the needs of the company and identifying gaps in the board's desired capabilities. A list is then assembled of potential candidates whose qualifications fill the identified gaps. The method for assembling this list varies among companies. Some rely extensively on the personal and professional networks of existing board members and the CEO. Others rely on a third-party consultant or search firm to assemble a list of candidates among a broader pool. According to the NACD, approximately 50 percent of companies use a search firm. However, this varies with firm size. Eighty-two percent of large companies (market capitalization greater than $10 billion) use a search firm, while smaller firms are considerably less likely to do so.[26]

Although intuition might suggest that board candidates identified by search firms would be more qualified on average than candidates identified through a personal network (because they come from a broader pool and are less likely to be selected because of personal biases of existing board members), this is not necessarily the case. Existing directors often have an extensive network that is equal in breath and insight to the network a third-party consultant uses. To our knowledge, no rigorous studies have compared the qualification of board candidates deriving from each source, primarily because the role of search firms in selecting directors is not a required disclosure by firms.

The director recruitment process differs from the recruitment process for senior executives in one key manner. When recruiting executives, the company assembles a list of top candidates, interviews them, and then makes a selection based on an evaluation of which is best qualified. When recruiting directors, the company assembles a list of top candidates, ranks them in preferential order, and approaches the candidates one at a time. In effect, the board (or the nominating and governance committee) decides who it wants to nominate before meeting face-to-face with the candidates. This requires a more careful evaluation of the skills and experience of the individual, without the benefit of meeting in advance. The meeting is more of an invitation to join the board than it is an interview. This is done because it is considered inappropriate to approach a qualified candidate (one who has been highly successful in a professional career) only to reject him or her in favor of another. Although some people might cringe at this as reminiscent of an "old boys' network," it is not clear whether a competitive process would improve board quality or whether the most qualified candidates would choose not to engage in interviews.

When assembled, the composition of the board should satisfy the diverse strategic, operating, and functional needs of the company. It's also important that the culture of the board reflect that of the organization, and that board members have good rapport among themselves and with senior management. Recruiters recommend against companies selecting directors based on regulatory and compliance expertise. (One exception is that a company embroiled in extensive legal troubles might specifically bring on a director to help the company navigate through this period.) Generally, directors can be taught compliance more readily than they can be taught domain expertise. Perhaps for this reason, more than half of all boards are open to recruiting directors with no previous board experience.[27]

According to the NACD, directors are satisfied with the board recruitment process. Eighty-seven percent of directors believe their companies are effective or highly effective in handling director recruitment, and only 13 percent believe they are not effective.[28]

Finally, the director recruitment process is unique, in that companies do not tend to engage in succession planning among board members. To our knowledge, most companies do not maintain an updated list of potential board candidates in anticipation of an unplanned or emergency succession. Although companies might feel that the board can continue to function with the loss of a single member, it seems that director succession planning should be a key responsibility of the nominating and governance committee (see following sidebar). This is especially true if the company has a shortage of qualified board candidates.

Outgoing CEOs on the Board

Should the outgoing CEO remain on the board as a director after stepping down from it as an executive? Proponents of the practice say that it can lend stability to the transition process. The former CEO is available to provide advice and mentor the incoming CEO and can help him or her manage boardroom dynamics. This might be particularly valuable if the incoming CEO has not had previous CEO experience. Critics of the practice say that it undermines the credibility and leadership of the incoming CEO. To the rest of the board, the former CEO might still seem like "the boss" and the incoming CEO a more junior executive.

According to a survey by Korn/Ferry Institute, 72 percent of directors believe that the former CEO should not sit on the board.[29] A separate survey finds that only 14 percent of companies have a retired CEO as a board member. This figure has fallen over time as the practice has become less common. Perhaps surprisingly, 20 percent of companies have a policy restricting the former CEO from serving on the board.[30]

Evans, Nagarajan, and Schloetzer (2010) found that companies that retain nonfounder, former CEOs on the board exhibit significantly worse operating and stock price performance during the two years following the succession event. By contrast, they see no deterioration in performance when the former CEO was also a founder. They interpret the results "as indicative of a powerful former CEO holding the influential board chairman position but lacking the pecuniary and nonpecuniary attachment to the firm that founder CEOs typically possess."[31] Therefore, the evidence suggests that retaining nonfounder former CEOs on the board might lead to a reduction in governance quality, although any decision should be based on the company's specific situation.

Director Compensation

Directors require compensation for the time, responsibility, and expense of serving as directors. Recruiters suggest that most directors would be unwilling to do this work on a *pro bono* basis (directors at nonprofits is one exception). Therefore, the amount of compensation must be sufficient to attract and retain qualified professionals with the knowledge required to advise and monitor the corporation. It should also be structured to motivate directors to act in the interest of shareholders and stakeholders. As a result, understanding the payment structure is important for evaluating the incentives directors have to contribute to a sound governance system.

Director compensation covers not only time directly spent on board matters, but also the cost of keeping the director's calendar open in case of unexpected events, such as an unsolicited takeover bid, financial restatement, or emergency CEO succession. In addition, it covers the personal risk that comes with serving on a board. For example, although we have seen that directors are unlikely to incur out-of-pocket payments for legal liability or expenses, lawsuits still demand substantial time and attention. They also bring reputational risk and take an emotional toll on those involved.[32]

Directors of the largest U.S. corporations receive approximately $230,000 in total compensation, on average. Compensation packages comprise approximately 55 percent cash (in annual retainer and committee fees) and 45 percent equity (stock options and stock awards). Director compensation is $133,000 at medium-sized companies and $72,000 at small companies. The mix of compensation is approximately 70 percent cash and 30 percent equity (see Table 4.2).[33]

Compensation mix is approximately similar across industries, with a slightly lower mix of equity awards in utilities and a slightly higher mix of equity in technology companies.[34] This suggests that some relation exists between compensation risk and reward, based on the nature of the industry.

Table 4.2 Director Compensation

	Revenues > $20 Billion	Revenues $1 Billion to $2.5 Billion	Revenues < $500 Million
Annual Retainer	$80,000	$45,000	$26,000
Total Committee Fees	$10,500	$16,200	$10,600
Total Retainer and Fees	$105,900	$70,200	$46,600
Nonretainer Equity	$105,800	$57,800	$15,100
Total Compensation	$229,900	$132,600	$72,000
Distribution:			
Board Retainer	47%	34%	42%
Board Meeting Fees	2%	8%	10%
Committee Fees	6%	12%	16%
Stock Options	10%	12%	10%
Restricted Stock	14%	22%	15%
Deferred Stock	15%	5%	3%
Outright Stock	6%	7%	4%

Median figures. Might not sum to total compensation.

Source: Aon Hewitt Outside Director Compensation, (2010).

Many companies pay directors supplemental fees for serving on committees. These figures are included in the total compensation figures cited in Table 4.2. Committee fees might be an annual retainer or might be awarded on a per-meeting basis. Committee fees average between $10,000 and $15,000 per year. Fees are higher for directors who serve on the audit committee because committee members are required to have financial expertise. They also bear a higher risk of being named in shareholder litigation, and they might have a bigger workload when assigned to this committee (see Table 4.3).

Table 4.3 Director Committee Fees

	Revenues > $20 Billion	Revenues $1 Billion to $2.5 Billion	Revenues < $500 Million
Audit Committee			
Retainer	$10,000	$10,000	$7,250
Meeting Fee	$2,000	$1,500	$1,000
Retainer (Chairman)	$20,000	$12,500	$10,000
Compensation Committee			
Retainer	$9,500	$5,000	$5,000
Meeting Fee	$2,000	$1,500	$1,000
Retainer (Chairman)	$15,000	$8,250	$6,000
Nominating/Governance Committee			
Retainer	$9,000	$5,000	$5,000
Meeting Fee	$2,000	$1,500	$1,000
Retainer (Chairman)	$10,000	$7,500	$5,500
Median figures. Includes only companies that pay fees.			

Source: Aon Hewitt Outside Director Compensation (2010).

Nonexecutive chairmen and lead independent directors also receive supplemental pay. The average total compensation for nonexecutive chairmen is approximately 80 percent higher than that paid to other directors. Lead independent directors receive total compensation that is approximately 20 percent higher. These pay multiples hold true for small, medium, and large companies, and are intended to compensate for the increased responsibilities that come from leadership roles.[35]

One important question is whether the level of director fees is reasonable or appropriate from the perspective of shareholders. As is the case with most compensation issues, this is a difficult question to answer. One simple way to think about it is to consider the opportunity cost to these directors. If they were not directors, what might they earn for their services? We know that directors spend approximately 20 hours per month on board-related duties.[36] At $230,000 per year, this translates into an hourly rate of approximately $1,000. This is comparable to the hourly rate of individuals with similar professional backgrounds (such as business, finance, consulting, and law), and on that basis we might conclude that director pay is reasonable.

From the corporation's perspective, the cost of board member compensation can be a significant portion of the total direct cost of maintaining a governance system (the auditor fee represents another significant direct cost). According to a study of companies in Silicon Valley, small companies incur total costs for nonexecutive board compensation of around $750,000, and large companies incur $1.8 million. These figures represent 0.5 percent of revenue for the small companies and less than 0.1 percent at the large companies. They also represent 0.16 percent of the market capitalization of the small companies and 0.02 percent of the large companies.[37] Although smaller companies get less leverage out of the direct cost of their board, they are perhaps in a stage of growth in which strong monitoring systems and sound strategic advice are more important. Considering the importance that many experts place on having effective corporate governance, these costs are not very significant.[38]

Another important question is whether the mix of director compensation is appropriate. To answer this, shareholders should consider various factors, including the company's growth prospects, industry, risk profile, and cash position. For example, a small startup might offer a mix that is heavily comprised of stock options if the company is cash starved, in growth phase, and can benefit from the strategic advice of directors. For these companies, cash is critical for survival, and shareholders likely prefer that the cash be invested in the company, not paid out to board members. This type of pay structure also attracts certain types of directors: those who can deal with risk, who have the valuable strategic insights for the company, and who are willing to work hard to make the company a success. Conversely, large, steadily growing companies might choose to offer a high cash component along with some type of equity payment (such as restricted stock units).

Finally, in evaluating compensation, investors should remember that directors are not managers and that their compensation mix should be consistent with their serving an advisory and oversight function (see following sidebar). We discuss the incentive value of compensation for executives in Chapter 8, "Executive Compensation and Incentives."

Director Compensation

The Coca-Cola Company: All-or-Nothing Plan

In 2006, The Coca-Cola Company adopted a new and unique director compensation plan. Directors did not receive guaranteed cash compensation. Instead, they received equity units with a stated value of $175,000. The equity units came with a three-year performance trigger: They would vest if the company achieved its publicly stated goal of 8 percent per year earnings-per-share growth. If the target was met at the end of three years, the directors would receive $175,000 in cash. If the target was not met, the directors would receive nothing.[39]

Investors evaluating this plan must ask themselves a few questions. First, should director compensation at a large and steadily growing company be entirely performance-based? Step-function payments have the potential to encourage individuals either to bank excess profits when they have overachieved their yearly goals or to get aggressive when they are barely underachieving their yearly goals to meet the cliff payout thresholds. Second, is earnings per share the correct performance measurement for contingent compensation? The risk in using a single performance metric is that it is more easily subject to manipulation. An ethical risk might exist if the performance metric is a GAAP-based metric, which the audit committee of the board is responsible for reviewing. Third, is it in the best interest of the company to compensate a director this way? After all, directors are not in a position to ensure that the company executes its strategic goals (as managers are), so it is hard to see how the directors can directly contribute to achieving the company's performance targets. However, this "all or nothing" plan puts directors in the same financial position as shareholders. In this way, it is a gesture to show that if the shareholders suffer from underperformance, the directors will suffer as well.

Ultimately, Coca-Cola achieved its earnings objective and directors received the promised equity awards. The compensation plan has since been replaced with a more traditional mix of cash and equity, although the equity awards still retain a performance-based element.[40]

SPX Corporation

In 2002, SPX Corporation offered cash bonuses to directors and executives in which bonuses were earned based on the company's ability to exceed certain return-on-capital targets. The targets were calculated using the metric **economic value added** (EVA). EVA is calculated as after-tax operating profit minus the company's estimated cost of capital. At SPX, if the company was able to generate EVA greater than a certain target, executives and directors earned a cash bonus, some of which was paid out immediately; the rest was deferred for future payout.

For 2003, SPX increased the size of the bonus payments by modifying the calculation used to compute EVA. The company made adjustments to exclude certain pension costs, differences between the cash tax rate and the accrued tax rate assumption, and "the negative impact of industry factors beyond management control." After making these adjustments, the CEO received a total bonus credit of $10.2 million, $6.7 million of which was paid out immediately (his salary was $1.4 million). Independent directors also received a bonus of almost $100,000, five times higher than the annual target, and a $40,000 retainer and 4,000 stock options (estimated fair market value $109,000).[41]

Activist investors targeted the company, alleging that management received unjustified awards, that the bonus plan was unnecessarily complex, and that it provided incentive for value-destroying capital allocation decisions.

Ownership Guidelines

Many companies require that directors maintain personal ownership positions in the company's common stock during their tenure on the board (**ownership guidelines**). Such a requirement is intended to align the interests of directors with those of the common shareholders they represent, thereby giving directors an incentive to monitor management. For somewhat obvious reasons, shareholders (and governance experts) look favorably upon companies whose directors own stock. However, it is an open question what level of ownership is sufficient to mitigate agency problems between the board and shareholders.

According to Equilar, approximately 80 percent of the 250 largest companies in the United States have some form of director ownership guidelines.[42] Companies can structure these guidelines in a few ways. Some companies require that directors accumulate and retain a specified amount of company stock, either through open-market purchases or through the retention of restricted stock grants. The minimum amount of stock that directors are required to hold is defined as a multiple of their annual cash retainer. Other companies require that directors hold restricted stock grants for a minimum number of years. Directors are not required to meet these guidelines immediately upon assuming their board seat but are instead given time to accumulate the minimum ownership amounts. For example, directors at Pitney-Bowes have five years to accumulate their ownership requirement of 7,500 shares (approximately $250,000 in value).[43] Directors at McKesson are given three years to accumulate shares valued at four times their annual retainer (approximately $300,000 in share value).[44] On average, companies give directors five years to meet ownership guidelines.[45]

Requiring directors to own company shares might not always be a good idea. First, directors are not managers. They are advisors and monitors. Paying directors similar to management might compromise their ability to provide effective oversight. A director might be unwilling to approve a project or acquisition that risks depressing the company share price in the near term, even if the project will create long-term value, if the director's personal financial portfolio cannot accommodate stock price volatility. In this way, stock ownership might encourage directors to make decisions through the lens of their personal financial interest instead of the long-term interest of the corporation. Similarly, directors with a large equity position might be less likely to oppose low-level manipulation of accounting results (such as the smoothing of earnings or accelerated booking of revenue) if they believe that stock price will suffer from their detection. Finally, ownership guidelines are not usually calibrated for the wealth of the individual director. A guideline that specifies a $100,000 investment carries a different weight for a director with a net worth of $1 million than it does for a director with a net worth of $100 million.

The evidence on this issue is mixed. Mehran (1995) did not find a relationship between director stock ownership and either increased operating performance or increased firm value.[46] However, Mikkelson and Partch (1989) demonstrated that when a director with a major ownership position sits on the board, the company is more likely to agree to a takeover bid. This suggests that director stock ownership might decrease management entrenchment.[47] Cordeiro, Veliyath, and Neubaum (2005) and Fich and Shivdasani (2005) found that equity ownership among directors is positively associated with future stock price performance and firm value.[48] They saw this as evidence that equity-based compensation gives directors greater incentive to monitor managerial self-interest. However, Brick, Palmon, and Wald (2006) found a positive correlation between director compensation and CEO compensation and that above-average compensation is associated with lower future firm performance. They saw this as evidence of "mutual back scratching or cronyism."[49]

Board Evaluation

A **board evaluation** is the process by which the entire board, its committees, or individual directors are evaluated for their effectiveness in carrying out their stated responsibilities. The concept of a board evaluation was among the key recommendations of the Higgs Report, which stated that "every board should continually examine ways to improve its effectiveness."[50] In the United States, annual board evaluations are a listing standard of the New York Stock Exchange (NYSE), which requires that the nominating and governance committee "oversee the evaluation of the board and management." Furthermore, each committee (audit, compensation, and nominating and governance) is required to perform its own self-evaluation.[51]

That said, companies are not required to perform an evaluation of *individual* directors. Some companies do this, but many do not. A study by Korn/Ferry found that although about 76 percent of senior officers believe individual directors *should* be evaluated on a regular basis, only 45 percent of companies do. The practice of performing evaluations of individual directors varies across countries. Although 45 percent of U.S. companies perform individual assessments, 75 percent of companies do in the United Kingdom (this is likely related to the recommendations of the Higgs Report and the Revised Combined Code). In Japan, the figure is 30 percent.[52]

Evaluations—whether at the board, committee, or individual level—are important because they enable the board to understand whether it is meeting its own expectations for performance. For example, a board might discover that it is effective in compliance and regulatory oversight but that it dedicates insufficient time to overseeing the company's operations or strategy. Evaluations also help the board to understand the performance of directors and whether they are exhibiting the skills, knowledge, and expertise that is expected of them. If a director is not adequately engaged, the evaluation process can be an effective tool for initiating a discussion about improvement or replacement.

Furthermore, board evaluations vary significantly in terms of the process and scope. The following is a list of some of the choices companies make in designing evaluations:

- Are the board and committees evaluated only as a whole or at the level of the individual director?
- Is the board evaluated against the company's own policies or against the practices of highly successful peers?
- Are individual directors subjected to peer evaluation, self-evaluation, or a combination?
- Are evaluations conducted by interview or by survey?
- Are evaluations conducted by an internal officer (such as a human resources executive), an outside law firm, or a third-party consultant?

In addition, evaluations can address a variety of topics, including these:

- **Composition**—Does the board have the expertise it needs to fulfill all its responsibilities? Is the process for selecting new directors satisfactory? Are individual board members contributing broadly and in their areas of expertise? Is the board taking full advantage of the skills and experiences of its directors?
- **Accountability**—Is the board effective in fulfilling its responsibilities? Has the board set an appropriate strategy? Has the board ensured the relationship integrity among the company's vision, mission, strategy, business model, and key performance metrics? Has the board set realistic long-term objectives? Does

the board successfully monitor performance? Does the board successfully monitor and advise the CEO?

- **Information**—Is the board getting the information it needs? Is information accurate and timely?

- **Meetings**—Are meetings appropriately structured? Is sufficient time dedicated to all necessary topics? Is discussion open and honest? Are directors adequately prepared?

- **Relations**—Are directors honest and open in their discussion with one another? Are directors honest and open in their discussion with management? Do boardroom relations encourage optimum decision making? Does management receive appropriate support from the board? Does management receive sufficient oversight from the board?[53]

Finally, just because an evaluation is comprehensive in scope does not mean that it leads to effective outcomes.[54] Practically speaking, it is difficult for the professionals conducting the evaluation to give constructive feedback, even if they are third-party consultants. The consultants that perform these evaluations indicate that many directors, given the success they have achieved in their professional lives, do not welcome commentary about their shortcomings, and consultants' advice for improvement is often ignored. This is unfortunate, as it can lead to outcomes in which ineffective directors remain on the board when they should either improve or retire. To this end, a survey by *Corporate Board Member* magazine found that almost a quarter of officers have directors on their boards whom they feel should be replaced. Thirty-six percent of those respondents believe the directors lack the necessary skill set, 31 percent believe that the directors are not engaged, and the remainder believe that the directors either are unprepared for meetings or have been on the boards too long.[55] For governance quality to improve, these board members should hear this feedback firsthand.

Removal of Directors

For a variety of reasons, a director might want to leave a corporate board. These reasons can be benign (such as a desire to pursue new opportunities or retire) or more troublesome (such as a fundamental disagreement with fellow board members over the direction of the company—see the following sidebar). Similarly, the company might have either benign or troublesome reasons for wanting to replace a director. The company could decide that, after many years of service, it is time to find a new director who can look at strategy and operations from a different perspective. Or the company might feel that a particular director is negligent in his or her services and is therefore unfit to oversee the organization.

That said, a director leaving unwillingly is extremely rare. (Audit Analytics counts only 106 dismissals out of the entire population of public directors in 2009.)[56] Generally directors leave voluntarily. However, it is usually unclear what has prompted a director to step down when that director leaves for reasons other than reaching a mandatory retirement age.

Director Resignations

Director resignations in protest occur infrequently. However, they send a strong signal to the market that the management or oversight of the company might be deficient.[57]

Fair, Isaac & Co.

In 2001, Robert Sanderson resigned from the board of Fair Isaac. As required, the company released a copy of his resignation letter in an 8-K filing with the SEC:

"I hereby resign as a Director of Fair Isaac effective immediately. I am resigning because I disagree with the rest of the Board's willingness to grant 100,000 stock options to Tom Grudnowski in fiscal 2001. This was an incorrect decision for two principal reasons. First, the Company's 1992 Long-Term Incentive Plan limits the number of options which may be granted to any one employee to 50,000 a year. While it may be legal to grant Mr. Grudnowski 100,000 options, doing so would violate the spirit of the agreement among the Company, the Board, and the shareholders embodied in the plan. Second, Mr. Grudnowski doesn't deserve the grant. He was hired to get the Company growing again and to develop Internet-based new business. During his tenure as CEO, revenue growth has been below the Company's long-term record, and revenues from new business have been miniscule. He has not earned the reward of an extraordinary option grant. It is my hope that the Board will conclude, as I have, that the Company will not achieve long-term success with Mr. Grudnowski in charge, and that the best way to increase shareholder value is to sell the Company."[58]

Surge Components

In 2001, James Miller sent the following resignation letter to the board of directors:

"Since joining the board of directors of Surge, I have on numerous occasions expressed my belief that I have not been given appropriate and relevant information necessary for me to perform my duties. It has been difficult for me to receive requested information either in a timely manner or at all. Furthermore, it has come to my attention that there were significant events and actions taken which were not properly disclosed to me. Case in point: the company recently filed two Q's without my advice, review, or approval. This is particularly disturbing given the fact that I am chairman of the audit committee. As a result of these and other unacceptable circumstances, I do not believe I can discharge my responsibilities in the manner in which the shareholders deserve."[59]

Agrawal and Chen (2008) found that two-thirds of director resignations are related to governance issues (such as board members being given insufficient information on issues; being asked to vote on a matter that they are unfamiliar with; or having disputes over hiring, compensating, or firing a CEO). The remaining resignations occur because of disagreements over strategy or financing decisions. As we might expect, they found substantial negative abnormal stock price returns surrounding disclosure of a resignation.[60]

Fahlenbrach, Low, and Stulz (2010) found that director resignations are correlated with decreased share price, decreased operating performance, greater likelihood of future financial restatement, and greater likelihood of a securities lawsuit.[61]

The board may not remove a fellow director, even if the director is performing poorly. Shareholders may remove a director at the annual meeting. This is rare, however, outside of a contested election. During 2009, only 93 directors failed to win majority support.[62] Shareholders may also remove a director between annual meetings, if permitted under the company's charter. This, too, is rare. The most common way a director is removed is not to be renominated for election (see the following sidebar).[63]

Director Removal

Dow Chemical

In 2007, J. Pedro Reinhard, director of Dow Chemical and former chief financial officer of the company, negotiated with J.P. Morgan and an Omani sovereign wealth fund to engage in a leveraged buyout of the company. Reinhard did not notify either the CEO of Dow Chemical or his fellow board members of his actions. When the board discovered these actions, Reinhard was fired from his consulting and advisory contract with the company. He remained on the board, however, until the end of his term. At the next annual meeting, the governance committee reduced the number of board seats from 12 to 11, and Reinhard was not renominated.[64]

To our knowledge, a well-developed body of research on the removal of directors does not exist. Most studies focus on the resignation of directors following a significant negative event, such as a lawsuit or financial restatement, and not removal during the due course of business. For example, Srinivasan (2005) found that director turnover is significantly higher for firms that undergo a major financial restatement (48 percent during the subsequent three-year period), compared to firms that undergo a technical restatement (18 percent). Furthermore, he found that these board members tend to lose their other directorships as well. The phenomenon is most pronounced for audit committee members.[65]

Similarly, Arthaud-Day, Certo, Dalton, and Dalton (2006) found that director and audit committee members are 70 percent more likely to turn over if the company experiences a restatement. They explained that forced turnover of senior officers sends a signal that the company is disassociating itself from its past errors and that it is committed to restructuring control and oversight mechanisms to prevent future recurrence. They noted that although these actions do not fully repair reputational damage, they are meant to reassure shareholders that they can rely on the company going forward.[66]

Finally, people debate whether directors and officers of failed companies should be elected to directorships at other firms or whether their failure to properly monitor one firm should disqualify them from other boards. To this end, shareholders raised questions when Xerox named former chairman and CEO of Citigroup Charles Prince to its board, and when Alcoa named former chairman and CEO of Merrill Lynch Stanley O'Neil to its board and audit committee. Nonexecutive directors at Lehman Brothers, Wachovia, Washington Mutual, Bear Stearns, and AIG all gained new directorships after their companies failed.[67] On one hand, failure brings meaningful experience that might be valuable in another corporate setting. On the other hand, if the failure was caused by a lapse in judgment or ineffective monitoring, legitimate questions arise over whether a possible recurrence is worth the risk to the corporation. According to one expert, "When selecting individuals to oversee an organization, what criteria should we be using other than their previous performance on a corporate board? [I]f there's no accountability here, then what is the system of accountability?"[68]

Endnotes

1. National Association of Corporate Directors and The Center for Board Leadership, "NACD Public Company Governance Survey" (2008). See www.nacdonline.org/.

2. Mark Cheffers and Don Whalen, "Audit Analytics, Director Departures: A Five-Year Overview" (2009). Accessed October 14, 2010. See www.auditanalytics.com/0000/custom-reports.php.

3. Egon Zehnder International, "Global Board Index 2008" (2008). Accessed July 15, 2009. See www.egonzehnder.com/global/thoughtleadership/hottopic/id/43700172/publication/id/43700177; Spencer Stuart, "Spencer Stuart U.S. Board Index 2007" (2007). See www.spencerstuart.com/research/boards/955/.

4. Corporate Board Member and PricewaterhouseCoopers LLC, "Special Supplement: What Directors Think 2009, Corporate Board Member/ PricewaterhouseCoopers LLC Survey" (2009). Accessed January 20, 2010. See www.pwc.com/us/en/corporate-governance/publications/what-directors-think-survey-highlights.jhtml.

5. National Association of Corporate Directors and The Center for Board Leadership, "NACD Public Company Governance Survey" (2009). See www.nacdonline.org/.

6. Spencer Stuart, 2007.

7. John Greenwald and Lois Gilman, "CEOs to Boards: We're Outta Here, Corporate Board Member First Quarter" (2009). Accessed March 2, 2009. See http://www.boardmember.com/MagazineArticle_Details.aspx?id=3070.

8. Spencer Stuart, "Spencer Stuart U.S. Board Index 2008" (2008). Accessed May 4, 2010. See www.spencerstuart.com/research/.

9. David F. Larcker, Eric C. So, and Charles C. Y. Wang, "Boardroom Centrality and Stock Returns," Rock Center for Corporate Governance at Stanford University working paper no. 84, *Social Science Research Network* (July 24, 2010). See http://ssrn.com/abstract=1651407.

10. Egon Zehnder International.

11. Betsy Atkins, "How Boards Should Do Deal Making—and Don't," *Forbes.com* (October 12, 2010).

12. FindLaw, "Nomination and Observer Agreement—Excite Inc. and Intuit Inc." (June 25, 1997). Accessed November 4, 2010. See http://contracts.corporate.findlaw.com/corporate/govern/289.html.

13. Napera, "About Us: Board of Directors." Accessed November 4, 2010. See www.napera.com/about-us/board-of-directors.

14. Editors of DiversityInc., "Fortune 500 Black, Latino, Asian CEOs" (2008). Accessed November 11, 2010. See http://diversityinc.com/content/1757/article/3895/. Catalyst Inc., "Women CEOs of the Fortune 1000, November 2010" (2010). Accessed November 4, 2010. See www.catalyst.org/publication/322/women-ceos-of-the-fortune-1000.

15. Boris Groysberg and Deborah Bell, "2010 Board of Directors Survey, Sponsored by Heidrick & Struggles and WomenCorporateDirectors (WCD)" (2010). Accessed October 7, 2010. See www.heidrick.com/PublicationsReports/PublicationsReports/HS_BOD_Survey2010.pdf.

16. Korn/Ferry Institute, "34th Annual Board of Directors Study" (2007). Accessed November 4, 2010. See www.kornferry.com/Publication/9955.

17. National Association of Corporate Directors and The Center for Board Leadership, 2009.

18. American Express Co., Inc., Form DEF 14-A, filed with the Securities and Exchange Commission March 15, 2007.

19. Wikipedia, "Allan Leighton." Accessed November 14, 2010. See http://en. wikipedia.org/wiki/Allan_Leighton.

20. Eugene H. Fram, "Are Professional Board Directors the Answer?" *MIT Sloan Management Review* 46 (2005): 75–77.

21. However, one could argue that professional directors have greater incentive for this same reason. If they do a poor job at one firm, they might lose multiple directorships.

22. Securities and Exchange Commission, "17 CFR PARTS 229, 239, 240, 249, and 274. Proxy Disclosure Enhancements [RELEASE NOS. 33-9089; 34-61175; IC-29092; File No. S7-13-09]." Accessed November 4, 2010. See www.sec.gov/rules/final/2009/33-9089.pdf.

23. SunTrust Banks, Form PRE DEF 14A, filed with the Securities and Exchange Commission February 23, 2010.

24. Analog Devices, Inc., Form DEF 14A, filed with the Securities and Exchange Commission February 3, 2010.

25. Covidien, Form DEF 14A, filed with the Securities and Exchange Commission January 25, 2010.

26. National Association of Corporate Directors and The Center for Board Leadership, 2009.

27. Corporate Board Member and PricewaterhouseCoopers LLC.

28. National Association of Corporate Directors and The Center for Board Leadership, 2009.

29. Korn/Ferry Institute.

30. National Association of Corporate Directors and The Center for Board Leadership, 2009.

31. John Harry Evans, Nandu J. Nagarajan, and Jason D. Schloetzer, "CEO Turnover and Retention Light: Retaining Former CEOs on the Board," *Journal of Accounting Research* 48 (2010): 1,015–1,047.

32. One example is the board of the Hewlett-Packard Company following the "pre-texting" scandal in 2006. See Alan Murray, "Directors Cut: H-P Board Clash Over Leaks Triggers Angry Resignation," *Wall Street Journal* (September, 6, 2006, Eastern edition): A.1.

33. Compensation figures represent median averages. Unless otherwise cited, compensation data in this section comes from Aon Hewitt Associates, LLP, "2010 Analysis of Outside Director Compensation" (2010). Accessed October 17, 2010. See http://www.hewittassociates.com/_MetaBasicCMAssetCache_/Assets/Articles/2010/2010_Outside_Director_Compensation.pdf.

34. Compensation mix for technology companies from Frederic W. Cook & Co. Inc., "2007 Director Compensation: NASDAQ 100 vs. NYSE 100," (2007). Accessed July 24, 2008. See www.fwcook.com/alert_letters/2008_Director_Comp.pdf.

35. Frederic W. Cook & Co. Inc.

36. Corporate Board Member and PricewaterhouseCoopers LLC.

37. Compensia, "Silicon Valley 130: Board of Directors Compensation Practices, October 2007" (2007). Accessed November 14, 2007. See www.compensia. com/surveys/SV130-BOARD.pdf.

38. The Sarbanes–Oxley Act of 2002 contributed to a significant rise in director compensation in recent years. Linck, Netter, and Yang (2008) found that director compensation at large companies rose almost 50 percent between 1998 and 2004 (measured as a percentage of sales). They also found a substantial increase in the cost of Director and Officer (D&O) insurance premiums (which are paid by the firm). See James S. Linck, Jeifry M. Netter, and Tina Yang, "The Effects and Unintended Consequences of the Sarbanes–Oxley Act on the Supply and Demand for Directors," *Review of Financial Studies* 22 (2009): 3,287–3,328.

39. The Coca-Cola Company, Form DEF-14-A, filed with the Securities and Exchange Commission March 13, 2007.

40. The Coca-Cola Company, Form DEF-14-A, filed with the Securities and Exchange Commission March 5, 2010.

41. SPX Corporation, Form DEF-14-A, filed with the Securities and Exchange Commission March 17, 2004.

42. Equilar Inc., "2010 Director Stock Ownership Guidelines Report," Equilar, an Executive Compensation Research Firm (2010). Accessed August 4, 2010. See http://insight.equilar.com/app/pub_serv.

43. Pitney-Bowes Inc., Form DEF 14A, filed with the Securities and Exchange Commission March 27, 2008.

44. McKesson Corporation, "Corporate Governance Guidelines" (amended July 28, 2010). See www.mckesson.com/en_us/McKesson.com/Investors/ Corporate%2B Governance/Corporate%2BGovernance%2BGuidelines.html.

45. Equilar Inc.

46. Hamid Mehran, "Executive Compensation Structure, Ownership, and Firm Performance," *Journal of Financial Economics* 38 (1995): 163–184. As cited in Clifford Holderness, "A Survey of Blockholders and Corporate Control," *Economic Policy Review—Federal Reserve Bank of New York* 9 (2003): 51–63.

47. Wayne H. Mikkelson and Megan Partch, "Managers' Voting Rights and Corporate Control," *Journal of Financial Economics* 25 (1989): 263–290. As cited in Clifford G. Holderness, "A Survey of Blockholders and Corporate Control," *Economic Policy Review—Federal Reserve Bank of New York* 9 (2003): 51–63.

48. James J. Cordeiro, Rajaram Veliyath, and Donald O. Neubaum, "Incentives for Monitors: Director Stock-Based Compensation and Firm Performance," *Journal of Applied Business Research* 21 (2005): 81–90. Eliezer M. Fich and Anil Shivdasani, "The Impact of Stock-Option Compensation for Outside Directors on Firm Value," *Journal of Business* 78 (2005): 2,229–2,254.

49. Ivan E. Brick, Oded Palmon, and John K. Wald, "CEO Compensation, Director Compensation, and Firm Performance: Evidence of Cronyism?" *Journal of Corporate Finance* 12 (2006): 403–423.

50. Dechert LLP, "The Higgs Report on Nonexecutive Directors: Summary Recommendations" (2003). Accessed December 5, 2007. See www.dechert.com/library/Summary%20of%20Recommendations1.pdf.

51. New York Stock Exchange, "Corporate Governance Standards." See www.nyse.com/regulation/nyse/1101074746736.html.

52. Korn/Ferry Institute.

53. Adapted from: Richard M. Furr and Lana J. Furr, "Will You Lead, Follow, or Develop Your Board As Your Partner?" (2005). Accessed November 5, 2010. See http://boardanddirectors.com/art_lead.asp.

54. We are not aware of any large-scale research studies on the performance consequences of board member evaluation methods.

55. Corporate Board Member and PricewaterhouseCoopers LLC.

56. Mark Cheffers and Don Whalen.

57. Anup Agrawal and Mark A. Chen, "Boardroom Brawls: An Empirical Analysis of Disputes Involving Directors," 3rd Annual Conference on Empirical Legal Studies Papers, *Social Science Research Network* (2008): 1–60. Accessed November 4, 2010. See http://ssrn.com/abstract=1101035.

58. Fair, Isaac & Co., Form 8-K, filed with the Securities and Exchange Commission, June 1, 2001.

59. Surge Components, Inc., Form 8-K, filed with the Securities and Exchange Commission August 1, 2001.

60. Anup Agrawal and Mark A. Chen.

61. Rüdiger Fahlenbrach, Angie Low, and Rene M. Stulz, "The Dark Side of Outside Directors: Do They Quit When They Are Most Needed?" Charles A. Dice Center working paper no. 2010-7; Swiss Finance Institute research paper no. 10-17; ECGI–Finance working paper no. 281/2010, *Social Science Research Network* (2010): 1–8. Accessed November 4, 2010. See http://ssrn.com/abstract=1585192.

62. Gibson Dunn, "Considerations for Public Company Directors in the Current Environment" (October 15, 2009). Accessed November 15, 2010. See gibsondunn.com/Publications/Pages/ConsiderationsforPublicCompanyDirectorsintheCurrentEnvironment.aspx.

63. William Meade Fletcher, "§ 351. Common Law Right to Remove for Cause," *Fletcher Cyclopedia of the Law of Corporations* (St. Paul: Thomson/West, 1931-).

64. Roger Parloff, "Inside Job," *Fortune* (July 7, 2008): 94–108.

65. Suraj Srinivasan, "Consequences of Financial Reporting Failure for Outside Directors: Evidence from Accounting Restatements and Audit Committee Members," *Journal of Accounting Research* 43 (2005): 291–334.

66. Marne L. Arthaud-Day, S. Trevis Certo, Catherine M. Dalton, and Dan R. Dalton, "A Changing of the Guard: Executive and Director Turnover Following Corporate Financial Restatements," *Academy of Management Journal* 49 (2006): 1,119–1,136.

67. Susanne Craig and Peter Lattman, "Companies May Fail, but Directors Are in Demand," *Dealbook.NYTimes.com* (September 14, 2010).

68. Rakesh Khurana, as cited in Susanne Craig and Peter Lattman.

5

Board of Directors:
Structure and Consequences

In this chapter, we examine the structural attributes of the board of directors and determine which contribute to board effectiveness. Despite what you might read in the popular press or professional literature, this is not a simple exercise.

Our objective is to take you through the evidence. We critically examine the importance of several salient features of a board of directors: separation of roles between the chairman and the CEO, the appointment of a lead director, board size, board committee structure, boards with directors that serve on other boards (that is, "busy" directors), female directors and diverse boards, and others. We also examine what impact, if any, these attributes have on the board's ability to perform its advising and monitoring functions. If these attributes are important, we should see that they are associated with improved outcomes (such as superior operating performance or increased stock returns) or other observable metrics (such as higher takeover premiums, fewer accounting restatements, less shareholder litigation, and more rational executive compensation). If no improvements are observed, it is difficult to claim that these attributes are important.

Two caveats are important. First, we do not provide a complete review of the literature on each topic in this chapter. The relevant body of work is too expansive to be summarized in one place. Still, we aim to provide a fair reflection of the general research results. Second, as mentioned in Chapter 1, "Introduction to Corporate Governance," the results discussed in this chapter are "on average" results across a large sample of companies. They do not tell us what will happen for an individual company. A company might find that a certain board structure is perfectly suitable, given its specific situation, even though the evidence from academic and professional literature suggests that it leads to worse outcomes on average. Where applicable, we cite examples that attempt to draw out these contradictions and, in doing so, enable the reader to draw conclusions about the relative importance of individual attributes. Finally, it is difficult to infer that any change in the board of directors will "cause" a change in organizational performance. In reading this chapter, keep in mind the famous dictum that "correlation does not imply causation."

Board Structure

The structure of a board of directors is generally described in terms of its prominent structural attributes: its size, professional and demographic information about the directors serving on it, their independence from management, number of committees, and director compensation.

According to Spencer Stuart, the board of an average large U.S. corporation has approximately 11 directors. (Boards usually have an odd number of directors to reduce the likelihood of a tie vote.)[1] The average age of directors is 61 years. More than 80 percent of directors meet the independence standards required by U.S. listing exchanges. Sixty-one percent have a chairman who is also CEO, and only 16 percent have a chairman who is fully independent.

Boards meet (in person and telephonically) between eight and nine times per year, on average. Audit committee members meet nine times, and compensation committee members six times. The Sarbanes–Oxley Act of 2002 mandated that all members of these committees be independent directors and that at least one member of the audit committee have expertise in finance and accounting.

Approximately three-quarters of boards have a mandatory retirement age, which is usually 70 years or older (see Figure 5.1).

Are these the right levels? Would outcomes improve if companies were compelled, through either regulation or shareholder activism, to change the composition of their boards? We consider several attributes:

- Independence of the chairman
- Lead independent director
- Outside (nonexecutive) directors
- Independence standards
- Independent committees of the board
- Representation on the board by selected constituents (bankers, financial experts, politically connected individuals, and employees)
- Companies whose directors sit on multiple boards (**busy boards**)
- Companies whose senior executives sit reciprocally on each other's boards (**interlocked boards**)
- Board size
- Diverse boards
- Boards with female directors

Chairman of the Board

The **chairman** presides over board meetings. He or she is responsible for scheduling meetings, planning agendas, and distributing materials in advance. In this way, the chairman shapes the timing and manner in which the board addresses governance matters. The chairman also plays a critical role in communicating corporate priorities, both internally and externally, and in managing stakeholder concerns. The chairman is expected to participate in or lead the discussion of several high-level items, including long-term strategic planning, enterprise risk management, management performance evaluation, management and director compensation, succession planning, director recruitment, and merger-related activity.

	2008	2003	1998	5-year % change	10-year % change	Comments
Board composition						
Average board size	10.8	10.9	12.0	-1%	-10%	Boards shrinking over past 10 years
Boards with 12 or fewer directors	80%	74%	68%	8%	18%	Continued trend toward smaller boards
Independent directors	82%	79%	78%	4%	5%	Boards becoming more independent
Average age of boards (independent directors)	61.2	60.3	60.0	1%	2%	Average age creeping up
New independent directors						
Total number	380	393	505	-3%	-25%	Number varies from year to year
Women	18%	19%	16%	-5%	13%	Down slightly in recent years but up longer term
Active CEOs/COOs/presidents/vice chairs	31%	32%	49%	-3%	-37%	Downward trend since late 1990s
Division/subsidiary presidents/ other corporate executives	19%	12%	9%	58%	111%	Continued rise in non-CEO directors
Women directors						
Women as percentage of all directors	16%	13%	n/a	20%	n/a	Rising share of female directors
Boards with at least one woman director	89%	85%	n/a	5%	n/a	Nearly 90% of boards have at least one woman
CEO profile						
Average number of other corporate directorships	0.7	1.0	2.0	-30%	-65%	CEOs serving on fewer boards
Women CEOs	14	9	4	56%	250%	Number of female CEOs tripled over past decade
Boards where CEO is the only nonindependent	44%	35%	23%	26%	90%	Increasingly, CEO is sole insider
Average age	55.4	55.3	57.0	0%	-3%	Down slightly from 10 years ago
Average tenure with company	14.4	14.7	17.0	-2%	-15%	Continued decline in tenure with company
Average tenure as CEO	6.4	6.3	7.0	2%	-9%	Down slightly from 10 years ago

Figure 5.1   Structure of the board of directors of U.S. corporations.

	2008	2003	1998	5-year % change	10-year % change	Comments
Chairman independence						
CEO is also chairman	61%	77%	84%	−20%	−27%	Growing separation of chair/CEO roles
Independent chairman	16%	n/a	n/a	n/a	n/a	Up from 10% in 2006
Boards with lead or presiding director	95%	36%	n/a	n/a	n/a	Nearly all boards have lead or presiding director
Board meetings						
Average number of board meetings	8.7	7.8	7.0	12%	24%	Continued increase
Median number of board meetings	8.0	7.0	7.0	14%	14%	Continued increase
Retirement age						
Boards with mandatory retirement age	74%	66%	45%	12%	64%	More boards establish mandatory retirement age
Boards with mandatory retirement age of 72+	72%	46%	37%	57%	95%	But age caps keep rising
Boards with mandatory retirement age of 70	27%	51%	58%	−47%	−53%	Fewer boards requiring retirement by 70
Committee independence	2008	2003	1998	5-year % change	10-year % change	Comments
Nominating/governance committee	100%	91%	67%	10%	49%	All members are independent
Compensation committee	100%	96%	97%	4%	3%	All members are independent
Audit committee	100%	98%	92%	2%	9%	All members are independent
Committee meetings						
Average number of audit meetings	9.1	7.3	n/a	25%	n/a	Audit committees meeting more frequently
Average number of compensation meetings	6.6	5.8	n/a	14%	n/a	Compensation committees meeting more frequently
Audit chairmen						
Active chair/president/CEO/vice chair	15%	28%	n/a	−46%	n/a	Fewer active CEOs serving as audit chairs
Retired chair/president/CEO/vice chair	28%	20%	n/a	40%	n/a	Retired CEOs filling the gap
Active/retired CFO/treasurer/financial manager	15%	4%	n/a	275%	n/a	More boards tapping financial executives for this role
Active/retired accountant	9%	3%	n/a	200%	n/a	Accountants also in demand

Source: Spencer Stuart, "Spencer Stuart U.S. Board Index 2008" (2008).

Professional studies suggest that certain personal characteristics might be correlated with an individual being more effective in this role. These include good communication and listening skills, a clear sense of direction, business acumen, an ability to bring people together, an ability to get to key issues quickly, and an ability to gain shareholder confidence.[2] Although these have not been thoroughly tested, anecdotes of successful public company chairmen tend to support them. For example, John Pepper, nonexecutive chairman of the Walt Disney Company, is known for being an effective chairman who restored relations with shareholders and stakeholders following the tumultuous ending to Michael Eisner's long run as CEO of that company. As one friend described Pepper, "He is very balanced and mature and can deal with all kinds of people. He can take a position in the middle of a dispute, but people will feel like he's listened and considered a position even if he comes out on the other side."[3]

Many governance experts assert that it is important that the position of chairman be separated from the position of CEO. This approach is widely adopted in the United Kingdom and other countries. It was also required of companies in the United States that received extraordinary assistance under the Troubled Asset Relief Program (TARP) in 2008, and it was proposed as a requirement of all publicly traded companies under Sen. Charles Schumer's Shareholder Bill of Rights.[4] Prominent shareholder groups, pension funds, and proxy advisory firms generally support shareholder proposals to create an independent chairman. According to The Corporate Library, a governance rating agency, "A split between the roles of chairman and CEO is gaining widespread support as a corporate governance best practice that many business leaders believe should be adopted by more, if not all, public companies in the United States."[5]

Having an independent chairman includes several potential benefits:

- It leads to clearer separation of responsibility between the board and management.
- It eliminates conflicts in the areas of CEO performance evaluation, executive compensation, long-term succession planning, and the recruitment of independent directors.

- It gives clear authority to one director to speak to shareholders, management, and the public on behalf of the board.
- It gives the CEO time to focus completely on the strategy, operations, and culture of the company.

Advocates of an independent chairman believe that it is particularly important in these situations:

- The company has a new CEO, particularly an insider who has been promoted and therefore has no previous experience as CEO.
- Company performance has declined and significant changes to the company's strategy, operations, or culture are needed that require management's complete attention while the board considers whether a change in leadership or sale of the company is necessary.
- The company has received an unsolicited takeover bid, which management might not be able to evaluate independently without considerations for their own job status.

However, having an independent chairman can also cause several potential disadvantages (see the accompanying sidebar):

- It can be an artificial separation, particularly when the company already has an effective chairman/CEO in place.
- It can make recruiting a new CEO difficult when that individual currently holds both titles or expects to be offered both titles.
- It can create duplication of leadership and internal confusion.
- It can lead to inefficient decision making because leadership is shared.
- It can create new costs to decision making because specialized information might not easily transfer from the CEO to the chairman (the **information gap**).
- It can create a second layer of monitoring costs because the new chairman also poses a potential agency problem.
- It can weaken leadership during a crisis.[6]

The Trouble with Separating the Chairman and CEO

Bank of America

In September 2009, Ken Lewis, chairman and CEO of Bank of America, unexpectedly announced that he would retire from the company by the end of the year.[7] At the time, the company was struggling to repay federal funds received through TARP. It was also involved in a Securities and Exchange Commission (SEC) lawsuit for inadequate disclosure relating to its acquisition of Merrill Lynch one year earlier. Robert Kelly, chairman and CEO of Bank of New York Mellon, was reportedly interested in the job. One analyst wrote, "He would be terrific [for the job.] He's an extraordinary manager with a lot of experience and integrity, and has a great deal of respect on Wall Street as well as with other bankers."[8] However, Kelly did not receive the job, partly because he wanted to retain the dual title of chairman and CEO, whereas the U.S. Treasury department wanted Bank of America to split these roles.[9]

General Motors

In June 2009, General Motors named Edward Whitacre, former chairman and CEO of AT&T, to the post of chairman. The company had just emerged from Chapter 11 bankruptcy and was operating under TARP. As such, the company was required to have an independent chairman. Whitacre's primary responsibility was to ensure that the company could meet its obligations to repay the U.S. government. However, by December 2009, the company continued to struggle. Whitacre and the board decided to fire CEO Fritz Henderson. Whitacre was named interim CEO (retaining the title of chairman) while a search for a permanent successor was underway. One month later, the board called off the search and Whitacre was formally given both titles. No explanation was given for the change. Whitacre said simply that General Motors "needs stability."[10]

Researchers have studied the impact of separating the chairman and CEO roles. Most studies have found little or no evidence that separation leads to improved corporate outcomes. For example, Baliga, Moyer, and Rao (1996) found that companies that announce a separation (or combination) of the roles do not exhibit abnormal positive (or negative) stock price returns around the announcement date. They also found no evidence that a change in the independence status of the chairman has any impact on the company's future operating performance, and they found only weak evidence that it leads to long-term market value creation. They concluded that although a combined chairman/CEO "may increase potential for managerial abuse, [it] does not appear to lead to tangible manifestations of that abuse."[11] Similarly, Boyd (1995) provided a meta-analysis of several papers on chairman/CEO duality and found, on average, no statistically significant relationship between the independence status of the chairman and operating performance.[12]

Research also suggests that companies are more likely to separate the chairman and CEO roles for succession purposes and are less likely to do so to improve management oversight. Grinstein and Valles Arellano (2008) examined a sample of companies that created nonexecutive chairs between 2000 and 2004. They found that the majority did so with the outgoing chairman/CEO retaining the title of chairman until his or her successor as CEO gained sufficient experience. In these cases, adopting a nonexecutive chairman was a means of providing stability during a period of transition. Only in a minority (20 percent) of the sample did an independent director assume the chairmanship. In these companies, the appointment of an independent chairman was more likely to follow a period of poor operating performance and, therefore, likely was driven by an attempt to improve corporate oversight.[13]

Brickley, Coles, and Jarrell (1994) reached similar conclusions. They found that firms that separate the chairman and CEO roles almost always appoint a former officer with relatively high stock ownership to the chair. They argued that this structure reduces the cost of sharing information. The authors also found that companies use the chairmanship as a reward to newly appointed CEOs who perform well during a preliminary period. They concluded that a dual chairman/CEO is an important tool in succession planning and that forcing a separation likely creates costs that outweigh the benefits.[14]

The evidence therefore suggests that an independent chairmanship is likely not a governance practice that definitively improves corporate outcomes. However, it is also not a structure that has been shown to destroy shareholder value.[15] The circumstances under which this structure is beneficial will likely vary depending on the specific situation, so the decision of whether to split the chairman and CEO roles is best left to the discretion of the company and its stakeholders. Research does not support mandating the split for all companies.

Lead Independent Director

The position of lead independent director has emerged as somewhat of a compromise between allowing companies to maintain dual chairman/CEO positions and forcing companies to separate these roles and appoint an independent chairman. The position evolved from the role served by the director who presides over executive sessions of the board. The New York Stock Exchange (NYSE) requires that nonexecutive directors meet outside the presence of management in regularly scheduled **executive sessions** and that an independent director preside over these meetings. In recent years, this director has assumed a more prominent role with expanded powers and has come to be known as the **lead independent (presiding) director**.

Many corporate governance experts recommend that companies formally appoint a lead independent director, particularly those in which the CEO also serves as chairman of the board. The expectation is that the lead independent director can serve as an important counterbalance to the chairman/CEO. However, beyond presiding over executive sessions, the responsibilities of this role are still being defined and vary widely across companies.

According to Spencer Stuart, the lead director at most companies serves as liaison between the chairman/CEO and independent directors. This person also plays a prominent role in the evaluation of corporate performance, CEO succession planning, director recruitment, and board and director evaluations. Sometimes the lead director serves as the main contact to receive and address shareholder communications.[16] He or she can particularly be important during times of crisis, including periods of increased government or regulatory scrutiny, hostile takeover attempts, and contentious proxy battles. In these situations, the lead director brings clarity of communication and clear leadership to internal and external stakeholders.

To be effective, the lead director needs many of the same attributes required of the chairman, including communication and listening skills, diplomacy, and an ability to gain confidence. The lead director must also be willing to take stands that are counter to those of management and, in doing so, compel change. According to one director, "The person has to care for the spirit of the board. He or she needs to be committed to integrity, loyalty, and equanimity. [Y]ou need someone in this role who calls for candor and makes people feel safe about asking the tough and proverbial 'dumb' questions."[17] However, the lead director should not become too involved in management issues, particularly during a crisis.

Experts believe that lead directors can contribute to improved corporate performance in these ways:

- Taking responsibility for improving board performance
- Building a productive relationship with the CEO
- Supporting effective communications with shareholders
- Providing leadership in crisis situations or in turbulent times
- Ensuring that the board is engaged effectively in developing corporate strategy
- Leading the board in succession planning for the CEO and senior management and for the board and its leaders[18]

Although the board should already be discussing these items, appointing a lead director might accelerate the process. Anecdotal evidence suggests that this can be accomplished by concentrating responsibility for selected matters in the hands of one capable director and granting him or her authority to act. Several examples of successful lead directors can provide a model for other companies to emulate. However, as these examples indicate, the lead director is likely to succeed only if given sufficient autonomy and if the chairman or other board members don't undermine his or her authority (see the following sidebar).

Lead Directors in Action

The Home Depot

Bonnie Hill was head of the compensation committee at Home Depot during the controversy over compensation paid to former CEO Robert Nardelli. In that role, she fielded a high number of complaints from institutional investors who were dissatisfied with the seeming disconnect between pay and performance. Hill decided that it was in the best interest of the company to proactively reach out to investors. She and fellow nonexecutive directors organized a town hall meeting where approximately 40 institutional shareholders were invited to voice their concerns. Importantly, management did not participate in the meeting. Following the town hall meeting, the company adjusted its compensation program to better align pay and performance. Because of the positive reception Hill received from shareholders, she was named lead independent director. She used that position to foster closer communication with shareholders on a wide variety of additional governance matters.[19]

Royal Dutch Shell

In 2004, it was revealed that Royal Dutch Shell had overstated its estimate of proved oil and gas reserves by nearly four billion barrels, or 20 percent. During the investigation that followed, disturbing details came to light regarding management's complicity in hiding the matter from the board and the public. The board appointed Sir John Kerr, nonexecutive director of Shell Transport and former European diplomat, to lead a steering committee of independent directors in a comprehensive review of the company's organizational structure and governance. In the months that followed, Kerr met with institutional investors who held more than 50 percent of the company's common stock. He met with some investors multiple times. Kerr took detailed notes in these meetings and was able to refer to and follow up on specific suggestions made previously. His approach gained the considerable confidence of investors, who believed that the company was truly listening to them. In October 2004, Kerr's steering committee recommended a complete overhaul of the company's organizational and governance systems, based in part on shortcomings investors had identified.[20]

The research literature on lead independent directors is modest because it is difficult to distinguish between companies that have a truly empowered lead director and those that grant that title to the director who presides over executive sessions. Still, some evidence suggests that lead independent directors improve governance outcomes. Larcker, Richardson, and Tuna (2007) found that appointing a lead independent director, in combination with other factors, is associated with improved future operating performance and stock price returns.[21]

The benefit of a lead director likely will depend on the governance situation of the firm and the personal qualities of the director selected, instead of the simple fact that the role was created.

Outside Directors

As discussed in Chapter 2, "International Corporate Governance," securities regulations in most developed countries require that companies have a majority of **outside (nonexecutive) directors.** Outside directors are expected to execute their duties without undue influence from management because they have no reporting lines to the CEO and do not rely on the company for their livelihood. They are also expected to draw on their professional backgrounds and lend functional expertise to advise on the company strategy and business model. Therefore, they are expected to be better suited to fulfill the advisory and monitoring functions of the board than inside directors.

However, outside directors are likely to be less informed about the company than inside directors. We referred to this earlier as the "information gap" and noted that such a gap is more likely to occur when specialized knowledge is required to run the company. When an information gap occurs, decision making can suffer. Decision making can also suffer through lack of independence. Although companies are required to meet the independence standards of listing exchanges, it doesn't guarantee that outside directors who meet these standards in a technical sense are truly independent. Some governance experts point out that insiders can coopt the board by nominating outside directors who appear to be independent but are not.[22] Alternatively, outside directors might be independent but not adequately engaged or qualified. When this occurs, numerical targets for outside representation become ineffective (see the following sidebar).

Independent ... but Qualified?

Lehman Brothers

In 2008, the board of directors of Lehman Brothers had 11 directors, of which 10 were outsiders and 1 was an insider (chairman and CEO Richard Fuld). Of the 10 outside directors, only 1 had recent experience leading a large U.S. bank (Jerry Grundhofer, former CEO of U.S. Bancorp). The other outside directors were

- John Macomber, 80, former McKinsey consultant, with experience as a CEO in the chemicals industry
- John Akers, 74, former CEO of IBM
- Thomas Cruikshank, 77, former CEO of Halliburton
- Henry Kaufman, 81, former chief economist of Salomon Brothers
- Sir Christopher Gent, 60, former CEO of Vodafone
- Roger Berlind, 75, theater producer
- Roland Hernandez, 50, former CEO of Telemundo
- Michael Ainslie, 64, former CEO of Sotheby's
- Marsha Johnson Evans, 61, former head of the Red Cross[23]

The composition of this board is notable for the number of retired executives. Although retired executives have more time than current executives to dedicate to board matters, their knowledge of industry dynamics and regulations is potentially outdated. The board is also notable for its average age. Older directors are not necessarily less effective than younger directors, but the ultimate bankruptcy of the company does suggest that this board was not properly equipped to advise on or monitor firm strategy and risk. Indeed, the career profiles of the outside directors indicate that they might have been selected for reasons other than their financial industry expertise.[24]

Research indicates that investors generally look favorably upon companies that add outside directors to the board. Rosenstein and Wyatt (1990) found that adding an outside director to the board leads to a statistically significant increase in stock price around the announcement date.[25] Interestingly, the addition of an insider to the board is greeted with a negative reaction by shareholders if the insider owns only a small amount of company stock, but is greeted with a positive reaction if the insider owns a large amount of stock. Apparently, investors understand the potential tradeoff between the information advantage of insiders and their potential for self-dealing, and they expect high stock ownership to help mitigate this risk.

The impact of outside directors on the long-term operating performance of the company is less clear. Bhagat and Black (2002) found almost no relationship between the percent of outsiders on a board and the long-term performance of the company's stock.[26] In contrast, Duchin, Matsusaka, and Ozbas (2010) found that the effectiveness of outside directors depends on the cost of acquiring information about the firm.[27] When it is easy for outsiders to gain expertise on the firm (because the firm is in a straightforward industry), company performance increases following the appointment of outsiders to the board. When it is difficult for outsiders to gain expertise, company performance decreases following their appointment. These findings tend to support the idea that outside directors are more effective when it is easy to close the information gap between insider and outsider knowledge.

Boards with a higher percentage of outside directors might also make better decisions regarding mergers and acquisitions. Cotter, Shivdasani, and Zenner (1997) found that when a company announces an acquisition, the stock price change of the acquiring firm is more negative if its board consists largely of executive directors than if the board consists mostly of nonexecutive directors. The expectation is that an acquisition is more likely to destroy value through empire building if executive directors have negotiated the purchase price. Similarly, companies receive a higher takeover premium if the board of the target company is independent.[28] Byrd and Hickman (1992) found similar results. The results suggest that a board comprised of outsiders is more likely to negotiate arms-length transactions, thereby ensuring that the targets and takeover prices are rational.[29]

Finally, it is not clear whether boards with a higher percentage of outsiders negotiate more rational compensation packages with CEOs.

Boyd (1994) found an unexpected positive relationship between the level of CEO compensation and the percentage of outside directors.[30] However, Finkelstein and Hambrick (1989) found no relationship between these variables.[31]

Clearly, outside directorships have both positive and negative aspects. Outsiders have the potential to bring expertise and independence to the board, which can reduce agency costs and improve firm performance. However, outsiders operate at an information disadvantage that can decrease their effectiveness. The research results on this point is mixed, but the potential information disadvantage of outside directors should be a critical concern for shareholders.

Board Independence

The NYSE requires that listed companies have a majority of independent directors. **Independence** is defined as having "no material relationship with the listed company (either directly or as a partner, shareholder, or officer of an organization that has a relationship with the company)."[32] A director is not considered independent if the director or a family member

- Has been employed as an executive officer at the company within the last three years.
- Has earned direct compensation in excess of $120,000 from the company in the last three years.
- Has been employed as an internal or external auditor of the company in the last three years.
- Is an executive officer at another company where the listed company's present executives have served on the compensation committee in the last three years.
- Is an executive officer at a company whose business with the listed company has been the greater of 2 percent of gross revenues or $1 million within the last three years.

These standards are intended to ensure that directors execute their duties with independent judgment.[33] Independence is important for both the advisory and monitoring functions of the board. It enables a director to objectively evaluate the top executives, strategy, business model, and risk-management policies proposed by senior management. It also enables them to be objective when measuring operating and financial results against predetermined targets. Independence means that compensation arrangements are established through arms-length negotiation and that acquisitions are determined in the best interest of shareholders. Directors who maintain material relations with the company or otherwise rely on the company for their livelihood are less likely to be independent in these areas.

The risk for investors is that the independence standards of the NYSE (or other listing exchanges) do not reliably produce directors with truly independent judgment. The NYSE acknowledges this risk:

> It is not possible to anticipate, or explicitly to provide for, all circumstances that might signal potential conflicts of interest, or that might bear on the materiality of a director's relationship to a listed company .... Accordingly, it is best that boards making "independence" determinations broadly consider all relevant facts and circumstances.[34]

Effectively, NYSE guidelines draw a line in the sand. For investors, this means that some directors will meet independence standards and not be independent in their perspectives, while others will not meet these standards yet be perfectly capable of maintaining independence. Stated differently, there is a risk that the structural characteristics used in the NYSE test for independence are a misleading measure of the independence of an individual director (see the following sidebar).

Business Relations and "Independence"

Three of the NYSE standards for independence are aimed at weeding out individuals who have a personal relationship with C-level executives. These include restrictions on former executives, former auditors, and executives who have a relationship through outside compensation committees. These are reasonable approximations for relationships that might compromise judgment.

However, the other two restrictions are somewhat arbitrary. Why does a $120,000 salary compromise judgment? It is a relatively large figure, but most salaries, regardless of level, are material to the people who earn them. Likewise, why does the fact that a director's firm relies on the company for 2 percent of gross revenue compromise the judgment of that director? Business partners surely want to see their customers or suppliers succeed financially. Although some directors might abuse their position of influence for gain, others will have a vested interest in ensuring that the company on whose board they sit prevents insider abuse and remains viable. (See the sidebar "The Re-election of Warren Buffett" in Chapter 12.)

Most studies fail to find a significant relationship between formal board independence and improved corporate outcomes. We cited some of these studies in the previous section on outside directors. In aggregate, they tend to demonstrate either a modest relationship or no relationship between independence and market returns or long-term performance. Some evidence suggests that independence leads to more rational merger-and-acquisition activity. The relationship between independence and CEO compensation is not clear. We suspect that the structural shortcomings of the NYSE standards of independence confound the data used in most studies and at least partially explain the weak results.

Hwang and Kim (2009) recognized this shortcoming and attempted to correct it by designing a study that takes into account situational or psychological factors beyond NYSE guidelines that risk compromising a director's judgment. The authors made a distinction between directors who are independent according to NYSE standards (**conventionally independent**) and those who are independent in their social relation to the CEO (**socially independent**). They used the board of Cardinal Health to illustrate this distinction:

> In the year 2000, this board had 13 directors, 10 of whom were conventionally independent of the CEO. However, one conventionally independent director was not only from the same hometown, but also graduated from the same university as the CEO (incidentally, this director provided a job, at his own firm, for the CEO's son). Another conventionally independent director graduated from the same university and specialized in the same academic discipline as the CEO. Similarly,

3 others shared informal ties with the CEO and, ultimately, only 5 of the 13 directors were conventionally *and* socially independent of the CEO.

The authors identified six areas where the independence standards of the NYSE might fail to take into account social relationships that could compromise independence if the director and the CEO have the following in common:

1. Served in the military
2. Graduated from the same university (and were born no more than three years apart)
3. Were born in the same U.S. region or the same non-U.S. country
4. Have the same academic discipline
5. Have the same industry of primary employment
6. Share a third-party connection through another director to whom each is directly independent

The authors posit that people who share these social connections feel a psychological affinity that might bias them to overly trust or rely on one another without maintaining sufficient objectivity. Among a sample of directors of Fortune 100 companies between the years 1996 and 2005, the authors found that 87 percent are conventionally independent, but only 62 percent are both conventionally and socially independent. They found that social dependence is correlated with higher executive compensation, lower probability of CEO turnover following poor operating performance, and higher likelihood that the CEO manipulates earnings to increase his or her bonus. They concluded that social dependence compromises the ability of the board to maintain arms-length negotiations with management.[35]

Although this type of analysis is certainly not easy, it demonstrates a level of critical thinking that is sometimes absent in the debate on corporate governance. Their findings suggest that an expanded and more sophisticated assessment of independence is likely to lead to better understanding of governance quality than simply checking for adherence with regulatory guidelines.

Independent Committees

The Sarbanes–Oxley Act of 2002 required that the audit, compensation, and nomination and governance committees of U.S. publicly traded companies include only independent directors. By contrast, other specialized committees of the board—such as finance and investment committees, credit committees, and science and technology committees—carry no such restrictions and often have a combination of inside and outside directors.

The issues regarding committee independence are similar to those regarding general board independence. Independent committees have the potential to objectively monitor managerial behavior and corporate performance, but committees with inside directors might have firm-specific knowledge that can improve their contribution to long-term operating performance. Independence standards mandated by the Sarbanes–Oxley Act are intended to balance these trade-offs. Committees with a primary charter to monitor the performance of management (audit, compensation, and nomination and governance) carry a legal mandate for independence. All other committees that serve both an advisory and a monitoring function (finance, environmental, science and technology, and others) don't carry these mandates.

The research literature produces some evidence that independent directorships improve the monitoring ability of the audit committee. Klein (2002) found that companies with a majority of independent directors on the audit committee have higher earnings quality than companies with a minority of independent directors on this committee. However, she did not find that a standard of 100 percent independence improves results compared to a simple majority. (The sample period preceded NYSE requirements for 100 percent independence.) She concluded that although independence on the audit committee might be important, "a wholly independent audit committee may not be necessary."[36]

In a separate study, Klein (1998) tested whether insiders on the investment and finance committees improve firm performance. She reasoned that although the audit committee is intended as an oversight body to mitigate agency costs, investment and finance committees are focused on strategic growth, so they should benefit from an insider's firm-specific knowledge. She found slight evidence in support of this hypothesis: Companies with a higher percentage of executive directors on the investment and finance committees tend to exhibit slightly better operating returns and stock market performance. She did not find this same correlation for audit and compensation committees.[37]

These studies suggest that the independence level of committees bears some influence on corporate outcomes. They also support the thesis that having inside directors on committees is neither uniformly positive nor uniformly negative. As we might expect, it depends on the function of the committee.

Bankers on the Board

Bankers play a prominent role on many corporate boards. They bring expertise regarding a firm's capital structure, financing options, financial risk, and mergers and acquisitions. They also bring industry knowledge gained from serving clients in similar businesses. During times of trouble, they can help facilitate access to capital, particularly when a company is "priced out" of the public markets because of a low credit rating. Bankers also bring monitoring expertise that comes from having a creditor perspective, with an emphasis on compliance with covenants and excess coverage. This enables them to detect and address early signs of trouble.

However, bankers might not be fully independent monitors because they have a divided loyalty between their employers and the company on whose board they sit. Some might use their positions to steer business toward their banks. This is in violation of fiduciary duty but is often hard to detect. Also, when the banker's employer provides financing to the company, the bank's interest as creditor might conflict with the interest of shareholders.

Research on the contribution of bankers to company boards is not very favorable. Güner, Malmendier, and Tate (2008) found that adding commercial bankers to the board leads to increased leverage, and adding investment bankers to the board leads to value-destroying acquisitions:

- **Commercial bankers**—Companies that add commercial bankers to the board tend to increase their borrowing activity but do not realize a corresponding increase in firm value. The evidence suggests that the increase in borrowing activity is encouraged to generate low-risk profits for the lending institution. Furthermore, the authors found no evidence that companies gain access to funds that they could not otherwise receive on their own.

- **Investment bankers**—Companies that add investment bankers to the board tend to make worse acquisitions. Stock price returns for the acquiring firm are about 1 percent less on the announcement date when investment bankers are on the board. This conflicts with the notion that investment bankers can create value by negotiating better deals.

The findings suggest that bankers who sit as outside directors put the interest of their employers above their obligation to company shareholders.[38] Studies on the impact of bankers in Germany and Japan arrive at similar conclusions.[39]

Financial Experts on Board

Section 407(b) of the Sarbanes–Oxley Act requires that companies appoint a **financial expert** to the audit committee. To qualify as a financial expert, the director must have experience as a public accountant, auditor, principal financial officer, comptroller, or principal accounting officer at an issuer. The director also is required to have an understanding of accounting principles, the preparation of financial statements, internal controls, and audit committee functions.[40]

The evidence suggests that adding a financial expert to the audit committee improves governance quality. Defond, Hann, and Hu (2005) found that the market reacts favorably when a financial expert is added to the audit committee. They also divided the sample of financial experts into two groups and found that the market reacts positively to the appointment of experts with accounting backgrounds but not those with nonaccounting financial backgrounds. Their results indicate that shareholders value audit committee members who can directly improve the integrity of financial statements.[41] Similarly, Agrawal and Chadha (2005) found that companies have fewer restatements when an audit committee member has a CPA or similar degree.[42]

Politically Connected Boards

Some companies believe that it is beneficial to add a politically connected director to their board. The director can use his or her professional network or knowledge to help secure government contracts or improve relationships with regulators. Other companies establish political connections when a senior officer leaves the company to take a high-level appointment in the administration or a federal agency.

Modest evidence indicates that investors look favorably upon politically connected boards. Faccio (2006) and Hillman, Bierman, and Zardkoohi (1999) found that investors react positively to news that a company CEO or board member has received a political appointment.[43] Similarly, Goldman, Rocholl, and So (2009) found that companies whose board members were affiliated with the Republican party exhibited positive stock price returns following the election of George W. Bush in 2000.[44]

However, these connections might not yield tangible benefits. Fisman, Fisman, Galef, and Khurana (2006) studied the influence of firm connections to former U.S. Vice President Richard Cheney, who previously served as CEO of Halliburton. They found no evidence that companies benefited from these ties.[45] Faccio (2010) found that companies with political connections have lower taxes and greater market power, but that they also have lower return on assets and lower market-to-book ratios than peers.[46] Studies of French companies have come to similar conclusions.[47]

Employee Representation

German law requires that the supervisory boards of German corporations have 33 percent employee representation when the company has 500 or more employees and 50 percent employee representation when the company has 2,000 or more employees. This requirement is considered an employee's **right of codetermination** and ensures that employees participate in decisions that impact workplace matters such as work rules and schedules, methods for appraising and hiring personnel, the design of health and safety work standards, wage and benefits agreements, and the process for introducing technology into production. Through board seats, employees also have input into high-level corporate matters such as strategy, operations, capital structure, and management oversight. Codetermination has the potential to give employees a real voice in the governance process.

A prudent level of employee involvement can be desirable for decision making. Employees have valuable information about daily business processes, customers, and suppliers. Board representation can facilitate the flow of this information between employees and management. Employee representation can also improve internal relations and reduce work stoppages. In addition, employee representation can reduce agency costs through better oversight of management compensation and perquisites. However, board representation puts employees in a position to engage in higher levels of rent extraction (such as demanding artificially inflated wages or employment numbers). This can reduce a company's competitive position.

The academic evidence on employee representation is mixed. Gorton and Schmid (2004) found that the stock of German companies with higher levels of employee representation (50 percent of directors) trade at lower prices than the stock of companies with lower levels of employee representation (33 percent of directors).[48] Fauver and Fuerst (2006) found that employee representation is positively related to market valuation in industries that require high levels of coordination (such as manufacturing, transportation, and wholesale or retail trade) and in concentrated industries with less competition. Modest evidence shows that the benefits of employee representation form an "inverse U," meaning that some level of employee representation improves firm valuation, but beyond a certain threshold, it leads to diminishing returns. Finally, companies with employee representation are more likely to pay a dividend, which reduces expropriation of capital by management.[49]

These studies involve German corporations, so it is not clear how they translate to the United States, where employee representation is not required. However, studies that have examined firms that are essentially employee owned through employee stock ownership plans (ESOPs) tend to reach negative conclusions. Faleye, Mehrotra, and Morck (2006) examined the performance of companies in which labor owns at least 5 percent of shares and, therefore, has a voice in corporate decision making. They found that such firms have lower valuations, invest less in long-term assets, are more risk averse, exhibit slower growth, have lower employment growth, and have lower labor productivity. They concluded that employee influence conflicts with an objective of maximizing shareholder value.[50]

However, anecdotal evidence suggests that employee participation in corporate decision making, at either the board or managerial level, can be beneficial in certain circumstances. For example, Southwest Airlines is notorious for granting significant autonomy to pilots and flight crews to make adjustments that improve efficiency and increase customer satisfaction. Whether board representation is required for operational benefits to be realized is not clear. We suspect that the effectiveness of employee board representation depends on the nature of the existing relations between management and labor, and the culture and competitive positioning of the firm.

Boards with "Busy" Directors

The vast majority (83 percent) of board members in the United States serve on just one corporate board. A fair number sit on two or three boards, but the numbers drop off significantly beyond that. According to *Corporate Board Member*, less than 1 percent of directors sit on five or more boards (see Figure 5.2).[51]

No. of Directorships	Directors
7	2
6	13
5	73
4	254
3	1,020
2	3,583
1	24,144
Total Unique Directors	**29,089**

Source: Corporate Board Member and PricewaterhouseCoopers, LLP (2009).

Figure 5.2   Number of directorships per director

Researchers refer to directors who hold multiple board seats as **busy directors**. The numeric threshold that constitutes a "busy" director is subject to discretion, although researchers generally consider it to be three or more board seats. Similarly, academics refer to a "busy" board as one in which a significant number of directors are busy.

Having a busy director can bring potential benefits. Busy directors are likely to have first-hand access to important information about operations, strategy, and finances at related companies. They are also likely to have broad social and professional networks, which are valuable for recruiting directors, evaluating executive talent, dealing with regulators, and forging partnerships. In addition, busy directors might have high integrity and sound reputations, which are driving factors in the demand for their services. However, busy directors also have the potential to be lax in their oversight or unavailable at critical moments because of outside obligations (see the following sidebar). Recognizing these risks, some companies place restrictions on the number of boards that their directors can sit on simultaneously. According to Spencer Stuart, slightly more than half of S&P 500 companies had such a restriction in 2008.[52]

Profile of a Busy Director

In 2009, Irvine Hockaday, Jr. was on the board of three publicly traded companies (Crown Media Holdings, Estee Lauder, and Ford Motor). Hockaday is the former president and CEO of Hallmark Cards, a position he held from 1986 to 2001. He is also a lifetime trustee of the Aspen Institute, former chairman of the Federal Reserve Bank of Kansas City, and a prominent citizen in the Kansas City area. Hockaday is described by one colleague as "an independent thinker who doesn't get swept along in the tide. If it doesn't ring right, he's quick to ask for clarification. He sure doesn't sit there like a bump on a log."[53] At one time, Hockaday served on six boards (including Dow Jones, Sprint Nextel, and Aquila).

Hockaday has performed many valuable services as a board member. He has been the lead independent director of Ford and was instrumental in recruiting Alan Mulally to that company. He also played an important role in forcing the resignation of Sprint CEO

William Esrey and COO Ronald LeMay after it was discovered that the two men used illegal tax shelters designed by the company's tax auditor, Ernst & Young. He was also head of the compensation committee of Dow Jones, where he emphasized pay for performance and reportedly did not miss a board meeting in 12 years. At five of the six public boards he has served on, he took compensation in stock instead of cash, believing that it better aligned his interest with those of shareholders.

However, Hockaday has been involved in controversies. For example, he was the head of the compensation committee of Aquila when it awarded a controversial severance package of $7.6 million to outgoing CEO Robert Green following an ill-timed foray into the energy trading markets and a collapse of the company's stock price.[54]

Recently, Hockaday reduced his directorships. In May 2009, Hockaday stepped down from the board of Sprint and noted that "being a director is more demanding than it once was."[55]

Researchers have studied the relationship between busy boards and governance quality, which is one of the few areas of research on board structure that yields consistent and convincing results: Companies with busy boards tend to have worse long-term performance and worse oversight. Fich and Shivdasani (2006) found that companies with busy boards have lower market-to-book ratios and lower return on assets. They also found that companies with busy boards are less likely to fire an underperforming CEO than companies that do not have busy boards. In addition, they demonstrate that investors react positively to news that a busy director is resigning from the board and negatively to news that an outside director is assuming an additional directorship. Investor response is most negative if the outside director or the board itself becomes "busy" after assuming the additional directorships.[56]

Many other studies have found similar results. For example, Core, Holthausen, and Larcker (1999) examined a variety of governance variables (busy directors, old directors, directors appointed by the CEO, and so on) to measure their impact on future firm operating performance and other variables, such as CEO compensation.

They found that busy boards award larger compensation packages to CEOs than nonbusy boards. Companies with busy boards also exhibit lower one-, three-, and five-year operating performance (measured as return on assets) and stock market returns.[57]

Interlocked (or Connected) Boards

An **interlocked board** is one in which an executive of one firm sits on the board of another and an executive of the second firm sits on the board of the first. According to one estimate, 8 percent of boards are interlocked through reciprocal CEO representation. When the definition is expanded to include retired CEOs and other current senior executives, the percentage of companies with interlocked boards increases to 20 percent.[58]

Interlocking creates a network among directors that can lead to increased information flow, which, in turn, improves decision making. Best practices in corporate strategy and firm oversight can be transferred more efficiently across companies that have shared board representation. Director networks also serve as a source of important business relationships, including new clients, suppliers, sources of capital, political connections, regulators, and director and executive referrals.

However, obvious drawbacks exist in this arrangement. Interlocking can become anticompetitive if proprietary information is shared among competing firms that use this information to collude on market actions.[59] Furthermore, interlocking creates a dynamic of reciprocity. For example, if the CEO of one firm approves a large compensation contract to the CEO of another firm, it is difficult for the second CEO not to reciprocate. As such, interlocks can compromise the objectivity of directors and weaken their monitoring capability.

Research demonstrates the positive effects of network connections among firms. Hochberg, Ljungqvist, and Lu (2007) found that such connections improve performance of companies in the venture capital industry.[60] Fracassi and Tate (2010) found that companies that share network connections at the senior executive and the director level have greater similarity in their investment policies and higher profitability. These effects disappear when the network connections are terminated.[61] Larcker, So, and Wang (2010) found that companies with a well-connected board have greater future operating performance and higher future stock price returns than companies whose boards are less connected. These effects are most pronounced among companies that are newly formed, have high growth potential, or are in need of a turnaround.[62]

However, evidence also indicates that network connections lead to decreased monitoring. Hallock (1997) found some weak evidence that CEOs of companies with interlocked boards earn higher compensation than the CEOs of companies with noninterlocked boards.[63] Nguyen (2009) found that CEOs whose firms are connected through interlocked boards are less likely to be fired following poor performance.[64] Finally, Santos, Da Silveira, and Barros (2009) found evidence that companies with interlocked boards in Brazil have lower market valuations. The results are especially strong for boards that are both interlocked and "busy."[65]

Board Size

The size of the board of directors tends to be related to the size of the corporation. Companies with annual revenues of $10 million have 7 directors, on average, and Companies with revenues of more than $10 billion have 11 directors, on average.[66]

Large boards have more resources to dedicate to both oversight and advisory functions. They allow for greater specialization to the board through diversity of director experience and through functional committees. However, large boards bring additional costs in terms of compensation and the coordination of schedules. In addition, large boards suffer from slow decision making, less candid discussion, diffusion of responsibility, and risk aversion. Given the tradeoffs, many experts believe a theoretically optimal board size exists. For example, Lipton and Lorsch (1992) argued that boards of directors should have either eight or nine members and should not exceed ten.[67]

Researchers have examined the relationship between board size and corporate performance. Yermack (1996) measured the relationship between board size and firm value (measured as the ratio of market-to-book value). He found that as board size increases, firm value falls (after controlling for factors such as firm size and industry). The largest deterioration in value occurs between boards of five and ten directors, suggesting that inefficiencies grow the most within this range. Yermack (1996) also found that larger boards are less likely to dismiss underperforming CEOs, they are less likely to award compensation contracts that correlate with shareholder value, and shareholders respond negatively to announcements that a company is increasing its board size. The author concluded that "an inverse association between board size and firm value" exists.[68]

However, as with other structural board variables that we have considered, the truth is more complicated. Coles, Daniel, and Naveen (2008) argued that a variety of other factors likely influence the relationship between board size and firm value. They identified "complexity" as one such variable. The authors argued that complex companies (those with many business segments, those that require external contracting relationships, leveraged firms, and those in specialized industries) might benefit from large boards because they bring more information to the decision-making process. As an example, they cited the board of Gulfstream Aerospace, which included at one point Henry Kissinger, Donald Rumsfeld, and Colin Powell. The authors speculated that "most likely these directors were selected not for monitoring, but for their ability to provide advice in obtaining defense contracts." If this is the case, a large board should have positive performance effects at complex companies where incremental expertise is needed. The authors tested this hypothesis by separating complex firms from so-called "simple" firms and repeating Yermack's analysis. They found that complexity brings added explanatory power: Board size is negatively correlated with firm value for simple firms and positively correlated for complex firms (with diminishing benefits beyond a certain point). They concluded, "At the very least, our empirical results call into question the existing empirical foundation for prescriptions for smaller, independent boards. [O]ur evidence casts doubt on the idea that smaller boards with fewer insiders are necessarily value enhancing."[69]

The research conducted by Coles, Daniel, and Naveen (2008) is an excellent example of how multiple factors can influence the relationship between a structural attribute and governance outcomes. At first glance, the data suggest that board size and corporate outcomes are strictly linearly related, but in reality the relationship is more nuanced. Complexity is one explanatory variable that early research did not properly consider, and other variables also likely bear consideration when exploring composition and structure.

Board Diversity

Many stakeholders advocate that corporate officers should increase the ethnic diversity of their boards so that their composition more closely reflects the diversity of the broader U.S. population. Ethnic diversity might improve decision making by ensuring that the board has the full array of knowledge in terms of market dynamics, customer behavior, and employee concerns to succeed operationally and culturally. According to social psychologists, diversity helps boards overcome tendencies toward **groupthink**, in which directors reach a consensus too quickly because of the way social similarities shape their perception and decision making. Diversity can also encourage healthy debate by making directors more likely to challenge one another's viewpoints without excessive concern for maintaining harmony because of social similarity. From the standpoint of public policy, diversity is an important social value and one that is consistent with equality.[70]

However, some evidence suggests that boardroom diversity might detract from the quality of decision making. Social psychologists have shown that heterogeneous groups exhibit lower levels of teamwork. Differences among team members can lead to less information sharing, less accurate communication, increased conflict, lower cohesiveness, and an inability to agree upon common goals.[71] If this dynamic manifests itself in the boardroom, both advice and monitoring might suffer.

Considerable professional and academic research focuses on the relationship between boardroom diversity and corporate outcomes. Not surprisingly, the results are mixed. Erhardt, Werbel, and Shrader (2003) found a significant positive relationship between diverse gender and minority board representation and corporate performance.[72] Similarly, Carter, D'Souza, Simkins, and Simpson (2010) found that board diversity is correlated with higher market-to-book ratios.[73] By contrast, Wang and Clift (2009) found no relationship between boardroom diversity and corporate performance, and Zahra and Stanton (1988) found a negative relationship.[74] As we have discussed before, a key problem with these studies is that it is very difficult to establish causality—do firms with diverse board members achieve better performance, or are more successful firms better positioned to attract diverse board members?

Similarly, the research on diversity and corporate decision making is inconclusive. Westphal and Zajac (1995) found that demographic similarity between the CEO and the board is correlated with higher levels of CEO compensation.[75] This is consistent with the idea that social similarity can lead to reciprocity, and implies that diversity in the boardroom might improve independence and oversight. However, Belliveau, O'Reilly, and Wade (1996) found that it is not social similarity, but the social status of the CEO relative to other board and compensation committee members that leads to higher compensation.[76] This implies that CEO power is the greater determinant of boardroom dynamics.

Female Directors

Women are significantly under-represented on boards of directors relative to the general population. According to Catalyst, a nonprofit research organization dedicated to expanding opportunities for women in business, just 15 percent of the directors of Fortune 500 companies are women, compared with 50 percent of the general population and 47 percent of the workforce. Boards might lack female directors because women are under-represented at the senior executive level. Only 17 percent of corporate officers are women.[77]

In recent years, several countries have made it a priority to increase female representation on corporate boards. In 2003, Norway passed a law requiring that approximately 40 percent of the directors of publicly traded companies be female (the actual percentage is a function of board size). Companies not compliant with the law risk being delisted from exchanges. The law has had an immediate impact on female board membership. In 2002, only 7 percent of directors at Norwegian companies were women. By late 2007, the figure had risen to 35 percent.[78] Other European countries have followed suit. Spain has enacted a 40 percent requirement starting in 2015. France recently passed similar legislation. Sweden has asked companies to voluntarily increase female directorship to 25 percent or risk a legal mandate.

The arguments for increased female board representation are similar to those put forth by diversity advocates. One is based on simple economics. If we assume that managerial talent is evenly dispersed across men and women, restricting board members to include only (or predominantly) men eliminates a significant portion of qualified talent. Given the scarcity of talent that we saw in Chapter 4, "Board of Directors: Selection, Compensation, and Removal," it makes strong sense to increase the candidate pool. Furthermore, greater female representation on boards might improve board performance. For example, female board representation can enhance independence by reducing social similarities that lead to premature consensus. Women might also exhibit higher levels of trustworthiness and cooperation than men, thus leading to better boardroom dynamics. In addition, they might evaluate information and consider risk and reward differently than men, thereby leading to enhanced decision making. Finally, obvious social benefits exist for increasing gender equality on the board.

However, risks also exist with higher female board representation. The primary risk occurs when companies, in an effort to appear more gender-balanced, recruit underqualified directors. This is referred to as **tokenism** and is similar to the risk of appointing outside directors with the sole purpose of satisfying perceived external demand for diversity.

Evidence is inconclusive whether female board representation improves corporate performance. Catalyst (2007) divided Fortune 500 companies into quartiles based on female board representation. They found that the quartile with the highest percent of females outperformed the lowest quarterly percentile in return on equity (13.9 percent versus 9.1 percent), net margin (13.7 percent versus 9.7 percent), and return on invested capital (7.7 percent versus 4.7 percent). They also found that companies with three or more female directors performed well above average along all three financial metrics. Unfortunately, this study did not include control variables, so it likely omits important explanatory factors, such as industry, company size, or capital structure.[79] More rigorous studies find no relationship between female board representation and performance.[80]

However, modest evidence supports the idea that female representation can improve governance quality. Adams and Ferreira (2009) found that female directors have better attendance records than and that male directors have fewer attendance problems when women also serve on the board. They also found that boards with female representation are more likely to fire an underperforming CEO and award more equity-based compensation. However, they did not find a positive correlation between female board representation and either operating performance or market valuation.[81]

Finally, evidence suggests that female board representation can be detrimental when encouraged primarily to meet arbitrary quotas. Ahern and Dittmar (2010) examined the impact of the Norwegian law on female board representation. They found that the law led to considerable changes in board composition, in terms of not only gender, but also age, education, and experience. They found that the somewhat arbitrary governmental constraints of the law led to a significant decrease in firm value. They found that the loss in firm value was not primarily attributable to a greater number of female directors, but to the inexperience of new directors.[82] This demonstrates the unintended consequences that can arise from artificial changes to board structure.

Summary

Table 5.1 presents a high-level summary of the evidence discussed in this chapter. A casual reading of this information indicates that very modest evidence supports the adoption of many of these attributes. Although this might be surprising to many readers and is in direct contrast to the "best practices" experts and proxy advisory firms advocate, it is characteristic of the current debate on governance that is insufficiently grounded in empirical research. (We discuss this in more detail in Chapter 14, "Summary and Conclusions.")

Table 5.1 Summary of Performance Effect for Selected Board Structural Characteristics

Board Structure Attribute	Findings from Research
Independent chairman	No evidence
Lead independent director	Modest evidence
Number of outside directors	Mixed (information gap is critical)
Independent directors	No evidence
Independence of committees	Evidence for audit committee primarily

Board Structure Attribute	Findings from Research
Representation of:	
Bankers	Negative evidence
Financial experts	Positive for accounting professionals only
Politically connected directors	No evidence
Employees	Modest evidence
Busy boards	Negative evidence
Interlocked boards	Evidence for performance, against monitoring
Board size	Evidence for small boards (in simple companies) and larger boards (in complex companies)
Diversity	Mixed evidence
Female directors	Mixed evidence

Source: The authors.

Endnotes

1. Spencer Stuart, "Spencer Stuart U.S. Board Index 2008" (2008). Accessed May 4, 2010. See www.spencerstuart.com/research/.

2. Directorbank, "What Makes an Outstanding Chairman? The Views of More Than 400 Directors." Accessed October 6, 2008. See www.directorbank.com/library/files/Chairman_s_Report.pdf.

3. Laura M. Holson, "Former P&G Chief Named Disney Chairman," *New York Times* (June 29, 2006): C13.

4. The final version of the Dodd–Frank Act did not include this provision, although it was included in earlier versions of the legislation.

5. Corporate Compliance Insights (CCI), "Corporate Governance Best Practices: Chairman-CEO Split Gains Support," *CorporateComplianceInsights.com* (March 30, 2009). Accessed November 8, 2010. See www.corporatecomplianceinsights.com/2009/corporate-governance-best-practices-chairmain-ceo-split-millstein-center. The CCI article cites a separate Corporate Library report that concludes that the adoption of the chairman/CEO split as a corporate governance best practice is spreading throughout the United States.

6. For more on this debate, see Millstein Center for Corporate Governance and Performance, "Chairing the Board: The Case for Independent Leadership in Corporate North America, Policy Briefing No. 4," *Yale School of Management* (2009). Accessed October 12, 2009. See http://millstein.som.yale.edu/2009%2003%2030%20Chairing%20The%20Board.pdf.

7. Greg Farrell, "Struggle to Find Successor for Lewis at BofA," *Financial Times* (November 12, 2009): 16.

8. Bradley Keoun and David Mildenberg, "Bank of New York CEO Said to Want Bank of America Job," *Bloomberg.com* (December 12, 2009).

9. Dan Fitzpatrick and Deborah Solomon, "Last Days of BofA's Hunt for a CEO: Pay, Politics," *Wall Street Journal* (December 18, 2009, Eastern edition): C.1.

10. Jeff Bennett and Joann S. Lublin, "Chairman of GM Taps CEO: Himself," *Wall Street Journal* (January 26, 2010, Eastern edition): A.1.

11. B. Ram Baliga, R. Charles Moyer, and Ramesh S. Rao, "CEO Duality and Firm Performance: What's the Fuss?" *Strategic Management Journal* 17 (1996): 41–53.

12. Brian K. Boyd, "CEO Duality and Firm Performance: A Contingency Model," *Strategic Management Journal* 16 (1995): 301–312.

13. Yaniv Grinstein and Yearim Valles Arellano, "Separating the CEO from the Chairman Position: Determinants and Changes after the New Corporate Governance Regulation," *Social Science Research Network* (2008). Accessed October 10, 2009. See http://ssrn.com/abstract=1108368.

14. James A. Brickley, Jeffrey L. Coles, and Gregg A. Jarrell, "Corporate Leadership Structure: On the Separation of the Positions of CEO and Chairman of the Board," Simon School of Business working paper FR 95-02 (1994). Accessed February 26, 2009. See http://hdl.handle.net/1802/4858.

15. David F. Larcker, Gaizka Ormazabal, and Daniel J. Taylor, "The Market Reaction to Corporate Governance Regulation," *Journal of Financial Economics* (forthcoming).

16. Spencer Stuart, "A Closer Look at Lead and Presiding Directors," *Cornerstone of the Board: The New Governance Committee* (2006) Accessed September 25, 2008. See http://content.spencerstuart.com/sswebsite/pdf/lib/Cornerstone_LeadPresiding_Director0306.pdf.

17. Spencer Stuart.

18. Jeff Stein and Bill Baxley, "The Role and Value of the Lead Director—A Report from the Lead Director Network," *Harvard Law School Corporate Governance Blog* (August 6, 2008).

19. Joann S. Lublin, "Theory & Practice: New Breed of Directors Reaches Out to Shareholders; Treading a Fine Line Between Apologist, Sympathetic Ear," *Wall Street Journal* (July 21, 2008, Eastern edition): B.4.

20. Chris Redman, "Shell Rebuilds Itself," *Corporate Board Member* (March/April 2005). See www.shellnews.net/week12/corporate_board_member_magazine 21march05.htm. See also David F. Larcker and Brian Tayan, "Royal Dutch/Shell: A Shell Game with Oil Reserves," Stanford GSB Case No. CG-17 (2009). Copyright 2009 by the Board of Trustees of the Leland Stanford Junior University. All rights reserved. Used with permission from the Stanford University Graduate School of Business.

21. Those factors include a lead director, greater proportion of blockholders, a compensation mix that is weighted toward accounting performance, smaller boards, and fewer busy directors. See David F. Larcker, Scott A. Richardson, and Írem Tuna, "Corporate Governance, Accounting Outcomes, and Organizational Performance," *Accounting Review* 82 (2007): 963–1,008.

22. Roberta Romano, "The Sarbanes–Oxley Act and the Making of Quack Corporate Governance," *Yale Law Review* 114 (2005): 1,521–1,612.

23. Lehman Brothers, Form DEF-14A, filed with the Securities and Exchange Commission March 5, 2008.

24. Dennis K. Berman, "Where Was Lehman Board?" *Wall Street Journal Blog, Deal Journal* (September 18, 2008). Accessed November 9, 2010. See http://blogs.wsj.com/deals/2008/09/15/where-was-lehmans-board/.

25. Stuart Rosenstein and Jeffrey G. Wyatt, "Outside Directors, Board Independence, and Shareholder Wealth," *Journal of Financial Economics* 26 (1990): 175–191.

26. Sanjai Bhagat and Bernard Black, "The Noncorrelation Between Board Independence and Long-Term Firm Performance," *Journal of Corporation Law* 27 (2002): 231.

27. Ran Duchin, John G. Matsusaka, and Oguzhan Ozbas, "When Are Outside Directors Effective?" *Journal of Financial Economics* 96 (2010): 195–214.

28. James F. Cotter, Anil Shivdasani, and Marc Zenner, "Do Independent Directors Enhance Target Shareholder Wealth During Tender Offers?" *Journal of Financial Economics* 43 (1997): 195–218.

29. John W. Byrd and Kent A. Hickman, "Do Outside Directors Monitor Managers?" *Journal of Financial Economics* 32 (1992): 195–221.

30. Brian K. Boyd, "Board Control and CEO Compensation," *Strategic Management Journal* 15 (1994): 335–344.

31. Sydney Finkelstein and Donald C. Hambrick, "Chief Executive Compensation: A Study of the Intersection of Markets and Political Processes," *Strategic Management Journal* 10 (1989): 121–134.

32. NYSE, "Corporate Governance Listing Standards, Listed Company Manual Section 303A.02, Independence Tests" (2010). Amended November 25, 2009. See www.nyse.com/regulation/nyse/1101074746736.html.

33. Marty Lipton makes the following fascinating historical comment: "It is interesting to note that it is not at all clear that director independence is the fundamental keystone of 'good' corporate governance. The world's most successful economy was built by companies that had few, if any, independent directors. It was not until 1956 that the NYSE *recommended* that listed companies have two outside directors, and it wasn't until 1977 that they were *required* to have an audit committee of all independent directors." See Martin Lipton, "Future of the Board of Directors," paper presented at the Chairman & CEO Peer Forum: Board Leadership in a New Regulatory Environment, New York Stock Exchange (June 23, 2010).

34. NYSE Euronext.

35. Byoung-Hyoun Hwang and Seoyoung Kim, "It Pays to Have Friends," *Journal of Financial Economics* 93 (2009): 138–158.

36. Earnings quality is measured using the metric abnormal accruals. Generally, abnormal accruals represent the difference between generally accepted accounting principles (GAAP) earnings, which are measured on an accrual basis, and GAAP cash flow, which represents cash generated by the business. When a large discrepancy exists between these two figures during a sustained period of time, the company's accounting is considered to be lower quality because the company is systematically recording more net income than it is generating on a cash basis. Research has shown that large abnormal accruals are correlated with an increased likelihood of future earnings restatements. This correlation is modest but still significant. Many academic studies that measure accounting quality use abnormal accruals as a measurement. Although not perfect, it is a standard measure that can be applied across firms. See April Klein, "Audit Committee, Board of Director Characteristics, and Earnings Management," *Journal of Accounting & Economics* 33 (2002): 375–400.

37. April Klein, "Firm Performance and Board Committee Structure," *Journal of Law and Economics* 41 (1998): 275–303.

38. A. Burak Güner, Ulrike Malmendier, and Geoffrey Tate, "Financial Expertise of Directors," *Journal of Financial Economics* 88 (2008): 323–354.

39. Ingolf Dittmann, Ernst Maug, and Christoph Schneider, "Bankers on the Boards of German Firms: What They Do, What They Are Worth, and Why They Are (Still) There," *Review of Finance* 14 (2010): 35–71. See Randall Morck and Masao Nakamura, "Banks and Corporate Control in Japan," *Journal of Finance* 54 (1999): 319–339. See http://search.ebscohost.com/login. aspx?direct=true&db=bth&AN=1556607&site=ehost-live.

40. Sarbanes–Oxley Act of 2002, Section 407(b).

41. Mark L. Defond, Rebecca N. Hann, and Xuesong Hu, "Does the Market Value Financial Expertise on Audit Committees of Boards of Directors?" *Journal of Accounting Research* 43 (2005): 153–193.

42. Anup Agrawal and Sahiba Chadha, "Corporate Governance and Accounting Scandals," *Journal of Law and Economics* 48 (2005): 371–406.

43. Mara Faccio, "Politically Connected Firms," *American Economic Review* 96 (2006): 369–386. See Amy J. Hillman, Leonard Bierman, and Asghar Zard-koohi, "Corporate Political Strategies and Firm Performance: Indications of Firm-Specific Benefits from Personal Service in the U.S. Government," *Strategic Management Journal* 20 (1999): 67–81.

44. Eitan Goldman, Jörg Rocholl, and Jongil So, "Do Politically Connected Boards Affect Firm Value?" *Review of Financial Studies* 22 (2009): 2,331–2,360.

45. David Fisman, Ray Fisman, Julia Galef, and Rakesh Khurana, "Estimating the Value of Connections to Vice-President Cheney," Columbia and Yale University, working paper (2006). Accessed August 23, 2008. See http://fairmodel. econ.yale.edu/ec483/ffgk.pdf.

46. Mara Faccio, "Differences Between Politically Connected and Nonconnected Firms: A Cross-Country Analysis," *Financial Management* (Blackwell Publishing Limited) 39 (2010): 905–928.

47. Marianne Bertrand, Francis Kramarz, Antoinette Schoar, and David Thesmar, "Politicians, Firms, and the Political Business Cycle: Evidence from France," (2007). Accessed February 23, 2011. See http://www.crest.fr/ckfinder/userfiles/ files/Pageperso/kramarz/politics_060207_v4.pdf..

48. Gary Gorton and Frank A. Schmid, "Capital, Labor, and the Firm: A Study of German Codetermination," *Journal of the European Economic Association* 2 (2004): 863–905. See http://search.ebscohost.com/login.aspx?direct=true&db= bth&AN=14835919&site=ehost-live.

49. Larry Fauver and Michael E. Fuerst, "Does Good Corporate Governance Include Employee Representation? Evidence from German Corporate Boards," *Journal of Financial Economics* 82 (2006): 673–710.

50. Olubunmi Faleye, Vikas Mehrotra, and Randall Morck, "When Labor Has a Voice in Corporate Governance," *Journal of Financial & Quantitative Analysis* 41 (2006): 489–510. See http://search.ebscohost.com/login.aspx?direct=true& db=bth&AN=22232120&site=ehost-live.

51. Corporate Board Member, "Special Supplement: What Directors Think 2009. The Corporate Board Member/PricewaterhouseCoopers LLC Survey," *Corporate Board Member Magazine* (2009). See http://www.boardmember.com/ Article_Details.aspx?id=4480&terms=what+directors+think+2009.

52. Spencer Stuart.

53. Jennifer Mann, "Outgoing Hallmark CEO Reflects on Successes, Setbacks," *Kansas City Star* (October 9, 2001).

54. David F. Larcker and Brian Tayan, "Executive Compensation at Aquila: Moving Utility Services to Power Trading," Stanford GSB Case No. CG-14 (2008). Copyright 2009 by the Board of Trustees of the Leland Stanford Junior University. All rights reserved. Used with permission from the Stanford University Graduate School of Business.

55. Anonymous, "Hockaday Stepping Down from Sprint's Board," Associated Press (March 27, 2009).

56. They categorize a board as "busy" if 50 percent or more of the outside directors sit on three or more boards. See Eliezer M. Fich and Anil Shivdasani, "Are Busy Boards Effective Monitors?" *Journal of Finance* 61 (2006): 689–724.

57. John E. Core, Robert W. Holthausen, and David F. Larcker, "Corporate Governance, Chief Executive Officer Compensation, and Firm Performance," *Journal of Financial Economics* 51 (1999): 371–406.

58. Kevin F. Hallock, "Reciprocally Interlocking Boards of Directors and Executive Compensation," *Journal of Financial and Quantitative Analysis* 32 (1997): 331–344.

59. For this reason, the Clayton Antitrust Act of 1914 prohibits board locking between directly competing firms (such as railroads, steel producers, or banks). However, the act does not broadly prohibit the practice.

60. Yael Hochberg, Alexander Ljungqvist, and Yang Lu, "Whom You Know Matters: Venture Capital Networks and Investment Performance," *Journal of Finance* 62 (2007): 251–301.

61. Cesare Fracassi and Geoffrey A. Tate, "External Networking and Internal Firm Governance," AFA 2010 Atlanta meetings paper and *Social Science Research Network* (2010). Accessed November 9, 2010. See http://ssrn.com/abstract=1213358.

62. David F. Larcker, Eric C. So, and Charles C. Y. Wang, "Boardroom Centrality and Stock Returns," Rock Center for Corporate Governance at Stanford University, working paper no. 84, *Social Science Research Network* (2010). See http://papers.ssrn.com/sol3/papers.cfm?abstract_id=1651407.

63. Kevin F. Hallock.

64. Bang Dang Nguyen, "Does the Rolodex Matter? Corporate Elite's Small World and the Effectiveness of Boards of Directors," *Social Science Research Network* (2009). Accessed November 8, 2010. See http://ssrn.com/abstract=864184.

65. Rafael Liz Santos, Alexandre Di Miceli Da Silveira, and Lucas Ayres B. de C. Barros, "Board Interlocking in Brazil: Directors' Participation in Multiple Companies and Its Effect on Firm Value," *Social Science Research Network* (2009). Accessed November 9, 2009. See http://ssrn.com/abstract=1018796.

66. Corporate Board Member and PricewaterhouseCoopers LLC (2007).

67. Martin Lipton and Jay W. Lorsch, "A Modest Proposal for Improved Corporate Governance," *Business Lawyer* 48 (1992): 59–77. See http://search.ebscohost.com/login.aspx?direct=true&db=bth&AN=5963897&site=ehost-live.

68. David L. Yermack, "Higher market valuation of companies with a small board of directors," *Journal of Financial Economics* 40 (1996): 185–211.

69. Jeffrey L. Coles, Naveen D. Daniel, and Lalitha Naveen, "Boards: Does One Size Fit All?" *Journal of Financial Economics* 87 (2008): 329–356.

70. See Deborah Rhode and Amanda K. Packel, "Diversity on Corporate Boards: How Much Difference Does Difference Make?" Rock Center for Corporate Governance at Stanford University working paper no. 89, *Social Science Research Network* (2010). See http://ssrn.com/abstract=1685615.

71. Charles A. O'Reilly III, Katherine Y. Williams, and Sigal Barsade, "The Impact of Relational Demography on Teamwork: When Differences Make a Difference," *Academy of Management Proceedings & Membership Directory* (1999): G1–G6. See http://search.ebscohost.com/login.aspx?direct=true&db=bth&AN =27622078&site=ehost-live.

72. Niclas L. Erhardt, James D. Werbel, and Charles B. Shrader, "Board of Director Diversity and Firm Financial Performance," *Corporate Governance: An International Review* 11 (2003): 102–111.

73. David A. Carter, Frank D'Souza, Betty J. Simkins, and W. Gary Simpson, "The Gender and Ethnic Diversity of U.S. Boards and Board Committees and Firm Financial Performance," *Corporate Governance: An International Review* 18 (2010): 396–414.

74. Yi Wang and Bob Clift, "Is There a 'Business Case' for Board Diversity?" *Pacific Accounting Review* (Emerald Group Publishing Limited) 21 (2009): 88–103. Shaker A. Zahra and Wilbur W. Stanton, "The Implications of Board Directors' Composition for Corporate Strategy and Performance," *International Journal of Management* 5 (1988): 229–236.

75. James D. Westphal and Edward J. Zajac, "Who Shall Govern? CEO/Board Power, Demographic Similarity, and New Director Selection," *Administrative Science Quarterly* 40 (1995): 60–83. See http://search.cbscohost.com/login.aspx?direct=true&db=bth&AN=9506192216&site=ehost-live.

76. Maura A. Belliveau, Charles A. O'Reilly III, and James B. Wade, "Social Capital at the Top: Effects of Social Similarity and Status on CEO Compensation," *Academy of Management Journal* 39 (1996): 1,568–1,593.

77. Catalyst Inc., "Statistical Overview of Women in the Workplace," *Catalyst Quick Takes* (2010). See www.catalyst.org/publication/219/statistical-overview-of-women-in-the-workplace.

78. Joann Lublin, "Behind the Rush to Add Women to Norway's Boards," *Wall Street Journal* (December 10, 2007, Eastern edition): B.1.

79. Joy Lois, Nancy M. Carter, Harvey M. Wagner, and Sriram Narayanan, "The Bottom Line: Corporate Performance and Women's Representation on Boards," Catalyst Inc. (2007). Accessed June 10, 2008. See www.catalyst.org/publication/200/the-bottom-line-corporate-performance-and-womens-representation-on boards.

80. Kassim Hussein and Bill M. Kiwia, "Examining the Relationship Between Female Board Members and Firm Performance—a Panel Study of U.S. Firms," *African Journal of Finance and Management* and *Social Science Research Network* (2009). Accessed November 9, 2010. See http://ssrn.com/abstract=1596498. Toyah Miller and María del Carmen Triana, "Demographic Diversity in the Boardroom: Mediators of the Board Diversity–Firm Performance Relationship," *Journal of Management Studies* 46 (2009): 755–786.

81. Renée Adams and Daniel Ferreira, "Women in the Boardroom and Their Impact on Governance and Performance," *Journal of Financial Economics* 94 (2009): 291–309.

82. Kenneth R. Ahern and Amy K Dittmar, "The Changing of the Boards: The Value Effect of a Massive Exogenous Shock," *Social Science Research Network* (2010). Accessed October 21, 2010. See http://ssrn.com/abstract=1364470.

Interlude

In the preceding chapters, we have taken a critical look at the board of directors. We have examined the operations and legal obligations of the board; the process of recruiting, compensating, and removing directors; and the research evidence on how board structure impacts firm performance. In doing so, we have referenced certain functional responsibilities of the board, such as approving corporate strategy and ensuring the integrity of financial statements. However, we have not yet defined these responsibilities in any detail. We focus on these topics next.

In each of the following chapters, we take a specific topic and examine the manner in which the board fulfills its responsibilities:

- Monitor firm strategy and risk (in Chapter 6, "Organizational Strategy, Business Models, and Risk Management")
- Plan for and select a new executive (in Chapter 7, "Labor Market for Executives and CEO Succession Planning")
- Structure executive compensation and equity ownership (in Chapters 8, "Executive Compensation and Incentives," and 9, "Executive Equity Ownership")
- Ensure the integrity of published financial statements (in Chapter 10, "Financial Reporting and External Audit")
- Determine whether to restrict acquisition of the company (in Chapter 11, "The Market for Corporate Control")
- Represent the interests of shareholders (in Chapter 12, "Institutional Shareholders and Activist Investors")

Each of these activities has an important bearing on governance quality. When the board performs these functions well, agency costs decrease and firm value is enhanced. When the board performs these functions less well, agency costs increase and firm value is destroyed.

We start with the first major responsibility: the oversight of firm strategy and risk.

6

Organizational Strategy, Business Models, and Risk Management

As we mentioned in Chapter 3, "Board of Directors: Duties and Liability," the Organization for Economic Cooperation and Development (OECD) states that one of the primary responsibilities of the board is to "ensure the strategic guidance of the company." The Higgs Report recommends that directors "constructively challenge and contribute to the development of strategy."[1] Furthermore, survey data from the National Association of Corporate Directors (NACD) indicates that directors themselves consider strategic planning and oversight to be their most important responsibility—more than financial oversight, CEO succession planning, compensation, and shareholder relations.[2]

Consensus holds that strategic oversight is crucial, but the manner in which the board is expected to perform this function is less clear. The confusion arises primarily because it is not the board's responsibility to develop the strategy—that is management's job. Instead, the board is expected to scrutinize the strategy to make sure that it is appropriate for the company's shareholders and stakeholders, and then to monitor the contribution of corporate activities to the strategic plan.

We break the discussion of strategy development and oversight into four parts:

1. Defining the corporate strategy
2. Developing and testing a business model that verifies how the strategy translates into shareholder or stakeholder value

3. Identifying key indicators to measure corporate performance
4. Identifying and developing processes to mitigate risks to the strategy and business model

Organizational Strategy

Developing the corporate strategy begins with identifying the organization's overarching **mission** and specific objectives. It answers questions such as, "Why are we in business?" and "What do we hope to achieve?" For example, Lockheed Martin publishes on its Web site a mission statement that outlines corporate vision and values:

> **Lockheed Martin's Vision:**
>
> Powered by innovation, guided by integrity, we help our customers achieve their most challenging goals.
>
> **Lockheed Martin's Value Statements:**
>
> *Do What's Right*
>
> We are committed to the highest standards of ethical conduct in all that we do. We believe that honesty and integrity engender trust, which is the cornerstone of our business. We abide by the laws of the United States and other countries in which we do business; we strive to be good citizens and we take responsibility for our actions.
>
> *Respect Others*
>
> We recognize that our success as an enterprise depends on the talent, skills, and expertise of our people and our ability to function as a tightly integrated team. We appreciate our diversity and believe that respect—for our colleagues, customers, partners, and all those with whom we interact—is an essential element of all positive and productive business relationships.
>
> *Perform with Excellence*
>
> We understand the importance of our missions and the trust our customers place in us. With this in mind, we strive to excel in every aspect of our business and approach every challenge with a determination to succeed.[3]

The mission statement becomes the basis for developing the corporate strategy.

The **corporate strategy** is how a company expects to create long-term value for shareholders and stakeholders, within the confines of the corporate mission. It answers questions such as, "What business are we in?" and "How can we create value by being in this business?" Strategic considerations include new market entry, acquisitions and divestures, branding, reorganizations, and other similar transformational decisions.

An organization considers multiple aspects when developing its corporate strategy:

- **Scope**—What is the scope of activities that the business will participate in over the long term?
- **Markets**—What markets will the business participate in?
- **Advantage**—What advantages does the company have to ensure that it can compete?
- **Resources**—What resources does the company have (in terms of property, plant, and equipment; human and intellectual capital; customer and supplier networks; and finances) that are required to compete?
- **Environment**—What factors in the market environment influence how the company competes?
- **Stakeholders**—Who are the internal and external stakeholders that influence the business, directly or indirectly?[4]

For example, we can imagine that Lockheed Martin's strategy is to provide cutting-edge innovation in defense, equipment, and technology to give its customers (primarily the U.S. government) a competitive advantage in security and combat. The company achieves an advantage by capitalizing on a base of technological sophistication and proprietary knowledge that it has built up during decades of research and development funding and proven success in attracting and retaining highly specialized engineering talent.

As we stated earlier, it is management's responsibility to define the corporate strategy. Various models assist in this task, such as those outlined in *Strategic Management,* by Saloner, Shepard, and Podolny (2005), and *Competitive Strategy,* by Porter (1998).[5] In some cases, a management consulting firm is retained to bring objectivity and third-party expertise to the exercise (see the following sidebar).

Considerations in Developing the Strategy

Many describe the strategy-development process as though it is always produced through a formal, linear, and logical exercise. First agree on corporate objectives, then develop the plan for achieving those objectives, and finally identify and deploy the necessary resources. The reality in most firms is quite different. Many companies develop a strategy through a nonlinear or iterative process. For example, they might develop a pilot program and then improve or refine the strategy based on the results. Other companies stumble upon a strategy, either at inception or over time, and only later articulate it into a clearly defined corporate strategy.

The strategy-development process can also be biased through cultural and psychological factors. For example, management might anchor on current activities, because they are comfortable with them and know how to manage them. If so, such an approach can lead to modest, incremental strategic change that binds the company's future too closely to its current way of conducting business. Incrementalism can be particularly detrimental when a company is faced with an unanticipated crisis or change in market environment that requires a more radical reassessment of corporate direction. The strategy-development process can also suffer from poor coordination, with the strategy, finance, and operating groups planning in isolation and experiencing serious communication disconnects.[6] Without proper information sharing, corporate planners fail to understand the true dynamics, pressures, and resources required to achieve company objectives. When this occurs, substantial risk exists that corporate strategy will not create shareholder value.[7]

Strategy Implementation Process

The board of directors needs to understand and evaluate the key elements of the strategy identification and implementation process. We illustrate this process using the generic example of a consumer products company. For simplicity, we follow a linear approach:

- Establish the overarching objective of the firm. If the board takes a purely shareholder perspective, the objective might be to produce total shareholder returns (TSR) that are superior to those of its direct competitors. If it takes a stakeholder perspective, it might establish additional objectives that are of concern to nonshareholder constituents (such as maintaining present employment levels, protecting the environment, and so on).

  Example: Target long-term TSR of 10 percent per year.

- Determine the outcomes that are necessary to achieve the TSR target. Management might propose explicit goals for sales growth, return on capital, free cash flow, and other economic metrics that are consistent with the TSR target. The finance group in consultation with officers in the functional areas of the company performs the analysis that supports these goals. The group will likely take into account the growth prospects of the industry and the relationship between financial returns and shareholder value. Board members test the assumptions underlying these computations to ensure that these goals are reasonable and that the relationship between the economic results and value creation is correct.

  Example: Sales growth of 6 percent per year, free cash flow growth of 8 percent, and return on equity of 15 percent.

- Assess the viability of specific strategies to achieve the company's economic targets.

  Example: Develop products at three price points: basic, middle-tier, and premium. The company seeks to increase adoption and encourage consumers to migrate up the value chain, thereby delivering increased sales and profitability. Higher margins, productivity increases, and economies of scale will drive growth in free cash flow.

- Assign targets (both financial and nonfinancial) that will enable the company to measure the success of its strategy over time.

Example: The company might set financial targets for cash flow
and revenue growth from new products and nonfinancial targets for market share, pricing, product attributes, advertising
support, research and development productivity, customer satisfaction, brand awareness and strength, and so on. If targets
are achieved, the company expects to succeed in its revenue
and profitability goals, and ultimately achieve its TSR target.

To satisfy itself that company goals are achievable, the board
needs to review a causal business model of the organization. A **causal
business model** links specific financial and nonfinancial measures in
a logical chain to delineate how the corporate strategy translates into
the accomplishment of stated goals. The board should evaluate the
business model for logical consistency, realism of targets, and statistical evidence that the relationships between performance measures
and stated goals are valid.

The board might test management assumptions by asking questions such as these: If we launch a product with the desired attributes, backed by a pricing, packaging, and advertising strategy, will we
achieve the customer satisfaction levels that we anticipate? Will customers engage in repeat purchases? Will we achieve the desired
sales volumes? What evidence (statistical, not anecdotal) do we have
that these relationships are valid for our company? What metrics will
we put in place to measure our progress, and how will we capture
this data?

This task is extremely difficult because it requires input and
agreement from all major functional areas of the firm. For example,
analysis should be performed by marketing (What does it take to get
the right customers?), human resources (What does it take to get the
right employees?), manufacturing (What needs to be done so that we
can produce the units in a timely manner?), and engineering (How
can we increase new product development?).

The business model serves an important purpose: It specifies how
management expects to create long-term value. The business model
lays out a concrete plan (value propositions) that the board can test
and evaluate when approving the corporate strategy. From a governance perspective, the business model is an important tool that the
board can rely on to fulfill its oversight function. By examining the

logical chain presented by management, the board can challenge assumptions and eventually recognize that the corporate strategy is sound. This model also provides the basis for measuring management performance and awarding compensation. To perform this function adequately, directors must have the requisite industry knowledge and business background to carefully examine the model and use informed judgment (see the following sidebar).

Considerations in Developing the Business Model

Companies that explicitly develop a causal business model will likely encounter substantial challenges. First, instead of dedicating the time necessary to do a thorough job, management might take shortcuts. One example is to rely on general "best practice" ideas that are assumed to work, without considering whether these ideas actually fit the organization. Sometimes this takes the form of off-the-shelf technology—such as customer resource management (CRM) and enterprise resource programs (ERP)—that alone is not capable of developing business models. Second, relevant data might be difficult to obtain. If the company does not have a system in place for tracking financial and nonfinancial metrics, it needs to be established. This might involve breaking down silos within the organization and convincing managers from across the organization to work collaboratively and share data. Third, managers might resist the concept of a formal business model, particularly if it requires that they fundamentally change how they do business. They might also resist implementation if they are underperforming and therefore want to avoid rigorous performance measurement, or if the modeling process leads to a restructuring that dramatically alters or reduces their area of responsibility. It is the board's responsibility to ensure that organizational inertia does not impede the business modeling process.

Business Model Development and Testing

Following are two real-world examples that illustrate how companies have used statistical data analysis to explore the causal relationship between financial and nonfinancial performance drivers and future operating performance. In each case, the board of directors sought specificity in understanding how such performance would be achieved (that is, they wanted management to tell them a convincing story). The results of the analysis were used to redefine the corporate strategy, based on a robust business model, and to track subsequent performance through key performance measures. Boards would be well advised to ask for this type of analysis from management to enable them to evaluate and monitor the corporate strategy. Simply looking at consolidated or business unit financial statements is not adequate; the board needs to see the underlying linkages that drive results.

Example 1: Fast-Food Chain and Employee Turnover

The board of directors and the senior management team at a major fast-food restaurant chain decided that the company was not growing fast enough, based on peer-group comparisons and discussion with sell-side and buy-side analysts. Market trends and competitive data suggested that the company could do much better. At the request of the board, senior-level executives across the various functional areas of the company convened to examine how and why the company was falling short. In these sessions, executives outlined what they believed to be a simple causal model of how the company made money (see Figure 6.1).[8]

Consensus Business Model

Source: Authors.

Figure 6.1   Consensus business model.

The group built this model based on an assumption that customer satisfaction was a key driver of operating performance. Satisfied customers made repeat visits, which increased purchase frequency and, therefore, sales. Dissatisfied customers did not come back. Company executives thought they had previously verified this relationship through statistical analysis although the supporting analysis and report could not be found and were not made available to this cross-functional group.

The question facing the group became, "What factors contribute to customer satisfaction?" The group hypothesized that employee performance played a critical role. Their reasoning was as follows: Employees have substantial influence over the in-store experience. They prepare the food, interact with customers, and maintain the cleanliness and efficiency of each location. Without diligent employee effort, customer satisfaction would likely decline. Carrying this reasoning further, the group brainstormed the factors that contributed to employee performance. They settled on two: 1) the hiring and staffing process, and 2) the level of employee satisfaction. The group agreed that the company needed to do a better job of attracting quality employees to the store and, after they were hired, keeping them satisfied.

To this point, most of the work done by the group was based on professional intuition. The underlying premise—that employees contributed to customer satisfaction—was not explored through formal data analysis, and the group did not interview customers. Nevertheless, the company decided to act on this model. Executives launched a series of strategic initiatives to improve employee performance. These initiatives centered on improving employee hiring practices and improving employee satisfaction. They measured the success of these initiatives through a nonfinancial performance indicator: employee turnover. Again, they selected this performance measure without testing. As one executive explained at the time, "We just know this is the key driver." They reasoned that a reduction in employee turnover would indicate that the company was succeeding in the recruitment and retention process. This would then lead to an improvement in employee performance, which would result in more frequent customer visits and purchases. As a result, employee turnover became a primary measure by which decisions were made. To support a reduction in turnover, the company began to implement an expensive human resource program that included retention bonus awards for all restaurant employees.

Only subsequently did the company undertake a detailed statistical analysis at the store level. They analyzed stores based on sales, profitability, and turnover. The results were not what they had expected. They discovered that groups of stores with the same over-all employee turnover rates exhibited very different financial performance. They also found that several high-profit stores had employee turnover that was significantly above average. These find-ings contradicted the premise of their causal model. The correlation they had expected between employee turnover and store perform-ance simply did not exist. Drilling into the data, the executives learned that the true driver of store performance was not general turnover, but *turnover among store managers*. The restaurant suf-fered a drop-off in performance when the supervisory personnel turned over. This was because a change in manager impacted consis-tency of training, food preparation, cleanliness, and other operating processes—at least until the new store manager got up to speed with the new responsibilities.

Based on these findings, senior management shifted its priority from reducing the turnover of all store employees to reducing the turnover of store managers. To reinforce this priority, retention bonuses were put in place at the store manager level. Further analy-sis provided an estimate for the financial cost of turnover, which was used to create an upper bound for the size of the retention bonus.

This somewhat simple business model provided new insights into the value-creation process at this company. Moreover, it became a tool for strategic discussions with the board of directors. Going for-ward, the key assumptions in the strategy were more easily identified, and the board was provided with the "vital few" predictive perform-ance indicators, including store manager turnover (in place of the litany of performance measures included in a typical board book of meeting materials).

Example 2: Financial Services Firm and Investment Advisor Retention

A large financial services organization had a goal of being a "world leader in financial advisory and brokerage services to retail investors." From prior statistical analyses, executives and the board knew that customer retention and assets under management were key success indicators that directly impacted economic results (see Figure 6.2).

Furthermore, this analysis revealed that the level of satisfaction with the investment advisor was positively correlated with the level of assets that the customer entrusted to the company.

Advisor Rating and Assets Invested

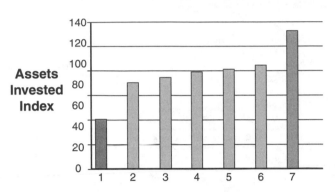

Customer Satisfaction with Investment Advisor

Source: Authors.

Figure 6.2   Relationship between customer satisfaction and asset investment levels.

At the board's request, management undertook further statistical analysis to better understand the factors that contributed to a customer's satisfaction with an investment advisor. They found several, including the advisor's trustworthiness, responsiveness, and knowledge. However, one factor in particular was the most important: advisor turnover. Customers wanted to deal with the same advisor over time, and when they were shuttled around from one advisor to the next, they became dissatisfied—even if the new advisor scored high on the personal attributes mentioned earlier (see Figure 6.3).

Management used this knowledge to explore the factors that contributed to advisor turnover. Statistical analysis revealed that they were (in decreasing order) compensation level, work environment, challenging career opportunities, quality of branch management, and work/life balance. The company used these insights to develop a human resources plan to address the compensation issues (changing the level and mix of short- and long-term remuneration). More important, senior management and the board now had a rigorous business model to filter strategic planning decisions and key perform-ance metrics to track management performance. Going forward, the board's review of corporate performance included not only the tradi-tional metrics of profitability and assets under management (AUM), but also the newly devised metrics of customer satisfaction, advisor satisfaction, and advisor turnover.

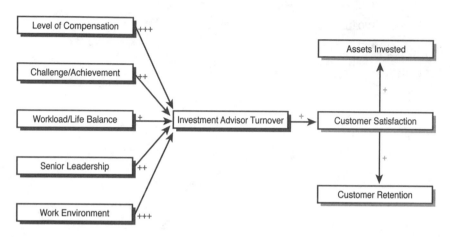

Source: Authors.

Figure 6.3   Statistical analysis of factors contributing to customer satisfaction.

Key Performance Measures

As highlighted in these two examples, an important output from the business model is that it serves as the basis for identifying key per-formance measures that the board can later use to evaluate manage-ment performance and award bonuses. **Key performance measures**, or **key performance indicators (KPIs)**, include both financial and nonfinancial metrics that validly reflect current and future corporate performance. For example, in the financial services firm example, the business model highlighted the need to use invest-ment advisor turnover and satisfaction, and customer satisfaction—in addition to traditional financial measures—as KPIs.

The board also uses key performance measures to evaluate man-agement performance and award compensation. For example, if a company believes that the success of a new product launch should be measured in terms of market share, brand awareness, gross margins, and sale volume, these should be the metrics that the board follows *both* to determine management's success *and* to award compensation.

KPIs are roughly grouped into two categories: financial and non-financial. **Financial KPIs** include measures such as total shareholder return; revenue growth; earnings per share; earnings before interest, taxes, depreciation, and amortization (EBITDA); return on capital; economic value added (EVA); and free cash flow. **Nonfinancial KPIs** include measures such as customer satisfaction, employee satisfaction, defects and rework, on-time delivery, worker safety, environmental safety, and research and development (R&D) pipeline productivity. Because of their common usefulness, certain KPIs are broadly used by many companies. Others are used by a more limited set of companies—because of the specificity of their line of business—and include both financial and nonfinancial measures, such as sales per square foot (retailing), R&D productivity (science and technology), and factory downtime (manufacturing). Whatever KPIs a company selects, it is important that they be closely tied to the company business model (see Table 6.1 for commonly used KPIs).

Table 6.1 Measures to Determine Corporate Performance

	Overall Prevalence[1]
Number of companies	343
Profit measures	**77%**
Earnings per share	29%
EBIT/EBITDA	19%
Net income	16%
Operating income	15%
Pretax profit	7%
Return measures	**14%**
Return on capital	6%
Return on assets	3%
Return on equity	3%
Return on investment	2%
Return on net assets	2%

Table 6.1   Measures to Determine Corporate Performance (continued)

Corporate Measures Used for Corporate Employees (Industrial and Service Companies)	Overall Prevalence[1]
EVA/cash flow measures	**26%**
Cash flow	16%
Economic value added (EVA)/economic profit	8%
Working capital	3%
Cash value added (CVA)	1%
Other measures	**62%**
Individual objectives	23%
Sales/revenue/revenue growth	20%
Customer satisfaction	8%
Service/quality	6%
Strategic goals/projects	6%
Discretionary	4%
Expense reduction	3%
Safety	3%
Employee satisfaction	2%
Total shareholder return	1%
Other various/combinations of measures[2]	28%

[1] Percent totals exceeding 100% indicate multiple responses.
[2] Some of the other measures used included inventory turnover, operating expenses, and process/product improvement.
Source: Confidential survey in 2005. Proprietary sample.

Research has shown that companies tend to use multiple performance measures, including a mix of financial and nonfinancial KPIs. De Angelis and Grinstein (2010) found that the KPIs used to award executive bonuses tend to be weighted toward accounting measures, particularly those related to corporate profitability—such as earnings per share, net income growth, and earnings before interest and taxes (EBIT).[9] Ittner, Larcker, and Rajan (1997) and Kim and Yang (2010) found that companies rely on a mix of quantitative and qualitative factors in awarding bonuses. Qualitative factors include those related to strategic development, individual performance, customer satisfaction, employee satisfaction, and workplace safety.[10]

Although nonfinancial measures are important, boards must be aware of the risks involved in using them. By their nature, nonfinancial measures are more easily subject to measurement error or manipulation. Others are difficult to track with precision. Following are some of the key factors for the board to consider when relying on performance measures:[11]

- **Sensitivity**—How sensitive is the metric to corporate performance? How sensitive is the metric to management action?

- **Precision**—How much measurement error is embedded in the measure? What is the potential for intentional manipulation?

- **Verifiability**—Can the measure be audited or otherwise independently verified?

- **Objectivity**—Is the measure objective (such as number of safety incidents) or subjective (such as level of employee commitment)? Do these different categories of measures have similar sensitivity, precision, and verifiability?

- **Dimension**—Are the results expressed as a percentage, survey scale, number of occurrences, or binary outcome? Would the metric lend itself to different interpretation if expressed in a different manner?

- **Interpretation**—What specific attribute does the data measure? (For example, does product failure rate measure the quality of the manufacturing process or the quality of the product design?)

- **Cost**—What is the cost to develop and track this metric? Does it provide sufficient value to the board, compared to the cost?

Research evidence supports the importance of these efforts. Ittner and Larcker (2003) found that companies that develop a causal business model based on KPIs exhibit significantly higher returns on assets and returns on equity during five-year periods than those that do not.[12] The authors identified three benefits of this process: enhanced internal communication on strategic assumptions, better identification and measurement of strategic value drivers, and improved resource allocation and target setting. Gates (1999) found that companies with a formal set of strategic performance measures tend to exhibit superior stock price returns compared to companies that do not have such measures.[13] Relative performance is even more favorable when such measures are regularly shared with the board of directors, investors, and analysts.

Furthermore, it is important that companies consider using both financial and nonfinancial measures. Researchers have repeatedly shown that nonfinancial KPIs can be a leading indicator of subsequent financial performance. For example, Ittner and Larcker (1997b) found that customer satisfaction was a leading indicator of future financial performance in a sample of banking and telecommunications companies.[14] Banker, Potter, and Schroeder (1993) demonstrated a similar relationship between customer satisfaction and future financial results in the hospitality industry.[15] Nagar and Rajan (2001) demonstrated a correlation between manufacturing quality measures and future revenue growth in manufacturing firms.[16] As such, it is critical that boards understand the relationship between nonfinancial measures and subsequent financial performance when deciding on a set of KPIs.

However, the importance of nonfinancial targets depends on the company's strategy and operating environment. For example, Ittner, Larcker, and Rajan (1997) found that nonfinancial measures take on greater importance when a company is pursuing an innovation strategy (such as new ventures that are cash-flow negative) or a quality strategy (such as the implementation of total quality management [TQM] or lean manufacturing).[17] Said, HassabElnaby, and Wier (2003) supported these findings. They found a greater prevalence of nonfinancial measures among companies that are pursuing an "innovation" or "quality" strategy, companies whose products are subject to long development cycles (such as aircraft manufacturers), companies that are in highly regulated industries (such as railroads), and companies in financial distress.[18] These studies suggest that nonfinancial measures are particularly important when a company's current strategy does not lend itself well to short-term financial targets.

How Well Are Boards Doing with Performance Measures and Business Models?

Deloitte undertook one of the most detailed analyses of this subject in a two-part study titled "In the Dark: What Boards and Executives Don't Know about the Health of Their Businesses" (2004 and

2007).[19] Based on a sample of 250 directors and executives at large international corporations, the report found a surprising disconnect between the metrics that board members and executives say are important drivers of firm performance and the KPIs that the companies actually use to track results.

More than 90 percent of respondents claimed that both financial and nonfinancial factors are critical to their company's success. Commonly cited nonfinancial measures included customer satisfaction (97 percent), product or service quality (96 percent), and employee commitment (92 percent). Yet when asked to assess the quality of information they receive regarding each of these measures, respondents claimed to have good visibility into only one: financial results (91 percent). The quality of information regarding nonfinancial measures was rated much lower, including product or service quality (52 percent reporting "excellent" or "good" information), customer satisfaction (46 percent), and employee commitment (41 percent). That is, evidence points to a shockingly large disconnect between the information that is important for understanding value creation and the information that is actually being supplied to the board.

More surprisingly, board members did not appear to have an explanation for why they were not receiving this information. The most frequently cited reason was that the company has "undeveloped tools for analyzing such measures" (59 percent). That is, information on these performance measures was not captured because no one has taken the time to formulate a proper system for tracking them. If true, this is a serious lapse in oversight on the part of directors. The study concluded that a "gap [exists] between awareness and action, rhetoric and reality":

> Until this gap narrows, board directors, managers, and investors remain less well-informed about the true state of their companies' health than they would otherwise. [N]onfinancial measurements of performance ... can provide the board and management with a vital guide to help steer the company toward long-term success. Yet too many companies focus their attention on financial data and too few rigorously monitor other performance measures.

Ittner, Larcker, and Randall (2003) also found similar results. The metrics that are the most important drivers of long-term organizational success suffer from very low measurement quality (see Figure 6.4). According to the study, the only measure that had higher measurement quality than importance is short-term financial accounting results. By contrast, metrics about customer satisfaction, product quality, innovation, and other important drivers were not tracked through reliable metrics. These measures had higher importance than measurement quality.[20]

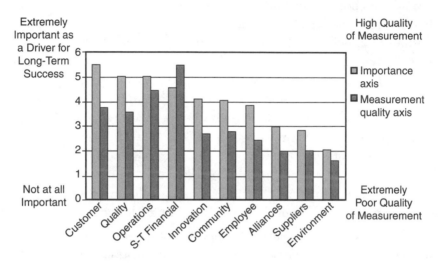

Adapted from Christopher D. Ittner, David F. Larcker, and Taylor Randall (2008).

Figure 6.4   The importance of metrics vs. the quality of their measurement.

All this suggests that many boards might be falling short of their duty to oversee firm strategy and performance. They can redress this deficiency by demanding more detailed information about the full set of KPIs that contribute to future operating success and then tracking those measures to assess the performance of management. With this information, boards can better understand the factors contributing to success or failure, as well as manage organizational risks.

Risk and Risk Management

The notion of risk is largely absent from the preceding discussion. Our focus was on the *desired* outcome instead of the *range* of outcomes that might occur. Although we emphasized the positive outcomes that arise from establishing a sound strategy and valid business model, we did not consider the loss of value that occurs when things do not work out as planned. Nor did we discuss the policies and procedures that a company might put in place to mitigate such losses. Now we take up that discussion.

First, we define the concept of risk in terms of its relationship to the corporate strategy and business model. Then we discuss what is meant by risk management. Finally, we consider the role the board plays in both understanding organizational risk and implementing the policies and procedures necessary to ensure that it is managed properly.

It is important to highlight that when we speak of *risk management* in this chapter, we are not talking about simple compliance with laws and regulations. We are treating it as a minimum standard that organizations attempt to conduct their affairs within the guidelines established by governments and federal agencies. When we speak of risk management, we are addressing the bigger picture involving outcomes or events that can reduce a company's profitability, lead to severe underperformance, or otherwise threaten an organization's success or viability.

The importance of this topic has been underscored by the large number of corporate failures that occurred following the financial crisis of 2008. Many casualties of the crisis—such as American International Group, Bear Stearns, and Lehman Brothers—simply did not understand the risks they were exposed to because of their business models. Had they been aware of these risks in advance, they might have conducted their affairs differently to protect themselves from the collateral damage they ultimately faced. Unfortunately, according to a recent survey, less than half of senior executives are confident that their organization understands the range of risks it faces, the severity of those risks, the likelihood of their occurrence, or their potential impact.[21] As might be expected with the financial crisis, Congress has also been actively engaged in the risk-management debate—risk committee requirements were proposed in both the Schumer Shareholder Bill of Rights and the Ellison Corporate Governance Reform Act (although ultimately omitted from the Dodd-Frank Act).[22] Risk management is now defined in much broader terms than was formerly the case, and includes CEO succession planning and the structure of executive compensation. (We discuss these issues in Chapters 7, 8, and 9.)

Risk and Risk Tolerance

The **risk** facing an organization represents the likelihood and severity of loss from unexpected or uncontrollable outcomes. This includes both the typical losses that occur during the course of business and losses from extremely unlikely and unpredictable events (so-called **black swans**, or **outliers**). Risk arises naturally, both from the nature of the activities that the corporation participates in and from the manner in which it pursues its objectives. Risk cannot be separated from the strategy and operations of the firm but instead is an integral feature of organizational decision making.

Each company must decide how much risk it is willing to assume through its choice of strategy. It is not possible to pursue a risk-free strategy, nor is risk management about removing all risk from the firm. Obviously, if managers were to remove all the risk, they should be able to earn no more than the risk-free interest rate, which is not in the interest of shareholders. Instead, firms succeed when they are better able to manage risk than their competitors.

In making this decision, each company must determine its own tolerance for risk (**risk tolerance**). This decision should involve the active participation of the board of directors. If the board (as representatives of shareholders) is willing to accept greater uncertainty and variability in future cash flows in exchange for potentially higher economic returns, then a risky strategy might be appropriate. If not, then either a safer strategy or an entirely new strategy is appropriate. The company must strike its own balance between aggressiveness and conservativeness. This balance can be achieved only when the riskiness of the corporate strategy and business model is properly understood. The risks that the firm is willing to accept should be properly managed in the context of its strategy. The risks that the firm cannot handle on its own or is not good at managing should be hedged or otherwise transferred to a third party. The management of the company and the board of directors need to understand the nature, cost, and repercussions of adverse or unexpected outcomes and manage those accordingly.

Risk to the Business Model

Boards and executives commonly focus on generic risks facing the firm.[23] However, the real risks are extensive and relate to all its activities, including these:

- **Operational risk**—This reflects how exposed the company is to disruptions in its operations. Operational risk is reflected in such factors as concentration of suppliers, concentration of buyers, redundancy in the supply chain, and the extent to which the company monitors its supply chain.

- **Financial risk**—This reflects how much the company relies on external financing (including the capital markets and private lenders) to support its ongoing operations. Financial risk is reflected in such factors as balance sheet leverage, off-balance-sheet vehicles, contractual obligations, maturity schedule of debt obligations, liquidity, and other restrictions that reduce financial flexibility. Companies that rely on external parties for financing are at greater risk than those that finance operations using internally generated funds.

- **Reputational risk**—This reflects how much the company protects the value of its intangible assets, including corporate reputation. Reputational risk is reflected in investing in product brand development, investing in corporate brand development, monitoring the use of brands, monitoring supplier and customer business practices, performing community outreach, and handling stakeholder relations.

- **Compliance risk**—This reflects how much the company complies with laws and regulations that otherwise would damage the firm. Compliance risk is reflected in such factors as labor practices, environmental compliance, and consideration given to the regulatory requirements that govern the company's products, processes, or publicly listed securities.

To understand the risks associated with the organizational strategy, the board must probe deeper than generic risk categories. Survey data suggests that companies are aware of the financial, political, regulatory, and economic risks facing their organizations and the risks associated with loss of human capital. However, they exhibit somewhat lower awareness of the risks that are inherent to their business models.[24]

The business modeling process discussed earlier provides a rigorous framework for doing so. Stress testing the key linkages and assumptions in the business model enables the board and management to better determine what might go wrong with the corporate strategy and the consequences of these problems. A causal business model focuses the risk management discussion by enabling corporate officials to think about how a disruption in one area or function could have cascading effects throughout the organization. The company then can develop policies and procedures to mitigate these risks.

Following up on the example of the fast-food company described previously, what would happen to earnings and cash flow if the company could not attract qualified store managers at the present wage rate? What would happen if the caloric content of the meals became more important to customers than cleanliness and efficiency?

In the example of the financial services company, what would happen to the company if life–work balance became a more important component of advisor satisfaction than level of compensation or work environment? How would the company respond to ensure that its advisors remained satisfied?

If the company has a well-developed business model, it is possible for the board and management to develop very detailed risk-management analyses of key issues such as these. The company should generally seek to mitigate risk to the extent that it is cost-effective to do so. Risks that the company is not willing to accept should be hedged or otherwise transferred to a third party through insurance or derivative contracts. However, other risks are desirable to retain and might be associated with the firm's competitive advantages, including labor talent, manufacturing processes, brands, patents, and intellectual property. Obviously, good corporate governance requires that risks retained by the company be properly disclosed to shareholders.

Risk Management

Risk management is the process by which a company evaluates and reduces its risk exposure. This includes actions, policies, and procedures that management implements to reduce the likelihood and severity of adverse outcomes and to increase the likelihood and benefits of positive outcomes. To accomplish this, the organization must define and develop a **risk culture**. A risk culture involves setting the tone for risk tolerance in the organization and ensuring that risk consideration is a key part of all decisions. Survey data suggests that strong leadership, clear parameters surrounding corporate risk taking, and access to information about potential risks are necessary for this to occur.[25]

Various professional frameworks can guide the company in the risk-management processes. For example, the Committee of Sponsoring Organizations (COSO) framework, originally developed in 1990, has become a respected framework for risk management.[26] COSO recommends that risk management be incorporated into strategy planning, operational review, internal reporting, and compliance. As such, risk should be considered at the enterprise, division, and business unit levels. COSO outlines its recommendations in an eight-step framework:

1. **Internal environment**—Establish the organization's philosophy toward risk management and risk culture.

2. **Objective setting**—Evaluate the company's strategy and set organizational goals based on the risk tolerance of management and the board.

3. **Event identification**—Examine the risks associated with each potential business opportunity.

4. **Risk assessment**—Determine the likelihood and the severity of each risk.

5. **Risk response**—Identify the organizational actions taken to prevent or deal with each risk.

6. **Control Activities**—Establish policies and procedures to ensure that risk responses are carried out as planned.

7. **Information and communication**—Create an information system to capture and report on the organization's risk-management process.

8. **Monitoring**—Review data from the information system and take actions as appropriate.

Note that the first steps of this framework are consistent with the argument we have made so far that risk should be discussed in terms of its strategic and operating components. Also note that the information-collection and monitoring steps are consistent with the manner in which we have described performance measurement using KPIs. That is, the risk-management process should be integrated with the processes the company uses for development and oversight of the strategy, business model, and performance measurement (see the following sidebar).

Organizational Risk Management

Heinz Company exemplifies this comprehensive approach to risk management. The company has defined its primary objectives to protect its reputation and shareholder value. To this end, the company's efforts focus on the long-term sustainability of the organization in a manner that enables it to achieve both short-term and long-term financial objectives. *Risk* at Heinz is therefore defined as "anything that can prevent the company from achieving its objectives."

The company groups risk into two categories: operational risk and nonoperational risk. Operational risk areas include product quality, environment and sustainability, employee health and safety, facility and product security, business continuity, and asset conservation. Nonoperational risk areas include strategy and market, corporate governance and ethics, finance, legal, information services, and human resources.

From an organizational perspective, the company maintains an Office of Risk Management, which consists of a chief quality officer, a director of enterprise risk management, and a director of operational risk management and sustainability. The Office of Risk Management has ties to the audit committee of the board, the disclosure committee, and internal audit. In addition, the company maintains a Risk Council, which consists of senior executives in each functional area. As a result, risks are evaluated *both* by compliance officers, whose primary responsibility is risk management, and by functional leaders, whose primary responsibility is managing the company's operations.

The objectives of these two groups (Office of Risk Management and Risk Council) are to identify, prioritize, measure, and manage key risks, and to ensure that these processes are owned and understood at the business unit level. Finally, the company emphasizes that its managers be "risk aware but not risk averse, with a primary focus on protecting and thereby maximizing enterprise value and brand equity."[27]

To date, little research rigorously examines the relation between risk management and future firm performance.[28] However, survey data suggests that shareholders place great value on comprehensive risk management. According to a survey by Ernst & Young, more than 80 percent of institutional investors responded that they were willing to pay a premium for companies with good risk-management practices. Similarly, a majority of respondents claimed that they had passed up the opportunity to invest in a company because they believed risk management was insufficient.[29]

Oversight of Risk Management

Although management is ultimately responsible for implementing and enforcing risk management, the board must ensure that these activities are carried out effectively. How is the board expected to satisfy this responsibility? What does it mean to "oversee" risk management?

The risk oversight responsibilities of the board can be roughly divided into four categories. First, the board is responsible for determining the risk profile of the company. As we have discussed, this includes considering macroeconomic, industry-related, and firm-specific risk. The board should determine the risk profile of the company in consultation with management, shareholders, and other key stakeholders. In heavily regulated industries—such as financial services, insurance, and utilities—discussions should include regulators. The board should weigh downside costs against long-term market opportunities and consider the likelihood of both success and failure.

Second, the board is responsible for evaluating the company's strategy and business model, to determine whether they are appropriate, given the firm's appetite for risk. The board should be satisfied that the company has identified risks to the strategy and business model and is effectively managing them. The board should confirm that viable contingency plans have been drawn up to deal with potential financial or operational interruptions. In addition, the board should consider whether appropriate hedges and insurance are in place to deal with risks that are not well managed by the firm.

Third, the board is responsible for ensuring that the company is committed to operating at an appropriate risk level on an ongoing basis. Does the company's culture encourage or discourage risky behavior? Are the company's operations assuming more risk than intended by the strategy and business model? Developing internal reporting systems that capture risk data can help answer these questions. Risk metrics should be included among the key performance indicators that the board uses to monitor firm performance. The board should be facile in interpreting this data and attentive to emerging trends (see the following sidebar).

Finally, the board should determine that management has developed the necessary internal controls to ensure that risk-management procedures remain effective. A lot of this activity is mundane, including ensuring that reporting relationships are well defined, communication channels work, and reporting data is tested for accuracy. Nevertheless, these are important steps for ensuring that risk management practices are effective. Tying executive compensation not only to strategic performance measures but also to the company's risk measures will help ensure that this work is performed appropriately. (This is discussed more fully in Chapters 8 and 9.)

Is Risk the Responsibility of a Committee or the Full Board?

According to a survey by the NACD, 59 percent of companies assign risk management to the audit committee, 5 percent to a special risk committee, and 30 percent to the full board.[30]

A company might assign risk management to the audit committee for several reasons. In recent years, much of the regulatory focus on "risk" has centered on financial statement risk and inaccurate disclosures. In fact, the listing requirements of the New York Stock

Exchange (NYSE) require that the audit committee review the firm's risk policies.[31] Companies are also required to disclose "risk factors" that could materially impact financial results; the audit committee oversees this disclosure on the 10-K. The risk-management function within the company typically reports to the chief financial officer and, by extension, the audit committee; the audit committee, therefore, should be well versed in its activities. Finally, the CFO and audit committee are familiar with financial hedges and insurance contracts that the company uses to protect the value of its assets. To reduce redundancies, many companies might choose to consolidate all risk-management activities with the audit committee.

A company might choose to set up a separate risk committee. If risk is operational instead of purely financial, it makes sense that oversight be given to a group of directors who view risk primarily through the lens of operations and firm performance instead of financial results and accounting statements. The audit committee might be burdened with so many regulatory requirements that it cannot possibly dedicate the requisite time to monitor operational risk. Furthermore, much risk is specialized in nature and requires specialized knowledge to evaluate. For this reason, companies such as Aegon (insurance), Duke Energy (utilities), and JP Morgan Chase (banking/finance) all have dedicated risk committees.[32]

However, forming a risk committee does not address a key issue identified earlier in this chapter: Risk management should not be an isolated function within the company. Any consideration of risk—financial or operational—should be made in conjunction with a comprehensive review of the company's strategy, business model, and performance measurement. As such, risk management is likely best handled by the entire board, not a subset of directors. Isolating risk to an audit or risk committee effectively denigrates the function. It also implies that strategy and risk are separate considerations, which, as we have seen in this chapter, is not the case.

Assessing Board Performance on Risk Management

Little rigorous research assesses the general effectiveness of risk-management programs and the performance consequences of these programs. However, survey data indicates that companies can stand to improve considerably in this area.

A 2007 study conducted by the Conference Board found that most companies have not integrated risk management into strategic planning and general operations.[33] Only 58 percent of companies ensure that risk issues are considered when making decisions, and only 32 percent integrate enterprise risk management into their general corporate processes. Furthermore, less than 25 percent of companies coordinate risk management with strategic planning, operational planning, annual budgeting, or management performance evaluations. Instead, risk management at most companies is treated as an isolated function that internal audit or the risk-management department carries out and is not under the jurisdiction of operational managers.

Other professional surveys have findings consistent with this. A survey by PricewaterhouseCoopers LLP found that only 20 percent of chief executive officers understand their responsibilities to manage risk.[34] Similarly, a study by McKinsey and *Directorship* magazine found that the board of directors generally gives nonfinancial risk only "anecdotal treatment."[35] Without a commitment from the top, it is understandable why risk-management processes are seriously underdeveloped at many companies.

Finally, survey data indicates that many professionals don't believe that their company has effective risk-management expertise. According to a survey by the American Institute of Certified Public Accountants and the Chartered Institute of Management Accountants, 84 percent of financial officers rated the risk oversight process at their companies as either "very immature," "immature," or "moderately immature."[36] In addition, a survey of senior executives found that audit committee members and business unit managers are not perceived as having effective risk expertise. Only 47 percent of respondents considered the audit committee to be effective or very effective in this regard; 44 percent of respondents said the same for business unit managers. Even the CEO, who receives the highest rating among corporate officers, is considered effective or very effective by only 72 percent of respondents.[37] These results highlight a very

real problem. Without adequate risk expertise and rigorous procedures, it is difficult to believe that firms are subject to proper oversight (see the following sidebar).

Risk Management and the Financial Crisis of 2008

The 2008 financial crisis clearly illustrated the failure of risk management at many companies. Major financial institutions—including Lehman Brothers, Bear Stearns, and Citigroup—collapsed in
part because their business and trading strategies assumed more
risk than either the boards or management realized. Consider a
summary report from the OECD:

"When they were put to a test, corporate governance routines did
not serve their purpose to safeguard against excessive risk taking in
a number of financial services companies. A number of weaknesses have been apparent. The risk management systems have
failed in many cases due to corporate governance procedures
rather than the inadequacy of computer models alone: Information about exposures in a number of cases did not reach the board
and even senior levels of management, while risk management was
often activity- rather than enterprise-based. These are board
responsibilities. In other cases, boards had approved strategy but
then did not establish suitable metrics to monitor its implementation. Company disclosures about foreseeable risk factors and about
the systems in place for monitoring and managing risk have also
left a lot to be desired, even though this is a key element of the
[OECD] Principles. Accounting standards and regulatory requirements have also proved insufficient in some areas, leading the
relevant standard setters to undertake a review. Last but not least,
remuneration systems have in a number of cases not been closely
related to the strategy and risk appetite of the company and its
longer-term interests."[38]

As Andrew Ross Sorkin explains in his book *Too Big to Fail* (2009),
the management of some of these organizations simply did not
understand the risks of their operations. Worse, they took little
interest in risk management and even excluded risk officers from
important discussions:

"As both Gregory (COO [of Lehman Brothers]) and Fuld (CEO [of Lehman Brothers]) were fixed-income traders at heart, they weren't entirely up to speed on how dramatically that world had changed since the 1980s. Both had started in commercial paper, probably the sleepiest, least risky part of the firm's business. Fixed-income trading was nothing like Fuld and Gregory knew in their day: Banks were creating increasingly complex products many levels removed from the underlying asset. This entailed a much greater degree of risk, a reality that neither totally grasped and showed remarkably little interest in learning more about. While the firm did employ a well-regarded chief risk officer, Madelyn Antoncic, who had a Ph.D. in economics and had worked at Goldman Sachs, her input was virtually nil. She was often asked to leave the room when issues concerning risk came up at executive committee meetings, and in late 2007, she was removed from the committee altogether."[39]

Research suggests that, when properly implemented, risk-management functions can effectively lower the risk levels of the organization. For example, Ellul and Yerramilli (2010) found that bank holding companies with strong risk-management functions had lower enterprise risk.[40] Similarly, Ormazabal (2010) found that firms with observable risk-management activities (such as a risk committee, enterprise risk-management function, chief risk officer, risk-management policies, or other organizational structure related to risk oversight) had less volatility during the financial crisis.[41]

Endnotes

1. Dechert, LLP, "The Higgs Report on Nonexecutive Directors: Summary Recommendations" (2003). Accessed December 5, 2007. See www.dechert.com/library/Summary%20of%20Recommendations1.pdf.

2. See National Association of Corporate Directors and The Center for Board Leadership, "NACD Public Company Governance Survey" (2009). Accessed at www.nacdonline.org/. Sample includes survey responses from 632 corporate directors between April and June 2009, of which 97.5 percent of respondents considered strategic planning and oversight to be either critical or important.

3. Lockheed Martin, "Corporate Vision and Value Statements." Accessed October 21, 2010. See www.lockheedmartin.com/aboutus/ethics/VisionValueStatements. html.

4. Adapted from Gerry Johnson, Kevan Scholes, and Richard Whittington, *Exploring Corporate Strategy: Text & Cases,* 8th ed. (Essex: Pearson Education Limited, 2008).

5. Garth Saloner, Andrea Shepard, and Joel Podolny, *Strategic Management,* rev. ed. (New York: John Wiley & Sons, 2005); Michael E. Porter, *Competitive Strategy* (New York: Free Press, 1998).

6. Forbes Insights, "The Powerful Convergence of Strategy, Leadership, and Communications: Getting It Right," FD Corporate Communications (June 2009). Accessed November 8, 2010. See http://images.forbes.com/ forbesinsights/StudyPDFs/PowerfulConvergenceofStrategy.pdf.

7. Eric Olsen, Frank Plaschke, and Daniel Stelter, "The 2008 Value Creators' Report: Missing Link Focusing Corporate Strategy on Value Creation," The Boston Consulting Group (2008). Accessed December 8, 2008. See www.bcg. com/documents/file15314.pdf.

8. This is similar to the insightful work done by James L. Heskett, W. Earl Sasser, and Leonard A. Schlesinger, *The Service Profit Chain* (New York: Free Press, 1997).

9. David De Angelis and Yaniv Grinstein, "Pay for the Right Performance," *Social Science Research Network* (2010). Accessed May 26, 2010. See http://ssrn.com/ abstract=1571182.

10. See Christopher D. Ittner, David F. Larcker, and Madhav V. Rajan, "The Choice of Performance Measures in Annual Bonus Contracts," *The Accounting Review* 72 (1997): 231–255. Daniel Sungyeon Kim and Jun Yang, "Beating the Target: A Closer Look at Annual Incentive Plans," *Social Science Research Network* (2010). Accessed October 21, 2010. See http://ssrn.com/ abstract=1361814.

11. Adapted in part from Christopher D. Ittner and David F. Larcker, "Extending the Boundaries: Nonfinancial Performance Measures," in *Handbook of Management Accounting Research,* edited by Christopher S. Chapman, Anthony G. Hopwood, and Michael D. Shields (Oxford: Elsevier, 2009).

12. Christopher D. Ittner and David F. Larcker, "Coming Up Short on Nonfinancial Performance Measurement," *Harvard Business Review* 81 (2003): 88–95. Also Christopher D. Ittner and David F. Larcker (2005).

13. Stephen Gates, "Aligning Strategic Performance Measures and Results," The Conference Board, research report 1261-99-RR (October 1999). Accessed March 15, 2010. See www.conference-board.org/publications/ publicationdetail.cfm? publicationid=438.

14. The function linking customer satisfaction to financial performance is "S-shaped" and not a simple linear relation. There are likely to be diminishing returns to increases in customer satisfaction and other similar measures. See Christopher D. Ittner and David F. Larcker, "Are Nonfinancial Measures Leading Indicators of Financial Performance? An Analysis of Customer Satisfaction," *Journal of Accounting Research* 36 (1997(b) Supplement): 1–35.

15. Rajiv D. Banker, Gordon Potter, and Roger G. Schroeder, "Reporting Manufacturing Performance Measures to Workers: An Empirical Study," *Journal of Management Accounting Research* 5 (1993): 33–55.

16. Venky Nagar and Madhav V. Rajan, "The Revenue Implications of Financial and Operational Measures of Product Quality," *Accounting Review* 76 (2001): 495–514.

17. Christopher D. Ittner, David F. Larcker, and Madhav V. Rajan, "The Choice of Performance Measures in Annual Bonus Contracts," *Accounting Review* 72 (1997): 231.

18. Amal A. Said, Hassan R. HassabElnaby, and Benson Wier, "An Empirical Investigation of the Performance Consequences of Nonfinancial Measures," *Journal of Management Accounting Research* 15 (2003): 193–223.

19. Deloitte Touche Tohmatsu, "In the Dark: What Boards and Executives Don't Know about the Health of Their Businesses. A Survey by Deloitte in Cooperation with the Economist Intelligence Unit" (2004). Accessed September 2, 2008. See www.deloitte.com/dtt/article/0,1002,cid%253D157828,00.html. Deloitte Touche Tohmatsu, "In the Dark II: What Many Boards and Executives Still Don't Know About the Health of Their Businesses. Executive Survey Results from Deloitte and the Economist Intelligence Unit" (2007). Accessed September 7, 2010. See www.deloitte.com/view/en_US/us/Services/audit-enterprise-risk-services/governance-regulatory-risk-strategies/Governance-Services/4e3e344d9a0fb110VgnVCM100000ba42f00aRCRD.htm.

20. Christopher D. Ittner, David F. Larcker, and Taylor Randall, "Performance Implications of Strategic Performance Measurement in Financial Services Firms," *Accounting, Organizations & Society* 28 (2003): 715.

21. Anonymous, "Beyond Box-ticking: A New Era for Risk Governance; A Report from the Economist Intelligence Unit Sponsored by ACE and KPMG," *The Economist* (2009). Accessed November 8, 2010. See www.kpmg.com/LU/en/IssuesAndInsights/Articlespublications/Documents/Beyond-box-ticking.pdf.

22. Ormazabal (2010) found a positive stock market response to these legislative events for companies that had not disclosed risk-management activities. See Gaizka Ormazabal, "An Examination of Organizational Risk Oversight," Ph.D. dissertation, Stanford University, Graduate School of Business (2010).

23. Public companies give a laundry list of "risk factors" in the annual 10-K. It is unclear whether these are the real risks the company faces or disclosures that provide the basis of a legal defense in case something bad happens to the firm. The challenge for the board is to push management to precisely articulate the fundamental risks that can have a devastating impact on shareholders and stakeholders.

24. *The Economist* (2009).

25. Ibid.

26. See COSO, Committee of Sponsoring Organizations of the Treadway Commission, "About Us." See www.coso.org/aboutus.htm.

27. Jim Traut, "Enterprise Reputation and Risk Management at H. J. Heinz," Enterprise Risk Management Initiative (October 3, 2008). Accessed November 5, 2010. See www.mgt.ncsu.edu/erm/index.php/articles/entry/jim-traut-roundtable/.

28. Ormazabal (2010) found some evidence that volatility decreases when firms include risk management. His risk-management index is computed using publicly available data on the existence of a risk-management board committee, whether this committee has any members that have risk-management expertise, and other similar variables. See Gaizka Ormazabal (2010).

29. Ernst & Young, "Investors on Risk: The Need for Transparency," Ernst & Young Risk Survey Series (2006). Accessed August 6, 2008. See www.ey.com/GLOBAL/content.nsf/International/Global_Risk_-_Risk_Research_-_.

30. National Association of Corporate Directors and The Center for Board Leadership (2009).

31. New York Stock Exchange (NYSE) regulations require that the audit committee discuss risk-management policies and practices. However, the NYSE allows companies to assign primary responsibility for risk management to another committee, as long as the audit committee plays a continuing role in the process.

32. Financial companies, in particular, are likely to have a risk committee because financial risk is almost the same as operational risk for these companies. Even energy companies such as Duke Energy are exposed to commodity price risk, which is both financial and operational.

33. The Conference Board, "Risky Business: Is Enterprise Risk Management Losing Ground?" The Conference Board, research report 1407 (2007). Accessed August 5, 2008. See www.conference-board.org/.

34. PricewaterhouseCoopers LLP, "Managing Risk: An Assessment of CEO Preparedness," 7th Annual Global CEO Survey (2004): 27. Accessed November 8, 2010. See www.pwc.fr/7th_annual_global_ceo_survey_managing_risk.html.

35. Robert Felton and Mark Watson, "U.S. Director Opinion Survey on Corporate Governance 2002," McKinsey & Co. (2002).

36. It's likely that the majority of these companies were small or mid-sized businesses, which likely influenced responses. Cited in Alix Stuart, "They'll Take Their Chances: Many Companies Have No Intention of Adopting Enterprise Risk Management, A Survey Finds, While Many Others Have Less-Than-Robust ERM Processes," CFO.com (September 17, 2010). Accessed November 8, 2010. See www.cfo.com/article.cfm/14524925/c_14524808.

37. *The Economist* (2009).

38. Grant Kirkpatrick, "The corporate governance lessons from the financial crisis", OECD Journal: Financial Market Trends, Vol. 2009: 1-30. http://dx.doi.org/10.1787/fmt-v2009-art3-en.

39. Andrew Ross Sorkin, *Too Big to Fail: The Inside Story of How Wall Street and Washington Fought to Save the Financial System—and Themselves* (New York: Penguin, 2009).

40. Andrew Ellul and Vijay Yerramilli, "Stronger Risk Controls, Lower Risk: Evidence from U.S. Bank Holding Companies," NBER working paper series w16178, *Social Science Research Network* (2010). Accessed November 1, 2010. See http://ssrn.com/abstract=1636647.

41. Gaizka Ormazabal (2010).

7

Labor Market for Executives and CEO Succession Planning

In this chapter, we examine the labor market for executives and the CEO succession process. Corporations have a demand for qualified executives who can manage an organization at the highest level. A supply of individuals exists who have the skills needed to handle these responsibilities. The **labor market for chief executives** refers to the process by which the available supply is matched with demand. For the labor market to function properly, information must be available on the needs of the corporation and the skills of the individuals applying to serve in executive roles.

The efficiency of this market has important implications on governance quality.[1] When it is efficient, the board of directors will have the information it needs to evaluate and price CEO talent. This leads to improved hiring decisions and reasonable compensation packages. It also tends to increase discipline on managerial behavior—that is, when managers know they can lose their jobs for poor performance, they have greater incentive to perform. When this market functions inefficiently, management faces less pressure to perform and distortions can arise in the balance of power between the CEO and the board, or in excessive compensation. Executives can also be matched to the wrong job, causing inefficiencies and loss of shareholder value.[2]

In this chapter, we start by considering the factors that contribute to CEO turnover and the evidence on how likely boards are to terminate underperforming CEOs. Next, we examine the CEO selection process. We then evaluate the manner by which companies plan for and implement succession at the CEO level, including both internal and external candidates.

Labor Market for Chief Executive Officers

A discussion of the labor market for CEOs is relevant in a book about governance for several reasons. First, the chief executive officer is the primary agent responsible for managing the corporation and ensuring that long-term value is preserved and enhanced. The board of directors has a "duty" to make sure that the right person is selected for the job.

Second, if a manager knows that he or she can be replaced for poor performance, self-interested behavior is limited. In this way, the concept of a "market for labor" is similar to the concept of a "market for corporate control" (which we discuss in Chapter 11, "The Market for Corporate Control"). In the market for corporate control, the board must decide whether the company is better off under current ownership or whether it should be sold to a third party who can better manage the assets. In the labor market for chief executives, the board is asked to determine whether it is economically better to retain the current CEO, given his or her performance, or try to replace that individual with someone who may be better suited to the company's needs. In both cases, the CEO is aware that a failure to perform can lead to loss of employment, through either termination or the sale of the company.

Third, the efficiency of the labor market sets the stage for how much compensation is required to attract and retain a suitable CEO. Ultimately, a matching process takes place between the attributes that the company desires (in terms of skill set, previous experience, risk aversion, and cultural fit), the price the company is willing to pay for these attributes, and the compensation package executives are willing to accept. If these issues are clear and the relevant information is available to all parties, the market has the potential to be efficient. In principle, executives and the board will engage in an arm's-length negotiation and the resulting pay levels will be neither too high nor too low.[3]

However, it is not at all clear that the labor market for CEOs is especially efficient. For starters, executive skill sets can be difficult to evaluate. An executive who performs effectively at one company is not necessarily guaranteed to repeat this performance at another company. Even if the executive has the requisite qualifications, the board needs to control for differences in industry, the operating and financial condition of the previous employer, cultural fit, work style, predilection toward risk taking, and competitive drive before it can make a selection. For these reasons, it is difficult to predict in advance whether a candidate will succeed. This contrasts with many other labor markets, such as those for accountants or factory workers, in which the skills of an employee are more readily identifiable and easier to transfer across companies.

In addition, the efficiency of the CEO labor market is limited by its size and by the ability of executives to move among companies. A job opening for a sales manager might attract hundreds of applicants, dozens of whom have the requisite skills and are willing to consider an offer. If the company's preferred candidate turns down an offer for salary reasons, the company can either increase its offer or make an offer to a second- or third-choice candidate. Contrast this with the search for the head of a publicly traded multinational corporation, such as IBM. How many executives were capable of managing IBM when Lou Gerstner was brought in to turn the company around in 1993? Some executive recruiters have speculated that the number might have been no more than ten.[4] Regardless of whether this estimate is accurate, the limited size and liquidity of the labor market clearly influences the CEO recruitment process (see the following sidebar).

"Brain Drain" to Private Equity

The balance between supply and demand for executive talent appears to have been altered in recent years through the trend of successful CEOs moving from publicly traded companies to private-equity owned firms. Although this can potentially further distort labor market efficiency, the actual impact has not been clearly measured.

Still, some prominent examples signal just how significant the trend has been. James Kilts, former executive at both Kraft Foods and Nabisco Holding Company, later led a successful turnaround at Gillette. After the sale of Gillette to Procter & Gamble in 2005, Kilts' name surfaced as a leading CEO candidate for several consumer product companies. Instead, he left the sector of public companies and joined the advisory board of private equity firm Centerview Partners. David Calhoun, then vice chairman of General Electric, was in similar demand as a CEO candidate. Having turned down several offers, he ultimately accepted a position at market research firm VNU (owners of A.C. Nielsen and Nielsen Media Research), which was private-equity owned. He reportedly received a compensation package worth $100 million. This amount is significantly above what most public corporations can afford and serves as further indication that the deep pockets of private equity firms can induce a "brain drain" from publicly traded enterprises.[5] With available talent leaving the labor pool, the boards of publicly traded companies are potentially at a disadvantage in competing for qualified executives.

The efficiency of the labor market is also limited by a lack of uniformity among corporate circumstances and practices. Some companies are looking to develop and promote talent from within; others are looking to bring in an outsider as a catalyst for needed change. If the company is in crisis, an emergency CEO might be required to serve on an interim basis while a long-term successor is groomed. The CEO being replaced may be one who has suddenly died, been forced out for underperformance, or long scheduled to step down on a specific retirement date. In all these situations, the board is charged with finding a successor; however, the number and quality of candidates available may vary, thereby limiting the company's options.

Labor Pool of CEO Talent

The United States has more than 6,000 CEOs of publicly traded companies.[6] The average CEO has been employed at his or her company for 14 years, 5 of those years in the CEO position itself and the other years in other roles. CEO tenure varies greatly across companies, depending on the age at which a person was promoted, firm performance during CEO tenure, and perhaps the personal relationships between the board and the CEO. Although the average tenure is about five years, the distribution is highly skewed by some long-serving CEOs (see Figure 7.1).[7] Furthermore, CEO tenure has been falling in recent years as executives spend fewer years with the same company. This contrasts with broad labor market trends in which employee tenure has remained relatively constant over the past 25 years.[8]

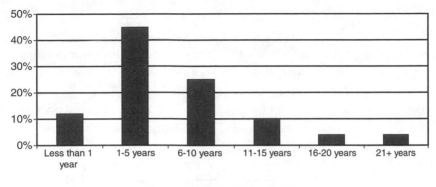

■ 2007 S&P 500 CEO Position Tenure

Source: Meghan Felicelli, "Route to the Top," Spencer Stuart (2007).

Figure 7.1   Number of years in CEO position.

In terms of experiential background, no standard career path to becoming a CEO exists. According to one study, 22 percent of the CEOs of large U.S. corporations had a background in finance, 20 percent in operations, 20 percent in marketing, 5 percent in engineering, 5 percent in law, 4 percent in consulting, and 6 percent in "other."[9] Only a third of U.S. CEOs have international experience.[10]

In terms of educational background, 21 percent of CEOs earned an undergraduate degree in engineering, 15 percent in economics, 13 percent in business administration, 8 percent in accounting, and 8 percent in liberal arts. The most commonly attended undergraduate institutions are Harvard, Princeton, Stanford, University of Texas, and University of Wisconsin. Just less than half have a master's degree in business administration. Only a small fraction of CEOs have military experience.[11] Based on interview data, executive recruiters believe that educational background is an important indicator of an individual's ability to deal with the higher levels of complexity and decision making that are required as the head of a corporation. They also believe that personal attributes, such as whether a candidate played team sports in college or whether they were the oldest child—are indicative of an individual's leadership ability. (Of course, it is not clear whether these attributes translate into better performance.) Still, primary emphasis is placed on the executive's professional track record and management style.

CEO Turnover

A CEO may leave the position for a variety of reasons, including retirement, recruitment to another firm, dismissal for poor performance, or departure following a corporate takeover. In 2009, CEO turnover was 14.3 percent on a worldwide basis.[12] Although this figure has plateaued in recent years, it has risen considerably over the last decade. For example, in 1998, the turnover rate was approximately 8 percent (see Figure 7.2).[13]

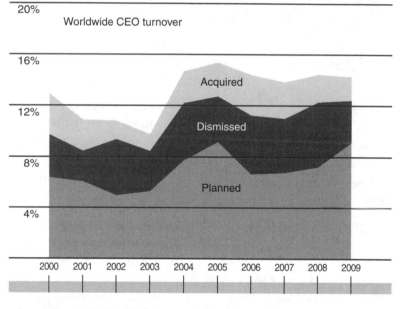

Source: Favaro, Ken, Per-Ola Karlsson, and Gary L. Neilson (2010).

Figure 7.2   CEO turnover rate.

Extensive research has examined the relationship between CEO turnover and performance.[14] Studies show that CEO turnover is inversely proportional to corporate operating and stock price performance.[15] That is, the CEOs of companies that are not performing well are more likely to step down than CEOs of companies that are performing well. We would expect this from a labor market that rewards success and punishes failure. However, the literature also finds that CEO termination is not especially sensitive to performance. Some

CEOs are unlikely to be terminated no matter how poorly they perform.[16]

This point is clearly illustrated in a study by Huson, Parrino, and Starks (2001). The authors grouped companies into quartiles based on their operating performance during rolling five-year periods. They then compared the frequency of forced CEO turnover (terminations) across quartiles. They found that, although considerable disparity in operating performance exists between the top and bottom quartiles, termination rates are not materially different. For example, during the measurement period 1983–1988, companies in the bottom quartile realized an average annual return on assets (ROA) of –3.7 percent, while companies in the highest quartile realized an average ROA of 12.0 percent, a difference of almost 16 percentage points. Still, the termination rate in the lowest quartile was a meager 2.7 percent per year, versus 0.8 percent in the highest quartile. That is, the probability of the CEO being terminated increased by only 2 *percentage points,* even though the lowest quartile delivered significantly worse profitability. Results were similar in different measurement periods and when companies were grouped by stock market returns.

For our purposes, this study suggests that labor market forces are not always effective in removing senior-level executives. Although the probabilities are correlated with performance, they remain very low. Other studies have produced similar findings. A study by Booz & Co. found that even though companies in the lowest decile in terms of stock returns underperform their industry peers by 45 percentage points over a two-year period, the probability that the CEO is forced to resign increases by only 5.7 percent.[17] Booz & Co. concluded that despite corporate governance getting "better" over time, little change has occurred in the sensitivity of termination to performance.

More recent research by Jenter and Lewellen (2010) found greater sensitivity between performance and forced termination. The authors found that 59 percent of CEOs who perform in the bottom quintile over their first five years are terminated, whereas 17 percent of those in the top quintile are terminated. The difference is even greater for "higher-quality" boards (defined as smaller boards with fewer insiders and higher stock ownership among directors). These findings differ from those of previous studies because Jenter and Lewellen measured CEO-specific relative performance over a longer time period and had a more refined measure of involuntary turnovers.[18]

Similarly, a proprietary survey by one of the authors found that 50 percent of professional executives and board members say they would terminate a CEO after four quarters of poor earnings performance. "Poor earnings performance" is defined as failure to meet internal and analyst forecasts for quarterly earnings. More than 90 percent say they would terminate a CEO after eight quarters of poor results. This data also suggests that termination is perhaps more closely related to performance than some of the studies cited earlier.[19]

Furthermore, evidence suggests that companies with strong governance systems are more likely to terminate an underperforming CEO. Fich and Shivdasani (2006) found that busy boards (boards on which a majority of outside directors serve on three or more boards and presumably do not have the time to be an effective monitor for shareholders) are significantly less likely to force CEO turnover following a period of underperformance than boards that are not busy.[20] This is consistent with evidence that we saw in Chapter 5, "Board of Directors: Structure and Consequences," that busy boards are less attentive to corporate performance than boards whose directors have fewer outside responsibilities.

Studies have also found that companies with a high percentage of outside directors, companies whose directors own a large percentage of shares, and companies whose shareholder base is concentrated among a handful of institutional investors are all more likely to terminate an underperforming CEO. This is consistent with a theory that independent oversight reduces agency costs and management entrenchment. Companies with lower-quality governance tend to "hold on" to underperforming CEOs too long. Strong oversight (by either the board or shareholders) is critical to holding CEOs accountable for company performance. Conversely, companies whose managers own a significant percentage of equity and companies whose CEO is a founding family member are less likely to see their chief executive terminated.[21]

As we would expect from even modestly efficient capital and labor markets, shareholders react positively to news that an underperforming CEO has been terminated and replaced by an outside successor.

Huson, Parrino, and Starks (2001) found excess stock returns of positive 2 to 7 percent following such announcements.[22]

Newly Appointed CEOs

Most newly appointed CEOs are internal executives. According to Booz & Co., approximately 80 percent of successions involve an internal replacement.[23] A variety of reasons explain why shareholders and stakeholders might prefer an insider. Internal executives are familiar with the company, and the board has the opportunity to evaluate their performance, leadership style, and cultural fit on a first-hand basis, giving them greater confidence that the executives will perform to expectations. Insiders bring continuity, which, if the company has been successful, can lead to a smooth transition and less disruption to operations and staffing. For this reason, well-managed companies invest in developing internal talent so that key positions can be filled following unexpected departures.

An external successor might be preferable under other circumstances. The board might be dissatisfied with recent performance or decide that the company needs to change direction. The company might lack insiders with sufficient talent or might prefer an outsider with unique experience (such as one who has successfully navigated an operational turnaround, financial restructuring, regulatory investigation, or international expansion), given the current state of the company. Because an outsider is not wedded to the company's current mode of operations or to its existing management team, an executive from outside the company might be more effective in bringing change.

The decision to recruit an external candidate, however, generally comes at a cost. According to Equilar, external CEOs receive first-year total compensation that is approximately 50 percent higher (median average) than that given to internal candidates.[24] Among small-cap companies, the disparity is even greater (see Figure 7.3). Part of the premium comes from the fact that external candidates tend to have proven experience as CEO, whereas internal candidates are promoted to the position for the first time. Furthermore, companies that recruit a candidate from the outside tend to be in financial trouble. As such, these executives require some sort of "risk premium" to take on a job that involves a higher chance of failure. Finally, external candidates must be bought out of existing employment agreements. This involves making them whole for unvested, in-the-money options, the value of which can be quite substantial. For example, when Hewlett-Packard recruited Carly Fiorina to be CEO in 1999, it offered her equity incentives worth almost $90 million, partly to compensate her for options forfeited at Lucent Technologies.[25]

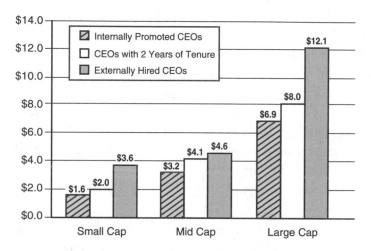

Source: Equilar Inc., "Executive Compensation Trends," (July 2008). Equilar is an executive compensation research firm.

Figure 7.3   CEO median total compensation ($MM).

The trend of looking outside the company for a CEO has increased in recent years. Murphy (1999) found that only 8.3 percent of new CEOs at S&P 500 companies were outsiders during the 1970s. By the 1990s, that figure had risen to 18.9 percent.[26] Studies have also shown that the likelihood of an external successor is inversely related to firm performance. Parrino (1997) found that approximately half of all CEOs who were forced to resign for performance reasons were replaced by an outsider, compared with only 10 percent of CEOs who voluntarily resigned or retired.[27]

Despite the promise that an outside CEO brings to many companies, considerable evidence indicates that external CEOs perform worse than internal CEOs. For example, a 2010 study by Booz & Co. found that internal CEOs delivered superior market-adjusted returns in seven out of the previous ten years.[28] Huson, Malatesta, and Parrino (2004) found improvements in operating performance (measured as ROA) following forced termination, but only mixed evidence that stock price improved.[29] However, results from these studies could be confounded by the fact that companies that require external CEOs tend to be in worse financial condition. Nevertheless, it is possible that either the practice of recruiting external candidates or the process itself is at least partly responsible for poor subsequent performance.

Models of CEO Succession

Broadly speaking, four general models of CEO succession exist:[30]

- External candidate
- President and/or COO
- Horse race
- Inside-outside model

External Candidate

The first model involves recruiting an external candidate. As discussed earlier, an external candidate is preferable when a company lacks sufficient internal candidates. Unlike internal executives, candidates recruited from the outside tend to have proven experience in the CEO role, thereby reducing the risk that they are unprepared for the responsibility. Also, because external executives are not involved in the decisions of their predecessors, they may have more freedom in making strategic, operational, or cultural changes to the firm. However, external candidates carry significant risk. Even though they are proven in terms of their ability to handle CEO-level responsibilities, they are not proven in terms of organizational fit. The work style that was successful in their previous environment might not necessarily translate well to another (see the following sidebar). External candidates are also more expensive because they need to be bought out of an existing employment contract. External candidates have greater bargaining power to negotiate compensation when they have no viable internal candidates to compete against.

Internal vs. External Succession

Nike

In November 2004, Nike announced the appointment of William Perez as president and CEO. Perez would succeed company founder Phil Knight, who retained the position of chairman.

It was not the first time Knight had tried to step away from the company he had closely managed for more than 30 years. In 1994, he had promoted insider Thomas Clarke to the position of president so he could assume a long-term strategic role as chairman and CEO. By 2000, it was clear that corporate performance was suffering, and Knight resumed control of day-to-day operations.

However, many were optimistic that the appointment of Perez would be different. First, Perez had enjoyed great success at family-controlled SC Johnson & Son, a company he had joined in 1970 and headed since 1996. His extensive experience in consumer marketing was seen as positive for a company that relied heavily on brand perception. He also had international experience, which was important as Nike expanded into new markets.

Some analysts, however, cautioned that Perez might have trouble fitting into the intensely sports-loving culture at Nike. Of particular concern was whether Perez would work well with Knight. Gerry Roche, the executive recruiter who conducted the search, was optimistic: "He gets along well with Phil. They click."[31]

Despite the optimism, Perez announced that he was stepping down just one year later. In his official statement, Perez said, "Phil and I weren't entirely aligned on some aspects of how to best lead the company's long-term growth. It became obvious to me that the long-term interests of the company would be best served by my resignation." For his part, Knight stated, "Succession at any company is challenging, and unfortunately the expectations that Bill and I and others had when he joined the company a year ago didn't play out as we had hoped."[32] It was an unusually candid assessment by both individuals.

The situation at Nike is one that recurs at many corporations when a founder or long-time CEO steps down but does not cede full control to the successor. Conflicts can result that disrupt the ability of the successor to implement new strategies or objectives. Perez touched upon this point in a subsequent interview:

"The fundamental issue was very basic. Phil didn't retire. When I joined Nike it was with the understanding that Phil was going to retire. I honestly believed he was going to step aside and let me move the ship in the right direction .... You don't need two CEOs. One is redundant, and I happened to be the redundant one."[33]

Perez was replaced by long-time insider Mark Parker, who had a more constructive relationship with Knight. Perez went on to become CEO of family-controlled Wrigley, where he successfully led the company until its sale to privately held Mars in 2008.

President and/or Chief Operating Officer

The second model of CEO succession is promoting a leading candidate to the position of president and/or chief operating officer (COO), where the executive can be groomed for eventual succession (see the following sidebar). This approach allows a company to observe how an executive performs when given CEO-level responsibility, without having to first promote that individual. In addition, it gives the executive experience interacting with the board, analysts, the press, and shareholders—constituents to whom he or she may not previously have had exposure. Because no standard set of responsibilities is associated with the COO role, the scope of the position can be customized to meet the needs of the company. In this way, the executive can be specifically tasked with overseeing a firm-wide initiative—such as product launch, international expansion, or restructuring—or trained to overcome a weakness or shortcoming. If he or she is successful, the executive can then be promoted.

At the same time, using a COO appointment in the succession process involves risks. Because it is not a standard role, the responsibilities of the position need to be well defined up front and clearly differentiated from those of the CEO. If not, decision making can suffer. Furthermore, the COO role adds structural and cultural complexity to the organization. If the direct reports of both the CEO and the COO do not clearly understand and support the leadership model of the company, internal divisions can form that undermine the success of the

COO. Finally, a clear timeline for succession needs to be established. If the COO remains in the position too long, he or she may become perceived as a "lifetime COO" and lose the internal and external support needed to win promotion.

President and COO As Chosen Successor

Verizon

In 2010, Verizon announced the appointment of Lowell McAdam as president and COO. McAdam had previously served as president of the company's wireless division. In his new role, McAdam would oversee all business groups and report to company chairman and CEO Ivan Seidenberg.

In a press release, Seidenberg stated that the move was made as part of the company's long-term succession planning: "The Board's selection of Lowell to this key, central position underscores its commitment to reward success while working with me to prepare our company for an executive transition in the future."[34] Although Seidenberg gave no indication of when he planned to step down, one insider expected that he would retire late the following year when he turned 65.[35]

Horse Race

The third model of CEO succession is the **horse race**. This model was famously used at General Electric to determine the successor to CEO Jack Welch in 2001. In a horse race, two or more internal candidates are promoted to high-level operating positions, where they formally compete to become the next CEO. Each is given a development plan to improve specific skills. Progress is measured over a specified period, with evaluations and feedback provided at predetermined milestones. At the end of the evaluation period, a winner is selected.

As with a COO appointment, a horse race allows the board to test primary candidates before granting a promotion. With this model, however, the board is not committing to a preferred successor in advance. Instead, the board has time to build consensus around a favorite.

The horse-race model also has drawbacks. Horse races tend to be highly public and bring unwanted media attention. They create a politicized atmosphere, in which board members, senior executives, and the CEO jockey to position their favored candidate to win. As such, they can be distracting to management and the organization. In addition, a horse race risks the precipitation of a talent drain. Losers of the race often leave because they do not want to report to the person they lost to and because they feel their only legitimate chance of becoming a CEO is with another company.[36]

Inside–Outside Model

In an **inside–outside model**, the company develops a forward-looking profile that lays out the skills and experiences required of the next CEO, based on the future needs of the company. Internal candidates are selected based on their potential fit with this profile. Each is given a preliminary assessment, and areas for development are identified. The candidates are then rotated into new positions where they can develop the skills and experiences needed to fill any gaps in their background. The inside–outside model is different from a horse race: While the internal evaluation is underway, the company identifies promising external candidates, who are also compared against their fit with the CEO profile. If an external candidate is demonstrably better, he or she is recruited to be CEO. If no external candidate is deemed demonstrably better, the leading internal candidate is selected. An external validation is useful in assuring the board that it is selecting the best CEO out of the entire labor market.

The inside–outside model neutralizes certain inefficiencies in the succession process. It levels the playing field between internal and external candidates. Interview data suggests that in many companies, board members are biased against internal executives because they first became acquainted with them in more junior roles and still think of them in a junior capacity. Board members do not have this bias against external candidates, even though external candidates have developed along similar career paths. The inside–outside model reduces this risk by giving the board significant exposure to internal candidates, where their leadership skills can be fully appreciated before they are compared to the external market. Experts recommend that an external candidate be selected only if he or she is 1.5 to 2 times better than the leading internal candidate.[37]

The risk of using the inside–outside model is that it requires significant planning and oversight. A common mistake occurs when the board lets the external process go on too long. When this occurs, internal candidates may feel that they are not the top choice, even if ultimately selected. This leads to an erosion of trust that affects the working relationship between the board and the new CEO well beyond the transition date.

The Succession Process

The succession-planning process relies on the full engagement of both the board of directors and senior management of the company. As a best practice, succession planning is an ongoing activity and includes preparation for both scheduled and unscheduled transitions. The most critical element of this is the continued development of internal talent. At any time, the company maintains a list of candidates that it can turn to in an emergency. It also maintains a list of primary candidates in line to replace the CEO in a planned succession.

At 37 percent of companies, the full board of directors has primary responsibility for succession; at 31 percent of companies, succession is the responsibility of the nominating and governance committee. Twenty percent of companies assign this duty to the chairman or lead director, and 11 percent of companies look to the CEO for this responsibility.[38]

When a succession event is scheduled, the board might choose to convene an ad hoc committee specifically tasked with handling the process. This committee is generally chaired by the most senior independent director. Experts recommend that directors be selected to the committee based on their qualifications and engagement rather than their availability. Qualified directors have overseen a succession or have participated in one as a CEO.[39] Because the new CEO will ultimately be selected by a vote of the full board, however, committee meetings should be open to all interested directors (see the following sidebar).

The Board-Led Search

Ford Motor

In 2006, William Ford Jr., chairman and CEO of the company his great-grandfather Henry Ford had founded more than 100 years before, hired a former Goldman Sachs executive to conduct a review of the company's operations. The review concluded that Ford's current strategy was insufficient to stem losses and that the senior executive team likely did not have the experience to bring needed change. As a result, William Ford decided to voluntarily step down as CEO and bring in an outsider to accelerate a turnaround.

Ford's actions were noteworthy in that it is rare for a founding-family CEO to voluntarily seek his or her own replacement. As Ford himself stated, "I have a lot of myself invested in this company, but not my ego."[40] The search process was also noteworthy in that it was entirely led by the board, without the help of an executive recruiter to source and screen candidates. Instead, the board identified one man—Alan Mulally of Boeing—to be Ford's chosen successor. Many boards would consider such an approach risky because it did not include a third-party expert to validate its decision.

At the time, Mulally was the head of the commercial airline division of Boeing. Although Mulally did not have experience in the automotive industry, he had significant experience at Boeing, where he had led product development for the company's 777 airline model. The board believed the two companies had many similarities: Both had long product cycles; capital-intensive operations; complex manufacturing; and similar management relations with customers, suppliers, and union employees.

As a first step, John Thornton, Ford Motor director and former president of Goldman Sachs, suggested that the company rely on an intermediary to gauge Mulally's interest. Richard Gephardt, former congressional leader, made the initial approach because the two men had worked together on labor issues. After those conversations, Thornton spoke directly with Mulally. Mulally expressed interest but noted that he had been at Boeing for almost 37 years and that he was excited to work on the company's fuel-efficient model, the 787 "Dreamliner." He agreed to discuss the opportunity further with William Ford.

Ultimately, Mulally accepted Ford's offer, and the company's head of human resources finalized the details. It was important to Mulally that he be made whole for the compensation he was fore-going by leaving Boeing. He also requested a significant incentive component that would reward him if his efforts were successful. His first-year compensation was $28 million: $2 million annual salary (prorated to $0.7 million), $18.5 million signing bonus, $1.0 million in stock awards, $7.8 million in options, and $0.3 million in other benefits.[41]

The selection of Mulally was ultimately deemed a success, as Ford was the only one of the Big Three Detroit automakers to avoid bankruptcy in 2009.

The outgoing CEO also plays an important role in the succession process. The CEO is responsible for developing talent, in the form of coaching and mentoring, and for assigning executives to areas of the organization where they can be challenged to learn new skills. This includes both job rotations and project-based work. Despite the important role the CEO plays, it is important that the board maintain primary control over the process because the board is responsible for its eventual success. This includes making sure that the CEO does not disrupt or influence the objectivity of the evaluation by advocating on behalf of a favored candidate or undermining a disfavored candidate (see the following sidebar).

Outgoing CEO Behaviors

According to research by Larcker and Miles (2011), the personality of the outgoing CEO can have an important impact on the success of a transition. To this end, they categorize CEOs into six groups based on the behaviors they exhibit during the succession process:

- **The Active Advisor**—The sitting CEO accepts that it is time to step down and is ready to do so. The CEO provides thoughtful insight into the selection process but does not overstep his or her role. The CEO limits opinions to when they are solicited and does not impose his or her "will" on the board. Disciplined, self-aware, and satisfied with the role as advisor, the CEO has full acceptance that the board will make the final decision.

- **The Aggressor**—The sitting CEO is relatively overt in his or her attempt to influence the selection decision. This type of CEO will "play nice" for most of the process only to attempt to steer the selection toward a handpicked candidate at a key decision point, undermining other candidates in the process. The CEO will take a strong position with the board and try to force the outcome he or she favors.

- **The Passive Aggressor**—The sitting CEO tries to influence the selection process in a covert manner. The CEO subtly undermines certain candidates by the way he or she positions them to the board. He or she will come across not as manipulative but instead as an advisor. If this behavior is undetected until late in the process, the board might have to start from the beginning and exclude the CEO.

- **The Capitulator**—When the board is close to making the final decision on a successor, the CEO changes his or her mind about retirement and requests to stay longer. This behavior essentially forces the board to choose between the present and the future leadership of the company. A nonexecutive director will need to meet with the CEO and firmly inform him or her that the board is moving forward with a successor.

- **The Hopeful Savior**—The sitting CEO largely identifies with the role of CEO and does not really want to retire. The CEO might actively promote successors in his or her own likeness. Alternatively, he or she might promote someone less capable in the hope that the successor will fail so that he or she can be swept back in to "save" the company.

- **The Power Blocker**—The sitting CEO also does not want to leave. He or she will throw up obstacles to slow or derail the process. The Power Blocker is different from the Hopeful Savior in the aggressiveness of approach. Whereas the Hopeful Savior is subtle, the Power Blocker is overt. He or she calls in favors with the board, makes direct personal appeals, or demands to stay.

Larcker and Miles recommend that rather than overlook the personality of the outgoing CEO, companies tailor their succession plan in part based on an assessment of how the outgoing executive might or might not attempt to influence the selection process.[42]

The next step in the succession process is to create a skills-and-experience profile. This profile is based on a forward-looking view of the company. If the future needs of the company are different from its present ones, the profile of the next CEO will be quite different from that of the outgoing CEO. The skills-and-experience profile is rooted in the company's strategy. The board identifies the attributes in terms of professional background and personal qualities required to successfully execute the strategy and achieve organizational objectives. The profile is used as a yardstick against which both internal and external candidates are benchmarked. In the case of long-term succession planning, the progress of internal candidates is measured over time. When it comes time for a succession event, either scheduled or unscheduled, the board will have a list of viable candidates, ranked in order of preference.[43]

After a new CEO has been selected and approved by a vote of the full board, the transition begins. Interviews with boards and search consultants indicate that transitions can be improved through open and honest dialogue between the CEO-elect and the board. Topics of discussion include how management and the board should interact on an ongoing basis, what each party expects from the other, the requirements for communication, what each party liked and did not like about the previous management, and how the board can support the CEO during both the transition and the tenure. This type of on-boarding activity builds trust and transparency, and lays the groundwork for a constructive relationship. The CEO-elect may also choose to improve his or her skills by engaging in coaching by a third-party professional. This allows him or her to collect additional feedback on leadership style and learn to correct behaviors that are not working. Finally, the outgoing CEO can facilitate the transition by remaining behind the scenes but accessible to the new CEO to answer questions that arise.

Interviews suggest that retaining ties to the former CEO is beneficial to the firm. This can be achieved either by inviting the departing CEO to serve (or remain) on the board or by establishing a consulting relationship. Such connections can be beneficial for two reasons. First, the outgoing CEO has unique insight into the firm that can improve the monitoring and advising functions of the boards. Second, extending ties to the outgoing CEO gives that person less incentive to take actions that boost short-term results at the expense of long-term performance in the months prior to departure. At the same time, companies face a risk that the outgoing CEO will exploit a position with the firm to extract agency costs (such as excessive perquisites) without providing substantive value to the firm.

Evans, Nagarajan, and Schloetzer (2010) found that 36 percent of companies invite the outgoing CEO to remain as director.[44] The study found that companies are more likely to retain the outgoing CEO as director when he or she retires voluntarily, is a founder or founding family member, or is succeeded by an insider without CEO experience. The company is also more likely to retain the outgoing CEO if the company has had strong stock price performance in the periods preceding the CEO transition.[45] (The performance implications of retaining a nonfounder CEO on the board are discussed more fully in Chapter 4.)

How Well Are Boards Doing with Succession Planning?

A recent survey by Heidrick & Struggles and the Rock Center for Corporate Governance at Stanford University took an inside look at CEO succession planning. Based on a sample of directors and CEOs at 140 public and private companies, the survey found a surprising lack of preparedness when it comes to succession. Only 51 percent of respondents reported that their company could name a permanent successor if called upon to do so immediately. A full 39 percent of respondents claimed to have zero viable internal candidates. Instead, respondents expected that it would take 90 days, on average, to find a permanent CEO. This raises serious questions about the attention boards are paying to this critical oversight responsibility. Many boards seem to be ignoring the intangible asset related to internal talent development.[46]

The shortcomings appear to stem from a lack of focus. On average, boards spend only two hours per year on succession planning. At most companies, the emphasis appears to be on planning for an emergency but not a permanent successor. A full 70 percent of companies have identified an emergency candidate to serve as CEO on an interim basis if the current CEO needed to be replaced immediately; however, the majority (68 percent) reported that the emergency candidate is not a candidate for the permanent position (see the following sidebar).

When a Current Director Becomes CEO

An interesting situation arises when the CEO resigns from the company and is replaced by a current director. Such a situation occurred at General Motors in 2009 (as discussed in Chapter 5). The benefit of appointing a current director to the CEO position is that the director can act as a hybrid inside-outside CEO. He or she is likely well versed in all aspects of the company, including its strategy, business model, and risk-management practices. A current director likely also has personal relationships with both the executive team and fellow board members. At the same time, this individual has not participated in the senior management team and thus does not have the legacy ties to the company that an insider would bring. On the other hand, appointing a current director to the CEO position has potential drawbacks. The most obvious of these is that it signals a lack of preparedness on the company's part to properly groom internal talent. It may also signal a lack of preparedness among the board to carry out a rigorous review process. As such, appointing a director to the CEO role could actually be an "emergency" succession in disguise.

Citrin and Ogden (2010) found that board members who become the CEO outperform all other types of candidates (including insiders, outsiders, former executives, and COO appointments). They measured performance using a combination of relative stock price returns, revenue growth, and profit growth. They concluded that "directors-turned-CEOs represent a strong blend of insider and outsider [attributes]."[47]

Survey data also suggests that only 50 percent of companies tie the succession plan to a written document that outlines the skills, competencies, and experiences required to be the CEO, based on the future needs of the company. Most companies appear to be looking for a CEO who is largely similar to the current CEO. Companies also fall short on internal talent development. Only 58 percent of companies rotate internal candidates into new positions to test their skills and further their growth as part of the grooming process. Finally, only half provide the new CEO with support during the on-boarding and transition process.

As this data indicates, many boards do not engage in rigorous succession planning. Instead, succession planning appears often to consist merely of "names in a box," aimed to satisfy compliance requirements but insufficient to handle an inevitable change in senior management. This may explain why so many companies seem ill-prepared when a CEO suddenly steps down. Succession planning would be improved if it were treated instead as an important element of risk management, with potential disruptions to the organization minimized by ensuring that internal talent is always being developed and external talent identified to manage the company in case of a sudden transition (see the following sidebar).

Succession as a Risk-Management Issue

In recent years, more attention has been paid to succession planning as a risk-management issue. In 2009, the Securities and Exchange Commission (SEC) began allowing shareholders to sponsor proposals on the annual proxy requiring companies to develop succession plans and disclose these plans to investors. Previously, such proposals could be excluded from the proxy under Rule 14a-8(i)(7), which allowed omission for matters "relating to the company's ordinary business operations."[48] In explaining its change of position, the SEC wrote that "we now recognize that CEO succession planning raises a significant policy issue regarding the governance of the corporation that transcends the day-to-day business matter of managing the workforce."[49] A handful of such proposals were put before shareholders in 2010, but the majority did not receive approval.[50]

Similarly, Moody's Investors Services includes CEO succession planning as one factor contributing to a company's overall credit rating: "[E]ffective succession planning—especially CEO succession planning—[is] critical to the sound management and oversight of an organization." Moody's lists the practices it sees as important for reducing transition risk:

- A track record of smooth transitions

- Active leadership-development programs

- Board involvement in succession, including frequent discussion and interaction with key executives

- An independent board

- Active CEO involvement

- Emergency plan in place[51]

The External Search Process

Approximately 10 to 20 successful external searches for a new CEO take place among Fortune 500 companies each year. In most of these searches, the board of directors hires a third-party recruiter. The need for an external search indicates that either these companies did not have sufficient internal talent development programs in place to groom a successor, the boards felt their companies required an external candidate to bring about change, or simply the use of an external expert was a necessary part of the due diligence process for selecting a CEO.

The external search market in the United States is characterized by significant concentration. Two firms handle the vast majority of external searches: Heidrick & Struggles and Spencer Stuart. Furthermore, searches are concentrated among just a few influential consultants.

Potential benefits come from a system dominated by a few well-connected search firms and consultants. Well-connected individuals can efficiently assemble information about the needs and capabilities of a vast number of companies and executives. Through their social and professional networks, they gain access to qualitative information about an executive's reputation and potential cultural fit with various firms. This information can be critical to understanding how an executive's proven track record and operation skills will translate into a different environment.

At the same time, market concentration has potential shortcomings. By relying on a select group of recruiters, companies could be limiting the size of the candidate pool. Despite the extensive networks of certain recruiters, experienced talent could be excluded while an established set of executives is recycled among firms. Stated another way, lack of competition among search firms may limit the competition among executives for CEO positions. For example, consider an anecdote related in a 2005 *Fortune* article about the influence of Gerry Roche of Heidrick & Struggles:

> In 2000, [Gerry Roche] was counseling [then-CEO Jack] Welsh on succession at General Electric, which gave him an edge when Jeff Immelt was anointed the next CEO. ... In a frenzied two-day period, he placed GE's also-rans Bob Nardelli and Jim McNerney, as CEOs at Home Depot and 3M, respectively. He got the gigs largely because he happened to be buddies with Home Depot co-founder and director Ken Langone and 3M director (and former Sears CEO) Ed Brennan.[52]

This anecdote raises questions over the suitability of matches made in a short period of time by recruiters who might not take the time to do a truly comprehensive search. If this is the case, it would tend to reduce the efficiency of the CEO labor market.

Some aspects of the process that might be potential problems include the following:

- The search consultant may have excessive influence over the selection of candidates. Although directors and other senior executives are invited to nominate qualified external candidates, the search consultant tends to determine who is identified and contacted.

- The search consultant is given considerable responsibility for assessing the pool of candidates and reducing it to a group of finalists. Board members generally do not participate in preliminary interviews, which are handled by the consultant.

- The board might not see enough finalists to make an informed decision. Typically, only three or four finalists are brought before the board committee for in-person interviews (sometimes only one candidate is). The board tends to make a decision after a handful of interviews, each lasting a few hours. Members of the senior management team are generally not invited to interview the finalists, and interaction with the broader team is not assessed to determine fit.

- The process for determining fair compensation might not be efficient (see the following sidebar). The search consultant (sometimes in conjunction with the candidate's personal compensation consultant or lawyer) provides input to the company regarding the necessary compensation for the deal to be consummated. Third parties might have a conflict of interest in negotiating compensation if their own compensation is expressed as a percentage of the CEO-elect's first-year compensation. Furthermore, both sides know that once a preferred candidate is identified, the board is unlikely to let the deal fall apart for salary reasons, given how time-intensive the search process is.

Severance Agreements

Under a **severance agreement** (or **golden parachute**), a CEO is entitled to additional compensation upon resignation or dismissal. The terms of the agreement are typically included in the broader employment agreement and must be disclosed to shareholders through SEC filings. The following are examples:

- **American Electric Power**—"In the event the Company terminates the Agreement for reasons other than cause, [CEO Michael] Morris will receive a severance payment equal to two times his annual base salary.... In January 2005, the Board adopted a policy to seek shareholder approval for any future severance agreement with any senior executive officer of the Company when any such agreement would result in specified benefits provided to the officer in excess of 2.99 times his or her salary and bonus."[53]

- **Home Depot**—"Mr. Nardelli and the Company have agreed in principle to the terms of a separation agreement which would provide for payment of the amounts he is entitled to receive under his pre-existing employment contract entered into in 2000. Under this agreement, Mr. Nardelli will receive consideration currently valued at approximately $210 million (including amounts which have previously been earned or vested). This consideration will include a cash severance payment of $20 million, the acceleration of unvested deferred stock awards currently valued at approximately $77 million and unvested options with an intrinsic value of approximately $7 million, the payment of earned bonuses and long-term incentive awards of approximately $9 million, the payment of account balances under the Company's 401(k) plan and other benefit programs currently valued at approximately $2 million, the payment of previously earned and vested deferred shares with an approximate value of $44 million, the payment of the present value of retirement benefits currently valued at approximately $32 million, and the payment of $18 million for other entitlements under his contract which will be paid over a four-year period and will be forfeited if he does not honor his contractual obligations."[54]

Considerable controversy exists over the use of severance agreements. Critics assert that severance payments have little incentive value because they are not associated with job performance (sometimes labeled as **pay for failure**). Severance agreements might also discourage or retard the process of dismissing an underperforming CEO. (Although not commonly discussed, interviews with board members suggest that directors often ask the cost to get rid of a poorly performing CEO.)

On the other hand, severance agreements may provide benefits to the firm. By promising compensation upon leaving the firm, severance agreements discourage management entrenchment (that is, there are financial incentives for the executive to leave the firm voluntarily). They also allow CEOs to take calculated risks to build shareholder value by promising compensation even if the efforts fail and result in termination. These incentives may be particularly valuable for younger CEOs who have not yet accumulated substantial wealth or reputation and would otherwise be more risk averse.

Yermack (2006) studied the use of severance agreements among Fortune 500 companies. He found that severance agreements are in place among 80 percent of executives, with a mean present value of $5.4 million. Payments made under these agreements take various forms: ongoing consulting or noncompete agreements (30 percent), lump-sum payments (21 percent), increases in the defined benefit pension plan (18 percent), equity award adjustments (16 percent), and other contracted severance payments (13 percent). Yermack found that shareholders tend to react negatively to the announcement of a severance agreement, suggesting that they are seen as destroying value or a form of rent extraction.[55]

One potential remedy for balancing the conflicting incentives of severance agreements is to assign them a limited term (say, the first three years of a new CEO's tenure). Such a move would protect the CEO from legitimate risks such as early sale of the company or irrational termination but would be phased out after the period of heightened risk has passed.

Endnotes

1. We loosely define an efficient labor market as one in which the right candidates are recruited into the right positions at the right compensation levels.

2. One method for estimating the efficiency of labor markets is to look at stock price performance following the unexpected death of a CEO. If the "right" executive is in the CEO position, the stock price should go down following an unexpected death. If the "wrong" executive is in the CEO position, the stock price should go up. Johnson, Magee, Nagarajan, and Newman (1985) found no uniform pattern across a sample of sudden deaths, but did find evidence that inappropriate appointments might take place at the company-specific level. Salas (2007) found similar results. See W. Bruce Johnson, Robert P. Magee, Nandu J. Nagarajan, and Harry A. Newman, "An Analysis of the Stock-Price Reaction to Sudden Executive Deaths—Implications for the Managerial Labor Market," *Journal of Accounting & Economics* 7 (1985): 151–174. Jesus M. Salas, "Entrenchment, Governance, and the Stock Price Reaction to Sudden Executive Deaths," *Journal of Banking & Finance* 34 (2010): 656–666.

3. Third-party agents are often involved in contract negotiations, which can distort the size and structure of compensation packages. Rajgopal, Taylor, and Venkatachalam (2008) found that CEOs who use a third-party agent receive first-year compensation that is significantly higher ($10 million) than those who do not. The study found that CEOs who use such agents tend to deliver superior operating and stock price performance, suggesting that premium compensation could be merited. See Shiva Rajgopal, Daniel Taylor, and Mohan Venkatachalam, "Frictions in the CEO Labor Market: The Role of Talent Agents in CEO Compensation?" working paper (2008). Accessed July 23, 2008. See www.stanford.edu/~djtaylor/research/RTV.pdf.

4. Interviews by the authors with executive recruiters, September 2008; proprietary data.

5. Rik Kirkland, Doris Burke, and Telis Demos, "Private Money," *Fortune* 155 (2007): 50–60.

6. Based on listings of companies trading on the NYSE (2,200), NASDAQ (3,200), and American Stock Exchange (460). See Securities and Exchange Commission.

7. Meghan Felicelli, "Route to the Top," Spencer Stuart (November 1, 2007). Accessed August 6, 2008. See http://content.spencerstuart.com/sswebsite/pdf/lib/Final_Summary_for_2008_publication.pdf.

8. Craig Copeland, "Employee Tenure, 2008," EBRI Notes 31 (January 2010): 1-20. *Social Science Research Network*. Accessed October 5, 2010. See http://ssrn.com/abstract=1532899.

9. Burak Koyuncu, Shainaz Firfiray, Björn Claes, and Monika Hamori, "CEOs with a Functional Background in Operations: Reviewing Their Performance and Prevalence in the Top Post," *Human Resource Management* 49 (2010): 869–882.

10. Meghan Felicelli.

11. Ibid. See also Efraim Benmelech and Carola Frydman, "Military CEOs," Harvard University working paper (2010). Accessed November 10, 2010. See www.defence-officers-in-business.com/resources/articles/military%20CEOs_Apr_2010.pdf. The authors found some evidence that military CEOs perform better during downturns.

12. Favaro, Ken, Per-Ola Karlsson, and Gary L. Neilson 2010. "CEO Succession 2000-2009: A Decade of Convergence and Compression." Booz & Company Inc., *strategy+business* 59, Summer 2010. http://www.strategy-business.com/article/10208. The sample included CEOs of the 2,500 largest publicly traded companies globally.

13. Chuck Lucier, Rob Schuyt, and Edward Tse, "CEO Succession 2004: The World's Most Prominent Temp Workers," Booz & Company, Inc., *strategy+business* 39 (Summer 2005). Accessed May 28, 2008. See www.strategy-business.com/article/05204?gko=664cd.

14. See James A. Brickley, "Empirical Research on CEO Turnover and Firm Performance: A Discussion," *Journal of Accounting & Economics* 36 (2003): 227–233.

15. Srinivasan (2005) found that more than half of CEOs step down following a restatement that requires the company to reduce net income. Similarly, Arthaud-Day, Certo, Dalton, and Dalton (2006) found that CEOs are almost twice as likely to be terminated in the two years following a major financial restatement; CFOs are almost 80 percent more likely to be terminated. See Suraj Srinivasan, "Consequences of Financial Reporting Failure for Outside Directors: Evidence from Accounting Restatements and Audit Committee Members," *Journal of Accounting Research* 43 (2005): 291–334. Marne L. Arthaud-Day, S. Trevis Certo, Catherine M. Dalton, and Dan R. Dalton, "A Changing of the Guard: Executive and Director Turnover Following Corporate Financial Restatements," *Academy of Management Journal* 49 (2006): 1,119–1,136.

16. It is difficult to determine from public sources whether a CEO has been terminated or voluntarily resigned. Most public announcements refer to CEO departures as retirements, and some "educated guesses" are needed to determine whether a departure was involuntary.

17. Per-Ola Karlsson, Gary L. Neilson, and Juan Carlos Webster, "CEO Succession 2007: The Performance Paradox," Booz & Company, Inc., *strategy+business* 51 (Summer 2007). Accessed July 7, 2008. See www.booz.com/global/home/what_we_think/reports_and_white_papers/ic-display/41901844.

18. Dirk Jenter and Katharina Lewellen, "Performance-Induced CEO Turnover," Stanford University, NBER, Tuck School at Dartmouth working paper (February 2010). Accessed September 29, 2010. See www.stanford.edu/~djenter/CEO_Turnover_February_2010.pdf.

19. David F. Larcker and Burson-Marsteller, proprietary study (2001).

20. Eliezer M. Fich and Anil Shivdasani, "Are Busy Boards Effective Monitors?" *Journal of Finance* 61 (2006): 689–724.

21. James A. Brickley.

22. Mark R. Huson, Robert Parrino, and Laura T. Starks, "Internal Monitoring Mechanisms and CEO Turnover: A Long-Term Perspective," *Journal of Finance* 56 (2001): 2,265–2,297.

23. Per-Ola Karlsson, Gary L. Neilson, and Juan Carlos Webster.

24. Equilar Inc., "Executive Compensation Trends," Equilar, an executive compensation research firm (2008). Accessed October 14, 2008. See www.equilar.com/newsletter/2008_06/2008_06_ect_main.html.

25. "New HP CEO to Get Stock and Options Worth $90 Million," *Reuters News* (September 21, 1999).

26. Kevin J. Murphy. "Executive Compensation," *Social Science Research Network* (1999). Accessed July 27, 2010.

27. Robert Parrino, "CEO Turnover and Outside Succession: A Cross-Sectional Analysis," *Journal of Financial Economics* 46 (1997): 165–197.

28. Ken Favaro, Per-Ola Karlsson, and Gary L. Neilson.

29. Comparisons were made to industry benchmarks. See Mark R. Huson, Paul H. Malatesta, and Robert Parrino, "Managerial Succession and Firm Performance," *Journal of Financial Economics* 74 (2004): 237–275.

30. Content in the following two sections is adapted with permission from David F. Larcker and Brian Tayan, "Multimillionaire Matchmaker: An Inside Look at CEO Succession Planning," Stanford GSB Case No. CG-21 (April 15, 2010). Copyright © 2010 by the Board of Trustees of the Leland Stanford Junior University. All rights reserved. Used with permission from the Stanford University Graduate School of Business.

31. Stephanie Kang and Joann S. Lublin, "Nike Taps Perez of S.C. Johnson to Follow Knight," *Wall Street Journal*, (November 19, 2004, Eastern edition): A.3.

32. Joann S. Lublin and Stephanie Kang, "Nike's Chief to Exit After 13 Months: Shakeup Follows Clashes with Co-Founder Knight; Veteran Parker to Take Over," *Wall Street Journal* (January 23, 2006, Eastern edition).

33. Stephanie Kang, "He Said/He Said: Knight, Perez Tell Different Nike Tales," *Wall Street Journal* (January 24, 2006, Eastern edition).

34. Verizon press release (September 20, 2010): "Verizon Clarifies Succession Plans; Names Lowell McAdam As COO." Accessed November 10, 2010. See http://newscenter.verizon.com/press-releases/verizon/2010/verizon-clarifies-succession.html.

35. Shayndi Raice, "Verizon to Name President, COO—Carrier Taps Wireless Chief McAdam for Roles, Revealing Likely Succession Plan for CEO Seidenberg," *Wall Street Journal* (September 20, 2010, Eastern edition).

36. See also James M. Citrin, "Is a 'Horse Race' the Best Way to Pick CEOs?" Wall Street Journal Online (August 3, 2009). Accessed November 10, 2010. See http://online.wsj.com/article/SB124898329172394739.html.

37. Stephen A. Miles and Jeffery S. Sanders, "Creating CEO Succession Processes," Directorship.com (posted January 27, 2010). Accessed November 10, 2010. See www.directorship.com/creating-ceo-succession/.

38. David F. Larcker and Stephen A. Miles, "2010 Survey on CEO Succession Planning," Heidrick & Struggles and the Rock Center for Corporate Governance at Stanford University (2010). See www.gsb.stanford.edu/cgrp/topics/succession/surveys.html. Copyright © 2010 by Heidrick & Struggles and the Board of Trustees of the Leland Stanford Junior University. All rights reserved.

39. Author interview with Stephen A. Miles, vice chairman of Heidrick & Struggles, September 30, 2009.

40. Monica Langley and Jeffrey McCracken, "Designated Driver Ford Taps Boeing Executive As CEO; Alan Mulally Succeeds Bill Ford, Who Keeps Post of Chairman; A Board Swings into Action," *Wall Street Journal* (September 6, 2006, Eastern edition).

41. Ford Motor Company, Form DEF 14-A, filed with the Securities and Exchange Commission April 4, 2008.

42. David F. Larcker and Stephen A. Miles (2011). Research in progress.

43. The board should not presume that its favored candidate, internal or external, will accept the job. For this reason, multiple candidates should always be considered, and contingency plans should be in place in case events do not unfold as anticipated. Recruiters recommend that companies engage in regular communication with internal candidates, but survey results suggest that only half of companies do so. A majority (65 percent) have not asked internal candidates whether they want the CEO job or, if offered, whether they would accept. See David F. Larcker and Stephen A. Miles (2010).

44. This study is based on John Harry Evans, Nandu J. Nagarajan, and Jason D. Schloetzer, "CEO Turnover and Retention Light: Retaining Former CEOs on the Board," *Journal of Accounting Research* 48 (2010): 1,015–1,047.

45. Jason D. Schloetzer, "Retaining Former CEOs on the Board," *The Conference Board,* Director Notes, no. DN-015 (September 2010). Accessed October 1, 2010. See www.conference-board.org/publications/publicationdetail.cfm?publicationid=1854.

46. David F. Larcker and Stephen A. Miles (2010).

47. James M. Citrin and Dayton Ogden, "Succeeding at Succession," *Harvard Business Review* 88 (November 2010): 29–31. Accessed November 17, 2010. See https://archive.harvardbusiness.org/cla/web/pl/product.seam?c=7105&i=7107&cs=5933466214cd23f7888714d905a6fe07.

48. Securities Lawyer's Deskbook, "Rule 14-8: Proposals of Security Holders." See www.law.uc.edu/CCL/34ActRls/rule14a-8.html.

49. SEC Staff Legal Bulletin 14E (CF), "Shareholder Proposals" (October 27, 2009). See www.sec.gov/interps/legal/cfslb14e.htm.

50. See David F. Larcker, and Brian Tayan, "CEO Succession Planning: Who's Behind Door Number One?" Stanford Closer Look Series, CGRP-05, (June 24, 2010). See www.gsb.stanford.edu/cgrp/research/closer_look.html. Copyright © 2010 by the Board of Trustees of the Leland Stanford Junior University. All rights reserved.

51. Christian Plath, "Moody's Corporate Governance: Analyzing Credit and Governance Implications of Management Succession Planning," Moody's Investor Service (May 15, 2008). Accessed November 6, 2010. See http://ssrn.com/abstract=1285082.

52. Patricia Sellers, Karen Keller, Patricia Neering, and Oliver Ryan, "Clash of the Corporate Kingmakers," *Fortune* 152 (July 25, 2005): 58–68.

53. American Electric Power, Form DEF-14A, filed with the Securities and Exchange Commission March 14, 2005. The IRS prohibits the tax deductibility of severance agreements that exceed 2.99 times the executive's base salary and bonus. See Internal Revenue Code Section 280G, "Golden Parachute Payments."

54. The Home Depot, Form 8-K, filed with the Securities and Exchange Commission January 4, 2007.

55. David Yermack, "Golden Handshakes: Separation Pay for Retired and Dismissed CEOs," *Journal of Accounting and Economics* 41 (2006): 237–256.

8

Executive Compensation and Incentives

In this chapter, we examine executive compensation and incentives. Executive officers develop the corporate strategy and business model, and oversee daily management of the firm. As with any employee, executives require compensation for their work.[1] Compensation packages must be sufficient in terms of their level and structure to attract, retain, and motivate qualified executives to create shareholder or stakeholder value.

The compensation committee and the independent directors on the board approve the compensation program. In theory, this should be a simple exercise. The "right" amount of compensation to be paid is the minimum amount it takes to attract and retain a qualified individual. After all, this is the same calculus that goes into setting compensation for all other job functions. However, several factors complicate how this works in practice. As we saw in the previous chapter, the labor market for chief executive officers does not appear to be highly efficient. Because of potential imbalances between supply and demand and the difficulty in evaluating the quality of candidates, it is not always easy for boards to identify the appropriate executive or the market wage necessary to attract this individual. Moreover, some board members might provide insufficient oversight (because of a lack of independence, insufficient engagement, or a lack of power relative to the CEO) during the compensation-setting process. These factors have the potential to distort executive compensation packages, in terms of both size and structure.

Further complicating the process is the large amount of scrutiny that this issue receives from the media and Congress.[2] Although some of this attention is merited, the intensity with which many observers have established their position has influenced the tone of the debate, making it difficult to arrive at a reasoned decision about how much compensation is appropriate.

The Controversy over Executive Compensation

Executive compensation has long been a controversial topic in corporate America. In the 1930s, economic depression coupled with enhanced disclosure laws mandated by the Securities and Exchange Commission (SEC) stoked popular outrage over some executive compensation packages. Particular ire was reserved for the compensation paid to executives of the industrial and financial powerhouses of the time, including Bethlehem Steel, General Motors, American Tobacco, and National City Bank, who each received compensation in excess of $1 million. The sentiment of the era is perhaps best encapsulated by Justice Thomas Swan of the Circuit Court of Appeals, who wrote that "no man can be worth $1,000,000 a year."[3]

However, the debate was more muted in the decades following World War II. This is primarily because executive compensation grew at more modest rates between the 1950s and 1970s, well below those of inflation and general wages.[4] High marginal income tax rates (more than 70 percent for top earners) helped to lower the overall size of executive salaries. Few executives received compensation more than the psychologically important $1 million mark.

However, the trend reversed itself in the 1980s. During a period characterized first by high inflation and then by rapid economic growth, executive compensation ballooned. The trend coincided with a compensation shift away from fixed salaries and annual bonuses toward variable pay tied to long-term performance targets and stock options.[5] Several executives received generous payouts. For example, in 1987, Charles Lazarus of Toys R Us, Michael Blumenthal of Unisys, and Lee Iacocca of Chrysler all received bonuses in excess of $10 million.[6] Investment bankers, Wall Street traders, and private equity partners saw similar increases in pay.

In the 1990s and 2000s, the widespread adoption of stock options accelerated the trend. Exploding corporate profits and a strong bull market enabled several executives to profit handsomely. According to the *Wall Street Journal,* 16 executives of major corporations received total stock option compensation in excess of $500 million between 1992 and 2005, including William McGuire of HealthSouth ($2.1 billion), Larry Ellison of Oracle ($1.5 billion), Sandy Weill of Citigroup ($980 million), and Michael Eisner of Disney ($920 million).[7] Furthermore, total compensation figures were increased by supplemental payments (those made beyond salary and bonuses) that were not always transparently disclosed to investors. Examples included deferred compensation, golden parachutes, and supplemental executive retirement plans (SERPs). The most famous payouts were made to Robert Nardelli of Home Depot ($210 million), Hank McKinnell of Pfizer ($83 million), Lee Raymond of ExxonMobil ($405 million), and Dick Grasso of the New York Stock Exchange ($187.5 million), all in conjunction with their retirements.[8]

Outside observers have decried the trend. According to the AFL–CIO "Executive PayWatch," the ratio of pay between the average CEO and the average company employee has grown to unacceptable levels, rising from 42 in 1980, to 525 by 2000, and down to 263 by 2009.[9] The union has blasted corporations for a large discrepancy in the structure and value of post-retirement benefits paid to executives compared to those received by the average employee. Even public company directors indicate that pay levels might have gotten out of hand. According to a survey by *Corporate Board Member* magazine, 60 percent of directors believe that U.S. company boards are having trouble controlling the size of CEO compensation.[10]

Critics believe that the problem is systemic. Bebchuk and Fried (2006) succinctly expressed this view:

> Flawed compensation arrangements have not been limited to a small number of "bad apples"; they have been widespread, persistent, and systemic. Furthermore, the problems have not resulted from temporary mistakes or lapses of judgment that boards can be expected to correct on their own; rather, they have stemmed from structural defects in the underlying governance structures that enable executives to exert considerable influence over their boards.[11]

Is this true? To find out, we review the size and structure of compensation packages. We consider the incentive value of certain compensation elements, including annual bonuses and equity-linked plans. We also identify potential areas of concern and highlight decisions the board can make to ensure that executive interests are aligned with those of the shareholder. We end with a discussion of regulatory and activist efforts to rein in executive compensation and consider the positive and negative effects of these efforts.

Components of Compensation

The compensation committee of the board of directors recommends the compensation of the chief executive officer and other senior executives. This work is typically performed in consultation with the human resources and finance departments and third-party compensation consultants. Compensation packages are approved by a vote of the independent directors of the full board of directors. A vote of shareholders must generally approve equity-based compensation plans (such as stock option plans and restricted stock awards).

The details of the compensation plan—including those that require shareholder approval and those that do not—are described in the annual proxy. This includes the "fair value" of the total compensation awarded to the chief executive officer and other named officers in each of the previous three years, and values realized by these individuals through the exercise or vesting of equity-based grants. The SEC has required that corporations also include a Compensation Discussion & Analysis (CD&A) section in the proxy. The CD&A includes information that might be useful to shareholders in evaluating the compensation program, including the company's compensation philosophy, elements of the pay package, total compensation awarded, the peer groups used for comparative purposes in designing compensation and measuring performance, performance metrics used to award variable pay, pay equity between the CEO and other senior executives, stock ownership guidelines, clawback policies, severance agreements, golden parachutes, and post-retirement compensation.[12]

A compensation plan serves three primary purposes.[13] First, it must *attract* the right people—those with the skill set, experience, and behavioral profile necessary to succeed in the position. Second, it must be sufficient to *retain* those individuals; otherwise they will leave to work at another organization that offers more appropriate compensation for their talents. Third, it must provide the right incentives to *motivate* them to perform appropriately. This includes encouraging behaviors that are consistent with the corporate strategy and risk profile of the organization and discouraging self-interested behavior.

The executive compensation package generally includes some or all of the following elements:

- **Annual salary**—Fixed cash payment made evenly during the course of the year. Section 162(m) of the Internal Revenue Code limits the tax deductibility of executive compensation greater than $1 million, unless such compensation is performance driven. The fixed salary is typically set at the beginning of the year.

- **Annual bonus**—Additional payment usually in the form of cash awarded if the yearly performance of the company exceeds specified financial and nonfinancial targets. The size of the bonus is commonly expressed as a percentage of base salary and might include a guaranteed minimum and specified maximum.

  The bonus computation might also include a discretionary element. This can be desirable because all aspects of performance cannot be forecast perfectly (for example, reasonable targets might be impossible to achieve when macroeconomic or industry factors change in a negative way). The board might want to reward executives for their efforts if they do well in a year when economic conditions impact their performance relative to what was expected when the goals were first established.[14] However, discretionary elements can have negative consequences if they reward executives without regard to performance. In this case, discretionary bonuses might indicate that the board has been coopted by management. The compensation committee must make the important choice of a formulaic versus subjective bonus plan, which is a necessary disclosure in the CD&A. Furthermore, a discretionary cash bonus requires disclosure through a Form 8-K upon adoption.[15]

- **Stock options**—Right to buy shares in the future at a fixed exercise price, generally equal to the stock price on the grant date. Stock options typically have vesting requirements (that is, they are "earned" in even batches over time or in blocks, such as 25 percent at the end of each of the next four years) and expire after ten years (with seven years being the next-most-popular term). Some companies adopt "hold to retirement" or "hold past retirement" requirements for equity awards. These features encourage long-term equity ownership and are intended to align the interests of executives with those of shareholders. Other companies structure their stock option programs to include above-market strike prices or performance-based features that require the company to achieve certain targets before the executive can realize value from the grants (see the following sidebar). These features can be especially effective because they have tougher targets and provide substantial rewards to executives only if firm performance is outstanding. Performance-based criteria are common practice in the United Kingdom and Australia but are still relatively rare in the United States. For example, a study by Frederic W. Cook found that among the top 250 firms, only 5 percent have performance vesting.[16]

Premium and Performance-Based Stock Options

Premium Options

Premium options are those with exercise prices higher than current market prices. In 1997, ADC Telecommunications structured its stock option program as follows: One-third of the options had a strike price equal to 120 percent of the market price of the stock on the grant date, one-third had a strike price that was 135 percent of market price, and one-third had a strike price that was 145 percent. Each set of options vested four years from the grant date and carried a seven-year term.[17] That is, executives could not realize any value from this program until a minimum shareholder return of 20 percent was created. At higher stock prices, the value grew in a stepped-up function. The payoff structure for these options is "convex" (that is, the payoff increases by a factor of three as the stock price moves from 120 percent to 145 percent of stock price at the grant date). This type of plan provides considerable incentives for executives to make strategic decisions (potentially highly risky ones) that will substantially increase stock price.

Performance-Vested Options (Based on Accounting Performance)

This variety of options has accelerated vesting provisions contingent upon achieving accounting-based performance metrics. In 1999, Perkin Elmer granted options to the CEO that carried a ten-year term and vested after six years. However, vesting would be accelerated if one of two targets was met: three consecutive years of a 15 percent per year growth in earnings per share or a 50 percent cumulative earnings-per-share growth during a two-year period (adjusted for acquisitions and divestitures).[18] In this case, the board might feel more comfortable paying realized stock option compensation only after superior accounting and operating performance.

Performance-Vested Options (Based on Stock Performance)

These options have accelerated vesting provisions contingent upon total stock price returns. In 1997, Enron granted 1,275,000 stock options in two batches to Chairman Kenneth Lay, each with at-market strike prices. Twenty percent of the options vested immediately, and the remaining 80 percent vested over seven years. The vesting schedule would accelerate if Enron's share price increased at 120 percent of the rate of the S&P 500 Index in calendar years 1997–1999.[19] This type of performance criterion guards against large stock option compensation when a company is simply following a general upward market trend.

Performance-Vested Options (Based on Nonfinancial Performance Metrics)

These options have accelerated vesting provisions contingent upon achieving major strategic goals. Advanced Tissue Sciences tied the acceleration of vesting to the U.S. Food and Drug Administration's approval of the experimental treatment Dermagraft, used to treat diabetic foot ulcers.[20] Strategic milestones should be highly correlated with firm value.

- **Restricted stock**—Outright grant of shares that are restricted in terms of transferability and are subject to a time-based vesting schedule. Performance accelerated vesting is relatively rare in the U.S., but it is common for firms outside of the U.S. When vested, they are economically equivalent to a direct investment in company stock.

As mentioned before, shareholders must approve equity-based compensation plans, including restricted stock and stock options. The frequency with which this occurs is shown in Table. 8.1.

Table 8.1 Number of Times Companies Have Sought Shareholder Approval for Equity-Based Compensation Plans (2001–2010)

Number of Votes	Number of Companies	Percent
0	1,038	21.5%
1	1,425	29.6%
2	973	20.2%
3	677	14.0%
4	391	8.1%
5	166	3.4%
6	79	1.6%
7	44	0.9%
8	11	0.23%
9	15	0.31%
10	2	0.04%

Two companies submitted an equity compensation plan for shareholder approval *every year* during the measurement period (Plantronics and Range Resources). Fifteen companies sought such approval every year except one, including Adobe, Chesapeake Energy, Electronic Arts, and eBay.

Source: Christopher Armstrong, Ian Gow, and David Larcker, "Consequences of Shareholder Rejection of Equity Compensation Plans," working paper (2010).

- **Performance units (shares)**—Cash (or stock) awards granted only after specified financial and nonfinancial targets are met during a three- to five-year time period. Performance units and performance shares work the same way, the difference being whether the final award is paid in cash or in stock. The size of the award is generally based on a percentage of base salary, similar to the method used to calculate the annual cash bonus. The maximum award is usually 200 percent of the target. In many ways, performance plans are simply a longer-term version of the annual bonus plan. The performance criteria generally include some type of profit measure (such as earnings-per-share growth or return on assets) or total shareholder return.

- **Perquisites**—Other amenities purchased or provided by the company, such as personal use of the company car or airplane, club memberships, or a home or apartment.

- **Contractual agreements**—Other cash or stock payments stipulated in the employment agreement, such as severance agreements, post-retirement consulting agreements, and golden parachutes (payments made upon a change in control).

- **Benefits**—Other benefits provided with employment, such as health insurance, post-retirement health insurance, defined contribution retirement accounts (401[k]), supplemental executive retirement plans (SERPs), life insurance, payment for the use of a personal financial planner, and reimbursement of taxes owed on taxable benefits.

The compensation package might also be subject to certain contractual restrictions:

- **Stock ownership guidelines**—The minimum amount of stock that an executive is required to hold during employment, generally expressed as a multiple of base salary. Among the Fortune 250 companies, 80.6 percent have stock ownership guidelines, typically of an amount equal to five times base salary.[21] (Executive stock ownership guidelines are discussed more fully in Chapter 9, "Executive Equity Ownership." Director stock ownership guidelines are discussed in Chapter 4, "Board of Directors: Selection, Compensation, and Removal.")

- **Clawbacks and deferred payouts**—Contractual provision that enables the company to reclaim compensation in future years if it becomes clear that bonus compensation should not have been awarded previously. Section 304 of the Sarbanes–Oxley Act enables companies to reclaim bonuses from the CEO and CFO if it is later determined that the bonuses were awarded on the basis of manipulated earnings.[22] Some companies use broader language to enable clawbacks under a wider set of circumstances, such as if the executive has acted unethically or violated a noncompete clause. Other companies defer the payout of bonuses until sufficient time has elapsed to determine whether the payment is economically justified (see the following sidebar). The prevalence of clawbacks has grown in recent years. In 2006, approximately 18 percent of the Fortune 100 companies had publicly disclosed clawback policies. By 2010, that figure increased to more than 82 percent.[23] Following the Dodd–Frank Financial Reform Act, companies are now required to develop, implement, and disclose a clawback policy.

Clawback and Deferred Payout Provisions

ExxonMobil

"Should the Corporation's reported financial or operating results be subject to a material negative restatement within five years, the Board would seek to obtain from each executive officer an amount corresponding to an incentive award or portion thereof that the Board determines would not have been granted or paid had the Corporation's results as originally reported been equal to the Corporation's results as subsequently restated."[24]

Citigroup

"Incentive awards ... are also subject to cancellation, forfeiture, or recovery by Citi if the committee determines that the employee (a) received an award based on materially inaccurate financial statements... (b) knowingly engaged in providing inaccurate information ... relating to financial statements or performance metrics, or (c) materially violated any risk limits established or revised by senior management. [I]ncentive compensation is also subject to cancellation by Citi if the employee's employment terminates on account of misconduct."[25]

McKesson

"As described in the Company's standard award documentation, the Compensation Committee may seek to recoup any economic gains from equity grants from any employee who engages in conduct which is not in good faith and which disrupts, damages, impairs, or interferes with the business, reputation, or employees of the Company or its affiliates."[26]

UBS

"Deferred awards generally vest over at least three years. Deferred awards are subject to forfeiture under certain circumstances, including if an employee's conduct or judgment results in material financial loss or restatement of results, breach of risk or compliance policies, or significant harm to the firm's business or reputation."[27]

Determining the Level of Compensation

The compensation committee and the board of directors are responsible for determining the level of compensation paid to the CEO and other officers. They must also select the mix of short-term and long-term elements to achieve a payout structure that is consistent with the firm's strategy. In theory, this should be a straightforward exercise, with the level of total compensation set to be commensurate with the value of services received. The process might work as follows: First, determine how much value the company expects to create during a reasonable time horizon (for example, five years). Then determine how much of this value should be attributable to the efforts of the CEO. Finally, determine what percentage of that value should be fairly offered to the CEO as compensation. Although many boards may implicitly follow this type of approach, it is exceedingly difficult to measure the value creation attributable to the efforts of a specific executive.

Instead, most boards determine compensation levels by benchmarking their CEO's pay against that of a set of companies that are comparable in size, industry, and geography (**peer group**). Interviews with compensation consultants reveal that companies commonly aim to provide cash compensation (base salary and annual bonus) at the 50th or lower percentile of the peer group and long-term incentives (primarily equity-based compensation) at the 75th percentile. These figures represent the board's assessment of the market wage opportunity of the CEO and other executive officers. The compensation committee also needs to make sure that the level of pay suggested by the benchmark has a similar level of risk as the compensation package being considered for the executive.

Although benchmarking presumably enables a company to remain competitive regarding the level of compensation, it has some obvious drawbacks. First, compensation levels might become inflated over time as companies increase pay to match amounts paid by peers. When multiple companies within a group try to meet or exceed the median, the median itself tends to increase, creating the well-known **ratcheting effect**. Second, benchmarking determines pay without explicit regard to value creation. This might encourage executives to engage in uneconomic behavior, such as acquiring a competitor purely to increase the size of the overall organization, resulting in a shift in the perceived peer group and, therefore, the CEO's own pay. Third, benchmarking can lead to very different pay packages, depending on the specific companies included in the peer group.

According to a study by Equilar, companies modify their peer groups regularly. Sixty-four percent of companies in the S&P 1500 made at least one change to their peer group in 2009. Furthermore, companies tend to select peers with revenues larger than their own. The median company had revenues at the 44th percentile of their group, and 77 percent had revenues at or below the 60th percentile.[28] Because compensation levels are correlated with size of the organization, selecting peers with larger revenues tends to increase the pay packages of senior executives.

Researchers have studied whether peer groups are selectively designed to extract excess pay. The results of these studies are mixed. Bizjak, Lemmon, and Naveen (2008) concluded that peer-group selection is a "practical and efficient mechanism" to determine the market wage for executives, and that it is not indicative of manipulation for personal gain.[29] However, Faulkender and Yang (2010) found that companies include unrelated firms in the peer group and that the inclusion of these firms increases pay.[30] As such, the process of peer group selection is under considerable scrutiny by securities regulators and shareholder activists (see the following sidebar).

> ## Benchmarking Compensation at Kroger and Safeway
>
> Kroger and Safeway are two grocery store chains that are fairly similar in terms of size and corporate strategy. However, they use very different peer groups for compensation benchmarking. Kroger has a peer group of mostly retail and grocery companies, but Safeway has a broader peer group consisting of department stores, food and beverage manufacturers, and clothing retailers (see Table 8.2).[31]

Table 8.2 Kroger and Safeway, Comparative Statistics

	Kroger	**Safeway**	
CEO total compensation	$8.25 million	$7.0 million	
Revenues	$66.1 billion	$40.2 billion	
Net income	$1.1 billion	$0.87 billion	
Five-year stock return (Kroger, Safeway)	28.3 percent	−16.0 percent	
Five-year stock return (peer group)	2.5 percent	11.8 percent	
Peer group	Albertson's	Best Buy	*Kroger*
	Costco	Colgate Palmolive	Limited Brands
	CVS	CVS	McDonald's
	Great A&P	Federated Department Stores	Office Depot
	Koninklijke Ahold	Fortune Brands	PepsiCo
	Marsh Supermarkets	Gap	Sears Holdings
	Safeway	General Mills	Sherwin-Williams
	SuperValue	Home Depot	Staples
	Target	IAC/Interactive	SuperValu
	Walmart	JCPenney	Target
	Walgreens	Johnson & Johnson	Walgreens
	Whole Foods	Kohl's	
	Winn-Dixie		

Source: The Kroger Company, Form DEF-14A, filed with the Securities and Exchange Commission May 15, 2007; Safeway, Inc., Form DEF-14A, filed with the Securities and Exchange Commission April 4, 2007.

It is interesting to speculate which company has the more appropriate peer group and why, given that they are in the same industry.

Compensation Consultants

Another area of popular concern is the use of third-party consultants to assist in the process of setting compensation. In 2009, the most frequently used consulting firms were Towers Perrin (now Towers Watson, 10 percent), Frederic Cook (9 percent), Mercer (7 percent), and Hewitt (now Aon Hewitt, 6 percent). At 74 percent of companies, the board of directors selects which firm to use, and at 7 percent of companies management makes this selection (20 percent of firms do not disclose this information in the annual proxy).[32]

Critics claim that a conflict of interest arises when the consulting firm used to structure the CEO compensation package is also used for other corporate services, such as designing benefits plans or managing pension assets. They allege that such consultants are less likely to recommend lower pay, for fear of losing contracts for the other services they provide to the company.[33] Although conflicts of interest should be a source of concern, no robust academic evidence suggests that compensation consultants who provide other services allow conflicts of interest to influence their determination of executive pay levels (see the next sidebar, "Disclosure on Compensation Consultants").

Conyon, Peck, and Sadler (2009) and Cadman, Carter, and Hillegeist (2010) found that total CEO pay is higher than predicted by economic determinants among companies that use compensation consultants, but they found no evidence that the higher pay is associated with governance quality. Murphy and Sandino (2010) examined CEO pay levels in a sample of companies that all have used compensation consultants. They found that CEO pay increases with the level of "influence" that the CEO has over the board, with influence measured by whether the CEO is also chairman and whether the CEO has appointed a high percentage of directors to the board.[34]

A forthcoming study by Armstrong, Ittner, and Larcker found that CEO pay is determined by the quality of governance at the firm and not by the use of a compensation consultant. Companies with weaker governance are more likely to both use compensation consultants and grant higher pay levels. They concluded that the difference in pay levels is driven by governance differences of the firms, not by the use of a consultant. Moreover, the authors found that pay levels do not vary between companies that retain specialized compensation consultants (who provide only compensation services) and those that use general human resources consultants (who offer a broad array of services). This finding raises some doubt about the belief that conflicts of interest facilitate excess pay levels.[35]

Although it is far from clear that compensation consultants are driving the growth in CEO compensation, they remain a convenient target for blame. That said, shareholders should be aware of who within the firm selected the compensation consultant. While it is appropriate for the compensation committee to retain an advisor to assist in structuring compensation, it is not appropriate for management (including a dual chairman-CEO) to recommend which firm to use.

Disclosure on Compensation Consultants

Wright Express

Companies are required to disclose whether they use a compensation consultant, the full set of services that the consultant provides, and the total payments made. For example, Write Express notes, "In 2008, the committee utilized Mercer, reporting directly to the committee, to provide advice regarding the Company's executive compensation practices" (see Table 8.3).

Table 8.3 Payments Wright Express Made to Mercer (2008)

Mercer Group	Services Provided	2008 Payments
Mercer Human Capital Business	Executive compensation consulting services provided to the compensation committee	$46,973
Mercer Health & Welfare Business	Health and welfare benefits consulting	$115,404
Mercer Retirement Risk and Finance	401(k) consulting	$15,000
Marsh, sister company of Mercer	Risk-management brokerage	$110,428
Total		**$287,805**

Source: Wright Express, Form DEF-14A, filed with the Securities and Exchange Commission April 9, 2009.

"Mercer's existing relationships with Wright Express were discussed by the committee during the compensation consultant selection process. The committee selected Mercer over other compensation consultants reviewed due to its breadth and depth of experience and its familiarity with our business model and Company goals."[36]

Compensation Levels

Based on a sample of 4,000 publicly traded U.S. companies, the median CEO receives expected total annual compensation of about $1.6 million. Among the largest companies, total compensation is $11.4 million.[37] Total compensation includes salary, cash bonuses, the fair value of equity-based incentives, pensions, benefits, and perquisites (see Table 8.4).

Note from the table that the median compensation is substantially smaller than the mean compensation of this same set of companies. Clearly, a relatively small number of "outliers" influences the mean average. For this reason, median average is a better descriptor of overall compensation because it represents the amount awarded at a typical company.

Note also that the calculation for compensation reflects the expected fair value of compensation *awarded* during the year. It does not reflect the value executives *realized* during that year. This is an important distinction. The fair value awarded is the value of compensation that the committee intends to pay to the executive in a given year. It measures equity-based incentives according to their expected value, with restricted stock valued at current market prices and stock options valued using an approved valuation method (either Black–Scholes or the binomial pricing model). The actual compensation that the executive receives when he or she ultimately sells the stock or exercises the options will likely be very different from the expected value. Realized compensation is a potentially problematic measure because it often reflects the combined value of stock and options granted during multiple years but exercised in a single year.

Company size (along with industrial sector) is a major determinant of executive compensation levels. Gabaix and Landier (2008) found that an increase in company size can almost entirely explain the increase in executive compensation in recent years. For example, they found that although CEO pay increased sixfold between 1980 and 2003, the market value of the companies they managed also increased sixfold during this period.[38] They concluded that "the rise in CEO compensation is a simple mirror of the rise in the value of large U.S. companies since the 1980s." Of course, simply demonstrating the correlation between compensation growth and company growth does not indicate that the compensation levels themselves are appropriate.

Table 8.4 Compensation Paid to CEOs in the United States

		Total Expected CEO Compensation ($)	Market Value ($ Millions)
Top 100	Mean	$13,527,125	$60,397
	Median	$11,357,478	$36,577
101 to 500	Mean	$8,862,514	$8,723
	Median	$6,546,988	$6,928
501 to 1,000	Mean	$5,623,823	$2,192
	Median	$4,100,877	$2,057
1,001 to 2,000	Mean	$2,980,475	$708
	Median	$2,129,101	$639
2,001 to 3,000	Mean	$1,768,872	$186
	Median	$1,152,533	$175
3,001 to 4,000	Mean	$932,494	$39
	Median	$613,596	$35
1 to 4,000	Mean	$3,347,868	$2,889
	Median	$1,588,389	$332

Total compensation includes salary, annual bonus, other bonus, expected value of stock options, performance plans, restricted stock grants, pensions, benefits, and perquisites. In calculating stock option fair value, remaining terms are reduced by 30 percent to adjust for potential early exercise or termination. Market value is the value of common shares outstanding at fiscal year end.

Source: Equilar, Inc. compensation and equity ownership data for fiscal years from June 2008 to May 2009.

In a related study, Kaplan and Rauh (2010) found that the growth in executive compensation is largely consistent with the growth in compensation for other highly paid professionals, such as hedge fund managers, private equity managers, venture capitalists, lawyers, and professional athletes. The authors calculated that pay among these groups all grew by roughly the same order of magnitude during 1994–2005. They concluded that CEO compensation has increased because of market forces that contribute to general wage inflation among highly paid professionals, and that extreme compensation growth is not limited to the business world.[39]

However, we can find exceptions among individual companies that pay their CEOs more than the normalized level that might be expected, given their size and performance. Research suggests that weak governance systems are correlated with excessive compensation. Core, Holthausen, and Larcker (1999) found an inverse relationship between the quality of oversight that a board provides and the level of compensation within the firm.[40] They also found that companies that award inflated compensation tend to underperform their peers in terms of subsequent operating performance and stock price returns. They concluded that "firms with weaker governance structures have greater compensation and that firms with greater agency problems perform worse." That is, governance quality clearly has an impact on executive compensation levels.

Pay Inequity: Executive Officers

Critics of executive compensation levels point to two statistics to support their position. One is the large differential between the pay granted to the CEO and the pay granted to other senior executives. The other is the large differential between CEO pay and the average employee pay.

For example, in 2008, the Connecticut Retirement Plans and Trust Funds, which manages pension assets on behalf of state and municipal workers in Connecticut, filed shareholder resolutions at Abercrombie & Fitch and SuperValu that would require the companies to adopt policies to encourage greater pay equity between the CEO and other named executive officers (NEOs).[41] According to State Treasurer Denise Nappier:

Large gaps in pay between the chief executive officer and other NEOs may signal that the CEO is earning an excessively large share of the compensation paid to top executives or that the pay is not tied to performance, and this is rightly of concern to shareholders. It may also be a red flag for inadequate succession planning, as wide pay differentials sometimes reveal significant differences in contribution and ability, and this, too, is troubling.[42]

Nappier was referring to the fact that, in 2006, Abercrombie & Fitch Chairman and CEO Michael Jeffries earned total compensation of $26.2 million, compared with total compensation of between $2.4 million and $4.3 million for the other NEOs of the company.[43] After negotiation with Nappier, both companies agreed to enhance disclosure on the compensation paid to their CEOs relative to other NEOs, and the Connecticut Retirement Plans and Trust Funds dropped its shareholder resolutions.

Table 8.5 shows that the typical CEO of a publicly traded U.S. corporation earns roughly two times the total compensation of the second-most highly paid NEO.[44] The second-most highly paid NEO earns roughly 1.5 times as much as the third-most highly paid NEO.

Table 8.5 The Ratio of Pay among Senior Executives

	Ratio of Pay CEO vs. 2nd Highest Paid Executive	Ratio of Pay 2nd vs. 3rd Highest Paid Executive
Top 100	2.00	1.16
101 to 500	1.99	1.28
501 to 1,000	2.05	1.23
1,001 to 2,000	1.88	1.23
2,001 to 3,000	1.69	1.17
3,001 to 4,000	1.60	1.16
1 to 4,000	1.77	1.20

Based on median total compensation.

Source: Equilar, Inc., compensation and equity ownership data for fiscal years from June 2008 to May 2009.

Several factors might contribute to "pay inequity" within the executive suite. From a purely economic standpoint, the relative pay packages might simply reflect the different levels of value creation within the organization. The success of a very complex company might more heavily rely on the efforts of the CEO, so it might be appropriate to have a greater pay differential to attract a qualified leader.

Furthermore, large pay differentials might also reflect competitive dynamics within the organization. This explanation, known as **tournament theory**, was proposed by Lazear and Rosen (1981), who pointed out that senior executives not only serve a current operating function, but also compete in a tournament for promotion.[45] According to the authors, pay inequity serves as an incentive for executives to compete more aggressively for promotion. If they are successful, they receive a large payoff in terms of compensation. As a result, the executive's current salary is not his or her only incentive to perform. The potential for promotion is itself an incentive, and the value of this incentive is reinforced by a large pay differential between the current and potential positions.

However, pay inequity might indeed signal real problems within the company, such as those Nappier suggested. Large pay differentials might indicate **management entrenchment** (the ability of management to shield itself from market forces and pressures to perform from the board, shareholders, and stakeholders).[46] In this way, large differentials might indicate that the CEO is able to engage in rent extraction, which the corporate governance system has not adequately controlled against. Pay inequity might also be a source of discouragement for executives who believe they are not fairly compensated. If this is the case, talented senior executives might become unmotivated, which leads to higher turnover, reduced productivity, and a decrease in shareholder value. Finally, pay inequity might reflect a lack of talent development within the organization. That is, the NEOs of the company might simply receive low compensation because they have lower talent levels. If this is the case, the company might be at greater risk of a failed transition because it lacks a viable successor when the current CEO eventually steps down.

Determining the true causes of pay differentials within a company is difficult. Doing so requires precise measures of value creation at different executive levels and a comparison of that value creation against earned wages. However, evidence from fields outside business tend to support a theory that value creation plays some role in inequitable wage scales at the highest ranks of some organizations. For example, the distribution of compensation among professional athletes, law firms, hedge funds, and Hollywood entertainers all tend to follow a highly convex curve, with star performers earning compensation significantly higher than that earned by less successful peers. This indicates that tournament-like forces might be in play broadly when extreme talent is both rare and highly valuable. Moreover, the tournament structure might be an effective way to sort out the top performers from executives who appear similar but are less skilled.

However, evidence does support the fact that pay inequity is a real source of concern within some organizations. For example, healthcare information technology company Cerner Corporation has a policy that limits the cash compensation of the CEO relative to that of the second-most highly paid NEO. The board must approve exceptions to this policy in advance.[47] DuPont has also instituted "pay equity multiples" that limit total annual compensation of the CEO relative to that of the other NEOs. Cash compensation is limited to between two and three times that paid to the other NEOs, and total compensation (which includes long-term incentives) is limited to between three and four times.[48]

Boards need to decide how much they want compensation packages to vary across the executive hierarchy. External benchmarking is a useful first step for this decision, but ultimately this choice depends on the complexity of the business and its culture, types of executives, and competitive environment. Despite the efforts of some to strictly limit pay inequity, it is difficult to imagine a common standard that would work across firms without destroying shareholder value.

Pay Inequity: Average Employee

Critics of executive compensation also point to the large differential between the compensation paid to the CEO and the average employee. This metric is often cited in the press. For example, a 2004 article in *The New York Times* explained efforts by the Catholic Funds to enact say-on-pay policies at seven companies, including Cendant,

International Paper, and Viacom. A spokesperson is quoted as saying, "If the CEO is going to be paid more than 100 times the average worker, we want to know why." He goes on to say, "We are trying to get at the notion of economic injustice in what the CEO is making compared to the average worker. It's bad for the long-term performance of a company because it breaches the trust between top management and people who work for them."[49] Perhaps with these types of arguments in mind, the Dodd–Frank Financial Reform Act now requires companies to disclose the ratio of CEO pay to average employee pay in the annual proxy.

Unfortunately, this ratio suffers from several shortcomings. First, it is difficult to accurately and consistently calculate. Recent estimates have pegged this ratio at 180 times, 300 times, 411 times, or 531 times.[50] Differences in methodology and sample selection no doubt contribute to the disparity of results. For example, is mean or median compensation used in the computation? Is expected or realized compensation used? When the later is used, it tends to greatly overstate CEO compensation because the compensation realized in one year might stem from longer-term awards granted in multiple years previously and were exercised only in the current year.

Second, it is difficult to compare the results across companies. The ratio is influenced by a company's industry, size, location, and measurement period. We can illustrate this by comparing the ratios at Walmart and Goldman Sachs. In 2007, H. Lee Scott, former CEO of Walmart, earned roughly 750 times the pay of that company's average employee ($30 million versus $40,000).[51] That same year, Lloyd Blankfein, CEO of Goldman Sachs, earned roughly 140 times the pay of that company's average employee ($70 million versus $500,000).[52] Despite the considerable disparity between these two ratios, it is not clear whether we should conclude that one, both, or neither of these executives is overpaid. The disparity says more about the industry, size, and risk of these two enterprises than it does about the levels of pay.

Finally, even within a single company, the statistic is difficult to interpret. Should we examine the ratio from the standpoint of value creation? (That is, does Walmart's Scott create 750 times more in corporate value than the average employee?) Or should we look at it in terms of scale of job? (Does oversight responsibility for 2.1 million workers and $400 billion in revenue merit 750 times more compensation than the oversight responsibility of the average Walmart associate?) Or in terms of expendability? (Would Walmart choose to eliminate the CEO position or 750 other positions selected at random?) Although each of these questions puts the ratio of CEO pay to average employee pay in an economic context, it is not clear whether any of these questions is an appropriate lens for the board to look through in determining compensation levels.

It is dangerous to reduce a complicated debate to a single number. Instead, we believe that CEO compensation should be evaluated in terms of its overall appropriateness for attracting, retaining, and motivating qualified talent—just as it is for all other employees.

Compensation Mix

In addition to determining the level of compensation, the compensation committee must decide how to *structure* the compensation package to ensure that it provides incentives that are in line with the company's objectives. Ultimately, this is done by arriving at a mix of cash, equity, and other benefits with appropriate performance targets to attract, retain, and motivate qualified executive officers, across both short-term and long-term horizons.

Table 8.6 shows that the average company pays roughly 18 percent of the CEO's compensation in the form of salary, 17 percent in bonus, 49 percent in stock options and restricted stock, 12 percent in performance plans, and 5 percent in pension and benefits. One interesting statistic is that smaller companies appear to reduce bonuses and performance-based compensation in their compensation and increase the proportion from salary. This might be driven by personal consumption (that is, because the compensation packages are smaller, the executives need a higher mix of cash to support their families).

How appropriate are these compensation mixes? Do they encourage behaviors that appropriately balance risk and reward in pursuit of the corporate strategy? When should the board think about using a different mix of compensation?

Table 8.6   Mix of Compensation Paid to CEOs in the United States

	Salary	Bonus	Stock Options	Restricted Shares	Performance Plans	Other
Top 100	9.20%	17.91%	32.12%	18.34%	19.30%	3.13%
101 to 500	10.80%	18.09%	31.96%	19.65%	15.80%	3.69%
501 to 1,000	13.83%	18.57%	28.07%	23.87%	12.44%	3.21%
1,001 to 2,000	20.60%	15.76%	25.37%	23.61%	9.12%	5.54%
2,001 to 3,000	26.03%	13.24%	23.55%	20.45%	8.13%	8.61%
3,001 to 4,000	40.41%	12.74%	21.62%	15.45%	4.10%	5.69%
1 to 4,000	17.53%	16.64%	27.86%	21.10%	12.13%	4.73%

Source: Equilar, Inc. compensation and equity ownership data for fiscal years from June 2008 to May 2009.

Short-Term Incentives

Short-term incentives offer an annual payment (usually cash) for achieving predetermined performance objectives. The size of the bonus is expressed in terms of a **target award**. Most companies define the size of the target award as a percentage of the base salary (for example, the target award might be equal to 200 percent of the base salary). The actual payment that the executive receives might be limited by upper and lower bounds, in which case a minimum award and a maximum award are established (the minimum award might be equal to 50 percent of the target and the maximum award equal to 200 percent of the target). As a result, the executive stands to receive a cash payment with a payoff that increases in a stepwise function, with bounded upper and lower limits (see Figure 8.1.)

The bonus payment is awarded if certain performance criteria are achieved during the year. The compensation committee determines the performance criteria. As discussed in Chapter 6, "Organizational Strategy, Business Models, and Risk Management," one way to select the measures used to award compensation is to use those that were identified during the business modeling process as correlated with success in the corporate strategy. In general, these include a mix of accounting measures (such as economic value added, earnings-per-share growth, and return on assets), stock market measures (such as total shareholder return), and nonfinancial measures (such as customer satisfaction, product defect rates, and market share). As such, bonus plans provide executives with an explicit monetary incentive to improve the short-term performance of the firm by achieving operating targets that are known to be correlated with increased shareholder value (see the next sidebar).

Proper alignment of target performance and payouts is crucial to incentive plan success

▶ Threshold performance levels are typically very achievable (85%-90% chance of achievement)

▶ Target performance levels are more difficult to achieve (~60% chance of achievement)

▶ Maximum performance levels are "stretch" goals, and very difficult to achieve (10-15% chance of achievement)

Source: Michael Benkowitz, Mark A. Borges, and Thomas G. Brown (2008).

Figure 8.1   Minimum, target, and maximum awards for typical short-term bonus plans.

One potential concern with bonus plans is that annual performance targets might not be that difficult to achieve. According to a 2005 proprietary survey by a major compensation consulting firm, on average, companies pay bonuses equal to 103 percent of the target level. Only 20 percent of executives receive a bonus less than 75 percent of target levels. That is, bonus plans do not appear to be based on "stretch" goals. Research studies arrive at similar conclusions. Merchant and Manzoni (1989) found that internal budget targets used to award performance bonuses are met 80 percent to 90 percent of the time.[53] Indjejikian, Lenk, and Nanda (2000) found that performance targets are achieved 60 percent of the time.[54] As such, it is not clear that average performance hurdles are difficult to achieve or encourage above-average performance. It is important for the board to assess whether the performance targets are sufficiently difficult to attain so that what is termed a "performance-based" bonus is not actually some type of "disguised fixed salary."

In addition, bonus plans have the potential to produce a variety of undesirable executive behaviors. For example, the annual nature of bonus plans can give rise to excessive focus on short-term accounting results at the expense of long-term value creation. One example is delaying the investment in important projects with positive net present value to improve current period net income. This is of special concern when an executive is in the final few years with the company and is therefore unlikely to see the economic benefit of a long-term investment in his or her annual bonus. (We alluded to this in Chapter 1, "Introduction to Corporate Governance," in our discussion of self-interested behavior).

Similarly, the practice of bounding annual bonus plans with a stated maximum can also encourage inappropriate behavior. Healy (1985) and Holthausen, Larcker, and Sloan (1995) found that executives are more likely to manipulate earnings downward after they have achieved their maximum bonus payment.[55] They do so to defer corporate earnings to a later period because they no longer contribute toward their current bonus.

Finally, it is plausible that bonus plans can provide incentives for managers to manipulate accounting results to achieve targets that they would otherwise miss. (We discuss this topic in greater detail in the next chapter.)

These are all real concerns for the board of directors to consider, given the important role that the bonus plays in the overall compensation package. Fortunately, compensation committees also grant a variety of long-term compensation awards that can mitigate these potential problems.

Annual Incentives

Northrop Grumman

In 2006, Northrop Grumman assigned the following weightings in calculating the annual performance bonus for the CEO and other named executive officers of the company:[56]

- **Warranted equity value (40% weighting)**—WEV is a discounted cash-flow measurement that derives the intrinsic value of the company resulting from operating performance. Goals were based on achieving desired year-over-year growth in WEV. WEV growth goals were based on analysis of yearly total shareholder returns (TSR) generated by companies in the S&P 500. Maximum payout required a percentage increase in WEV that exceeded the top quartile performance level of returns.

- **Pension-adjusted operating margin (20% weighting)**—The goals were based on the implementation of a phased improvement program to drive operating margin performance beyond a weighted average of peer company performance levels. Goals were based on achieving specific operating margin dollar amounts (adjusted for net Financial Accounting Standards [FAS] and Cost Accounting Standards [CAS] pension expense) defined by improving year-over-year operating margin rates. In 2006, maximum payout required a 120 basis point improvement in operating margin rate compared to 2005.

- **Cash from operations (20% weighting)**—Goals are designed to reward the improved efficiency of converting earnings into cash, a key indicator of earnings quality and management's ability to generate operating cash. Goals were based on analysis of cash conversion rates (Cash from operations and earnings before interest, taxes, depreciation, and amortization [EBITDA]) for the S&P 100 nonfinancial companies and a peer group consisting of aerospace and defense companies. Cash conversion rates were translated into specific dollar amounts. Achieving maximum payout required cash generation that equated to the top quartile level of performance for the peer groups.

- **Supplemental goals for sector operating units (20% weighting)**—Goals were designed to maximize operational performance, which includes metrics such as customer satisfaction, new product development, new business initiatives, productivity, quality improvement, workplace diversity, employee management, leadership development, and environmental management. NEOs received the weighted average score of all sectors.

This is a complex annual bonus plan. Are the large number of financial and nonfinancial measures in this annual bonus plan really necessary? When does a plan become too complicated?

Long-Term Incentives

Long-term incentives are added to the compensation mix to encourage executives to select long-term investments that increase shareholder value. Long-term incentives extend the time horizon of the executive and mitigate the natural tendency of a risk-averse executive to reject risky investments. In Table 8.6, we saw that the value of long-term awards (in the form of stock options, equity, and performance plans) is more than three times the value of short-term awards—60 percent versus 17 percent at the average company. As such, long-term incentives can help mitigate short-term gamesmanship by refocusing the emphasis on long-term performance.[57]

For example, as executives approach retirement, they might be expected to reduce a company's investment in research and development to hit earnings targets that increase their own annual bonus. Because the annual bonus (along with salary) is a key input in calculating their pension benefits, the CEO will benefit by receiving larger annual payments throughout retirement. This is part of the reason firms put "hold until or past retirement" features in stock option and restricted stock programs. If the CEO rejects valuable research and development to boost the value of his or her pension, the executive will, in theory, be punished through a corresponding loss in the eventual value of options and shares owned.

Stock options are the primary compensation element that many companies use to create this longer-term horizon for value creation. Options have several desirable features that can help align the interests of executives with those of shareholders. First, options increase in value as the stock price increases. This motivates executives to add corporate value by identifying and implementing investments with positive net present value (NPV). Second, options increase in value with stock-price volatility. This motivates executives to accept risky, positive NPV investments that might otherwise be rejected if the compensation program were instead mostly fixed salary or short-term incentives. Third, because of vesting requirements, options have deferred payoffs that encourage a focus on long-term results. As such, stock options tend to be used in companies where there are substantial investment opportunities that are associated with considerable risk. Stock options will attract highly skilled executives with moderate risk tolerance that want to share in the value created by their work. Whether the company wants this type of employee depends on the firm's strategy. A firm operating in a stable and predictable environment might use more fixed salary and annual bonus compensation, but a company in a highly dynamic and risky industry might place greater emphasis on long-term equity-based compensation.

On the other hand, stock options can offer capricious financial rewards to executives when broad market factors cause changes in stock price that are not the result of the executive's individual effort. During much of the 1990s, a rising market tended to reward most executives who received options, regardless of the firm's operating performance. Conversely, most stock options granted in the late 1990s expired with zero value because of significant market declines, even in cases when some sort of payout was merited based on relative performance. This concern has motivated some companies to use relative performance in their stock option and restricted stock grants, such as those illustrated in the first sidebar in this chapter.

Some have argued that stock options encourage executives to engage in a variety of undesirable behaviors, such as the manipulation of earnings to increase the stock price and, therefore, the value of their holdings.[58] The incentive to engage in this behavior theoretically should be strongest when a majority of the executive's compensation and wealth is in the form of stock options. However, Armstrong, Jagolinzer, and Larcker (2010) found that larger stock option and equity holdings are associated with fewer accounting manipulations, suggesting that the risk to financial statement integrity might be overstated.[59] (We discuss the relationship between executive equity holdings and accounting manipulation in greater detail in the next chapter.)

Some evidence suggests that stock options encourage the investment in new, risky projects. (Risky projects are desirable to shareholders when they are consistent with the strategy and business model of the organization, and when such investments have expected positive net present value. They are negative when they are inconsistent with the company's business model or are unlikely to bring rewards that compensate for the associated risk.) Rajgopal and Shevlin (2002) found that stock options are an effective tool to encourage risk-averse managers to invest in higher-risk, higher-return investments. Executives understand that the expected value of a stock option increases with the volatility of the stock price, and they tend to respond to stock option awards by investing in riskier projects to create this volatility.[60] Sanders and Hambrick (2007) found that executives who receive stock options are more likely to increase investment in risky research and development, capital expenditures, and acquisitions. In addition, total shareholder returns at these companies are more likely to be extreme in their outcomes (extremely positive or extremely negative). Unfortunately, the authors found that results are more likely to be extremely negative than extremely positive. They concluded that "high levels of stock options appear to motivate CEOs to take big risks ... to 'swing for the fences.'"[61]

The issue of whether stock options might be related to excessive risk taking is an important consideration for boards and shareholders when deciding on executive compensation packages. (Congress and the media coined the term *excessive risk taking* following the financial crisis of 2008.) It is difficult to make an assessment of what is "excessive," and, to our knowledge, no standard methodology exists for measuring the risk level of compensation. (We provide one possible tool later in this chapter). To temper "excessive" risk-seeking behavior, the compensation committee might rationally add equity incentives with lower payout leverage to the compensation package, such as restricted shares or performance units. In theory, equity compensation with lower leverage would provide less incentive for managers to take "excessive" risk to earn an exponential payoff. However, such an approach would also substantially reduce executive incentives. The SEC now requires that companies discuss the relationship between selected compensation plans and organizational risk in the CD&A (see the following sidebar).

Disclosure on Compensation and Risk

Moog

"In light of the current global economic and financial situation, the Committee has considered how recent events might affect the Company's Executive Compensation program. After review, a determination was made that no modifications to the compensation programs need to be made at this time. There are no risks associated with the Company's incentive compensation programs which could threaten the value of the Company or its shareholders."[62]

It would be interesting to understand how the board reached this conclusion.

Lilly

"The committee noted several design features of the company's cash and equity incentive programs for all employees that reduce the likelihood of excessive risk-taking:

- The program design provides a balanced mix of cash and equity, annual and longer-term incentives, and performance metrics (revenue, earnings, and total shareholder return).
- Maximum payout levels for bonuses and performance awards are capped at 200 percent of target.
- All regular U.S. employees participate in the same bonus plan.
- Bonus and equity programs have minimum payout levels for nonexecutive officers.
- The company currently does not grant stock options.
- The compensation committee has downward discretion over incentive program payouts.
- The executive compensation recovery policy allows the company to "claw back" payments made using materially inaccurate financial results.
- Executive officers are subject to share ownership and retention guidelines.
- Compliance and ethical behaviors are integral factors considered in all performance assessments."[63]

Although eliminating stock options and capping bonuses might reduce "excessive" risk taking, these changes might also influence the managerial focus on innovation. The board must weigh the tradeoff between curbing potentially excessive risk taking and discouraging innovation.

Ameriprise Financial

"There are no objective tests to determine whether one type of incentive compensation plan encourages executive officers to take excessive and unnecessary risks while another type of plan encourages only prudent and appropriate risk taking. Nevertheless, we will continue to examine our incentive compensation plans during 2010 to identify any plan features that may be incompatible with our enterprise risk-management program. With that said, it is not always easy to categorize risks as excessive or appropriate, except with the benefit of hindsight. [T]he question we have been asking ourselves is this: 'Are the Company's enterprise risk-management framework and internal controls effective to prevent or to identify and mitigate risk taking by our executive officers that exceeds our risk tolerances, regardless of the incentive compensation plan in which he or she participates?' We believe that the answer to that question is 'Yes.' Nevertheless, we will continue to give additional attention to the subject of risk and compensation as we continue to enhance our enterprise risk-management program."[64]

Ameriprise highlights the importance of an active risk-management program. Even if a compensation program encourages "excessive" risk taking, a vigilant risk-management function can offset these risks by preventing poorly conceived ideas from being implemented.

Benefits and Perquisites

The CEO compensation package generally includes a mix of benefits, perquisites, and other contingent payments. The value of these awards is not negligible. On average, they constitute 3 percent of the total compensation (see Table 8.6). In some of the more extreme cases cited at the beginning of this chapter, they can ultimately prove to be quite valuable.

The research evidence on the incentive value of these payments is quite mixed. Rajan and Wulf (2006) found that companies consistently use perks as a means to improve executive productivity. They found that perks such as use of aircraft and chauffeur drivers are predominantly awarded to executives who stand to benefit the most from free time.[65] Sundaram and Yermack (2007) argued that defined benefit pension plans (which are a fixed claim on the firm similar to salary) can be seen as a risk-reducing form of compensation that offsets the risk-seeking incentives of equity compensation.[66]

However, other researchers argue that these perquisites and benefits are a form of "stealth compensation" that enriches executives at the cost of shareholders. As such, they can be seen as the very agency costs that corporate governance systems are meant to preclude. To this end, Yermack (2006) found that shareholders react negatively to disclosure that an executive is allowed personal use of company aircraft.[67] Grinstein, Weinbaum, and Yehuda (2010) found that the reported value of perquisites increased by 190 percent following enhanced SEC disclosure rules in 2006.[68] They also found that the reduction in shareholder value following the disclosure significantly exceeded the actual value of the perquisites, indicating that shareholders saw them as value destroying. They concluded that perquisite disclosure "conveys a more fundamental negative signal about the agency conflicts in these firms." Perquisites might not be an especially large dollar amount relative to the market capitalization of the firm, but they might provide a window into the workings of the board and governance quality of the firm.

Pay for Performance

One of the more controversial issues in corporate governance is whether executive compensation contracts exhibit "pay for performance."[69] We know that annual bonus and performance plans are explicitly linked to operating performance. We also know that stock options provide compensation only when executives have increased the stock price to the point at which the options trade "in the money." These simple observations indicate that, at some level, pay for performance must exist.

In discussing pay for performance, governance experts and the media often compare the size of the annual compensation package to recent changes in stock price. Their assumption is that if the executive receives a large compensation payment in a year when the stock price declines then there is no pay for performance; for there to be pay for performance, the executive must only receive large compensation when stock prices increase. However, this viewpoint is short-sighted because it overlooks the considerable wealth that an executive holds in equity stock options, restricted stock, and outright ownership of shares. A better way to judge pay for performance is to compute how much an executive gains or loses in total wealth as stock prices change.[70]

One way to make this calculation is to measure the change in CEO wealth over small changes in stock price.[71] Based on a sample of 4,000 publicly traded U.S. companies, the median CEO stands to gain roughly $54,000 in wealth for every 1 percent increase in stock price. Among the largest 100 companies, this figure approaches $600,000.[72]

Another way to assess the relationship between pay and performance is to measure the change in CEO wealth over large changes in stock price. For example, the median CEO will gain more than $5 million in wealth if the stock price doubles (median wealth of $4.6 million multiplied by 113 percent—see Table 8.7). Clearly, executives have significant economic incentive to perform in both the short and long term.

To better understand this relationship, we can go one step further and plot the percentage change in the CEO's equity portfolio against percentage changes in stock price ranging from –100 percent to +100 percent. The 0 percentage point on the x-axis is based on CEO wealth at prevailing market prices, and the –100 percentage point is where the value of equity goes to zero. By graphing this data and comparing these results to direct competitors or peer firms, observers can better understand the relative risk and reward that the total compensation package offers. (An example is provided in Figure 8.2.) Of particular note is the "convexity" of the payout curve.[73] For example, a manager who is rewarded predominantly in restricted stock or holds only stock will see a change in wealth that is essentially linear (low convexity) and coincides one-for-one with the change in wealth of the average shareholder. By contrast, a manager who is rewarded predominantly in stock options (especially those with blocks of stock options with progressively higher exercise prices) will see a change in wealth that has a much steeper payout curve (high convexity) and promises significant wealth for superior performance. Payout curves with high convexity will encourage more risk taking, and payout curves with low convexity will encourage less risk taking. This can be good or bad, depending on the strategy of the organization.

Table 8.7 Percentage Change in CEO Equity Wealth vs. Percentage Change in Stock Price (Median Values)

Firm Size	Market Cap ($ Millions)	Total CEO Pay ($)	Total CEO Wealth ($)	1% Change	50% Change	100% Change
Top 100	$36,577	$11,357,478	$41,416,000	1.43%	68.10%	141.50%
101 to 500	$6,928	$6,546,988	$20,703,000	1.35%	63.55%	130.00%
501 to 1,000	$2,057	$4,100,877	$12,240,500	1.27%	60.10%	122.00%
1,001 to 2,000	$639	$2,129,101	$7,531,000	1.17%	56.00%	113.00%
2,001 to 3,000	$175	$1,152,533	$3,312,500	1.15%	54.00%	109.00%
3,001 to 4,000	$35	$613,596	$720,000	1.11%	53.90%	109.00%
1 to 4,000	$332	$1,588,389	$4,628,000	1.17%	55.95%	113.00%

Calculations exclude personal wealth outside company stock. Total CEO compensation is the sum of salary, annual bonus, expected value of stock options granted, expected value of restricted stock granted, target value of performance plan grants, and other annual compensation. Calculations for compensation exclude changes in pension. Stock options are valued using the Black–Scholes pricing model, with remaining option term reduced by 30 percent to compensate for potential early exercise or termination and volatility based on actual results from the previous year.

Source: Equilar, Inc., compensation and equity ownership data for fiscal years from June 2008 to May 2009.

Measures percentage change in expected value of CEO stock and option portfolio with percentage change in company stock price.

Figure 8.2   Relationship between CEO wealth and stock price: Exelon vs. Southern Co.

As an example, consider the relationship between pay and potential performance for a series of direct competitors:

- **Regulated utilities**—As shown in Figure 8.2, if the stock price of Southern Company increases by 100 percent, the CEO of the company's Georgia Power division will realize a 235 percent increase in "wealth" (a ratio of 2.35). By comparison, the ratio at Exelon's ComEd division is 1.23. Compensation at Southern Company therefore seems to encourage more risk taking. Under what circumstances is it appropriate for a public utility to engage in risky activities?

- **Food companies**—The CEO of General Mills has convexity in his compensation of 2.98, and the CEO of Kraft has convexity of 1.18. However, the CEO of General Mills was newly appointed to the position. Although it can be appropriate to use options to help a CEO build wealth in the company at a faster rate, will a more aggressive compensation structure simultaneously, and perhaps undesirably, impact company strategy and risk (see Figure 8.3)?

- **Pharmaceutical companies**—The CEOs of Johnson & Johnson and Abbott Laboratories have higher convexity in their compensation (2.26 and 2.13, respectively) than the CEOs of Pfizer and Merck (1.78 and 1.67). Does a diversified healthcare model require more risk taking than a pure-play pharmaceutical model (see Figure 8.4)?

Figure 8.3   Relationship between CEO wealth and stock price: General Mills vs. Kraft.

Figure 8.4   Relationship between CEO wealth and stock price: Johnson & Johnson vs. Pfizer.

Although it is difficult for outside observers to determine whether these payout functions are appropriate, this is precisely the type of analysis that the compensation committee should conduct to make a reasoned assessment of whether compensation contracts are providing appropriate incentives for performance. They can also gauge whether "excessive" risk taking is being encouraged. Finally, it is important to note that these curves demonstrate the downside as well as the upside offered to the executive. If the value of the executive's wealth quickly approaches zero on the downside, this will provide a disincentive to engage in risky projects. The board should consider total (upside and downside) effects of risky investments on the executive's wealth.

Efforts to Reform Compensation

Many governance experts have offered remedies to "reform" executive compensation. Although some of these recommendations have promising elements, they also have potentially negative repercussions that stakeholders should be aware of.

- **Increase proxy disclosure**—In 2006, the SEC required that companies improve disclosure of executive compensation by including a Compensation Discussion & Analysis (CD&A) section in the proxy that explains the company's compensation philosophy, the elements of the compensation program, the total compensation offered, the peer group used to benchmark compensation, performance metrics used to award variable pay, pay equity between the CEO and other senior executives, stock ownership guidelines, clawback policies, and post-retirement compensation. The SEC intended the CD&A to provide a "plain English" discussion of these items. Although more detailed disclosure has been beneficial to investors, the CD&A section is often overly complex and difficult to navigate. Beucler and Dolmat-Connell (2007) found that the median disclosure length is nearly five times longer than the SEC envisioned (4,726 words versus an expectation of 1,000). They concluded that current disclosure is not very accessible to the average investor.[74] However, the complexity of disclosure might reflect the complexity of compensation packages in general.

- **Say-on-pay**—Shareholders are given an advisory (nonbinding) vote on executive and director compensation. Although the board is not required to follow the outcome of the vote, the process is intended to lead to more rational compensation and clearer communication on compensation policy (see the following sidebar). The United Kingdom, the Netherlands, Australia, Sweden, Norway, and India have adopted various forms of say-on-pay. The Dodd–Frank Financial Reform Act of 2010 also legislated it in the United States. Under Dodd–Frank, companies are required to hold a nonbinding vote on compensation at least once every three years. At least once every six years, companies are required to hold a vote to determine the frequency of say-on-pay votes (every one, two, or three years, but no less frequently). In addition, a vote is required on compensation related to a change in control.[75]

Research provides mixed evidence whether giving shareholders a vote on compensation reduces pay. A forthcoming study by Ertimur, Ferri, and Muslu examined the impact of "vote no" campaigns and compensation-related shareholder proposals in the United States. They found that support for shareholder initiatives restricting compensation is higher among companies with above-average CEO pay. Furthermore, they found that vote-no campaigns are associated with a subsequent reduction of $2.3 million in CEO pay, but only when institutional investors initiated the proxy proposal.[76] A forthcoming study by Cai and Walkling examined shareholder returns following the passage of the "Say-on-Pay Bill of 2007" by the U.S. House of Representatives. They found some evidence that share prices for firms with high excess compensation reacted in a positive manner to the regulatory announcement.[77] In contrast, Ferri and Maber (2009) found that say-on-pay regulation in the United Kingdom had some impact on the level of severance pay awarded to CEOs. It also reduced stock option "retesting," in which a company extends the time period of a performance-based grant to give the executive more time to meet the performance threshold. These effects began to show up when at least 20 percent of shareholders voted against the plan. However, the authors also found that say-on-pay has not reduced overall pay levels in the United Kingdom.[78] Larcker, Ormazabal, and Taylor (2010) found evidence that capping or regulating executive pay results in less efficient contracts and negatively affects shareholder wealth in firms that are likely to be affected.[79]

"Say-on-Pay"

Amgen

Amgen has implemented a unique method for soliciting share-holder feedback on executive compensation. The company's proxy invites shareholders to fill out a survey to provide input and feedback to the compensation committee regarding executive compensation.[80]

The survey asks questions such as

- Is the compensation plan performance based?

- Is the plan clearly linked to the company's business strategy?

- Are the plan's metrics, goals, and hurdles clearly and specifi-cally disclosed?

- Are the incentives clearly designed to meet the company's specific business challenges, in both the short and long term?

- Does the compensation of senior executives complement the company's overall compensation program, reinforce internal equity and promote the success of the entire business enterprise?

- Does the plan promote long-term value creation, which is the primary objective of shareholders?

- Does the plan articulate a coherent compensation philoso-phy appropriate to the company and clearly understood by directors?[81]

Each question allows for an open-text-field response and links to a pop-up box where shareholders are given expanded information.

This type of survey raises a variety of important questions. Do shareholders have the necessary information to make a correct judgment about these issues? What happens if shareholders indi-cate that they do not like some part of the compensation program? When does the board have a "duty" to make changes? What type of investor relations activity is needed to support this survey?

- **Set strict limits on compensation**—This approach suggests that legislative bodies should place explicit restrictions on compensation to reduce aggregate pay. The U.S. Congress veered toward such an approach by limiting the compensation of executives whose companies received federal money through the Troubled Asset Relief Program (TARP). Under the Emergency Economic Stabilization Act of 2008, the tax deductibility of executive compensation at such firms was limited to $500,000.[82] Also these firms were prohibited from awarding executives "risky incentives," were prohibited from awarding golden parachute payments, and were required to increase clawback provisions. The downside of such an approach is that it tends to drive talent from public companies into private companies (the so-called "private equity brain drain"). Executives who believe that they will be better compensated elsewhere are likely to leave the firm. Furthermore, if an imbalance between the supply and demand for qualified CEOs exists, strict limits on pay would exacerbate the problem. For example, the time to limit the compensation of the CEO of General Motors is not when the company is in most dire need of attracting a qualified CEO to turn it around.

- **Take into account cumulative pay before setting future compensation**—This is a potentially more sophisticated way of setting strict limits on pay levels. Instead of looking at compensation on a yearly basis, advocates of this approach suggest that companies look at the cumulative pay that has been awarded to an executive during his or her tenure with the company. The board determines when "enough" compensation has been awarded. Future compensation packages are then reduced. For example, after having paid CEO Henry Herrmann approximately $70 million in compensation during a 36-year period, the board of Waddell & Reed Financial decided that it would no longer contribute to his retirement account.[83] The risk with such an approach is that seasoned executives might object to having their future compensation curtailed and decide instead to move to a new firm where they would be able to continue their current earnings level. This approach would also not prevent relatively unseasoned executives from reaping excessive compensation in their early years with a firm.

- **Decrease flexibility of executives to cash in on earned or accrued long-term incentives**—Under this approach, directors would restrict a portion of payouts until it is clear that they are truly merited. Restrictions might include requiring executives to retain a portion of their equity holdings well past retirement, prohibiting executives from using cashless exercises of stock options, or deferring the payout of cash bonuses earned. (UBS made these types of restrictions—see the second sidebar in this chapter). This approach would help reduce the incentives for executives (or traders in financial institutions) to generate a short-term gain that will not persist into the future. However, requiring executives to retain too much exposure to the firm can induce high levels of risk aversion, leading to a reduction in the pace of innovation or insufficient investment in new initiatives. A delicate balance exists between imposing risk on managers to mitigate agency problems and causing (typically undiversified) managers to become hyper–risk averse.

Assuming that a problem exists, it is unlikely that there is a "silver bullet" solution that will reform executive compensation. As with other governance issues, a one-size-fits-all solution is likely to fail. Governmental "reform" through SEC regulation or Congressional legislation has generally been met with mixed success (at best). A better solution is to continue to improve governance quality and corporate transparency to discourage the practices that allow for excessive pay.

Endnotes

1. Exceptions do exist in which CEOs work for no pay, as a result of either public pressure or moral duty, but they are obviously rare. See Moira Herbst, "The Elite Circle of $1 CEOs: Apple's Steve Jobs and Google's Eric Schmidt Are Just Two of the CEOs Who Work for a Buck. Why Do Top Executives Give Up Their Salaries?" *Business Week Online* (May 10, 2007). Accessed November 10, 2010. See www.businessweek.com/bwdaily/dnflash/content/may2007/db20070509_ 992600.htm.

2. A 2007 report prepared by Congressman Waxman (California) asserted that compensation consultants were a cause of excessive CEO compensation. However, the analysis did not control for other explanatory factors (such as size of the company). When properly controlled, these associations disappear. As a result, the causality attributed in this report was misleading, at the very least. See Henry A Waxman, et al., "Executive Pay: Conflicts of Interest Among Compensation Consultants," United States House of Representatives Committee on Oversight and Government Reform (December 2007). Separately, Core, Guay, and Larcker (2008) found that while the media places a lot of attention on executive compensation, it actually has relatively little influence in affecting compensation levels. See John E. Core, Wayne Guay, and David F. Larcker, "The Power of the Pen and Executive Compensation," *Journal of Financial Economics* 88 (2008): 1–25.

3. See Harwell Wells, "No Man Can Be Worth $1,000,000 a Year: The Fight over Executive Compensation in 1930s America," *University of Richmond Law Review* 44 (January 2010): 689.

4. Carola Frydman and Raven E. Saks, "Executive Compensation: A New View from a Long-Term Perspective, 1936–2005," *Review of Financial Studies* 23 (2010): 2,099–2,138.

5. Amanda Bennett, "Executives Face Change in Awarding Pay, Stock Options: More Managers Find Salary, Bonus Are Tied Directly to Performance," *Wall Street Journal* (February 28, 1986, Eastern edition): 1.

6. Anonymous, "Highest Paid CEOs," *USA Today* (May 17, 1988). Accessed November 10, 2010. See http://infoweb.newsbank.com/iw-search/we/InfoWeb.

7. Measured in terms of the amount realized through stock option exercises and the value of unexercised in-the-money options. See Standard & Poor's Execu-Comp data, cited in: Mark Maremont and Charles Forelle, "Open Spigot: Bosses' Pay: How Stock Options Became Part of the Problem; Once Seen as a Reform, They Grew Into Font of Riches and System to Be Gamed; Reload, Reprice, Backdate," *Wall Street Journal* (December 27, 2006, Eastern edition): A.1.

8. David F. Larcker and Brian Tayan, "Executive Compensation at Nabors Industries: Too Much, Too Little, or Just Right?" Stanford GSB Case No. CG-5 (February 2, 2007).

9. AFL-CIO, "Trends in CEO Pay, 1980–2009," *Corporate Watch, Executive Pay Watch* (2010). Accessed November 10, 2010. See http://www.aflcio.org/corporatewatch/paywatch/pay/index.cfm.

10. Corporate Board Member & PricewaterhouseCoopers LLC, "Special Supplement: What Directors Think 2009. The Corporate Board Member/PricewaterhouseCoopers LLC Survey," *Corporate Board Member Magazine* (2009): 1–16. Accessed November 2, 2010. See www.pwc.com/us/en/corporate-governance/assets/what-directors-think-2009-supplement.pdf.

11. Lucian A. Bebchuk and Jesse M. Fried, "Pay Without Performance: Overview of the Issues," *Academy of Management Perspectives* 20 (2006): 5–24. Lucian A. Bebchuk and Jesse M. Fried, *Pay Without Performance: The Unfulfilled Promise of Executive Compensation* (Cambridge, Mass.: Harvard University Press, 2006).

12. For examples of each of these, see Equilar, Inc., "CD&A Overview: An Examples-Based Review of Key CD&A Elements," Equilar, an executive compensation research firm (2009). Accessed June 23, 2009. See www.equilar.com/.

13. When reading this section, it is useful to consider whether all the different components of compensation are really necessary. For a comparison of compensation packages paid today against those of 50 years ago, see David F. Larcker and Brian Tayan, "A Historical Look at Compensation and Disclosure," Stanford Closer Look Series, CGRP-04 (June 15, 2010). See www.gsb.stanford.edu/cgrp/research/closer_look.html.

14. For an excellent analysis regarding the role of discretion, see Madhav V. Rajan and Stefan Reichelstein, "Subjective Performance Indicators and Discretionary Bonus Pools," *Journal of Accounting Research* 44 (2006): 585–618. See also Christopher D. Ittner, David F. Larcker, and Marshall W. Meyer, "Subjectivity and the Weighting of Performance Measures: Evidence from a Balanced Scorecard," *Accounting Review* 78 (2003): 725–758.

15. U.S. Securities and Exchange Commission (SEC), Division of Corporate Finance, "Current Report on Form 8-K: Frequently Asked Questions," (November 23, 2004): Question 12. See www.sec.gov/divisions/corpfin/form8kfaq.htm.

16. Frederic W. Cook & Co., Inc., "The 2009 Top 250—Long-Term Incentive Grant Practices for Executives," (2009). Accessed October 8, 2009. See www.fwcook.com/alert_letters/2009_Top-250-Report.pdf.

17. ADC Telecommunications, Inc., Form DEF-14A, filed with the Securities and Exchange Commission February 24, 1998.

18. Perkin Elmer, Inc., Form DEF-14A, filed with the Securities and Exchange Commission April 25, 2000.

19. Enron, Inc., Form DEF-14A, filed with the Securities and Exchange Commission May 6, 1997.

20. Advanced Tissue Sciences, Form DEF-14A, filed with the Securities and Exchange Commission May 25, 1999.

21. Equilar, Inc., "Executive Stock Ownership Guidelines Report," Equilar, an executive compensation research firm (2010). Accessed July 28, 2010. See www.equilar.com/.

22. Sarbanes–Oxley Act of 2002 §304, 15 U.S.C. § 7243 (2006).

23. Equilar, Inc., "Clawback Policy Report: An Analysis of Compensation Recovery Policies at Fortune 100 Companies," Equilar, an executive compensation research firm (2010). Accessed October 22, 2010. See www.equilar.com/.

24. ExxonMobil Corp., Form DEF-14A, filed with the Securities and Exchange Commission April 10, 2008.

25. Citigroup, Inc., Form DEF-14A, filed with the Securities and Exchange Commission March 12, 2010.

26. McKesson Corp., Form DEF-14A, filed with the Securities and Exchange Commission June 23, 2008.

27. UBS AG, Form 20F, filed with the Securities and Exchange Commission March 15, 2010.

28. Equilar, Inc., "S&P 1500 Peer Group Report: An Analysis of Peer Groups at S&P 1500 Companies," Equilar, an executive compensation research firm (2010). Accessed September 16, 2010. See www.equilar.com/.

29. John M. Bizjak, Michael L. Lemmon, and Lalitha Naveen, "Does the Use of Peer Groups Contribute to Higher Pay and Less Efficient Compensation?" *Journal of Financial Economics* 90 (2008): 152–168.

30. Michael Faulkender and Jun Yang, "Inside the Black Box: The Role and Composition of Compensation Peer Groups," *Journal of Financial Economics* 96 (2010): 257–270.

31. The Kroger Company, Form DEF-14A, filed with the Securities and Exchange Commission May 15, 2007. Safeway, Inc., Form DEF-14A, filed with the Securities and Exchange Commission April 4, 2007.

32. Since then, Towers Perrin has merged with Watson Wyatt. Both Towers Watson and Hewitt (now Aon Hewitt) have spun off their compensation consulting practice to avoid potential perceived conflicts with doing pension outsourcing and compensation consulting for the same clients. See Chris S. Armstrong, Christopher D. Ittner, and David F. Larcker, "Corporate Governance, Compensation Consultants, and CEO Pay Levels," *Review of Accounting Studies* (forthcoming).

33. A similar argument has been made about the same firm providing both audit- and nonaudit-related services to a client. We discuss this in greater detail in Chapter 10, "Financial Reporting and External Audit."

34. See Martin J. Conyon, Simon I. Peck, and Graham V. Sadler, "Compensation Consultants and Executive Pay: Evidence from the United States and the United Kingdom," *Academy of Management Perspectives* (2009): 2,343–2,355. Brian Cadman, Mary Ellen Carter, and Stephen Hillegeist, "The Incentives of Compensation Consultants and CEO Pay," *Journal of Accounting & Economics* 49 (2010): 263–280. Kevin J. Murphy and Tatiana Sandino, "Executive Pay and 'Independent' Compensation Consultants," *Journal of Accounting & Economics* 49 (2010): 247–262.

35. Chris S. Armstrong, Christopher D. Ittner, and David F. Larcker, "Corporate Governance, Compensation Consultants, and CEO Pay Levels," *Review of Accounting Studies* (forthcoming).

36. Wright Express, Form DEF-14A, filed with the Securities and Exchange Commission April 9, 2009.

37. Includes the fair value of beneficially held stock and options (both vested and unvested). In calculating stock option fair value, remaining terms are reduced by 30 percent to adjust for potential early exercise or termination. See Equilar, Inc., proprietary compensation and equity ownership data for fiscal years from June 2008 to May 2009.

38. Xavier Gabaix and Augustin Landier, "Why Has CEO Pay Increased So Much?" *Quarterly Journal of Economics* 123 (2008): 49–100.

39. Steven N. Kaplan and Joshua Rauh, "Wall Street and Main Street: What Contributes to the Rise in the Highest Incomes?" *Review of Financial Studies* 23 (2010): 1,004–1,050.

40. Companies with weak board oversight are defined as those with dual chairman/CEO, boards with a large number of directors, boards with a large percentage of "gray" directors (directors who are not executives of the company, but who have other financial connections to the company or management as a result of serving as a lawyer, banker, consultant, or other provider of services), boards on which a large percentage of outside directors are appointed by the CEO, boards with a large percentage of old directors, and boards with a large percentage of busy directors. See John E. Core, Robert W. Holthausen, and David F. Larcker, "Corporate Governance, Chief Executive Officer Compensation, and Firm Performance," *Journal of Financial Economics* 51 (1999): 371–406.

41. Named executive officer is an SEC designation that includes the principal executive officer, the principal financial officer, and the three most highly compensated executive officers. See Securities and Exchange Commission, Executive Compensation and Related Person Disclosure. Section II.C.6. SEC Release 33-8732a § II.C.3.a. Accessed December 9, 2008. See www.sec.gov/rules/final/2006/33-8732a.pdf.

42. The Office of State Treasurer Denise L. Nappier, press release, "Nappier Says Four Companies Agree to Connecticut Pension Fund Resolutions, Setting New Standard for Disclosure of Executive Compensation in 2008 Proxies," (April 16, 2008). Accessed November 11, 2010. See www.state.ct.us/ott/pressreleases/press2008/pr04162008.pdf.

43. Abercrombie & Fitch, Form DEF-14A, filed with the Securities and Exchange Commission May 9, 2008.

44. Equilar, Inc., proprietary compensation and equity ownership data for fiscal years from June 2008 to May 2009.

45. Edward P. Lazear and Sherwin Rosen, "Rank-Order Tournaments As Optimum Labor Contracts," *Journal of Political Economy* 89 (1981): 841–864.

46. Moody's reviews CEO compensation as one factor contributing to a company's credit rating. The rating agency finds that large performance-based compensation packages might be indicative of lax oversight and lead to increased risk taking that ultimately increases the likelihood of corporate default. See Chris Mann, "CEO Compensation and Credit Risk," Moody's Investors Service, Global Credit Research Report no. 93592 (2005). Accessed August 11, 2005. See www.moodys.com/cust/content/content.ashx?source=StaticContent/Free%20pages/Credit%20Policy%20Research/documents/current/2003600000426617.pdf.

47. Cerner Corporation, Form DEF-14A, filed with the Securities and Exchange Commission April 17, 2008.

48. E.I. du Pont de Nemours & Co., Form DEF-14A, filed with the Securities and Exchange Commission March 20, 2008.

49. Gretchen Morgenson, "Explaining (or Not) Why the Boss Is Paid So Much," *New York Times* (January 25, 2004): BU1.

50. See Congressional Research Service, cited in Carol Hymowitz, "Pay Gap Fuels Worker Woes," *The Wall Street Journal* (April 28, 2008, Eastern edition): B.8. Carola Frydman of Harvard University and Raven Saks of the Federal Reserve, cited in Greg Ip, "Snow Rebuts Critics of Bush's Economic Record; Treasury Chief Says Many Benefit from Expansion; Some Data Show Otherwise," *Wall Street Journal* (March 20, 2006, Eastern edition): A.3. Institute for Policy Studies, cited in Phred Dvorak, "Theory & Practice—Limits on Executive Pay: Easy to Set, Hard to Keep," *Wall Street Journal* (April 9, 2007): B.1. Towers Perrin (now Towers Watson), cited in Gretchen Morgenson.

51. Walmart Corp., Form DEF-14A, filed with the Securities and Exchange Commission April 22, 2008.

52. Goldman Sachs Group, Inc., Form DEF-14A, filed with the Securities and Exchange Commission March 7, 2008.

53. Kenneth A. Merchant and Jean-Francois Manzoni, "The Achievability of Budget Targets in Profit Centers: A Field Study," *Accounting Review* 64 (1989): 539–558.

54. Raffi J. Indjejikian, Peter Lenk, and Dhananjay Nanda, "Targets, Standards, and Performance Expectations: Evidence from Annual Bonus Plans," *Social Science Research Network* (2000). Accessed October 16, 2008. See http://ssrn.com/abstract=213628.

55. Paul M. Healy, "The Effect of Bonus Schemes on Accounting Decisions," *Journal of Accounting & Economics* 7 (1985): 85–107. Robert W. Holthausen, David F. Larcker, and Richard G. Sloan, "Annual Bonus Schemes and the Manipulation of Earnings," *Journal of Accounting & Economics* 19 (1995): 29–74.

56. Northrop Grumman, Form DEF-14A, filed with the Securities and Exchange Commission April 12, 2007.

57. Long-term performance plans appear to have a positive impact on managerial behavior and firm performance. For example, Larcker (1983) found that managers are likely to increase long-term capital investment following the adoption of a performance plan. He also found positive stock market response to the adoption of these plans, indicating that shareholders believe that they align managerial and shareholder interests. See David F. Larcker, "The Association Between Performance Plan Adoption and Corporate Capital Investment," *Journal of Accounting and Economics* 6 (1983): 3–29.

58. See Jared Harris and Philip Bromiley, "Incentives to Cheat: The Influence of Executive Compensation and Firm Performance on Financial Misrepresentation," *Organization Science* 18 (2007): 350–367. Jap Efendi, Anup Srivastava, and Edward P. Swanson, "Why Do Corporate Managers Misstate Financial Statements? The Role of Option Compensation and Other Factors," *Journal of Financial Economics* 85 (2007): 667–708. Daniel Bergstresser and Thomas Philippon, "CEO Incentives and Earnings Management," *Journal of Financial Economics* 80 (2006): 511–529.

59. Christopher S. Armstrong, Alan D. Jagolinzer, and David F. Larcker, "Chief Executive Officer Equity Incentives and Accounting Irregularities," *Journal of Accounting Research* 48 (2010): 225–271.

60. Shivaram Rajgopal and Terry Shevlin, "Empirical Evidence on the Relationship Between Stock Option Compensation and Risk Taking," *Journal of Accounting & Economics* 33 (2002): 145–171.

61. W. M. Sanders and Donald C. Hambrick, "Swinging for the Fences: The Effects of CEO Stock Options on Company Risk Taking and Performance," *Academy of Management Journal* 50 (2007): 1,055–1,078.

62. Moog, Inc., Form DEF-14A, filed with the Securities and Exchange Commission December 10, 2008.

63. Lilly, Inc., Form DEF-14A, filed with the Securities and Exchange Commission March 8, 2010.

64. Ameriprise Financial, Form DEF-14A, filed with the Securities and Exchange Commission March 19, 2010.

65. Raghuram G. Rajan and Julie Wulf, "Are Perks Purely Managerial Excess?" *Journal of Financial Economics* 79 (2006): 1–33.

66. Rangarajan K. Sundaram and David L. Yermack, "Pay Me Later: Inside Debt and Its Role in Managerial Compensation," *Journal of Finance* 62 (2007): 1,551–1,588.

67. David Yermack, "Flights of Fancy: Corporate Jets, CEO Perquisites, and Inferior Shareholder Returns," *Journal of Financial Economics* 80 (2006): 211–242.

68. Yaniv Grinstein, David Weinbaum, and Nir Yehuda, "The Economic Consequences of Perk Disclosure," Johnson School research paper, series no. 04-09, AFA 2011 Denver Meetings Paper, *Social Science Research Network* (2010). Accessed October 24, 2010. See http://ssrn.com/abstract=1108707.

69. Material in this section is adapted from: David F. Larcker and Brian Tayan, "Sensitivity of CEO Wealth to Stock Price: A New Tool for Assessing Pay for Performance," Stanford Closer Look Series, CGRP-10, (September 15, 2010). See www.gsb.stanford.edu/cgrp/research/closer_look.html. Copyright © 2010 by the Board of Trustees of the Leland Stanford Junior University. All rights reserved. Used with permission from the Stanford University Graduate School of Business.

70. For this approach to be valid, we must assume that the stock market is reasonably efficient in setting prices and that the change in corporate value created by management generally corresponds to the change in market value of the firm.

71. John Core and Wayne Guay, "The Use of Equity Grants to Manage Optimal Equity Incentive Levels," *Journal of Accounting & Economics* 28 (1999): 151–184. John E. Core, Wayne R. Guay, and Robert E. Verrecchia, "Price versus Nonprice Performance Measures in Optimal CEO Compensation Contracts," *Accounting Review* 78 (2003): 957–981.

72. Includes the fair value of beneficially held stock and options (both vested and unvested). In calculating stock option fair value, remaining terms are reduced by 30 percent to adjust for potential early exercise or termination. See Equilar, Inc., proprietary compensation and equity ownership data for fiscal years from June 2008 to May 2009.

73. For simplicity, we use the term *convexity* to mean the percentage return on the CEO's equity portfolio for a 100 percent change in the stock price. This is taking some liberty with the pure mathematical definition of convexity.

74. Erik Beucler and Jack Dolmat-Connell, "Pay Disclosure Rules: Has More Become Less?" *Corporate Board* 28 (2007): 1–5.

75. David Sasaki, and Tania Tovey, "Dodd–Frank Financial Reform Act: Preparing for 2011," Equilar (2010): 1–42.

76. Yonca Ertimur, Fabrizio Ferri, and Volkan Muslu, "Shareholder Activism and CEO Pay," *Review of Financial Studies* (forthcoming).

77. Jie Cai and Ralph A. Walkling, "Shareholders' Say on Pay: Does It Create Value?" *Journal of Financial and Quantitative Analysis* (forthcoming).

78. Fabrizio Ferri and D. Maber, "Say on Pay Votes and CEO Compensation: Evidence from the United Kingdom," working paper, New York University (2009).

79. David F. Larcker, Gaizka Ormazabal, and Daniel J. Taylor.

80. Amgen, Form DEF-14A, filed with the Securities and Exchange Commission March 29, 2010.

81. Amgen, Executive Compensation Survey. Accessed November 11, 2010. See www.amgen.com/executivecompensation/exec_comp_form_survey.jsp.

82. Joseph E. Bachelder III, "EESA Limits on Executive Pay At Affected Institutions," *New York Law Journal* (November 14, 2008).

83. Phred Dvorak, "Firms Measure a CEO's (Net) Worth—In Vetting Pay, Companies Take Stock of Accumulated Wealth; Directors Wrestle with 'Turning Off the Hose,'" Wall Street Journal Online (June 23, 2008). Accessed November 11, 2010. See http://online.wsj.com/article/SB121418172473595653.html.

9

Executive Equity Ownership

In this chapter, we examine the relationship between equity ownership and executive behavior. In theory, executives who hold equity in the companies they manage—either directly in the form of stock ownership or indirectly through options, restricted stock, and performance shares—have greater incentive to improve the economic value of the firm. In addition, equity holdings dissuade self-interested behavior, in that any action the executive takes that impairs firm value will inflict corresponding damage to the executive's personal wealth (although not on a "dollar-for-dollar" basis, given that executives are also compensated in forms other than equity). As a result, equity ownership is an important tool that companies use to mitigate agency problems.

This is the general idea, but it bears closer scrutiny. What behavior is actually observed among executives with significant stock holdings? Is company performance improved? Are agency costs reduced? What unintended effects might equity ownership encourage? What happens when executives sell or hedge their equity holdings to diversify personal wealth? Is there evidence that they rely on informational advantages to do so (insider trading)? In this chapter, we examine the evidence.

Equity Ownership by the CEO

As we discussed in the previous chapter, chief executive officers of the 4,000 largest U.S. companies hold equity positions in their company with a median value of about $4.6 million, comprising a mix of stock and stock options (refer back to Table 8.7). Although some executives make open-market purchases of company stock, they accumulate most of their equity ownership through compensation-related grants.[1]

These sums are significant. As we discussed in the previous chapter, a 1 percent change in company stock price changes CEO wealth by approximately $54,000. Among the largest 100 companies, this figure approaches $600,000.[2] Sizeable monetary incentives should encourage actions that lead to value creation and discourage actions that lead to value destruction.

Equity Ownership and Firm Performance

Extensive research has examined the relationship between executive equity ownership and company performance. One of the most widely cited studies comes from Morck, Shleifer, and Vishny (1988). The authors found a "see-saw shaped" relationship between ownership and firm performance. At low levels of managerial ownership (less than 5 percent), equity ownership and firm value are positively correlated.[3] The relationship is consistent with a hypothesis that managerial ownership provides positive incentive to improve firm performance. However, at higher ownership levels (between 5 percent and 25 percent), the relationship becomes negative. In this part of the function, higher ownership percentages appear to *decrease* firm value. The relationship here is consistent with a different hypothesis: Large ownership positions allow for management entrenchment and weakened oversight. Management is able to gain control of the firm and use its position of influence to extract personal wealth, with the other shareholders bearing the cost of its actions. However, at much higher ownership levels (above 25 percent), the relationship once again turns positive. One potential explanation of this second reversal is that when managers own such a large portion of the company stock, they bear a large share of the cost of their actions, which discourages personal rent extraction and reinforces incentives to enhance firm value. We therefore see evidence of both positive and negative effects of managerial ownership, depending on the level of ownership (see Figure 9.1).[4]

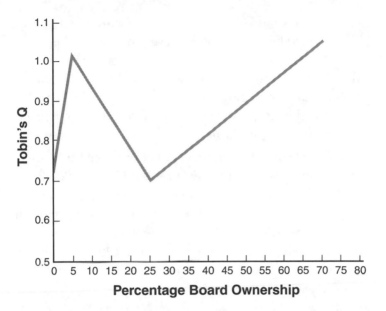

Percentage Board Ownership

The relationship between board ownership and Tobin's *Q* implied by the piecewise linear ordinary least squares regression of 1980 Tobin's *Q* on board ownership and other firm characteristics for 371 Fortune 500 firms.

Source: Morck, Shleifer, and Vishny (1988).

Figure 9.1   Relationship between executive ownership and firm value.

Other studies tend to find more positive benefits from executive equity ownership. For example, McConnell and Servaes (1990) found results similar to those of Morck, Shleifer, and Vishny (1988). However, in their study, the negative effects of higher ownership levels are largely muted. Managerial ownership became negative only at levels above 40 to 50 percent (a level that is rare for most public companies), and even then only to a slight degree. Their study is more consistent with a hypothesis that equity ownership aligns executive interests with those of shareholders.[5]

Elsilä, Kallunki, and Nilsson (2009) also found positive benefits from executive equity ownership. Instead of measuring executive incentives in terms of the percentage of the company that an executive owns, the authors measured them in terms of the personal wealth the executive had invested in the company. They explained: "A relatively small proportion of [a] firm's shares owned by the CEO may represent a significant proportion of her personal wealth, if the value

of the personal wealth is modest. Accordingly, a relatively large proportion of shares owned by CEOs may represent only a small proportion of her wealth, if the value of the wealth is large." The authors
hypothesized that CEOs with a large portion of wealth invested in the
firm have greater incentive to perform. This is what they found. The
ratio of CEO ownership to personal wealth is positively correlated
with both firm performance and firm value.[6]

Finally, if we simply plot the book-to-market ratio against the percentage of firm equity owned by the CEO for the largest 4,000 firms
in the United States, we observe the following results (see Figure
9.2). Not only is it difficult to see the "see-saw shaped" pattern
described by Morch, Shleifer, and Vishny (1988), but it is difficult to
see any discernable pattern. Here, the relationship between equity
ownership and firm performance is much more fragile than suggested in earlier works.

Calculations by the authors. Data from Equilar, Inc.

Figure 9.2   Relationship between equity ownership and firm valuation.

It seems plausible that managerial incentives are higher when
executives have some reasonable level of "equity skin in the game."
However, despite extensive efforts, researchers have not reached a
consensus on the relationship between equity ownership and firm
performance. One especially troublesome aspect of the research is

untangling the causal direction of the relation. Do equity incentives cause better future performance, or do firms that expect an improvement in future performance increase equity grants to executives in anticipation of this improvement?[7] Nevertheless, boards must make decisions regarding the appropriate level of equity ownership by executives.

Target Ownership Plans

A company can encourage equity ownership by adopting a **target ownership plan**, which requires that an executive own a minimum amount of company stock. The limit is generally expressed as a multiple of the annual salary and varies among executive officers, depending on their seniority. For example, in 2008, Kroger required that CEO David Dillon hold stock and options with a dollar value equal to at least five times his base salary of $1.185 million; the vice chairman and chief operating officer four times base salary; and executive vice presidents and nonexecutive directors three times base salary. The company explained that the guidelines were designed to "align the interests of the officers with [the] interests [of] shareholders" and "to [ensure] that the officers work within the framework of Kroger's long-term strategic objectives."[8] The company's target ownership plans do not require that these executives purchase their equity positions using personal wealth, but instead allow the executives to retain options or restricted shares granted through the regular compensation program to build up their ownership stake.

According to data from Fredric W. Cook, 83 percent of the largest 250 companies in the United States have executive stock ownership guidelines. This percentage is up significantly from just a few years ago. Among companies with target ownership plans, approximately half are expressed as a multiple of compensation (as in the case of Kroger). Thirty-five percent are expressed as **retention approaches**, in which executives are required to take a percentage of proceeds that they realize through option exercises and keep the money invested in company stock. The remaining plans are expressed as a fixed number of shares that executives are required to own.[9]

Researchers find generally positive benefits from the adoption of target ownership plans. For example, Core and Larcker (2002) measured the performance of 195 companies that first adopted target ownership plans. The study found that, before plan adoption, executives in the sample had low levels of direct equity ownership and the firms had inferior stock price performance relative to peers. Following plan adoption, however, these companies experienced a significant improvement in subsequent operating performance and stock price performance. Holding aside the difficulty of inferring causality, the findings suggest that companies with below-average executive ownership and poor performance might consider implementing a target ownership plan as one step toward improving executive incentives.[10]

Equity Ownership and Agency Costs

Equity ownership is intended to provide incentives that motivate managers to improve corporate performance, but it also has the potential to encourage undesirable behaviors. This occurs when an executive seeks to increase the value of equity holdings in ways other than through improvements in operating, financing, and investment decisions. Examples include these:

- Manipulating accounting results to inflate stock price or achieve bonus targets
- Manipulating the timing of option grants to increase their intrinsic value
- Manipulating the release of information to the public to correspond with more favorable grant dates
- Using inside information to gain an advantage in selling or otherwise hedging equity holdings

When these actions occur, they represent the very agency costs that equity ownership is intended to discourage.

Accounting Manipulation

As discussed more completely in the Chapter 10, "Financial Reporting and External Audit," plenty of evidence shows that accounting manipulations occur. Consider these prominent examples:

- Enron, which front-loaded revenues and hid liabilities through off-balance-sheet vehicles

- WorldCom, which capitalized expenses on the balance sheet that should have been treated as operating costs
- Royal Dutch/Shell, which inflated the size and value of proved oil reserves

An important question for boards and shareholders is whether such manipulations are *more likely* to occur in companies where executives own a large portion of company stock than in companies where executives own little or no stock. That is, do executives with considerable equity ownership inflate earnings to manipulate the market and produce a higher stock price?

The research evidence on this topic is mixed. For example, Harris and Bromiley (2007) found that financial restatements are more likely to occur at companies where executives are paid a large portion of compensation in the form of options.[11] However, Baber, Kang, Liang, and Zhu (2009) found no such evidence.[12] Johnson, Ryan, and Tian (2009) found that unrestricted equity holdings by executives are associated with a greater incidence of accounting fraud.[13] Erickson, Hanlon, and Maydew (2006) did not find this association.[14]

The mixed results appear to be due in part to methodological differences in these studies. Armstrong, Jagolinzer, and Larcker (2010) addressed these problems by applying more sophisticated statistical methods and a broader sample than those used in previous studies. They did not find evidence of a positive association between equity incentives and accounting irregularities. In fact, they found some evidence that firms in which the CEO has larger equity incentives have a *lower* frequency of accounting irregularities than firms in which the CEO has a relatively low level of equity incentives.[15] If true, these findings would support a conclusion that equity incentives tend to reduce agency costs and that equity holdings do not encourage manipulation of accounting results for personal gain. Still, shareholders and stakeholders should be cognizant of the potential for self-gain that comes through accounting manipulation ("cooking the books"). The potential for this problem would seemingly be most pronounced when executives have highly convex compensation plans (as discussed in the previous chapter).

Manipulation of Equity Grants

Equity ownership might also encourage executives to manipulate equity grants, to extract incremental value. This might occur in at least two ways:

- **Manipulating the timing of the grant**—The grant date either is delayed so that it occurs after a stock price decline has already taken place or is brought forward to precede an expected increase in stock price.

- **Manipulating the timing that information is released to the public**—The release of favorable information about the company (a new product, a new strategic relationship, stronger-than-expected sales) is delayed so that it occurs after a scheduled grant date; the executive benefits from an immediate increase in value when the favorable information is subsequently released. Likewise, unfavorable information is released early, to precede a grant date; the executive benefits by receiving the grant after the unfavorable news has already driven the stock price lower.

In both cases, the executive seeks to maximize the value received from an equity grant by taking actions that are not in the interests of shareholders.

When equity awards are granted on a purely random basis, no discernable pattern emerges in the stock price movement around the grant date. Stock price movements appear random and the relative favorability of the timing of the grant tends to be unpredictable. Many grants fit this pattern. However, at some companies, stock price movements follow a discernable pattern around the grant date. The grant either coincides with a relative low or immediately precedes a sudden increase in price, resulting in a V-shaped pattern.

Considerable research shows that such patterns occur for a large sample of firms. Yermack (1997) demonstrated a V-shaped pattern around stock option grant dates. Stock prices in that sample mirrored the market before option grant dates, but then exhibited above-market returns in the 50 days following the grant dates. Yermack concluded that some sort of manipulation took place, through either the release of information or the timing of grants, but he was unable to conclusively determine which.[16]

To test the hypothesis that executives might manipulate the release of information, Aboody and Kasznik (2000) examined stock price behavior around *scheduled* option grants. Scheduled option grants include those for which the option grants follow a predetermined schedule (for example, they might be regularly awarded the day after a board meeting). Their findings are similar to those of Yermack (1997): Stock prices exhibited a distinctive V-shaped pattern around the grant date. The authors concluded that executives might opportunistically time the release of company information to the market around grant dates.[17]

Lie (2005) tested a hypothesis that executives manipulate the timing of awards in their favor. He divided the sample into companies whose grants were clearly unscheduled (with the grant date made at the discretion of the board) and those whose grants were scheduled. Unexpectedly, Lie found that the V-shape pattern around *unscheduled* grants was more pronounced (see Figure 9.3). He posited that insiders were retroactively changing the grant date of unscheduled awards, to lower the exercise price and increase profits to executives. This practice has come to be known as **stock option backdating** (see the following sidebar).[18]

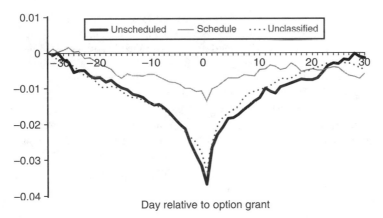

Day relative to option grant

Figure 9.3   Stock price movements around scheduled and unscheduled grant dates.

Stock Option Backdating

The *Wall Street Journal* reported the findings of Lie (2005) in a front-page article. The story soon triggered a wide-ranging investigation by the Securities and Exchange Commission (SEC). The article suggested that dozens of companies might be engaged in backdating.[19] By the end of 2006, more than 120 companies were implicated.[20] In a separate study, Bebchuk, Grinstein, and Peyer (2010) estimated that the practice was much more prevalent, occurring in approximately 12 percent of companies.[21] Although retroactive manipulation largely stopped with the passage of the Sarbanes–Oxley Act, which required that option grants to executives be reported within two days, alleged abuses have been uncovered stemming back as far as 1981. Still, it has been difficult for U.S. regulators to convict executives who were shown to engage in the practice. More important, backdating is an illustration of the types of executive behavior that the board needs to monitor when equity-based compensation plans are used (see Table 9.1).

Table 9.1 Selected Allegations of Backdating (continued)

Company	Allegations	Highlighted Results
Brocade Communications	The SEC charged the CEO and former Vice President of Human Resources with fraud for granting employees favorably priced options without recording the necessary compensation expense.	The CEO was sentenced to 18 months in prison and fined $15 million. The Vice President of Human Resources was sentenced to four months in prison and fined $1.25 million.
	Shareholders filed a class-action lawsuit claiming they suffered losses in the market because the company and its executives made false and misleading statements.	The two executives were convicted of criminal offenses. The CEO was sentenced to 21 months in federal prison. He has been out on bail pending the appeal.

Table 9.1   Selected Allegations of Backdating (continued)

Company	Allegations	Highlighted Results
KLA-Tencor	The SEC charged the company and former CEO with an illicit scheme to backdate options, alleging that the company had concealed more than $200 million in stock option compensation.	Without admitting or denying the charges, the company agreed to settle a derivative lawsuit and consented to a permanent injunction from further violations. The former general counsel was accused of altering options at **two** different companies (KLA-Tencor and Juniper Networks). SEC suit is still pending.
UnitedHealth Group	The SEC charged the CEO with repeatedly granting undisclosed, in-the-money stock options to himself and other UnitedHealth officers and employees without recording this in the company's books and without disclosing to shareholders material compensation expenses.	The CEO settled for $468 million. Settlement was the first with an individual under the "clawback" provision (Section 304) of the Sarbanes–Oxley Act. Separately, UnitedHealth and former CEO agreed to settle investor claims for approximately $1 billion,

Research by the authors and Stanford Law School, and Securities Class Action Clearinghouse in cooperation with Cornerstone Research. See http://securities.stanford.edu/.

Bernile and Jarrell (2009) found that the cost of backdating (in terms of reduced shareholder value) is well in excess of the associated fines and legal fees. Shareholders might perceive backdating to be one manifestation of broader agency problems within the firm, or they might be concerned about damage to the firm's reputation. Either way, backdating reflects a serious lapse in oversight by the board of directors.[22]

Other Examples of Value Extraction through Timing

Today the stock option backdating scandal has largely run its course. Regulatory changes, such as a shortened window for reporting transactions on Form 4, have widely eliminated the practice. Other practices, however, have been harder to prevent through regulatory actions, although they represent similar attempts to extract additional value from equity grants. Examples include these:

- **Spring-loading**—Awarding options immediately before the release of unexpected positive news that is likely to drive up the price of a stock.

- **Bullet-dodging**—Waiting to award options until after the release of unexpected negative news that is likely to drive down the price of a stock.

- **Exercise backdating**—Retroactively changing the exercise date of stock options to a date when the market price was lower, to reduce the reported taxable gain that the option holder would have to pay at an ordinary income tax level.[23]

In some instances, these actions result in only marginal increases in value for executives.[24] In others, the dollar amounts can be significant. Nevertheless, it is hard to see how they are justified on any grounds. Instead, they appear to run counter to the concept of stewardship and demonstrate that some executives will take advantage of weaknesses in oversight for personal gain.[25]

Equity Sales and Hedging

An executive employed at a company for a long period of time commonly accumulates a substantial ownership position in company stock (as reflected in Table 8.7 in Chapter 8). Furthermore, the ownership of this stock likely comprises a significant portion of the executive's total personal wealth. As such, an executive might want to limit his or her financial exposure and reduce portfolio risk. The board of directors might allow this diversification if it believes this type of transaction is in the best interest of the company and does not lessen incentives to perform (see the following sidebar).

Executives can achieve diversification through at least three mechanisms:

- Selling the company shares outright
- Hedging a portion of the ownership position through financial instruments
- Pledging a portion of shares as collateral for a loan that is used to purchase additional assets

In doing so, however, a risk arises that executives will engage in self-interested behavior to maximize the value of their holdings at the expense of shareholders.

Equity Ownership and Risk Aversion

A major retailer found itself in deep financial straits and close to insolvency.[26] The board hired a CEO with extensive industry experience to turn around the company. The CEO informed the board that he was looking for a large payout if his efforts proved successful. The board designed a compensation program that was heavily weighted with stock options, combined with a low salary and cash bonus. The package included one million stock options, with a ten-year term and strike price close to zero (the current market price of the stock). These economic incentives encouraged a solid turnaround.

The CEO took drastic measures to improve the company's situation, including selling noncore assets and expanding into new retail formats. The moves paid off, and within a few years, the stock price soared to $100 per share. The CEO was suddenly sitting on $100 million of in-the-money options.

At this point, his behavior changed. He brought forward fewer proposals for investments and acquisitions. The board realized that his significant wealth in the company was affecting his desire to take risk. Whereas originally he had nothing to lose, now failure to execute on new strategies could result in severe personal economic loss. The board therefore decided to allow the CEO to cash out his $100 million of options and grant him a new tranche of options at the current market price. This move allowed the executive to diversify his established wealth while still retaining equity incentives.

A key decision for the board of directors is to consider whether the executive's investment in company stock motivates him or her to make the right investment decisions on behalf of shareholders. Both excessive concentration and lack of ownership can influence decision making negatively.

Trading by Insiders

Executives can diversify their equity holdings by making open-market sales of company stock or by exercising stock options and selling the acquired shares. However, because executives have access to nonpublic information that could be material to valuing the company's stock, there is always a possibility that executives will use this information to gain an improper trading advantage over public shareholders. Examples include selling shares before the release of bad news that is expected to decrease the stock price and waiting to sell until after the release of good news that is expected to increase the stock price.

The SEC has established rules that dictate when and how sales by executives may occur. The SEC uses the term **insider** to identify individuals—corporate officers, directors, employees, and certain professional advisors—who have access to material financial and operational information about a company that has not yet been made public. Insiders are restricted in their ability to engage in transactions involving company securities (both purchases and sales) and may trade only when they are not in possession of material nonpublic information. Trades made on the basis of such information are considered illegal **insider trading** and, under various acts passed by Congress, are punishable with jail time and financial penalties (up to three times the profit gained or loss avoided from such activity).[27]

Insider trading lawsuits are prosecuted, in part, under SEC Rule 10b-5, "Employment of Manipulative and Deceptive Devices."[28] Prosecutors argue that the insider has committed fraud on the market by making false statements regarding the prospects of the company or by failing to make appropriate disclosures, thereby maintaining an artificially high share price at the time of sale. For example, in 2007, the SEC charged Joseph Nacchio, former chairman and chief executive officer of Qwest, with insider trading. He was accused of selling more than $100 million of Qwest shares in early 2001 while in possession of material inside information that the company would not meet aggressive financial targets. Qwest shares, which Nacchio sold at approximately $35 per share, subsequently fell below $10. He was sentenced to six years in prison and ordered to pay $19 million in fines and $44.6 million in forfeitures.[29]

To restrict executives from violating insider trading laws, companies typically designate a period of time known as a **blackout period**, in which insiders are restricted from making trades in the company stock. Blackout periods typically occur between the time when material information is known (such as quarterly earnings, a new product launch, or acquisition) and the time when it is released to the public. Blackout periods are specified in the company's insider trading policy.[30] A typical blackout window has a median length of 50 calendar days.[31] Trades within the blackout period are prohibited, and trades outside the blackout period (during the **trading window**) commonly require approval in advance by the general counsel's office. As a result, the general counsel plays a critical role in preventing trading abuses by insiders (see the following sidebar).

Trading Window

Crimson Exploration

"You may not trade in Company securities outside of a trading window. For purposes of this policy, a 'trading window' will commence after the close of trading two full trading days following the Company's widespread public release of quarterly operating results and ending at the close of trading on the last day of the second month of the current fiscal quarter. ... During a trading window, you may trade in Company securities only after obtaining the approval of the Compliance Officer. If you decide to engage in a transaction involving Company securities during a trading window, you must notify the Compliance Officer in writing of the amount and nature of the proposed trade(s) at least two business days prior to the proposed transaction, and certify in writing that you are not in possession of material nonpublic information concerning the Company. You must not engage in the transaction unless and until the Compliance Officer provides his approval in writing."[32]

Despite these restrictions, extensive evidence indicates that executives rely on nonpublic information to guide their trading. For example, Lakonishok and Lee (2001) found that open-market purchases of company stock by insiders are predictive of future price increases. The effects are particularly pronounced among small-capitalization companies.[33] Seyhun (1986) found both that insider stock purchases tend to precede a period of market outperformance and that sales tend to precede a period of underperformance. Insiders with access to more valuable information about the firm (such as the chairman or the CEO) are found to have a greater trading advantage than other insiders.[34] These and other studies suggest that insiders can earn substantial returns over a period of up to three years.[35]

Rule 10b5-1

The SEC adopted Rule 10b5-1 in 2000 to protect insiders whose position regularly exposes them to important nonpublic information. According to the agency:

> As a practical matter, in most situations it is highly doubtful that a person who knows inside information relevant to the value of a security can completely disregard that knowledge when making the decision to purchase or sell that security. In the words of the Second Circuit, "material information cannot lay idle in the human brain." Indeed, even if the trader could put forth purported reasons for trading other than awareness of the inside information, other traders in the market place would clearly perceive him or her to possess an unfair advantage. On the other hand, we recognize that an absolute standard based on knowing possession, or awareness, could be overbroad in some respects. Sometimes a person may reach a decision to make a particular trade without any awareness of material nonpublic information, but then come into possession of such information before the trade actually takes place.[36]

To protect executives in such a situation, the SEC adopted Rule 10b5-1 ("Trading 'on the Basis of' Material Nonpublic Information in Insider Trading Cases"), which outlines a set of procedures that, if followed, provide an "affirmative defense" against alleged violations of insider trading laws.[37]

Under Rule 10b5-1, insiders are allowed to enter into a binding contract that instructs a third-party broker to execute purchase or sales transactions on behalf of the insider (**10b5-1 plans**). The contract can be agreed to only during a period in which the insider does not have knowledge of material nonpublic information (that is, outside the blackout window). The insider is required to specify a program or algorithm that dictates the conditions under which sales are to be made; such factors might include the number of shares, the interval between transactions, or a share price limit. For example, a plan might call for the sale of 10,000 shares on a given day each month for one year. Alternatively, a plan might call for the sale of 10,000 shares each month at prices above a limit of $20 per share, with the timing of each trade subject to the broker's discretion. After the third-party broker received his or her instructions, the insider is not allowed to exercise any influence over the execution of the plan. From that point forward, the third-party broker has sole discretion (see the following sidebar).[38]

Approximately 80 percent of companies permit executives to trade using 10b5-1 plans. Approval by the general counsel is generally required in advance: Seventy-three percent of companies require such approval to set up a plan, and 59 percent require approval to modify or cancel a plan.[39] Insiders are not required to disclose to the public that they have entered into a 10b5-1 plan (although they are required to disclose each trade on a Form 4).

10B5-1 Plan Disclosures

Datalink Corporation

"On February 13, 2006, our Chairman, Greg R. Meland, established a pre-arranged, personal stock trading plan under SEC Rule 10b5-1 (the 'Plan') to sell a portion of his holdings of our Common Stock. Mr. Meland has advised us that he intends to use proceeds from sales under his Plan to diversify his personal investments. The Plan covers the sale of up to 120,000 shares over a one-year period. Subject to a minimum $3.00 per share price, Mr. Meland's broker will make sales under the Plan of up to 30,000 shares per month. Sales will take place only during the first ten business days of the month. Following completion of the planned sales, and assuming the broker sells all of the shares subject to the Plan, Mr. Meland will continue to own 3,330,690 shares of our Common Stock."[40]

McDATA Corporation

"On May 8, 2002, John A. Kelley, Jr., McDATA's President and COO, entered into a Rule 10b5-1 Stock Purchase Plan with Deutsche Bank Alex Brown to purchase $20,000 worth of McDATA Class B Common Stock on each of the following dates: May 29, 2002; June 26, 2002; July 31, 2002; August 28, 2002; and September 25, 2002, for an aggregate total amount of purchases equal to $100,000."[41]

When a plan is in place, the insider may not interfere with the execution of trades. However, he or she is allowed to make amendments to (or terminate) the plan at any time. Insiders may also trade outside the plan, although these trades are not offered the protections of Rule 10b5-1.

Through 10b5-1 plans, insiders are therefore able to make prearranged commitments to buy or sell securities that protect them from legal liability if the transactions occur while they are subsequently in possession of material nonpublic information. These plans are used almost exclusively for the purpose of selling securities. By ceding discretion and trading authority to a third-party broker, the insider is no longer seen to be trading "on the basis of" such inside information and, therefore, cannot be found to be deceiving or defrauding the public. The SEC has stipulated, however, that protection under Rule 10b5-1 is effective "only when the contract, instruction, or plan to purchase or sell securities was given or entered into in good faith and not as part of a plan or scheme to evade the prohibitions of this section."[42]

Research indicates that Rule 10b5-1 might not be achieving the outcome that the SEC envisioned. Jagolinzer (2009) found that insiders who execute sales through 10b5-1 plans outperform the market by an average of 6 percent over the six months following each trade. Moreover, the returns earned by executives using 10b5-1 plans are substantially higher than trades made without such plans. Finally, he found that sales transactions by plan participants systematically precede periods of underperformance by the company's share price and that early terminations of 10b5-1 sales plans systematically precede periods of outperformance.

He offered potential explanations for his findings:

1. Insiders might implement a 10b5-1 plan far enough in advance of pending adverse news that the public and regulators would have difficulty clearly establishing that the plan was initiated purposefully to profit from the news. Such a strategy would allow insiders to exploit longer-term nonpublic information.

2. Insiders might alter the timing of news releases to make pending 10b5-1 trades more profitable.

3. 10b5-1 participants might terminate their plans prematurely to take advantage of newly available material information before it is released to the public, thereby preventing trades that would otherwise be less profitable.[43]

All such explanations indicate a possible pattern of abuse that corporate governance systems are expected to prevent. To minimize insider abuse of 10b5-1 plans, experts recommend that companies adopt strict and transparent procedures to govern their use (see the following sidebar).

Procedures for Minimizing Abuse of Rule 10b5-1

- Disclose the implementation of 10b5-1 trading plans on Form 8-K.

- Require that a period of time (such as 30 days) elapse between the disclosure of a new plan and the first trade made under it. This minimizes the appearance of market timing.

- Note on each Form 4 that the sales were made pursuant to a 10b5-1 plan.

- Limit the number of modifications to a plan after it is adopted. If changes are made to a plan, require an additional lag period before the first trade made pursuant to the modified plan.

- Limit the number of plan suspensions and terminations. Encourage insiders to adopt shorter-duration plans (such as just six or nine months) to reduce terminations.

- Arrange for sales to take place in small lots, over a long period of time. Diversified sales minimize the appearance of market timing.

- Arrange for the 10b5-1 plan to be administered by a dedicated broker who is not the insider's broker for other personal holdings. The insider will have fewer reasons to communicate with the plan broker and will be less likely to convey inside information, advertently or inadvertently.

- Limit the number of trades made outside the 10b5-1 plan, while a plan is in place.[44]

Hedging

An executive might decide to **hedge** the value of his or her equity holdings rather than engage in an outright sale of shares or options. A decision to hedge is often the result of discussion with a personal investment advisor and could be motivated by diversification, tax planning, or a variety of other objectives. Hedging might also allow an executive to avoid the public scrutiny that comes from a substantial sale of company shares.

At the same time, obvious problematic issues are related to executive hedging. First, hedging unwinds equity incentives that the board presumably intended to align the interests of management with those of shareholders. If the board had preferred this compensation structure, it should have awarded this in the first place. Second, allowing an executive to hedge is costly to the company. Management will demand larger compensation for receiving risky equity incentives instead of risk-free cash compensation. Through hedging, however, the executive can translate the value of that premium to cash. This results in a higher compensation bill for the company.[45] Third, explaining to shareholders why it is in their interest to allow executives to hedge is exceedingly difficult. Hedging requires the executive to take a "short" position in the company's shares. Although it is illegal for an executive to short-sell, it is permissible to buy a put option on company stock. For obvious reasons, the compensation committee and the entire board need to proactively discuss and define the circumstances under which hedging is permissible.

Survey results suggest that hedging is a relatively infrequent occurrence. Only 7 percent of companies allow executives to hedge.[46]

Bettis, Bizjak, and Kalpathy (2010) found hedging transactions by 1,181 executives at 911 firms between 1996 and 2006 (also a relatively small number). The most common techniques for hedging are zero-cost collars and prepaid variable forward contracts.[47] (See the following sidebar for examples.)

- **Zero-cost collar**—The executive purchases a put option with an exercise price at or slightly below the current market price of the stock. The executive offsets the cost of the put option by selling a call option, with an exercise price generally 10 to 20 percent above the current market price. The executive has effectively reduced the downside risk and has given up much of the upside gains. In economic substance, the collar is similar to a sale, although taxes are not owed until option expiration and the eventual stock sale. The executive can also take out a loan against the value of the collar (not the underlying stock) and invest the proceeds in a diversified portfolio.

- **Prepaid-variable forward (PVF)**—The executive enters into a contract that promises future delivery of shares that he or she owns in company stock, in return for an upfront payment of cash. Two aspects of the PVF give it its name. First, the executive is prepaid for stock that he or she does not have to deliver to the investment firm until the end of the contract (generally two to five years). Because delivery is deferred, the cash payment is discounted from the current fair value of the stock (say, 15 percent less). The executive can take the cash payment and invest it in a diversified portfolio. As such, the payment is similar to a zero-coupon loan. The executive does not owe capital gains tax on the underlying shares until the end of the contract. Second, the forward contract is variable, in that the number of shares that the executive owes upon delivery is based on a sliding scale. If the price of the stock has fallen below some threshold, the executive is required to deliver all the shares. If the share price has risen, the executive is required to deliver only a fraction of the shares (subject to a minimum percentage defined up front). In some cases, the executive agrees to a cash payment at settlement rather than the delivery of shares. The PVF structure gives the executive full downside protection and allows for partial participation in the upside.[48]

Hedging Examples

Example of Zero-Cost Collar

In 2005, Alexander Taylor II, president and COO of Chattem, who beneficially owned approximately 200,000 shares of common stock, arranged a zero-cost collar on 50,000 shares of common stock. The collar comprised the purchase of a put option that gave Taylor the right to sell 50,000 shares at a price of $18.13 and the sale of a call option that gave the purchaser of the call the right to buy 50,000 shares at $34.48. The collar had a two-month term and expired on March 22.[49]

At the time, the company's common stock traded at a price of approximately $34. It had increased almost 80 percent, from $19 one year before.

Example of Prepaid-Variable Forward

In 2002, David Doyle, president of Quest Software, owned 12.8 million shares of company stock worth approximately $150 million.[50] In November 2002, he entered into a PVF contract with a two-year term. In the deal, he received an upfront cash payment of $9.6 million in exchange for a derivative on one million shares (market value $11.9 million). The derivative obligated Doyle to make delivery of shares, with the number of shares dependent upon the stock price in January 2005.

- If stock price ≤ $10.74 (floor), 1 million shares

- If stock price was between floor ($10.74) and cap ($12.88), number of shares = (floor/price) × 1 million shares

- If price > cap ($12.88), number of shares = [(stock price − cap + floor)/stock price] × 1 million shares[51]

If Doyle can earn a total return of 10 percent on the $9.6 million cash payment over two years, the pretax value of the PVF contract to Doyle is as follows. This payout is compared to the opportunity cost of holding the shares outright.

If the stock price falls below the floor, Doyle delivers one million shares but retains his diversified portfolio, which is assumed to have grown to $10.56 million in value. If the price rises above the cap, Doyle delivers a sliding number of shares and retains the remainder (the fraction of shares he retains decreases as the price increases); the value of the retained shares plus the value of the diversified portfolio remains fixed at $12.7 million. In between the cap and the floor, he earns a slight discount to what he would earn if he had not entered the PFV, but for practical reasons, he is somewhat indifferent between owning the PFV and owning the shares (see Figure 9.4).

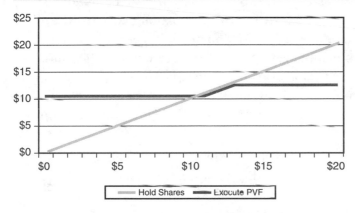

Assuming that the cash received was invested in the market with a 10 percent return over two years

Figure 9.4   Payout under the prepaid variable forward.

The Dodd–Frank bill requires companies to disclose whether they allow executives to hedge equity positions. Previously, this disclosure was not required. Guidelines for executive hedging (if they exist) are typically included in the Insider Trading Policy. Companies are not required to make this policy public, although it is not clear why a company would choose to keep this information private (see the following sidebar).

Hedging Policies and Disclosure

AirNet Systems

The Company considers it improper and inappropriate for any of our directors, officers, or team members to engage in short-term or speculative transactions in our securities or in other transactions in our securities that may lead to inadvertent violations of the insider trading laws. Therefore, it is our policy that directors, officers, and team members may not engage in any of the following transactions:

- **Short-term trading**—Short-term trading of our securities may be distracting to you and may unduly focus you on our short-term stock market performance instead of our long-term business objectives. For these reasons, any director, officer or other team member who purchases our securities in the open market may not sell any Company securities during the six months following the purchase. The prohibition applies only to purchases in the open market and does not apply to stock option exercises or other employee benefit plan acquisitions.

- **Short sales**—Short sales of our securities (sales of securities that are not then owned) evidence an expectation on the part of the seller that the securities will decline in value, and therefore signal to the market that the seller has no confidence in the Company or our short-term prospects. In addition, short sales may reduce the seller's incentive to improve our performance. For these reasons, short sales of our securities are prohibited. In addition, Section 16(c) of the Securities Exchange Act of 1934 prohibits our officers and directors from engaging in short sales.

- **Publicly traded options**—A transaction in options is, in effect, a bet on the short-term movement of our common shares and therefore creates the appearance that the director, officer, or team member is trading based on inside information. Transactions in options also may focus the director's, officer's, or team member's attention on short-term performance at the expense of our long-term objectives. Accordingly, transactions in puts, calls, or other derivative securities, on an exchange or in any other organized market, are prohibited.

- **Standing orders**—Standing orders should be used only for a very brief period of time. A standing order placed with a broker to sell or purchase our common shares at a specified price leaves you with no control over the timing of the transaction. A standing order transaction executed by the broker when you are aware of material nonpublic information may result in unlawful insider trading.

- **Hedging transactions**—Certain forms of hedging or monetization transactions, such as zero-cost collars and forward sale contracts, allow a director, officer, or team member to lock in much of the value of his or her common shares, often in exchange for all or part of the potential for upside appreciation in the common shares. These transactions allow the director, officer, or team member to continue to own the covered common shares, but without the full risks and rewards of ownership. When that occurs, the director, officer, or team member may no longer have the same objectives as our other shareholders. Therefore, directors, officers and team members are prohibited from engaging in any such transactions.[52]

Several studies on the prevalence and implications of hedging activity among senior executives exist. Bettis, Bizjak, and Lemmon (2001) studied the use of zero-cost collars and found that executives use these transactions to hedge approximately 36 percent of their total holdings. The number of shares hedged was approximately ten times greater than the number of shares sold by these executives through outright sales transactions. Hedges were put on during periods in which other insiders were executing a relatively high volume of sales. The authors did not, however, find evidence that executives using these transactions outperformed the market and thus conclude that hedges do not indicate trading on the basis of inside information.[53]

Jagolinzer, Matsunaga, and Yeung (2007) studied the use of prepaid-variable forward transactions. They found that the average PVF transaction hedged 30 percent of the executive's equity position. The number of shares involved in a PVF was approximately 50 times larger than the number of shares sold by these same insiders in outright sales transactions during the preceding year. Unlike Bettis, Bizjak, and Lemmon (2001), the authors found that PVF transactions preceded periods of abnormal stock returns and concluded that the hedges were used to protect against anticipated declines in the company stock, generally after a period of strong outperformance.[54]

Bettis, Bizjak, and Kalpathy (2010) found that executives tended to place hedges after the company share price made significant run-ups relative to the market. They also found that zero-cost collar and prepaid variable forward hedges tended to precede significant declines in the company share price, which might signal that they were acting on inside information.[55]

These studies raise questions regarding the desirability of executive hedging for shareholders. The change of incentive structure resulting from hedging activity does have a significant impact on the level of risk and reward that the executive has tied up in the company. This change has the potential to disassociate the interests of management from those of shareholders. If hedging is carried to the extreme, the executive receives almost no performance-based incentive value from equity ownership and might as well be paid entirely in cash. These are important considerations for the board of directors. Executive hedges will almost certainly need to be justified to shareholders and the media.

Pledging

Instead of selling or hedging, an executive might decide to **pledge** shares as collateral for a loan, the proceeds of which would be used either to purchase a diversified portfolio of assets, to enter new business activities, or for personal spending. As with hedging transactions, pledging might be more tax efficient than an outright sale. The interest rate on collateralized loans might also be relatively low. In addition, the executive does not necessarily have to sell shares to settle the loan and thus may maintain a high level of ownership in the company.

At the same time, the board of directors must understand why the executive wants to pledge shares. If the proceeds of the loans are used for personal consumption (such as paying college tuition or remodeling a home), the board might decide that it has minimal impact on managerial incentives. However, what does it say about the focus and dedication of the executive if the proceeds are used to launch a new business venture or finance risky investments? What would be the impact if these activities failed and the CEO went bankrupt? Is the board willing to offset these losses with additional compensation and equity grants? Clearly, pledging transactions deserve special consideration (see the following sidebar).

Companies are required to disclose whether executives have pledged shares in a brokerage account or used them as collateral for a loan. According to survey data, approximately 20 percent of companies allow their executives to pledge shares.[56] An electronic search of available proxy statements found that 982 executive officers have pledge disclosures. The median percent of total shares pledged was 44.4 percent. When executives pledge their shares, they tend to do so in an aggressive manner.

Pledging Policies and Disclosure

AirNet Systems

Margin Accounts and Pledges: "Securities held in a margin account or pledged as collateral for a loan may be sold without your consent by the broker if you fail to meet a margin call or by the lender in foreclosure if you default on the loan. Because a margin sale or foreclosure sale may occur at a time when you are aware of material nonpublic information or otherwise are not permitted to trade in our securities, you are prohibited from holding our securities in a margin account or pledging our securities as collateral for a loan. An exception to this prohibition may be granted where you wish to pledge our securities as collateral for a loan (not including margin debt) and clearly demonstrate the financial capacity to repay the loan without resort to the pledged securities. If you wish to pledge Company securities as collateral for a loan, you must submit a request for approval ... at least two weeks prior to the proposed execution of documents evidencing the proposed pledge."[57]

Chesapeake Energy

In October 2008, Aubrey McClendon, the chairman and CEO of Chesapeake Energy, was forced to sell 31.5 million shares, or 94 percent of his 5.8 percent stake in the company, to meet a margin call. Those shares had been worth $2.2 billion when McClendon bought them on margin just a few months earlier, but he sold them for only $569 million.[58]

Following the sale, the board temporarily suspended the company's stock ownership guidelines (five times annual salary plus cash bonus). The company also signed McClendon to a new five-year contract, even though he had committed to a five-year agreement in 2007. As part of the new agreement, McClendon received a cash bonus of $75 million.[59]

Repricing and Exchange Offers

A **repricing** or **exchange offer** is a transaction in which employees holding stock options are allowed to exchange those options for either a new option, restricted stock, or (less frequently) cash. Exchange offers generally occur when stock options are trading out-of-the-money to such an extent that they will not likely become profitable or offer value to employees in the foreseeable future.

Management typically initiates the exchange process by evaluating the profile of employee option holdings, the potential incentive and retention effects, shareholder considerations, and the cost of implementation. If shareholder approval is not required under the terms of the equity program, the board can approve and implement an exchange. If shareholder approval is required, the board must seek shareholder approval for the authority (but not the obligation) to implement an exchange. This authority expires after a specified period of time. Proposals are voted on in either the regular annual meeting or a special meeting. If the proposal is approved, the board can then decide to implement an exchange, but if market conditions change between plan inception and shareholder approval, or if there is executive or board turnover, the plan might not be implemented. In addition, employees are not required to accept an exchange offer made by the company; they have the right to retain unexercised options (both vested and unvested) if they choose to do so.

Once approved, the exchange may be made at a premium to fair value, at fair value, or at a discount to fair value (see the next sidebar).

- **Premium to fair value**—This is a straight repricing in which the exercise price of each option is reduced but no other terms of the option (including the number of shares) are changed. Alternatively, a firm may offer restricted shares worth more than the fair value of the underwater options, to provide the incentive needed for employees to accept the exchange.

- **Equal to fair value**—New awards are granted so that their value is exactly equal to the fair value of underwater options. When there are multiple outstanding tranches (with varying strike prices and remaining terms), implementing a fair-value program can be difficult. For example, should all the tranches be exchanged or only tranches that are deeply out-of-the-money?

- **Discount to fair value**—New awards are granted so that their value is less than the fair value of the underwater options.

New awards typically change the vesting terms of the old award, and some firms require additional vesting beyond the term of the forfeited awards, to extend the retention period. If fully vested options are being exchanged, a minimum level of vesting (such as six months) typically is attached to the new shares. The voting guidelines of proxy advisory firm RiskMetrics/ISS require that vesting terms be no less than the terms of the forfeited options and that new options not be exercisable for at least six months. If these and various other conditions are not met, RiskMetrics/ISS will recommend that shareholders vote against the exchange offer.

Exchange Offer

Citadel Broadcasting

"In the spring of 2002, the Board of Directors granted the 2002 Stock Options to [CEO Farid] Suleman in connection with his agreeing to serve as the Company's chief executive officer. The 2002 Stock Options are nonqualified stock options with a ten-year term. The options vested 25 percent at the date of grant and 25 percent over each of the next three years, and, as of March 16,

2006, the grant was fully vested and unexercised. There are approximately six years remaining on the full option term.

On March 16, 2006, ... the compensation committee approved the following:

- The cancellation of the 2002 Options and replacement of them with the Restricted Stock Units (RSUs)

- The cancellation of Mr. Suleman's option to purchase 400,000 shares of common stock of the Company at an exercise price of $16.94 granted to him under the Long-Term Incentive Plan on March 26, 2004

- The modification of the terms of Mr. Suleman's previously granted 1,250,000 time-vesting restricted shares ...

- The grant to Mr. Suleman of 1,131,994 performance shares under the Long-Term Incentive Plan, which vest in two equal portions annually, beginning on March 16, 2007, and subject to the same vesting requirements as Mr. Suleman's modified restricted share grant"[60]

An exchange offer can be an effective way to restore the incentive value of equity awards that have lost much of their value due to significant stock price declines. This is particularly true when the stock price declines are caused by general market factors (such as a recession or financial crisis) and not events that are specific to the firm (such as underperformance). Exchange offers can reduce voluntary turnover of key employees who might otherwise leave to work at other firms.

On the other hand, exchange offers might signal a culture of entitlement within the company. Frequent repricing encourages the expectation that risky incentives will pay out regardless of company performance. Repricings can create an investor relations problem for this same reason, with shareholders perceiving that employees will always receive generous compensation even when shareholders have lost money. In addition, there is no guarantee that an exchange will improve morale or reduce turnover.

The research results on exchange offers are somewhat mixed. Carter and Lynch (2001) found that firms reprice options as a result of company-specific (not industry-wide) performance problems. Still, they did not find evidence that exchange offers were driven by agency problems; instead, they found that exchanges were made to restore incentive value to employees and prevent turnover.[61] Chidambaran and Prabhala (2003) reached similar conclusions. They found that repricings occurred among companies with abnormally high CEO turnover, suggesting that they were not initiated by entrenched management. Furthermore, more than 40 percent of firms that repriced excluded the CEO in their exchange offers.[62]

Other studies have suggested that repricing might not benefit the firm or its stakeholders. Carter and Lynch (2004) found modest evidence that employee turnover is lower following repricing but that executive turnover is unaffected.[63] Brenner, Sundaram, and Yermack (2000) found that repricing is *negatively* correlated with subsequent firm performance, even adjusting for industry conditions.[64] Chance, Kumar, and Todd (2000) found that firms with greater agency problems, smaller size, and insider-dominated boards are more likely to reprice.[65] Finally, Callaghan, Saly, and Subramaniam (2004) found that repricings tend to precede the release of positive information about the firm or follow the release of negative information, suggesting that repricing events might be opportunistically timed to benefit insiders (similar to the manipulation of the timing of new grants).[66] The evidence therefore suggests that although exchange offers might not be uniformly good or bad, the benefits to shareholders are somewhat unclear.

Repricing and exchange offers are controversial decisions for the board and shareholders. Although infrequent, exchange offers are a continuing issue for companies that offer equity-based compensation, particularly during bear markets.

Endnotes

1. One exception to this is company founders who gain a significant ownership position in the early stages of capitalization.

2. Equilar, Inc., proprietary compensation and equity ownership data for fiscal years from June 2008 to May 2009.

3. The authors measured company performance using Tobin's Q, the ratio of market to book value. We discuss this ratio in Chapter 1, "Introduction to Corporate Governance". See Randall Morck, Andrei Shleifer, and Robert W. Vishny, "Management Ownership and Market Valuation: An Empirical Analysis," *Journal of Financial Economics* 20 (1988): 293–315.

4. Ibid.

5. John J. McConnell and Henri Servaes, "Additional Evidence on Equity Ownership and Corporate Values," *Journal of Financial Economics* 27 (1990): 595–612.

6. Anna Elsilä, Juha-Pekka Kallunki, and Henrik Nilsson, "CEO Personal Wealth, Equity Incentives, and Firm Performance," *Social Science Research Network* (2009). Accessed April 19, 2010. See http://ssrn.com/abstract=1342237.

7. See Stacey R. Kole, "Managerial Incentives and Firm Performance: Incentives or Rewards?" in *Advances in Financial Economics 2,* edited by Mark Hirschey and M. W. Marr (Greenwich: Jai Press Inc., 1996). John E. Core, Wayne R. Guay, and David F. Larcker, "Executive Equity Compensation and Incentives: A Survey," Federal Reserve Bank of New York, Economic Policy Review (April 2003): 27–50.

8. Kroger Company, Form DEF 14-A, filed with the Securities and Exchange Commission May 15, 2008.

9. Frederic W. Cook & Co., Inc., "The 2007 Top 250: Long-Term Incentive Grant Practices for Executives," (2007). Accessed February 5, 2008. See www.fwcook.com/alert_letters/2007_Top_250.pdf.

10. John E. Core and David F. Larcker, "Performance Consequences of Mandatory Increases in Executive Stock Ownership," *Journal of Financial Economics* 64 (2002): 317–340.

11. Jared Harris and Philip Bromiley, "Incentives to Cheat: The Influence of Executive Compensation and Firm Performance on Financial Misrepresentation," *Organization Science* 18 (2007): 350–367.

12. William R. Baber, Sok-Hyon Kang, Lihong Liang, and Zinan Zhu, "Shareholder Rights, Corporate Governance, and Accounting Restatement," *Social Science Research Network* (2009). Accessed November 12, 2010. See http://ssrn.com/abstract=760324.

13. Shane A. Johnson, Harley E. Ryan, Jr., and Yisong S. Tian, "Managerial Incentives and Corporate Fraud: The Sources of Incentives Matter," *Review of Finance* 13 (2009): 115–145.

14. Merle Erickson, Michelle Hanlon, and Edward L. Maydew, "Is There a Link Between Executive Equity Incentives and Accounting Fraud?" *Journal of Accounting Research* 44 (2006): 113–143.

15. Chris S. Armstrong, Alan D. Jagolinzer, and David F. Larcker, "Chief Executive Officer Equity Incentives and Accounting Irregularities," *Journal of Accounting Research* 48 (2010): 225–271.

16. David Yermack, "Good Timing: CEO Stock Option Awards and Company News Announcements," *Journal of Finance* 52 (1997): 449–476.

17. David Aboody and Ron Kasznik, "CEO Stock Option Awards and the Timing of Corporate Voluntary Disclosures," *Journal of Accounting & Economics* 29 (2000): 73–100.

18. Erik Lie, "On the Timing of CEO Stock Option Awards," *Management Science* 51 (2005): 802–812. Reproduced with permission of INST FOR OPERATIONS RESEARCH & THE MGMT SCIENCES in the format Tradebook via Copyright Clearance Center.

19. Charles Forelle and James Bandler, "The Perfect Payday—Some CEOs Reap Millions by Landing Stock Options When They Are Most Valuable; Luck—or Something Else?" *Wall Street Journal* (March 18, 2006, Eastern edition): A.1.

20. Alan Murray, "The Economy; Business: Will Backdating Scandal Thwart Effort to Roll Back Reforms?" *Wall Street Journal* (December 20, 2006, Eastern edition): A.2. See also "Perfect Payday: Options Scorecard," Wall Street Journal Online (2007). Last modified September 4, 2007. See http://online.wsj.com/public/resources/documents/info-optionsscore06-full.html.

21. Lucian A. Bebchuk, Yaniv Grinstein, and Urs C. Peyer, "Lucky CEOs and Lucky Directors," *Journal of Finance* 65 (2010): 2,363–2,401.

22. The practice of granting in-the-money options to executives is not illegal. Companies may do so with the prior approval of shareholders and as long as the grants are properly reported. Retroactively manipulating a grant date, however, violates generally accepted accounting principles, IRS tax rules, and SEC regulations. For more on backdating, see Christopher S. Armstrong and David F. Larcker, "Discussion of 'The Impact of the Options Backdating Scandal on Shareholders' and 'Taxes and the Backdating of Stock Option Exercise Dates,'" *Journal of Accounting & Economics* 47 (2009): 50–58. John Bizjak, Michael Lemmon, and Ryan Whitby, "Option Backdating and Board Interlocks," *Review of Financial Studies* 22 (2009): 4,821–4,847. Gennaro Bernile and Gregg A. Jarrell, "The Impact of the Options Backdating Scandal on Shareholders," *Journal of Accounting and Economics* 47 (2009): 2–26.

23. Definitions from Mark Maremont and Charles Forelle, "Open Spigot: Bosses' Pay: How Stock Options Became Part of the Problem; Once Seen as a Reform, They Grew into Font of Riches and System to Be Gamed; Reload, Reprice, Backdate," *Wall Street Journal* (December 27, 2006, Eastern edition): A.1. Note that exercise backdating works only for transactions that are executed through the firm, where there is a possibility of getting someone from within the firm to agree to retroactively change the exercise date. Exercise backdating does not work for cashless exercise through a broker.

24. Dhaliwal, Erickson, and Heitzman (2009) found that CEOs who engage in exercise backdating realized average (median) tax savings of $96,000 ($7,000). It is difficult to believe that executives would be motivated by this somewhat trivial magnitude of savings, especially when there is some chance of getting

caught by the board of directors or regulators. See Dan Dhaliwal, Merle Erickson, and Shane Heitzman, "Taxes and the Backdating of Stock Option Exercise Dates," *Journal of Accounting & Economics* 47 (2009): 27–49.

25. In 2008, the SEC investigated the stock option grant practices at Analog Devices. At issue was whether the company both backdated and spring-loaded options. Although the company agreed to pay a $3 million fine for backdating, no settlement was sought for spring-loading. An SEC commissioner indicated that spring-loading was not a form of illegal trading. See Kara Scannell and John Hechinger, "SEC, Analog Settle Case—'Spring-Loading' Options Complaint Isn't Included," *Wall Street Journal* (May 31, 2008, Eastern edition): B.5.

26. This example comes from consulting work performed by one of the authors. The names of the company and individuals have been disguised.

27. For most public purposes, the term *insider trading* refers to illegal activity. The SEC, however, considers all trading by insiders to be insider trading and distinguishes between legal and illegal insider trading. See Securities and Exchange Commission, "Insider Trading," www.sec.gov/answers/insider.htm. Last modified on April 19, 2001.

28. University of Cincinnati College of Law, "Securities Lawyer's Deskbook. General Rules and Regulations Promulgated Under the Securities Exchange Act of 1934: Rule 10b5—Employment of Manipulative and Deceptive Devices," www.law.uc.edu/CCL/34ActRls/rule10b-5.html.

29. Dionne Searcey, Peter Lattman, Peter Grant, and Amol Sharma, "Qwest's Nacchio Is Found Guilty in Trading Case; Ex-CEO's Conviction on 19 of 42 Counts Adds to Government's Wins," *Wall Street Journal* (April 20, 2007, Eastern edition). Also, "Judge Cuts Ex-Qwest CEO's Sentence by 2 Months." Reuters (June 24, 2010). Accessed November 12, 2010.

30. Recent survey data found that only 30 percent of companies disclose their insider trading policies. It is not clear why a company would not do so when the restrictions on managerial behavior are a key aspect of governance and directly relevant to shareholders' ability to assess the quality of controls in place. See David F. Larcker and Brendan Sheehan, "Executive Hedging and Pledging Survey," *Corporate Secretary Magazine* and the Rock Center for Corporate Governance at Stanford University (2010).

31. As we discuss later in this chapter, 10b5-1 plans can be used by executives to trade within the blackout window. Some evidence exists that this occurs. See Alan D. Jagolinzer, David F. Larcker, and Daniel J. Taylor, "The Impact of General Counsel on Insider Trading and Information Risk," working paper (2010).

32. Crimson Exploration, Inc., "Crimson Exploration Insider Trading Policy" (2010). Accessed November 12, 2010. See http://crimsonexploration.com/default/Insider_Trading_Policy_Preclearance_3_1_2010.pdf.

33. Josef Lakonishok and Inmoo Lee, "Are Insider Trades Informative?" *Review of Financial Studies* 14 (2001): 79–111.

34. Nejat H. Seyhun, "Insiders' Profits, Costs of Trading, and Market Efficiency," *Journal of Financial Economics* 16 (1986): 189–212.

35. See also James H. Lorie and Victor Niederhoffer, "Predictive and Statistical Properties of Insider Trading," *Journal of Law & Economics* 11 (1968): 35–53. Jeffrey F. Jaffe, "Special Information and Insider Trading," *Journal of Business* 47 (1974): 410–428. S. P. Pratt and C. W. DeVere, "Relationship Between Insider Trading and Rates of Return for NYSE Common Stocks, 1960–1966," in *Modern Developments in Investment Management,* edited by James H. Lorie and Richard Brealey (New York: Praeger, 1970). Joseph E. Finnerty, "Insiders and Market Efficiency," *Journal of Finance* 31 (1976): 1,141–1,148.

36. Securities and Exchange Commission, "Proposed Rule: Selective Disclosure and Insider Trading," (July 31, 1999). Modified January 10, 2000. See www.sec.gov/rules/proposed/34-42259.htm.

37. General rules and regulations promulgated under the Securities Exchange Act of 1934, Rule 10b5-1—Trading "on the Basis of" Material Nonpublic Information in Insider Trading Cases, Securities Lawyer's Deskbook, The University of Cincinnati College of Law. See http://taft.law.uc.edu/CCL/34ActRls/rule10b5-1.html.

38. The broker also is not permitted to execute trades under the 10b5-1 plan if he or she comes into possession of material nonpublic information.

39. David F. Larcker and Brendan Sheehan, "Executive Hedging and Pledging Survey," *Corporate Secretary Magazine* and the Rock Center for Corporate Governance at Stanford University (2010).

40. Datalink Corporation, Form 8-K, filed with the Securities and Exchange Commission February 13, 2006.

41. McDATA Corporation, Form 8-K, filed with the Securities and Exchange Commission May 13, 2002.

42. General rules and regulations promulgated under the Securities Exchange Act of 1934, Rule 10b5-1—Trading "on the Basis of" Material Nonpublic Information in Insider Trading Cases, Securities Lawyer's Deskbook, The University of Cincinnati College of Law. See http://taft.law.uc.edu/CCL/34ActRls/rule10b5-1.html.

43. Alan D. Jagolinzer, "SEC Rule 10b5-1 and Insiders' Strategic Trade," *Management Science* 55 (2009): 224–239.

44. Priya Cherian Huskins, "10b5-1 Trading Plans: The Next Stock Option Backdating Scandal?" Woodruff Sawyer and Co. (May 30, 2007).

45. Assume that a CEO requires compensation of $1 million. The board can offer either cash or equity. However, because equity has uncertain value, the executive will require a premium relative to cash (say, $1.2 million in expected value of stock options vs. $1 million riskless cash). Although the CEO might be indifferent between these two forms of payment, if he or she immediately hedges

the options, the $1.2 million in risky compensation will be converted to $1.2 million in riskless cash (minus transaction costs). In this case, the board overpaid because it could have satisfied the CEO with $1 million in cash instead of the $1.2 million in equity it gave up.

46. David F. Larcker and Brendan Sheehan, "Executive Hedging and Pledging Survey," *Corporate Secretary Magazine* and the Rock Center for Corporate Governance at Stanford University (2010).

47. J. Carr Bettis, John M. Bizjak, and Swaminathan L. Kalpathy, "Why Do Insiders Hedge Their Ownership and Options? An Empirical Examination," *Social Science Research Network* (March 2010). Accessed November 12, 2010. See http://ssrn.com/abstract=1364810.

48. Two other (less common) hedging devices are an equity swap and exchange-traded funds. An equity swap is an agreement between two parties to exchange cash flows associated with the performance of their specific holdings. The arrangement allows each party to diversify its income while still holding the original assets. An exchange-traded fund allows an investor to exchange his or her large holding of a single stock for units in a pooled (diversified) portfolio.

49. Chattem Inc., Form 4, filed with the Securities and Exchange Commission January 26, 2005.

50. Quest Software, Form DEF-14A, filed with the Securities and Exchange Commission April 30, 2002.

51. Quest Software, Form 4, filed with the Securities and Exchange Commission November 4, 2002.

52. In 2008, AirNet was purchased by private-equity firm Bayside Capital, a Division of HIG, and is now a privately held corporation. Airnet Systems, Inc., "Statement of Company Policy Regarding Securities Trades by Officers, Directors, and Team Members of AirNet Systems, Inc." (2004). Adopted by the board of directors February, 17, 2004. Accessed November 17, 2010. See www.investquest.com/iq/a/ans/cg/cg_tradepolicy04.pdf.

53. J. Carr Bettis, John M. Bizjak, and Michael L. Lemmon, "Managerial Ownership, Incentive Contracting, and the Use of Zero-cost Collars and Equity Swaps by Corporate Insiders," *Journal of Financial and Quantitative Analysis* 36 (2001): 345–370.

54. Alan D. Jagolinzer, Steven R. Matsunaga, and P. Eric Yeung, "An Analysis of Insiders' Use of Prepaid Variable Forward Transactions," *Journal of Accounting Research* 45 (2007): 1,055–1,079. Also J. Carr Bettis, John M. Bizjak, and Michael L. Lemmon.

55. J. Carr Bettis, John M. Bizjak, and Swaminathan L. Kalpathy.

56. David F. Larcker and Brendan Sheehan, "Executive Hedging and Pledging Survey," *Corporate Secretary Magazine* and the Rock Center for Corporate Governance at Stanford University (2010).

57. Airnet Systems, Inc.

58. Peter Galuszka, "Chesapeake Energy Not Alone in Margin Call Madness," *BNET Energy* (October 13, 2008). Accessed November 17, 2010. See www.bnet.com/blog/energy/chesapeake-energy-not-alone-in-margin-call-madness/313.

59. Posted by TraderMark on April 3, 2009: "Chesapeake Energy (CHK) CEO Aubrey McClendon with New Shady Compensation Deal; I Was Right in My Prediction." Accessed November 17, 2010. See www.fundmymutualfund.com/2009/04/chesapeake-energy-chk-ceo-aubrey.html.

60. Citadel Broadcasting, Form DEF-14A, filed with the Securities and Exchange Commission April 17, 2006.

61. Mary Ellen Carter and Luann J. Lynch, "An Examination of Executive Stock Option Repricing," *Journal of Financial Economics* 61 (2001): 207–225.

62. N. K. Chidambaran and Nagpurnanand R. Prabhala, "Executive Stock Option Repricing Internal Governance Mechanisms and Management Turnover," *Journal of Financial Economics* 69 (2003): 153–189.

63. Mary Ellen Carter and Luann J. Lynch, "The Effect of Stock Option Repricing on Employee Turnover," *Journal of Accounting & Economics* 37 (2004): 91–112.

64. Menachem Brenner, Rangarajan K. Sundaram, and David Yermack, "Altering the Terms of Executive Stock Options," *Journal of Financial Economics* 57 (2000): 103–128.

65. Don M. Chance, Raman Kumar, and Rebecca B. Todd, "The 'Repricing' of Executive Stock Options," *Journal of Financial Economics* 57 (2000): 129–154.

66. Sandra Renfro Callaghan, P. Jane Saly, and Chandra Subramaniam, "The Timing of Option Repricing," *Journal of Finance* 59 (2004): 1,651–1,676.

10

Financial Reporting and External Audit

In this chapter, we examine the process by which the board of directors assesses the integrity of published financial statements. As discussed in previous chapters, the accuracy of financial reporting is important for several reasons. First, this information is critical for the general efficiency of capital markets and the proper valuation of a company's publicly traded securities. Second, an informed evaluation of a company's strategy, business model, and risk level depends on the accurate reporting of financial and operating measures. This is true for both internally and externally reported data. Third, the board of directors awards performance-based compensation to management based on the achievement of predetermined financial targets. Accurate financial reporting is critical to ensuring that results are stated honestly and that management has not manipulated results for personal gain.

The audit committee must ensure that the financial reporting process is carried out appropriately. The committee does so in two ways: first, by working with management to set the parameters for accounting quality, transparency, and internal controls; and, second, by retaining an external auditor to test the financial statements for material misstatement.

In this chapter, we discuss both of these responsibilities. We start by considering the general obligation of the audit committee to oversee the financial reporting and disclosure process. What actions should the committee take to ensure that financial data is reported accurately? How can it decrease the likelihood of material misstatement or manipulation by management? How effective are these efforts?

Next, we evaluate the role of the external auditor. What is the purpose of an external audit? What is it expected to accomplish, and what is it not expected to accomplish? We then consider the impact that various factors have on audit quality, including the structure of the industry itself, the reliance on audit firms for nonaudit-related services, auditor independence, auditor rotation, and the Sarbanes-Oxley Act of 2002.

The Audit Committee

The audit committee has a broad range of responsibilities. These include the responsibility to oversee financial reporting and disclosure, to monitor the choice of accounting principles, to hire and monitor the work of the external auditor, to oversee the internal audit function, to oversee regulatory compliance within the company, and to monitor risk.

Many of these responsibilities are mandated by securities regulation or federal law. For example, the audit committee's oversight of the external audit is required by the Sarbanes-Oxley Act of 2002. Sarbanes-Oxley also mandates that the audit committee establish procedures for receiving and handling complaints about the company's accounting, internal controls, or auditing matters (including anonymous submissions by employees). By contrast, other responsibilities are not mandated by law but instead have evolved from historical practice. For example, the assignment of enterprise risk management to the audit committee is not a legal requirement but is an election that many companies have made of their own volition.[1]

To ensure that the work of the committee is carried out free from the influence of management, the audit committee must consist entirely of independent directors (see Chapter 3, "Board of Directors: Duties and Liability"). In addition, listing exchanges require that all members of the audit committee be financially literate and that at least one committee member qualify as a **financial expert**. A financial expert is defined as follows:

> [Someone who] has past employment experience in finance or accounting, requisite professional certification in accounting, or any other comparable experience or background which results

in the individual's financial sophistication, including being or having been chief executive officer, chief financial officer, or other senior officer with financial oversight responsibilities.[2]

The audit committee can retain external advisors or consultants as it deems necessary to assist in the fulfillment of its duties, with the cost borne by the company.

Accounting Quality, Transparency, and Controls

The work of the audit committee begins with establishing guidelines that dictate the quality of accounting used in the firm. **Accounting quality** is generally defined as the degree to which accounting figures precisely reflect the company's change in financial position, earnings, and cash flow during a reporting period.[3]

An outside observer might think that accounting quality should not be discretionary, but the nature of accounting standards somewhat requires that it be so. This is because oversight bodies—including the Financial Accounting Standards Board (FASB) in the United States and the International Accounting Standards Board (IASB) abroad—sometimes afford considerable flexibility to companies in the manner in which they interpret and apply accounting standards. They do so to allow for the fact that it is not always clear how transactions should be valued or when the costs and revenues associated with a transaction should be recognized. In many cases, these are subject to interpretation. For example, how should a company allocate the costs associated with completing a multiyear project? Should it be evenly over the life of the project, at the time of delivery, or in some other manner that takes into account the work performed during each reporting period? Correspondingly, should the company be aggressive or conservative in recognition of the associated revenues? The way a company answers these questions has a direct impact on accounting results.

In addition, the audit committee must establish the company's standards for transparency. **Transparency** is the degree to which the company provides details that supplement and explain accounts, items, and events reported in its financial statements and other public filings. Transparency is important for shareholders to properly understand the company's strategy, operations, risk, and performance of management. It is also necessary when shareholders make decisions about the value of company securities. As such, transparent disclosure plays a key role in the efficient functioning of capital markets.

On the other hand, transparency brings risks. When a company is highly transparent, it might inadvertently divulge confidential or proprietary information that puts it at a disadvantage relative to competitors. For example, competitors might be able to use information disclosed about a company's strategy (including the timing of a new product launch, distribution channels, pricing, marketing, and other promotion) to effectively dampen its success. Too much transparency might also weaken the bargaining position of a company. For example, counterparties could use disclosure about a company's potential exposure to litigation to gain leverage and extract additional concessions. For these reasons, the audit committee and the entire board of directors must weigh the costs and benefits of transparency when establishing guidelines for reporting and disclosure.

Finally, the audit committee is responsible for monitoring the internal controls of the corporation. **Internal controls** are the processes and procedures that a company puts in place to ensure that account balances are accurately recorded, financial statements reliably produced, and assets adequately protected from loss or theft. Effectively, internal controls act as the "cash register" of the corporation, a system that confirms that the level of assets inside the company is consistent with the level that should be there, given revenue and disbursement data recorded through the accounting system.

The audit committee determines the rigor of controls necessary to ensure the integrity of financial statements. A rigorous system is important for protecting against theft, tampering, and manipulation by management or other employees. It is also important for detecting potential regulatory violations or illegal activity, such as the payment of bribes, which are illegal under the Foreign Corrupt Practices Act of 1977.[4] Rigorous controls help ensure that employees do not make inappropriate adjustments to company accounts to create falsified results. If the company is too zealous in its internal controls, however, the results can be detrimental. Excessive controls can lead to bureaucracy, lost productivity, inefficient decision making, and an inhospitable work environment. As a result, the audit committee must strike a balance between proper controls that prevent inappropriate behavior and excessive controls that impact firm performance.

Survey data suggests that audit committees are confident in their ability to carry out these responsibilities. According to a study conducted by KPMG and the National Association of Corporate Directors (NACD), the vast majority of audit committee members believe they are effective or very effective in overseeing management's use of accounting (90 percent), company disclosure practices (93 percent), and internal controls (87 percent). The majority also believe they are effective in overseeing both the internal and external audit function (89 percent and 94 percent, respectively).[5]

Financial Reporting Quality

Several control mechanisms are in place to assist the audit committee in ensuring the integrity of financial statements. Companies hire an external auditor to test financials for material mis-statement based on prevailing accounting rules. The external auditor reports its findings directly to the audit committee to ensure that the audit process has not been compromised by management influence. Companies also employ an internal audit department, which is responsible for separately testing accounting processes and controls. Under Sarbanes-Oxley, management is required to certify that financial reports do not contain misleading information. Companies that violate accounting regulations face the risk of lawsuits from shareholders and regulators. Penalties for violation include fines and, in some cases, bans from serving as an officer of a publicly traded company or even prison time for corporate officers.

Audit committee members are confident that these controls are effective. According to the KPMG survey cited, 89 percent of audit committee members are confident or very confident that the company's internal audit department would report controversial issues involving senior management. Eighty-six percent are satisfied with the support and expertise they receive from the external auditor.[6]

Still, considerable empirical evidence suggests that accounting controls might not be as effective as audit committee members believe. Burgstahler and Dichev (1997) found that companies are much less likely to report a small decrease in earnings than a small increase in earnings, even though statistically the distribution between the two should be equal.[7] This suggests that management might manipulate or overstate results to meet targets. Other studies support this conclusion. For example, Carslaw (1988) examined the pattern that occurs in the second-from-left digit of net income figures. He found that zeros are overrepresented and nines are under-represented, suggesting that companies round up their earnings to convey slightly better results.[8] Similarly, Grundfest and Malenko (2009) examined the pattern that occurs when earnings per share figures are extended by one digit to include tenths of a penny. The authors hypothesized that if no manipulation is occurring, fours should occur in the tenth-of-a-penny digit just as often as other numbers. Instead, they found that fours are significantly under-represented, suggesting that managers manipulate results when possible so that they can report EPS figures that are one penny higher. The authors identified inventory valuation, asset writedowns, accruals, and reserves as areas that are particularly susceptible to manipulation.[9]

Although such behavior might allow management to meet short-term targets, it is generally detrimental to the corporation and provides some insight into the governance quality of the firm. Bhojraj, Hribar, Picconi, and McInnis (2009) found that companies that just beat earnings expectations with low-quality earnings have superior short-term stock price performance compared to companies that just miss earnings expectations with high-quality earnings. However, over the subsequent three-year period, these companies tend to underperform. The authors saw this as evidence that managers make "myopic short-term decisions to beat analysts' earnings forecasts at the expense of long-term performance."[10] Perhaps to discourage myopic behavior among management, some companies have implemented policies that they will not issue quarterly earnings guidance. Examples include AT&T, Coca-Cola, ExxonMobil, Ford, and Walt Disney.

Financial Restatements

A **financial restatement** occurs when a material error is discovered in the company's previously published financials. When such an error is discovered, the company is required to file a Form 8-K with the Securities and Exchange Commission (SEC) within four days. The

8-K alerts investors that previously published financials can no longer be relied upon and are under review for restatement. If an error is not material, the financial statements are simply amended.

According to proxy advisory firm Glass Lewis, between 200 and 500 publicly traded companies listed in the United States restate their earnings each year (approximately 5 to 12 percent of the total firms they follow).[11] The most frequent causes of a restatement include improper expense recognition (22 percent), misclassification of items (18 percent), tax accounting errors (11 percent), and improper revenue recognition (10 percent).[12] (See Table 10.1).

Table 10.1 Reasons for Financial Restatement (2004–2008) (continued)

Error Category	Description	Frequency (2004–2008)
Revenue recognition	Restatements due to improper revenue accounting. This category includes instances in which revenue was improperly recognized, questionable revenue was recognized, or any other number of related errors led to misreported revenue.	10%
Expense recognition	Restatements due to improperly recording expenses in the incorrect period or for an incorrect amount. This category includes restatements due to improper lease accounting and restatements due to misdated stock options.	22%
Misclassification	Restatements due to improperly classifying accounting items on the balance sheet, income statement, or statement of cash flows, including restatements due to misclassifications of short- or long-term accounts or misclassification of cash flows.	18%

Table 10.1 Reasons for Financial Restatement (2004–2008) (continued)

Error Category	Description	Frequency (2004–2008)
Equity	Restatements due to improper accounting for earnings per share, equity effects of stock-based compensation and stock options, warrants, convertible securities, beneficial conversion features, and other equity instruments.	6%
Other comprehensive income	Restatements due to improper accounting for other comprehensive income transactions, including derivatives and hedging transactions, foreign-currency items, unrealized gains and losses on investments in debt and equity securities, other financial instruments, and pension-liability adjustments.	8%
Tax accounting	Restatements due to errors involving tax provisions, improper treatment of tax liabilities, deferred tax assets and liabilities, tax contingencies, sales tax, and other tax-related items.	11%
Acquisitions/investments	Restatements due to improper application of purchase accounting for business combinations, other merger- or acquisition-related errors, and errors related to the appropriate accounting method for significant investments in other companies.	6%
Capital assets	Restatements due to asset impairments, asset place-in-service dates, writedowns, and depreciation and amortization.	6%
Inventory	Restatements associated with inventory-costing valuations, quantity issues, and cost-of-sales adjustments.	3%

Table 10.1   Reasons for Financial Restatement (2004–2008) (continued)

Error Category	Description	Frequency (2004–2008)
Reserves/allowances	Restatements due to errors involving bad-debt reserves for accounts receivable, reserves for inventory, valuation allowances, provisions for loan losses, or other types of allowances and reductions of assets.	3%
Liability/contingencies	Restatements due to errors in estimated liability claims, loss contingencies, litigation matters, commitments, certain accruals, or other types of obligations.	3%
Other	Restatements not covered by the other categories listed.	3%

Total does not equal 100 percent due to rounding.

Source: Adapted from Mark Grothe and Poonam Goyal (2009).

A restatement can be caused by human error, the aggressive application of accounting standards, or fraud. The distinctions are important because they have implications on the quality of internal controls and the steps that the company must take to improve oversight. For example, consider three restatements that occurred in the 1990s and 2000s:

- In 1991, Oracle restated second- and third-quarter earnings from the previous year when it was discovered that sales had been recorded prematurely. Investment analysts blamed the incident on management pressure to meet financial targets, which, in turn, caused sales associates to book contracts before they were fully closed. The practice occurred only in these two quarters, and total fiscal year results were unaffected by the timing shift.
- Between 1999 and 2001, Bristol-Myers Squibb used financial incentives to persuade wholesalers to purchase larger quantities of its drugs than needed. The company eventually reduced reported revenues by $2.5 billion because of so-called "channel stuffing" and paid fines.

- Between 1998 and 2000, the CEO and other senior executives of Computer Associates engaged in a systematic process of backdating customer contracts and altering sales documents to move revenue into earlier periods. When questioned about their actions, they lied to internal investigators, the SEC, and the FBI. Those involved went to jail—including the CEO, who was sentenced to a 12-year term.

The actions at Oracle and Bristol-Myers were due to aggressive behavior on the part of management and required a change in incentives and more effective internal controls. The actions at Computer Associates, however, were clearly fraudulent and stemmed from an ethical breakdown that pervaded the entire organization. As a result, it required a much more extensive overhaul of the governance system, including a complete change in senior leadership, dismissal of the external auditor, and fairly substantial turnover among board members.

The evidence indicates that investors differentiate between more and less egregious forms of manipulation. According to Glass Lewis, companies that announce "severe" restatements (defined as those affecting multiple annual periods) exhibit a 2.0 percent decrease in stock price in the two days following the announcement, compared with a 0.5 percent decrease for all companies announcing a restatement. Stock price performance tends to be the worst when the restatement is caused by improper revenue recognition. Furthermore, the effects of a severe restatement tend to be long lasting. These companies continue to underperform their benchmarks well beyond the announcement date.[13]

Similarly, Palmrose, Richardson, and Scholz (2004) found that companies exhibit a 9 percent average (5 percent median) decrease in stock price in the two days following a restatement announcement. Reaction is more negative when the restatement is due to fraud (–20 percent), was initiated by the external auditor (–18 percent), or reflects a material reduction in the company's previous earnings (–14 percent). The authors hypothesized that "the negative signal associated with fraud and auditor-initiated restatements is associated with an increase in investors' expected monitoring costs, while higher materiality is associated with greater revisions of future performance expectations" (see the following sidebar).[14]

Financial Restatement

Krispy Kreme

In July 2004, Krispy Kreme Doughnuts announced that the Securities and Exchange Commission was conducting an informal inquiry into the company's accounting practices.[15] In October, the status of the investigation was reclassified as formal. On January 4, 2005, Krispy Kreme filed a Form 8-K alerting investors that it intended to restate its financials, due to errors in the company's accounting for the acquisition of certain franchises:

"The Board of the Directors of the Company has concluded that the Company's previously issued financial statements for the fiscal year ended February 1, 2004, and the last three quarters of such fiscal year should be restated to correct certain errors contained therein, and, accordingly, such financial statements should no longer be relied upon."

When completed, the investigation revealed that the company had engaged in many questionable activities to increase reported income. For example, Krispy Kreme had failed to expense certain items associated with reacquired franchises. Items that should have been treated as operating expenses were instead capitalized on the balance sheet as intangible assets called "reacquired franchise rights." Among the costs capitalized were $4.4 million in compensation paid to the executive of a reacquired franchise, franchise management fees, and other costs. The company also had manipulated revenue accounts. In one transaction, the company had sold equipment to a franchisee immediately before reacquiring it. Krispy Kreme had included the sale of equipment as revenue and then purchased the company for a price that was increased by the cost of the equipment in what is known as a "round-trip transaction." The company had also "sold" equipment to franchises before it was needed. The unused equipment was not shipped for several months, and instead was stored in an off-site warehouse. The franchisees did not have to pay for the equipment until delivery.

The company's stock price fell from more than $30 per share before the investigation was initiated to less than $10 by the time it released restated financials in April 2006. Chairman and CEO Scott Lovegood resigned from the company. The company and its officers were named in multiple shareholder-derivative lawsuits, which were settled for $75 million. The cost of the company's external audit increased from $440,000 in fiscal 2004 to $3.5 million in 2006.[16]

Some evidence indicates that financial restatements are correlated with weak governance and regulatory controls. For example, Beasley (1996) found that companies with a lower percentage of outside directors are more likely to be the subject of financial reporting fraud. He also found that other governance features—low director ownership of company stock, low director tenure on the board, and busy board members—are correlated with fraud.[17] Farber (2005) found that firms that are found to have committed fraud have fewer outside directors, fewer audit committee meetings, fewer financial experts on the audit committee, and a higher percentage of CEOs who are also chairman.[18] Correia (2009) found that companies with low accounting quality spend more money on political contributions—particularly to members of Congress with strong ties to the SEC—and that these contributions are correlated with a lower likelihood of SEC enforcement action and lower penalties for firms found guilty of violations. She posited that companies at risk of financial statement fraud might use political contributions to reduce their regulatory exposure.[19]

However, the evidence that financial restatements are correlated with typical governance features is not conclusive. The Committee of Sponsoring Organizations of the Treadway Commission (COSO) reviewed fraud investigations occurring between 1998 and 2007 and found no relation to size of the board, frequency of meetings, or composition and experience of directors.[20]

A behavioral component likely is involved in financial reporting fraud. Magnan, Cormier, and Lapointe-Antunes (2009) argued that an exaggerated sense of self-confidence, encouraged by lavish media attention and praise, might encourage CEOs who are inclined to commit fraud to take increasingly aggressive actions without fear of detection or reproach. As they explained, "Almost all sample firms and/or their CEOs were the objects of positive media or analyst coverage in the period preceding or concurrent to the fraudulent activities. In our view, such coverage translated into a higher sense of self-confidence or invulnerability among the executives, i.e., managerial hubris. Managerial hubris either led guilty executives further down the path of deception and fraud or, alternatively, pulled their supervising executives away from efficient and effective monitoring." They recommend that more attention be paid to behavior cues and that auditors greet the appearances of good governance with skepticism (see the next sidebar).[21]

Dyck, Morse, and Zingales (2010) studied a comprehensive list of fraud cases between 1996 and 2004. They found that legal and regulatory mechanisms (such as the SEC and external auditors) and financial parties (such as equity holders, short sellers, and analysts) were less effective at detecting fraud than uninvolved third parties that are typically seen as less important players in governance systems. Employees, non-financial-market regulators, and the media were credited with uncovering 43 percent of the fraud cases, compared with 38 percent for financial parties and 17 percent for legal and regulatory agents. They offered two explanations for these findings. Employees and nonfinancial regulators might be more effective in discovering fraud because they have greater access to internal information and, therefore, lower costs of monitoring. Journalists might be effective monitors because of reputational gains.[22]

Decentralization and Internal Controls

In 1983, SEC Commissioner James Treadway, Jr., identified a decentralized organizational structure as a common feature among companies involved in financial reporting fraud:

"The single most significant factor to emerge from these cases is the organizational structure of the companies involved. I refer to a decentralized corporate structure, with autonomous divisional management. Such a structure is intended to encourage responsibility, productivity, and therefore profits—all entirely laudable objectives. But the unfortunate corollary has been a lack of accountability."

He identified certain characteristics as associated with financial fraud:

1. Autonomy among operating divisions

2. Unrealistic profit targets set by corporate headquarters without input from divisions

3. Pressure from headquarters to achieve those targets

4. A sense among divisions that profit targets cannot be achieved without aggressive action

5. Emphasis on sales and marketing by headquarters without concern for internal controls

6. Lack of emphasis on auditing, accounting, and internal controls

7. Limited communication between headquarters and divisions[23]

At the same time, several prominent examples exist of highly successful companies that operate under a decentralized structure. Board members must weigh the risks and benefits of decentralization in determining whether it is appropriate for their companies. Attention should be paid not only to the control mechanisms in place, but also to intangible factors such as culture, quality of management and personnel, incentives, reporting and communication structure, and opportunity for misbehavior. As with most governance systems, these are unique to each organization.

Models to Detect Accounting Manipulations

Researchers and professionals have put extensive effort into developing models to detect the manipulation of reported financial statements. Such tools are useful not only for auditors and the audit committee (and perhaps the board in general), but also for investors, analysts, and others who rely on credible financial reports. These efforts have been met with somewhat limited success, although in certain circumstances they have predictive ability in whether a restatement will occur.

One set of models measures accounting quality in terms of accounting accruals. Accrual accounting is based on the premise that the profitability of a corporation can be measured more accurately by recognizing revenues and expenses in the period in which they are realized instead of in the period in which cash is received or dispensed. Accrual accounting reduces the variability that is inherent in cash flow accounting and provides a more normalized view of earnings. Because accrual accounting relies more heavily on managerial assumption than cash flow accounting, however, it is more easily subject to manipulation. If management manipulates results over time, reported earnings will steadily diverge from cash flows. The difference between accruals and cash flows (after adjusting for the typical or normal accruals that will occur during the application of the accounting process), known as **abnormal accruals**, might be used as a measure of earnings quality.

Several researchers have developed models that use abnormal accruals to predict financial restatements. One widely used model was developed by Dechow, Sloan, and Sweeney (1995), based on a modification of Jones (1991).[24] Another was developed by Beneish (1999). His model uses the following metrics as inputs:

- The change in accounts receivables as a percent of sales over time
- The change in gross margin over time
- The change in noncurrent assets other than plant and equipment over time
- The change in sales over time
- The change in working capital (minus depreciation) over time, in relation to total assets

Beneish (1999) tested his model against both companies that have restated their earnings and those that have not. He found that excessive changes in these metrics have predictive power in whether a company is likely to restate earnings, and the results were statistically significant.[25] However, accrual-based models such as these tend to have a very modest success rate in predicting future restatements.

Audit Integrity has also developed a model with a slightly higher success rate in predicting financial restatements. The company uses a composite metric that aggregates both accounting and governance data to identify companies at risk of restatement and other negative outcomes such as fraud, debt default, and lawsuits.[26] The company computes Accounting and Governance Risk (AGR) scores on a scale of 0 to 100, with low ratings indicating a higher likelihood of restate-ment or adverse outcome. Audit Integrity claims that companies that are in the lowest decile according to its model account for almost 29 percent of all restatements, whereas those in the highest decile account for only 1.6 percent. In addition, it claims that "not only are the high-risk companies substantially more likely to face a restatement than the low-risk firms, but the estimated probabilities neither under-state nor overstate the actual likelihood of the restatement."

Independent testing has confirmed that Audit Integrity's models have some predictive power. Price, Sharp, and Wood (2010) found that AGR is more successful in detecting financial misstatements than standard accrual-based models, such as those discussed earlier.[27] Correia (2009) also found that AGR is slightly more effective (but sta-tistically equivalent) in predicting accounting restatements than accrual-based models. Still, the precision of both models is relatively low—no more than 10 percent.[28]

Finally, evidence indicates that adding linguistic-based analysis can improve the predictive ability of accrual-based models. Larcker and Zakolyukina (2010) studied the Q&A section of quarterly earn-ings conference calls. They found that certain linguistic tendencies are associated with future restatements:

- CEOs make fewer self-references (that is, they're less likely to use the pronoun *I*).
- They are more likely to use impersonal pronouns (such as *anyone, nobody,* and *everyone*).
- They make more references to general knowledge (such as "you know").
- They express more extreme positive emotions (*fantastic* as opposed to *good*).
- They use fewer extreme negative emotions.
- They express less certainty in their language.
- They are less likely to refer to shareholder value.

The predictive ability of the model using these cues is better than chance and better than the accrual models. The authors con-clude that "it is worthwhile for researchers to consider linguistic measures when attempting to measure the quality of reported financial statements."[29] However, this type of research is still in its infancy.

The External Audit

The **external audit** assesses the validity and reliability of publicly reported financial information. Shareholders rely on financial statements to evaluate a company's performance and to determine the fair value of its securities. Because management is responsible for preparing this information, shareholders expect an independent third party to provide assurance that the information they receive is accurate. The external auditor serves this purpose.

The external audit process is broken down as follows:[30]

1. **Audit preparation**—The external audit is tailored to the industry, the nature of operations, and the company's organizational structure and processes. Before the audit takes place, the auditor and the audit committee discuss and determine its scope. The auditor uses professional judgment to determine how best to perform its assessment. This involves identifying areas that require special attention, evaluating conditions under which the company produces accounting data, evaluating the reasonableness of estimates, evaluating the reasonableness of management representations, and making judgments about the appropriateness of the manner in which accounting principles are applied and the adequacy of disclosures.

2. **Review of accounting estimates and disclosures**—The audit is predicated on a sampling of accounts. Highest attention is paid to the accounts that are at the greatest risk of inaccuracy. These generally include the following:
   - Revenue recognition
   - Restructuring charges
   - Impairments of long-lived assets
   - Investments
   - Goodwill
   - Depreciation and amortization

- Loss reserves
- Repurchase obligations
- Inventory reserves
- Allowances for doubtful accounts[31]

In determining the reasonableness of management estimates, the auditor reviews and tests the processes by which estimates are developed, calculates an independent expectation of what the estimates should be and reviews subsequent transactions or events for further comparison. The auditor also evaluates the key factors or assumptions that are significant to the estimate and the factors that are subjective and susceptible to management bias.

3. **Fraud evaluation**—The main objective of the audit is to test for validity and reliability. The auditor does not explicitly focus on whether errors result from inadvertent mistakes or fraudulent action, but public shareholders and many board members expect that auditors will root out fraud if it exists. Auditing standards encourage auditors to use "professional skepticism" to determine whether fraud has occurred.[32] In the scope of the audit, auditors evaluate the incentives and pressures placed on management. They also review the opportunities for fraud to take place. Nevertheless, despite public conception to the contrary, it is not the explicit objective of the audit to identify fraud.[33]

4. **Assessment of internal controls**—Under Section 404 of Sarbanes-Oxley, the external auditor is required to perform an assessment of the company's internal controls.[34] The auditor assesses the design of entity-level controls, controls relating to risk management, significant accounts and their disclosure, the process for developing inputs and assumptions for management estimates, and the use of external specialists who assist in preparing estimates. To identify areas where internal controls can lead to material misstatement, the auditor pays particular attention to significant or unusual transactions, period-ending adjustments, related-party transactions, significant management estimates, and incentives that might create pressure on management to inappropriately manage financial results. In 2008,

approximately 8 percent of companies received an adverse opinion from their auditors regarding their internal controls.[35]

5. **Communication with the audit committee**—The external auditor discusses its findings with the audit committee. The auditor's communications with the committee include an assessment of the consistency of the application of accounting principles, the clarity and completeness of the financial statements, and the quality and completeness of disclosures. Particular attention is paid to changes in accounting policies, the appropriateness of estimates, unusual transactions, and the timing of significant items. The auditor reports directly to the audit committee and may also communicate and discuss its findings with the chief financial officer and other employees of the company.

6. **Expressed opinion**—The ultimate objective of the audit is to express an opinion on whether the company's financials adequately comply with regulatory accounting standards. If the auditor finds no reason for concern that the statements are materially misleading, the firm expresses an **unqualified opinion** that accompanies the financial statements in the annual report. (Alternatively, the auditor issues a **qualified opinion** and explains the reason for concern.) The unqualified opinion generally states that "the financial statements present fairly the financial condition, the results of operations, and the cash flows of the company [for specific years], in accordance with accounting principles generally accepted in the United States of America." The auditor also specifies whether the company can continue to operate profitably as a **going concern**. Qualified, adverse, or no opinions occur very infrequently (see Table 10.2).[36]

In summary, the external auditor is not responsible for the presentation or accuracy of financial statements but instead reduces the risk that statements are misleading by performing a check on management and its financial reporting procedures. The board of directors and company shareholders may expect the auditor to find all material errors and instances of fraud, but given the process of the audit, that is an unrealistic expectation (see the following sidebar).

Table 10.2   Auditor Opinions (2005–2009)

Year	Unqualified	Qualified	No Opinion	Additional Language	Adverse Opinion	Total
2005	7,108	0	3	2,486	1	9,576
2006	4,497	3	3	4,898	1	9,377
2007	4,496	3	2	4,544	1	9,022
2008	5,085	2	1	3,531	4	8,587
2009	5,273	3	2	2,674	2	7,915

Additional language might be used in an unqualified opinion to indicate an inconsistency in the application of an accounting principle, to emphasize a matter of importance, or to express concern about the company's ability to remain a going concern. An adverse opinion means that the company's financial statements are misstated. No opinion (or a disclaimer of opinion) means that the auditor could not complete the scope of the audit.

Source: Computed from *Standard & Poor's* Compustat.

Fraud and the External Auditor

HealthSouth

In Chapter 1, "Introduction to Corporate Governance," we told the story of HealthSouth, whose CEO, Richard Scrushy, and other corporate officers were accused of overstating earnings by at least $1.4 billion between 1999 and 2002. When their scheme unraveled in 2003, outside observers expressed outrage that Ernst & Young, the company's external auditor for more than a decade, had failed to detect the fraud. A committee member investigating the incident on behalf of the U.S. Congress declared that it "raises serious questions about the extent to which Ernst & Young was diligently performing its auditing duties."[37]

Ernst & Young defended its actions, stating, "When individuals are determined to commit a crime ... a financial audit cannot be expected to detect that crime .... The level of fraud and financial deception that took place at HealthSouth is a blatant violation of investor trust and Ernst & Young is as outraged as the investing public."[38] Knowing that the auditors were looking for material errors to their accounts, HealthSouth executives perpetrated fraud by making adjustments to small-dollar accounts that the auditors were less likely to examine: revenue accounts for clients reporting $5,000 or less in annual billings. Although each entry was not material, the accumulation of the adjustments created a significant misstatement of earnings. To meet quarterly earnings targets, executives had to make 120,000 fraudulent entries each quarter.[39] According to Ernst & Young, "[HealthSouth's] accounting personnel designed the false journal entries to the income statement and balance sheet accounts in a manner calculated to avoid detection by the outside auditors."[40] The firm claimed that its auditors followed appropriate procedures but were "provided fraudulent information as part of the criminal conspiracy specifically designed to defeat the audit process."[41]

Still, HealthSouth shareholders sued Ernst & Young, alleging that the firm had knowingly acquiesced to management and allowed for the improper booking of certain revenues, to secure additional nonaudit-related contracts.[42] Ernst & Young eventually settled the charges for $109 million.[43]

Audit Quality

Given the importance of the external audit, much attention has been paid to factors that might impact audit quality. These include consolidation among the major audit firms, whether conflicts exist when the auditor also provides nonaudit-related services to the client, whether conflicts exist when a member of the audit firm is hired into a senior finance role at the client, and how auditor rotations impact audit quality. We discuss these in the remainder of this chapter.

Structure of Audit Industry

The audit industry is characterized by extreme concentration among four main firms: Deloitte & Touche, Ernst & Young, KPMG, and PricewaterhouseCoopers. Together, these firms are known as the **Big Four**. The Big Four handle approximately 98 percent of the audits of large U.S. companies and earn 94 percent of total industry revenue for audit and audit-related services.[44] The rest of the industry is characterized by several midsize firms, such as Grant Thornton and BDO

Seidman, and thousands of boutique firms that cater primarily to local businesses.

As recently as the late 1980s, there were eight major accounting firms, but in the ensuing years, the industry has consolidated (see Figure 10.1).

Significant Mergers of the 1980s and 1990s

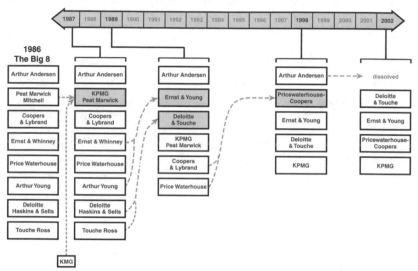

In 2002, the Department of Justice indicted Arthur Andersen on obstruction of justice charges for destroying documents relating to its audit of Enron. The firm was found guilty, lost its SEC license, and was forced to dissolve. In 2005, the U.S. Supreme Court overturned the verdict on procedural grounds. Nevertheless, it was too late to salvage the company.

Source: U.S. Government Accountability Office, "Audits of Public Companies: Continued Concentration in Audit Market for Large Public Companies Does Not Call for Immediate Action," GAO-08-163.

Figure 10.1   Consolidation among large accounting firms.

Several factors have contributed to concentration in the audit industry. First, scale among accounting firms is required to match the scale of international corporations. As companies expand around the globe, they require larger and more sophisticated accounting firms to resolve complex issues. These same firms are equipped to handle the complexity of an international audit. Scale is also important for the significant investment in information technology systems that are required to support a global audit. Second, because audit firms have deep expertise about their clients' accounting systems, their clients historically have hired them for nonaudit-related services, including tax, advisory, information technology systems, and consulting services. This has contributed to the global size and reach of the largest firms. Third, auditors are subject to intense legal scrutiny. Large firms are capable of surviving large legal penalties that would bankrupt smaller competitors. For example, between 1991 and 2009, the Big Four paid a combined total of $5.9 billion in legal settlements.[45]

Most countries require that audit firms be owned and managed by locally licensed auditors. As a result, the Big Four are not organized as a single corporation managed by a CEO and overseen by a board of directors. Instead, the Big Four consist of a collection of affiliated firms, each of which is locally owned and operated.[46] These firms benefit from the reputation and global resources of the Big Four but have the expertise of understanding country-specific regulations, accounting standards, and business practices. This structure allows them to cater to the local offices of multinational corporations and still maintain the economies of scale to make them globally competitive. It also means that, for the most part, when a Big Four firm is subject to shareholder or regulatory litigation, only the local office is named in the lawsuit.[47]

Much debate circulates over whether the concentration of market share among the Big Four has led to a decrease in competition and reduction in audit quality. In 2008, the GAO examined this issue and was unable to find a clear link between industry concentration and anticompetitive behavior. Still, 60 percent of the large companies that the GAO surveyed believed they did not have an adequate number of firms from which to choose their auditor. Smaller companies saw no such problem; 75 percent of them believed that the number of audit firms available to them was sufficient.

Respondents to the GAO survey also indicated that, although audit and audit-related fees have increased significantly in recent years, they did not believe that the increase in cost was due to anticompetitive behavior. Instead, they believed that it reflected the cost of compliance with stricter regulatory oversight (including Sarbanes-Oxley); the greater scope of the audit; and the cost of hiring, training, and retaining qualified professionals.

Finally, the GAO (2008) examined the possibility of requiring the Big Four to split into smaller firms, to increase competition and selection. Executives from large companies expressed concern that forced divestiture by the Big Four would reduce their expertise and decrease audit quality. Nevertheless, they agreed that further concentration among the Big Four might lead to insufficient choice. The GAO concluded its study with no recommendation for regulatory change.[48]

Impact of Sarbanes-Oxley

The audit industry in the United States has historically been self-regulated. For many years, auditing standards were developed by the American Institute of Certified Public Accountants (AICPA), a national association of accountants. These standards, known as Generally Accepted Auditing Standards (GAAS), set professional and ethical guidelines for auditors. Following the scandals of Enron, WorldCom, and others in 2001 and 2002, congressional leaders made efforts to formalize auditor oversight as a step toward improving investor confidence in published financial statements.

As such, the U.S. government passed the Sarbanes-Oxley Act of 2002 (SOX). Among its provisions, Sarbanes-Oxley established the Public Company Accounting Oversight Board (PCAOB) to regulate the audit industry. Prior to Sarbanes-Oxley, audit firms were subject to a peer review every three years, in which outside accountants tested the firm's compliance with quality-control systems for both accounting and audit. The peer review system was seen as deficient because it relied on industry self-policing and because the review was limited to testing control systems and did not examine the full scope of the audit firm's activities.[49] This system was replaced by one in which auditors are required to register with a public regulator (PCAOB), which inspects large audit firms every year and small audit firms every three years. PCAOB inspections differ from the peer review process in that they

- Are structured around a risk-based inspection (the audits subject to review are those seen as having the highest likelihood of a material omission or misstatement)
- Are given broad latitude to inspect any audit firm activity that might violate auditing standards or SOX

- Examine the "tone from the top" (attitude of the firm's management toward regulatory compliance)[50]

The PCAOB has the power to impose disciplinary measures when violations are detected. In addition to its inspection and enforcement powers, the PCAOB proposes auditing standards. Following passage of SOX, the PCAOB adopted the auditing standards of the AICPA while it drafted its own standards.[51]

Sarbanes-Oxley also enacted measures to reduce potential conflicts of interest between auditors and their clients. Section 201 of the law prohibits auditors from performing certain nonaudit services for their audit clients, including bookkeeping, financial information system design, fairness opinions, and other appraisal and actuarial work. These measures are intended to increase the independence of the external auditor by encouraging the auditor to stand up to management without fear of recourse that would come from losing a lucrative consulting relationship.

A number of studies have examined the impact of Sarbanes-Oxley or features restricted by SOX on audit quality. Interestingly enough, most of the research suggests that SOX restrictions on nonaudit-related service do nothing to improve audit quality. Romano (2005) provided a comprehensive review of the research literature and came to this conclusion. In the studies she reviewed, audit quality was measured in a variety of ways, including abnormal accruals, earnings conservatism, failure to issue qualified opinions, and financial restatements. She interpreted these results as indicating that marketplace factors (such as concern for reputation and competition for clients) deterred auditors from abusing their position to gain auxiliary revenue from nonaudit services.[52]

Romano (2005) also found that the U.S. Congress, in debating Section 201 of SOX, had ignored most of the research literature. Only one study was cited in congressional debate, and it was one that had already been largely disproven at the time.[53] None of the contravening evidence was considered, even though it was well understood by academics and professionals. She blamed this willful ignorance on a rush to respond to the collapse of Enron, a declining stock market, and upcoming midterm elections that compelled politicians to pass an important piece of legislation without "the healthy ventilation of issues that occurs in the usual give-and-take negotiations." Romano concluded that because the evidence does not support their effectiveness, the "corporate governance provisions of SOX should be stripped of their mandatory force and rendered optional for registrants."[54]

This is not to say that Sarbanes-Oxley has been entirely negative. In many ways, the legislation has focused the efforts of many constituents—including external auditors, internal auditors, audit committee members, managers, and shareholders—on practical methods to improve financial statement quality.

Still, these changes have come at a considerable cost. According to Audit Analytics, audit costs almost doubled among the 3,000 companies that came into compliance with SOX in the two years following enactment.[55] Furthermore, the amount of the increase was substantially higher than expected. Maher and Weiss (2010) found that the median cost of compliance with new provisions of SOX was between $1.3 million and $3.0 million annually in the four years following enactment. This compares with an original estimate of $91,000 by the SEC.[56] The largest increase in audit costs has been incurred by financial institutions, due to the complexity of their audits and internal controls. In addition, smaller companies have incurred higher costs (relative to revenues) than larger companies because of the considerable fixed-cost portion of an external audit.

Finally, Sarbanes-Oxley decreased the proportion of revenues that the Big Four received from nonaudit services. In 1975, the Big Eight received 11 percent of revenues from consulting services. By 1998, the proportion had increased to 45 percent. Following SOX, most of the Big Four divested their consulting divisions (Deloitte & Touche was an exception). As a result, consulting and advisory fees fell to approximately 25 percent of total revenues.[57]

External Auditor as CFO

A company might find it beneficial to offer a job to a member of the external auditing team, in either the finance, treasury, internal audit, or risk management departments. Hiring a former auditor has several advantages. These individuals are familiar with the company's business, internal practices, and procedures. They know (and presumably have good working relations with) other members of the staff. The company has had the opportunity to witness their working style, knowledge, and expertise first-hand. As such, hiring a former auditor allows a company to benefit from lower training costs and more reliable cultural fit.

Hiring a former auditor also has potential drawbacks. These individuals might feel an allegiance to their former employer and, therefore, be less willing to challenge their work. In addition, a former auditor has intimate knowledge of the company's internal control procedures and would be more adept at maneuvering around them without detection. As such, the company might find itself more greatly exposed to fraud. To address these concerns, Sarbanes-Oxley requires that former auditors undergo a one-year "cooling-off" period before they can accept an offer to work for a former client.

Some research evidence shows that audit quality suffers when a company hires a former auditor. Dowdell and Krishnan (2004) found that companies that hire a former auditor as their new CFO tend to exhibit a decrease in earnings quality. In addition, the authors found that a cooling-off period did not improve earnings quality. Observed decreases in earnings quality were not materially different whether the employee was hired more than or less than one year after leaving the audit firm.[58]

Other studies did not find significant evidence that hiring a former audit team member leads to a decrease in earnings quality. Geiger, North, and O'Connell (2005) examined a sample of more than 1,100 executives who were hired into a financial reporting position (CFO, controller, vice president of finance, or chief accounting officer) between 1989 and 1999. Of this group, 10 percent were hired from the company's current external audit firm. The authors compared the earnings quality of this group against three control groups: 1) executives who had not worked as an auditor immediately before being hired by the company, (2) executives who had worked for an audit firm that was not the company's current auditor prior to being hired, and (3) companies that had not made a new hire and instead retained their existing financial executives. They found no evidence that the source of hire had an impact on earnings quality. The authors concluded that even though "several recent highly publicized company failures have involved [so-called] 'revolving door' hires ... there does not appear to be a pervasive problem regarding excessive earnings management associated with this hiring practice."[59]

That is, even though hiring a former auditor as a financial officer might carry potential risks (such as occurred at HealthSouth), the evidence is weak that such a practice routinely compromises audit quality.

Auditor Rotation

Proposals have also been made that companies be required to rotate the external auditor periodically to ensure its independence and decrease the risk of fraud. Advocates of this approach argue that, over time, audit firms grow stale in their review of the same accounts and that a new audit firm brings fresh perspective to company procedures. Furthermore, they argue that members of the audit team develop personal relationships with company employees, further reducing their independence. Rotating the audit firm or the lead engagement partner is intended to counteract these tendencies. Critics of auditor rotation contend that it is overly costly to change audit firms or lead engagement partners because the new audit team must learn company policies and procedures from scratch. This can be time-consuming and can reduce audit quality while the new firm is going up the learning curve.

Regulators in many countries tend to view auditor rotation favorably. For example, Sarbanes-Oxley requires that audit firms rotate the lead engagement partner on all public company audits every five years.[60] The law stopped short of requiring that companies rotate their audit firm on a fixed schedule. Other countries have such regulations, however. For example, Italy, Brazil, and South Korea require audit firm rotation for all publicly traded companies. In India and Singapore, mandatory rotation is required only for domestic banks and certain insurance companies. Australia, Spain, and Canada previously required audit rotation but ultimately dropped the requirement.

The empirical evidence indicates that auditor rotation most likely does not improve audit quality. Cameran, Merlotti, and Di Vincenzo (2005) reviewed 26 regulatory reports and 25 empirically based academic studies on auditor rotation.[61] Only four of the regulatory reports concluded that auditor rotation is favorable; the rest determined that the costs of rotation outweighed its benefits. For example, the Association of British Insurers (ABI), American Institute of Certified Public Accountants (AICPA), European Federation of

Accountants and Auditors (EFAA), Fédération des Experts Comptables Européens (FEE), Institut der Wirtschaftsprüfer (IDW), and U.S. General Accounting Office (GAO) all found that mandatory auditor rotation is not cost-effective. Similarly, 19 of the 25 empirically based academic studies did not support mandatory rotation.[62]

Of course, some companies change auditors through the normal course of business.[63] The company might have grown to such a size or level of sophistication that it requires an auditor with greater expertise or geographical reach. The company might also simply be dissatisfied with the auditor's services or fees. When the company decides to replace its auditor, it is known as a **dismissal**. Dismissals can be concerning to investors because they might indicate that the company is seeking more lenient treatment of its accounting and controls procedures (**opinion shopping**). Alternatively, the auditor can resign from a client account. In this case, it is considered a **resignation**. Auditor resignations are potentially more troublesome for investors than dismissals in that they are more likely to indicate a disagreement over the application of accounting principles, company disclosure, or material weaknesses in the company's internal controls. Given the auditor's exposure to potential liability from a financial misstatement or fraud, the auditor might decide that it is easier to resign from an account than to continue to negotiate with management over accounting changes. Still, both a dismissal and a resignation can indicate deterioration in governance oversight.

Auditor changes must be disclosed to investors through an 8-K filing with the SEC. In the filing, the company outlines that a change in auditor has taken place and the reason for that change. The audit firm is required to report whether it agrees or disagrees with the company's explanation. The auditor must also report any concern about the reliability of the company's internal controls or financial statements.[64]

As we might expect, the market reacts negatively to auditor resignations. Shu (2000) found that a company's stock price significantly underperforms the market around the announcement of an auditor resignation but does not underperform following dismissals. She interpreted these results as indicating that investors react negatively to audit resignations because of their implication for future earnings or financial restatement risk.[65] Whisenant, Sankaraguruswamy, and Raghunandan (2003) reported similar findings. They found that the market reacts negatively when the auditor's resignation calls into question the reliability of financial statements but not when it suggests that the company might have insufficient internal controls. They speculated that auditor resignations due to a disagreement over the reliability of financial statements signals an "early warning" of accounting trouble to market participants, whereas a disagreement over insufficient internal controls is too imprecise for the market to react to.[66]

Endnotes

1. Under Sarbanes-Oxley, the audit committee is required to oversee the risks associated with internal controls and the preparation of financial statements, but not to oversee enterprise risk management, as defined in Chapter 6, "Organizational Strategy, Business Models, and Risk Management."

2. NASDAQ, "NASDAQ Rule Filings: Listed Companies—2002, SR NASD 2002 141." Accessed October 26, 2010. See www.nasdaq.com/about/RuleFilingsListings/Filings_Listing2002.stm.

3. Considerable disagreement exists among academics regarding how to measure accounting quality. Dechow and Schrand (2004) measured earnings quality in terms of the precision with which business operating performance is reported. This approach is consistent with a view that large noncash accruals denote low-quality earnings, in that earnings diverge from reported cash flows. Francis, Schipper, and Vincent (2003) measured earnings quality in terms of the precision with which the change in corporate value is reported. This view prescribes that the earnings should reflect the change in the market value of the balance sheet during a reporting period. The American Accounting Association (2002) takes a holistic assessment of earnings quality, including operating results; balance sheet valuation; earnings management; and the perspectives of external auditors, analysts, and international organizations. See Patricia M. Dechow and Catherine M. Schrand, "Earnings Quality," Research Foundation of CFA Institute (2004). Jennifer Francis, Katherine Schipper, and Linda Vincent, "The Relative and Incremental Explanatory Power of Earnings and Alternative (to Earnings) Performance Measures for Returns," *Contemporary Accounting Research* 20 (2003): 121–164. The Accounting Review Conference (January 24–26, 2002), and a special issue of *The Accounting Review* (Volume 77, Supplement 2002), edited by Katherine Schipper.

4. See David F. Larcker and Brian Tayan, "Baker Hughes: Foreign Corrupt Practices Act," Stanford GSB Case No. CG-18 (August 31, 2010).

5. Audit Committee Institute, "The Audit Committee Journey. Recalibrating for the New Normal. 2009 Public Company Audit Committee Member Survey," KPMG. Accessed November 11, 2010. See www.kpmginstitutes.com/insights/2009/highlights-5th-annual-issues-conference.aspx.

6.   Audit Committee Institute.

7.   David Burgstahler and Ilia Dichev, "Earnings Management to Avoid Earnings Decreases and Losses," *Journal of Accounting and Economics* 24 (1997): 99–126.

8.   Charles A. P. N. Carslaw, "Anomalies in Income Numbers: Evidence of Goal-Oriented Behavior," *The Accounting Review* 63 (1988): 321–327.

9.   Joseph A. Grundfest and Nadya Malenko, "Quadrophobia: Strategic Rounding of EPS Data," Rock Center for Corporate Governance at Stanford University working paper no. 65, *Social Science Research Network* (October 14, 2009). See http://ssrn.com/abstract=1474668.

10. Sanjeev Bhojraj, Paul Hribar, Marc Picconi, and John McInnis, "Making Sense of Cents: An Examination of Firms That Marginally Miss or Beat Analyst Forecasts," *Journal of Finance* 64 (2009): 2,361–2,388.

11. Mark Grothe and Poonam Goyal, "Trend Report Restatements: Restatement Dust Settles," Glass Lewis & Co., LLC (March 19, 2009).

12. Ibid.

13. Ibid.

14. Zoe-Vonna Palmrose, Vernon J. Richardson, and Susan Scholz, "Determinants of Market Reactions to Restatement Announcements," *Journal of Accounting & Economics* 37 (2004): 59.

15. The information in this sidebar is adapted with permission from Madhav Rajan and Brian Tayan, "Financial Restatements: Methods Companies Use to Distort Financial Performance," Stanford GSB Case No. A-198 (June 10, 2008). Copyright © 2008 by the Board of Trustees of the Leland Stanford Junior University. All rights reserved. Used with permission from the Stanford University Graduate School of Business. See Krispy Kreme Doughnuts, Forms 8-K, filed with the Securities and Exchange Commission July 30, 2004; October 10, 2004; January 4, 2005; August 10, 2005.

16. Krispy Kreme Doughnuts, Form 10-K, filed with the Securities and Exchange Commission October 31, 2006; and Forms DEF 14-A, filed April 14, 2004, and April 28, 2006.

17. Mark S. Beasley, "An Empirical Analysis of the Relation Between the Board of Director Composition and Financial Statement Fraud," *Accounting Review* 7 (1996): 443–465. Accessed October 27, 2010.

18. David B. Farber, "Restoring Trust After Fraud: Does Corporate Governance Matter?" *Accounting Review* 80 (2005): 539–561.

19. Maria M. Correia, "Political Connections, SEC Enforcement and Accounting Quality," Rock Center for Corporate Governance at Stanford University working paper no. 61, *Social Science Research Network* (July 1, 2009). See http://ssrn.com/abstract=1458478.

20. Mark S. Beasley, Joseph V. Carcello, Dana R. Hermanson, and Terry L. Neal, "Fraudulent Financial Reporting 1998–2007: An Analysis of U.S. Public Companies." Committee of Sponsoring Organizations of the Treadway Commissions (COSO) (May 2010). Accessed November 13, 2010. See www.coso.org/documents/COSOFRAUDSTUDY2010.pdf.

21. Michel Magnan, Denis Cormier, and Pascale Lapointe-Antunes, "Like Moths Attracted to Flames: Financial Reporting Frauds," American Accounting Association (2009). Accessed May 11, 2010. See http://aaahq.org/pubs.cfm.

22. Alexander Dyck, Adair Morse, and Luigi Zingales, "Who Blows the Whistle on Corporate Fraud?" *Journal of Finance* 65 (2010): 2,213–2,253.

23. Paraphrased SEC Commissioner James C. Treadway remarks made to the American Society of Corporate Secretaries, Inc., in Cleveland, Ohio on April 13, 1983, titled "Are 'Cooked Books' a Failure of Corporate Governance?"

24. Patricia M. Dechow, Richard G. Sloan, and Amy P. Sweeney, "Detecting Earnings Management," *Accounting Review* 70 (1995): 193–225. Jennifer J. Jones, "Earnings Management During Import Relief Investigations," *Journal of Accounting Research* 29 (1991): 193–228.

25. Other ratios in the analysis were not shown to have predictive power. These included leverage growth, the rate of change in depreciation, and changes in SG&A as a percent of sales. See Messod D. Beneish, "The Detection of Earnings Manipulation," *Financial Analysts Journal* 55 (1999): 24–36.

26. In 2010, Audit Integrity merged with GovernanceMetrics International. Going forward, the combined entity will be called GovernanceMetrics International. Audit Integrity, "The AGR Methodology," (2010). Accessed November 18, 2010. See www.auditintegrity.com/methodology.html.

27. Richard A. Price, Nathan Y. Sharp, and David A. Wood, "Detecting and Predicting Accounting Irregularities: A Comparison of Commercial and Academic Risk Measures," *Social Science Research Network* (September 2010). Accessed November 13, 2010. See http://ssrn.com/abstract=1546675.

28. Maria M. Correia.

29. David F. Larcker and Anastasia A. Zakolyukina, "Detecting Deceptive Discussions in Conference Calls," Rock Center for Corporate Governance at Stanford University working paper no. 83, *Social Science Research Network* (July 29, 2010). See http://ssrn.com/abstract=1572705.

30. Public Company Accounting Oversight Board, "PCAOB Staff Audit Practice Alert No. 3, Audit Considerations in the Current Economic Environment, December 5," (2008). Accessed March 5, 2009. See http://pcaobus.org/Standards/QandA/12-05-2008_APA_3.pdf.

31. American Institute of Certified Public Accountants (AICPA), Overview of Summary Fraud Conference held on January 31, 2006, entitled "Fraud ... Can Audit Committees Really Make a Difference?"

32. American Institute of Certified Public Accountants (AICPA), Statements on Auditing Standards: SAS No. 99, AU §316.02 Consideration of Fraud in a Financial Statement Audit. Statement on Auditing Standards No. 99. New York, NY: AICPA.

33. Still, many feel that the auditor should have greater accountability for rooting out fraud, and shareholder groups continue to press for liability. See Ian Fraser, "Holding the Auditors Accountable for Missing Corporate Fraud," QFinance blog posting September 22, 2010. Accessed November 13, 2010. See www.qfinance.com/blogs/ian-fraser/2010/09/22/holding-the-auditors-account-able-for-missing-corporate-fraud-auditor-liability.

34. Management, too, is required to produce an "internal controls report" that establishes that adequate internal controls are in place.

35. Audit Analytics, "404 Dashboard: Year 4 Update, December," (2008). Accessed November 9, 2010. See http://auditanalytics.com/doc/AuditAnalytics_SOX404_AICPA_Conf_12_08.pdf.

36. Standard & Poor's Compustat.

37. Jonathan Weil, "HealthSouth Becomes Subject of a Congressional Probe," *Wall Street Journal* (April 23, 2003, Eastern edition): C.1.

38. Jonathan Weil and Cassell Bryan-Low, "Questioning the Books: Audit Committee Met Only Once During 2001," *Wall Street Journal* (March 21, 2003, Eastern edition): A.2.

39. Aaron Beam and Chris Warner, *HealthSouth: The Wagon to Disaster* (Fairhope, Ala.: Wagon Publishing, 2009).

40. Jonathan Weil, "Accounting Scheme Was Straightforward but Hard to Detect," *Wall Street Journal* (March 20, 2003, Eastern edition): C.1.

41. Carrick Mollenkamp, "HealthSouth Figure Avoids Prison," *Wall Street Journal* (June 2, 2004, Eastern edition): A.2.

42. Carrick Mollenkamp and Ann Davis, "HealthSouth Ex-CFO Helps Suit," *Wall Street Journal* (July 26, 2004, Eastern edition): C.1.

43. Anonymous, "HealthSouth Corporation: Stockholder and Bondholder Litigation," Stanford Law School, Securities Class Action Clearinghouse in cooperation with Cornerstone Research. Accessed October 28, 2010. See http://securities.stanford.edu/1008/HRC98/.

44. United States Government Accountability Office (GAO), "Audits of Public Companies: Continued Concentration in Audit Market for Large Public Companies Does Not Call for Immediate Action: Report to Congressional Addressees," report no. GAO-08-163 (January 2008). Accessed May 20, 2010. See www.gao.gov/new.items/d08163.pdf.

45. These break down as follows: Deloitte ($1.2 billion), Ernst & Young ($1.9 billion), KPMG ($1.4 billion), and PwC ($1.3 billion). In addition, Arthur Andersen paid settlements of $0.8 billion before ultimately dissolving following the Enron scandal. See Mark Cheffers and Robert Kueppers, "Audit Analytics: Accountants Professional Liability Scorecards and Commentary," paper presented at the 21st Annual ALI-ABA, Accountants' Liability Conference, June 10–11, 2010.

46. In the United States, each of the Big Four is organized as a partnership, owned by the partners who run the firm. These partnerships are overseen by a governing board, which numbers approximately 20 directors, the majority of whom are certified public accountants.

47. However, plaintiffs' lawyers have attempted to name the international office in liability lawsuits. In 2004, Parmalat shareholders named Deloitte Touche Tohmatsu (the international association) along with Deloitte's Italian office, in a lawsuit alleging that the auditors were liable for failing to detect or report management fraud. Deloitte Touche Tohmatsu asked a U.S. District Court judge to remove its name from the case, claiming that it is a legally separate entity and provides no services to the local office. In a 2009 ruling, the judge ruled that the international association should remain defendants. He cited the marketing, financial, and quality control ties that the international association provided to the local office as evidence that a substantial connection exists between the entities. According to Stanford Law School professor and former SEC commissioner Joseph A. Grundfest: "All of them have structures designed to build fire walls [between the local office and the international association]. The question is, will the dikes hold when you have this kind of a flood?" See Nanette Byrnes, "Audit Firms' Global Ambitions Come Home to Roost," BusinessWeek Online (February 3, 2009). Accessed November 13, 2010. See http://search.ebscohost.com/login.aspx?direct=true&db=bth&AN=36427167&site=ehost-live&scope=site.

48. United States Government Accountability Office (GAO).

49. Public Oversight Board (POB), "The Road to Reform—A White Paper from the Public Oversight Board on Legislation to Create a New Private-Sector Regulatory Structure for the Accounting Profession," (March 19, 2002). Accessed November 13, 2010. See www.publicoversightboard.org/White_Pa.pdf.

50. Jerry Wegman, "Government Regulation of Accountants: The PCAOB Enforcement Process," *Journal of Legal, Ethical, and Regulatory Issues* 11 (2008): 75–94.

51. Louis Grumet, "Standards Setting at the Crossroads," *The CPA Journal* (July 1, 2003). Accessed November 13, 2010. See www.nysscpa.org/cpajournal/2003/0703/nv/nv2.htm.

52. Larcker and Richardson (2004) found that, for the subset of firms that have apparent accounting deficiencies, the problem is weak governance systems (such as low institutional holdings and higher insider holdings) rather than payments made to the auditor for nonaudit services. See Roberta Romano, "The Sarbanes-Oxley Act and the Making of Quack Corporate Governance," *Yale Law Review* 114 (2005): 1,521–1,612. See David F. Larcker and Scott A. Richardson, "Fees Paid to Audit Firms, Accrual Choices, and Corporate Governance," *Journal of Accounting Research* 42 (2004): 625–658.

53. That study is: Richard M. Frankel, Marilyn F. Johnson, and Karen K. Nelson, "The Relation Between Auditors' Fee for Nonaudit Services and Earnings Management," *Accounting Review* 77 (2002): 71–105.

54. Romano is referring to restrictions including audit committee independence, limits on corporate loans to executives, and executive certification of the financial statements. See Roberta Romano.

55. Mark Cheffers and Don Whalen, "Audit Fees and Nonaudit Fees: A Seven-Year Trend," *Audit Analytics* (March 2010): 1–12.

56. Michael W. Maher and Dan Weiss, "Costs of Complying with SOX—Measurement, Variation, and Investors' Anticipation," *Social Science Research Network* (October 29, 2010). See http://ssrn.com/abstract=1699828.

57. The U.S. Department of the Treasury, "Advisory Committee on the Auditing Profession, Final Report, October 6," (2008). Accessed November 13, 2010. See www.ustreas.gov/offices/domestic-finance/acap/docs/final-report.pdf.

58. Measured in terms of abnormal accruals. See Thomas D. Dowdell and Jagan Krishnan, "Former Audit Firm Personnel As CFOs: Effect on Earnings Management," *Canadian Accounting Perspectives* 3 (2004): 117–142. Beasley, Carcello, and Hermanson (2000) found that 11 percent of financial restatements due to fraud involved a CFO who had previously been employed at the company's audit firm. However, the authors do not provide descriptive statistics to determine whether this represents an above-average incidence rate. Mark S. Beasley, Joseph Y. Carcello, and Dana R. Hermanson, "Should You Offer a Job to Your External Auditor?" *Journal of Corporate Accounting & Finance* 11 (2000): 35–42.

59. Marshall A. Geiger, David S. North, and Brendan T. O'Connell, "The Auditor-to-Client Revolving Door and Earnings Management," *Journal of Accounting, Auditing & Finance* 20 (2005): 1–26.

60. The SEC audit review partner (or "concurring reviewer") also rotates every five years.

61. Mara Cameran, Emilia Merlotti, and Dino Di Vincenzo, "The Audit Firm Rotation Rule: A Review of the Literature," SDA Bocconi research paper, *Social Science Research Network* (September 2005). Accessed February 20, 2009. See http://ssrn.com/abstract=825404.

62. The authors reviewed 34 "academic" studies, 25 of which were based on empirical data and 9 of which were opinion based. Although the authors considered all 34 to be academic studies, we refer only to the 25 empirical studies here because the others did not test their conclusions against observable evidence. Interestingly, the authors noted that although 76 percent of the empirical studies concluded against mandatory auditor rotation, only 56 percent of the opinion-based reports opposed the practice. This is consistent with a general bias among thought leaders who advocate a best practice without regard to rigorous evidence.

63. For example, in 2008, there were approximately 50 audit firm changes among companies that use Big Four or other national accounting firms. Among all publicly traded companies, there are approximately 1,000 auditor changes each year. Audit Analytics, "Where the Audit Gains & Losses Came From: January 1, 2008–December 31, 2008," (2009): 35–42. See http://www.auditanalytics. com/0000/par-articles.php. Lynn E. Turner, Jason P. Williams, and Thomas R. Weirich, "An Inside Look at Auditor Changes," *The CPA Journal* (November 2005). Accessed November 13, 2010. See www.nysscpa.org/cpajournal/2005/1105/special_issue/essentials/p12.htm.

64. Securities Lawyer's Deskbook, "Standard Instructions for Filing Forms under the Securities Act of 1933, Securities Exchange Act of 1934, and Energy Policy and Conservation Act of 1975 Regulation S-K," The University of Cincinnati College of Law. Accessed October 29, 2010. See http://taft.law.uc.edu/CCL/regS-K/index.html.

65. Susan Zhan Shu, "Auditor Resignations: Clientele Effects and Legal Liability," *Journal of Accounting & Economics* 29 (2000): 173–205.

66. J. Scott Whisenant, Srinivasan Sankaraguruswamy, and K. Raghunandan, "Market Reactions to Disclosure of Reportable Events," *Auditing* 22 (2003): 181–194.

11

The Market for Corporate Control

A well-functioning governance system consists of more than a board of directors to provide oversight of the corporation and an external auditor to ensure the integrity of financial reporting. It includes all disciplining mechanisms—legal, regulatory, and market driven—that influence management to act in the interest of shareholders. For example, in Chapter 7, "Labor Market for Executives and CEO Succession Planning," we examined how a competitive labor market for CEOs puts pressure on management to perform or risk being replaced by another executive, either from within or outside the company, who can deliver better corporate results.

Instead of removing an executive, the board of directors (or in some cases shareholders directly) can decide to transfer ownership of the firm to new owners who will manage its assets more profitably. A change in control involves not only replacing management, but also possibly making substantial changes to firm strategy, cost structure, and capital structure. In theory, a change of control makes economic sense only when the value of the firm to new owners, minus transaction costs associated with the deal, is greater than the value of the firm to current owners. When this scenario occurs, the acquirer will attempt to purchase the target and capture the resulting economic gains. This general idea is called the **market for corporate control**.[1]

Of course, this discussion above is somewhat simplistic. Clearly, acquisitions also occur for non-strategic reasons. For example, management might want to increase the scope of operations simply for the sake of managing a larger operation. When this occurs, the acquiring company might receive less in value than it gives up. The management of the acquiring firm might be better off, but the economic impact on shareholders would be considerably less positive. Similarly, the management of the target firm might seek to impede a takeover—even one that makes economic sense—to protect their present jobs. If successful, these actions can lead to inefficiencies in the market for corporate control and can weaken the disciplining effects on managerial performance.

In this chapter, we explore this topic. We start by examining the market for corporate control. In general, how beneficial are acquisitions? Do they create or destroy value? Then we examine the steps companies take to protect themselves from unsolicited acquisitions. When is it appropriate for the firm to adopt antitakeover protections? Do they lead to enhanced shareholder value, or are they a source of value-destroying friction?

The Market for Corporate Control

The concept of a market for corporate control was succinctly described by Henry Manne: "The lower the stock price, relative to what it could be with more efficient management, the more attractive the takeover becomes to those who believe that they can manage the company more efficiently."[2] Manne's thesis was that the price of a company's stock partly reflects management performance. A low stock price indicates poor management of company assets and provides incentive to find alternative sources of capital to acquire the company, replace its management, and maximize its resources for their own gain.

Today we think of the market for corporate control as consisting of all mergers, acquisitions, and reorganizations, including those by a competitive firm, by a conglomerate buyer, or through a leveraged buyout (LBO), management buyout (MBO), or private equity firm. The company that makes the offer is known as the **acquirer** (or **bidder**). The company that is the subject of the offer is the **target**.

An acquisition attempt can either be friendly or hostile. **Friendly acquisitions** are those in which the target is open to receiving an offer from the acquiring firm. An acquisition might still be considered friendly if the target rejects the initial bid as inadequate but signals that it is willing to negotiate a higher takeover price. **Hostile takeovers** are those in which the target resists attempts to be acquired at any reasonable price. Management of the target firm might adopt a defense mechanism to protect itself from a takeover, or more likely, it might already have such a mechanism in place that management declines to remove. These are known as **antitakeover protections**, or **antitakeover defenses**.

Takeover offers can be structured in three basic forms. A **merger** occurs when two companies directly negotiate a takeover. Mergers tend to be friendly. A merger is complete when it has been approved by both companies' boards and shareholders. A **tender offer** occurs when the acquirer makes a public offer to acquire the shares of the target at a stated price. Tender offers tend to be hostile. In the absence of antitakeover defenses, a tender offer allows a hostile bidder to bypass the target's board of directors and seek approval directly from shareholders. When antitakeover defenses are in place, a tender offer is combined with a **proxy contest**. In the proxy contest, the acquirer asks the target shareholders to elect a board proposed by the acquirer to replace the incumbent board. If elected, the new board will disable the antitakeover defenses and allow the acquisition to go forward.[3]

Acquisitions occur for many reasons. The most frequently cited reason is that the acquiring firm believes it can enhance the profitability of the target company in a manner that the company could not achieve in its existing ownership structure. In this way, the firm's assets might be worth more to an acquirer than the company as a free-standing entity.[4] Examples include these:

- **Financial synergies**—An acquiring firm believes that it can increase profits through revenue improvements, cost reductions, or vertical integration that comes from combining the two companies' business lines.

- **Diversification**—Two companies whose earnings are uncorrelated (for example, because they are in unrelated or countercyclical industries) might benefit by merging because the capital generated when one business is thriving can help the other when it is under pressure. This is the logic behind the conglomerate structure. Conglomerates can also transfer noncash resources, such as management, among divisions.[5]

- **Change in ownership**—A new ownership group might be able to improve the profitability of the target through its access to capital, managerial expertise, and other business resources. For example, private equity firms dramatically change the capital structure and incentive plans in the target firm after acquisition (see the following sidebar).

Private Equity

Private equity firms are privately held investment firms that invest in companies for the benefit of retail and institutional investors. The private equity firm itself is generally structured as a limited liability corporation, while its investment capital is deployed through limited partnerships (with the private equity firm acting as general partner).[6] This structure allows the private equity firm to manage multiple funds, each with its own portfolio of assets. It also allows the firm to avoid liability to creditors if an investment in one of the funds fails.

Private equity firms invest in publicly traded businesses, privately held firms, and subsidiaries spun off from larger corporations. Their targets are generally mature companies that generate substantial free cash flow to support a leveraged capital structure. After they are acquired, these companies can undergo a complete change in management, board of directors, operating strategy, and capital structure. If successful, the private equity firm then sells the company, either back into the public markets through an IPO or to a strategic buyer that is interested in the improved operations.

Because private equity–backed companies are not publicly traded, they are not required to adopt the governance standards of the New York Stock Exchange, the Sarbanes–Oxley Act, or the Dodd–Frank Financial Reform Act. As a result, their governance structure tends to be very different from that of a publicly traded corporation. The board of directors is relatively small (five to seven individuals). The composition of the board is heavily represented by insiders (both executives of the portfolio company and members of the private equity firm) who own a majority of the firm. The private equity investors are closely involved in strategic and operating matters, and the focus of board meetings is on business, financial, and risk-management issues rather than compliance or regulatory issues. Executive compensation consists heavily of equity-based pay and, as we saw in Chapter 7, might approach very large numbers if the deal is successful, but will be very low if the deal does not work out. As a result, it offers extreme pay for performance.

Mixed evidence has emerged over whether private equity firms generate superior, risk-adjusted returns. Kaplan and Schoar (2005) found that median returns are 5 to 10 percent *below* the S&P 500. However, large private equity firms that have been in business for an extended time period have outperformed the index by 60 to 80 percent over a 17-year period.[7]

Companies can also merge for nonstrategic reasons, such as for empire building, management hubris, herding behavior, and compensation incentives. **Empire building** describes a situation in which the acquiring company's management seeks to acquire another company primarily for the sake of managing a larger enterprise. **Hubris** represents overconfidence on the part of management that it can more efficiently utilize the assets of a target to achieve greater revenues or cost savings than current owners can.[8] **Herding behavior** occurs when the senior management team of one company pursues acquisitions because its competitors have recently completed acquisitions.[9] **Compensation incentives** might encourage management to pursue deals that are not in the best interest of shareholders. Management of the acquiring company might pursue a deal because the executives will receive greater compensation for managing a larger enterprise.[10] Management of the target company might want to accept a takeover bid because the executives stand to receive large severance or change-in-control payments. According to a study by Equilar, the average CEO stands to receive $29 million in cash and accelerated equity grants following a change in control[11] (see the following sidebar).

The Personalities behind Mergers

Empire building—Empire building might have been the driving factor behind the series of acquisitions led by former Citigroup CEO Sandy Weill.[12] Weill, who took over as CEO of little-known Commercial Credit, aggressively expanded by purchasing Primerica (parent of the prestigious brokerage firm Smith Barney),

Travelers Insurance, Salomon Brothers, and Citicorp to create Citigroup—at one time, the largest financial institution in the world. Although improved service was often the stated motivation behind each acquisition, the emphasis was also on size. For example, upon announcing the Citicorp/Travelers merger, Weill asserted:

"Citicorp and Travelers Group bring together some of the best people in the financial services business, creating a resource for customers like no other—a diversified global consumer financial services company, a premier global bank, a leading global asset management company, a pre-eminent global investment banking and trading firm, and a broad-based insurance capability. Our ability to serve consumers, corporations, institutions, and government agencies, domestic and foreign, will be without parallel. This is a combination whose time has come."[13]

Hubris—Hubris might have driven AT&T CEO Michael Armstrong in his bold acquisition strategy in the late 1990s.[14] Armstrong joined the company in 1997 following an accomplished career at IBM and then after serving as CEO of Hughes Electronics. In the next few years, he moved aggressively to accumulate a significant collection of telecommunication assets—he spent more than $100 billion on cable companies TCI and MediaOne. Armstrong believed that by managing a diverse set of telecommunication assets under one roof, AT&T would be positioned to capitalize on a convergence between voice, data, and Internet technologies. However, the strategy largely failed: AT&T was unable to realize revenue and profit objectives, and the company struggled under significant debt. AT&T was steadily dismantled, and the company was sold to SBC in 2005.

Herding behavior—After pharmaceutical giant Pfizer agreed to acquire Wyeth in 2009 and Merck announced that it was merging with Schering Plough, the *Wall Street Journal* predicted that a "wave of acquisitions is likely as companies worry about their drug pipelines."[15] Senior management teams might justify copy-cat moves in economic terms (such as a "change in the competitive landscape"), but herding behavior is likely also driven by psychological tendencies, including envy, social proof, a desire for media attention, and reputational factors. Investment bankers also might exploit these tendencies to encourage deal making.

Compensation incentives—In 2005, Gillette Company agreed to sell itself to Procter & Gamble in a deal valued at $57 billion. Following the deal, Gillette CEO James Kilts received $185 million in severance and other benefits. Critics of the deal alleged that Kilts had put his own financial consideration above that of the company by agreeing to the acquisition. According to NYU Professor David Yermack, "Many [CEOs] really dip in and take an extra bonus, an extra augmentation of their contract at the eleventh hour, when there's very little ability of the shareholders or even their own directors to do anything about it." Kilts defended the deal by claiming that it was not done to "aggrandize management or myself, but to do what is right for shareholders and employees."[16] He pointed out that much of the gain was from appreciated equity compensation that he had accepted in lieu of cash during his tenure.

Stock Market Assessment of Acquiring and Target Firms

A vast research literature has examined the market for corporate control and the impact of the acquisitions on corporate performance. Here we summarize some of the basic results.

Who Gets Acquired?

Many researchers have attempted to develop models that predict which companies are likely to become acquisition targets, based on financial and stock price performance.[17] Palepu (1986) found some evidence that firms with poor performance, small size, and a need for resources for growth are more likely to be takeover targets. Still, he cautions that it is difficult to predict takeover targets with accuracy.[18]

Professional studies have also identified attributes that might be common across takeover targets:

- **Fundamentally weak performance**—The company can be purchased at a low price (relative to assets) and performance can be subsequently improved through managerial changes or capital infusions.
- **Companies in an industry with heightened merger activity**—Industry groups tend to experience merger activity

in waves. An example includes the casino industry in the 2000s. This might be caused by a shift in the marketplace that makes these firms more attractive or encourages consolidation. It might also be driven by psychological factors, such as the herding behavior discussed earlier.

- **Low debt levels**—Companies with low debt levels have greater financial flexibility. The acquirer can increase the debt levels of the target as part of the financial strategy.

- **Strong cash flows**—Companies with strong cash flows also have greater financial flexibility. Strategic buyers can use internally generated cash flow to fund expansion; private equity buyers can rely on cash flow to support a higher debt burden.

- **Valuable assets**—The target's assets might be underutilized, complementary to those of the acquirer, or have value that is not readily apparent to public shareholders (such as land, intellectual property, or patents that are not carried on the balance sheet at fair value).[19]

Researchers have also studied the practice of awarding change-of-control payments (**golden parachutes**) for their implications on takeover activity. Lambert and Larcker (1985) found that the stock market reacts positively to the adoption of a golden parachute provision in the executive employment contract. They suggested that shareholders might view such provisions favorably if they believe it means that a takeover is more likely or that management has greater incentive to negotiate a larger premium in a prospective deal.[20] Machlin, Choe, and Miles (1993) found that golden parachute provisions significantly increase the likelihood of a takeover and that the size of the payment positively influences the magnitude of the takeover premium. They saw no evidence that such payments are made as a form of rent extraction (that is, if they are awarded only after a deal is already pending), but instead concluded that "golden parachutes encourage managers to pursue shareholder interests."[21]

Finally, as mentioned earlier, it is necessary to offer a premium relative to the current stock price, to convince the target company to accept a deal. As we discussed in Chapter 3, "Board of Directors: Duties and Liability," the board of directors must evaluate the premium offered in relation to the standalone, long-term value of the company and make a decision that they believe is in the interest of shareholders. Eckbo (2009) calculated that the average takeover premium between 1973 and 2002 was about 45 percent (see Figure 11.1).[22]

Sample	Number of cases	Deal value ($ million)		% of contests where the winner is:			Average offer premium (%)	
		Mean	Median	Initial bidder	Rival	No bidder wins	Initial bid	Final bid
All contests	10,806	715	89	66.6	3.7	29.7	44.5	46.1
1973–1989	3,730	312	60	58.7	5.2	36.1	45.0	48.5
1990–2002	7,076	903	108	70.7	3.0	26.4	44.2	45.0
Merger bid	7,750	827	92	63.5	3.3	33.2	43.6	44.5
Tender offer	3,056	433	78	74.8	4.8	20.4	46.5	50.2
Acquirer public	6,726	902	112	75.6	3.2	21.3	46.1	47.5
Acquirer private	4,080	285	52	51.7	4.5	43.7	40.1	42.6
Single bidder	9,944	693	88	70.5	0.0	29.5	44.8	45.4
Multiple bidders	862	989	101	20.6	47.8	31.7	41.1	53.2
Target friendly	10,295	688	85	68.0	3.2	28.8	44.1	45.1
Target hostile	511	1,204	183	34.4	16.3	49.2	49.0	60.9
All cash	4,185	320	66	69.1	4.0	27.0	44.1	46.6
Stock/mixed	6,621	1,048	119	65.0	3.6	31.4	44.7	45.8

Source: B. Espen Eckbo (2009).

Figure 11.1 Initial and final offer premiums (1973–2002).

Who Gets the Value in a Takeover?

The benefits of a change in ownership are not evenly shared between the acquirer and the target. Research studies routinely have found that the incremental value anticipated by a merger tends to flow predominantly to the target, in the form of a large premium relative to past stock price. Jensen and Ruback (1983) reviewed 12 studies on successful tender offers and acquisitions. They found that target companies exhibit double-digit excess stock price returns between the announcement and consummation of a merger.[23] The amount of outperformance varies by the nature of the deal. For example, Servaes (1991) found that companies that are the target of a hostile bid outperform the market by 32 percentage points in the month following the takeover announcement, while companies that agree to a friendly merger outperform by 22 percent.[24] Gains also vary by the structure of the deal. Andrade, Mitchell, and Stafford (2001) found that mergers funded with equity result in lower excess returns for target companies than all-cash offers.[25]

At the same time, the benefits of a change in ownership are decidedly less favorable for the acquirer. Martynova and Renneboog (2008) found that the acquiring firm's shareholders enjoy no bump up in share price following the announcement of a takeover. Instead, the stock price returns of the acquirer are indistinguishable from those of the general market.[26] Studies also show that relative performance depends on the nature of the bid. Goergen and Renneboog (2004) found that hostile takeovers result in worse stock price performance for the acquirer than friendly deals.[27] Mergers financed with equity destroy more value for the acquiring firm than mergers financed with cash.[28]

However, these studies focus on the market's expectations for the merger based on stock price changes around the announcement date. But what does the evidence say about the long-term economics of deals? The evidence is fairly negative. Studies that measure long-term operating performance (such as earnings-per-share growth or cash flows over a one- to three-year period) largely find that firms tend to underperform their peers following an acquisition.[29] One obvious explanation is that the acquisition is simply a bad investment in which revenue and cost synergies do not meet expectations. If a target has multiple bids, the acquirer might experience the "winner's curse," in which the final bid is actually too high. Acquirers sometimes cut back on investment in working capital and capital expenditures following a deal, actions that can improve cash flow but destroy value. Furthermore, companies that acquire targets within the same industry enjoy no performance advantage over companies that acquire targets from an unrelated industry. Still, some evidence indicates that acquisitions financed with cash perform better than acquisitions financed with equity.[30]

Although much attention is paid to the economics of a merger, the merger process itself is equally important. Proposed mergers can be highly disruptive to both the target and the acquirer. This is particularly true of hostile takeover attempts, in which considerable resources are expended to mount or defend an unsolicited bid. The bidder must acquire a list of shareholders, contact major shareholders to assess their willingness to sell, and mail proxy materials to all parties. For its part, the target must contact shareholders and convince them not to sell. If the target believes that the threat is credible, it might engage in value-destroying behaviors to thwart the acquisition. All these actions detract from a focus on running day-to-day operations, and boards need to be especially diligent during these activities (see the following sidebar).

BASF vs. Engelhard

In January 2006, German chemical company BASF made an unsolicited offer to acquire Engelhard Corporation for $4.9 billion. At $37 per share, the offer represented a 30 percent premium over the current share price. Nevertheless, Engelhard's board rejected the offer as "inadequate," stating that corporate actions initiated by management would ultimately "deliver higher value to stockholders than BASF's offer."[31]

The rejection did not deter BASF, which made a tender offer directly to Engelhard investors. BASF would use the votes of the shares it received to launch a proxy fight to replace five of Engelhard's directors and force a new vote on its offer. Engelhard responded by initiating a competing tender offer for 20 percent of its shares at $45 each. BASF raised its bid to $38 and then $39. Engelhard's board withdrew its competing tender and accepted the higher offer in May 2006.

For all its efforts, Engelhard shareholders received payment that was 5.6 percent higher than the original offer. This increase came at several costs, however. First was the lost time value of money, in that the deal closed five months later. Second, Engelhard incured considerable expense hiring lawyers and bankers to implement a defense. Third, these efforts detracted from the management of the business.

Even successful deals result in considerable turmoil for the acquirer. For example, takeovers commonly lead to layoffs as acquirers seek to capture operating efficiencies by reducing labor expenses. Takeovers also lead to executive turnover as management teams are integrated. In fact, Krug and Shill (2008) found that executive turnover rates double following an acquisition, and that executive turnover remains elevated for ten years. The authors noted that "long-term leadership instability ... should be viewed as potentially harmful to integration and long-term performance."[32] Other studies have suggested that how well a company manages the integration process is a key determinant of whether a merger will ultimately generate economic benefits to the acquirer.[33]

Based on the evidence, considerable debate arises over whether acquisitions are a good idea for the acquiring firm. Consensus seems to have formed that the value of deals generally flows to shareholders of the target firm. Furthermore, experience shows that the surviving firm often fails to realize economic value. As a result, the board should carefully consider whether to allow management to complete large acquisitions. Although in some examples such deals lead to substantial value creation, the average results (discussed earlier) are considerably less compelling for shareholders.

On the other hand, target companies often go through considerable effort to protect themselves from being acquired. Why this is so, given the potential economic returns that target shareholders stand to receive, remains a question. In the second half of this chapter, we consider the actions that targets take to defend themselves from an unsolicited offer, and the impact of these actions on shareholder value.

Antitakeover Protections

A company that does not want to become the target of an unsolicited takeover can adopt defense mechanisms that discourage or dissuade potential bidders from making a formal offer. Several important economic reasons justify doing so:

- **Preservation of long-term value**—A company with attractive future growth prospects that is selling at a depressed market price might want to prevent another company from making a bid at artificially low prices. For example, the firm might have developed a new technology but has chosen not to disclose this information to the public, for competitive reasons. The current stock price will not reflect the value of this innovation. By remaining independent, the company will have time to commercialize this technology and deliver long-term value to current shareholders.

- **Acquirer myopia**—A company that is protected from unsolicited takeovers has greater flexibility to pursue risky, long-term projects that offer attractive future gains. Management is able to make investments with positive net present value that depress current earnings, without having to worry about being taken over before those investments have had time to pay off.

- **Enhanced bargaining power**—When a company implements antitakeover protections, a potential acquirer is more likely to be compelled to engage management rather than make a hostile bid. This increases management's negotiating leverage and offers the target the opportunity to secure a higher deal price.

However, antitakeover provisions can also be a manifestation of agency problems, such as **management entrenchment**. An entrenched management is one that erects barriers to retain its position of power and insulate itself from market forces. An entrenched management is able to extract rents from the company (through continued employment or excessive compensation and perquisites) when these are not merited based on performance.

The board must determine whether antitakeover provisions are truly in the interest of shareholders. Even with antitakeover protections in place, the board of directors has a fiduciary obligation to weigh all offers—both friendly and hostile.

Antitakeover Actions

The most common antitakeover defense is the **poison pill**—also known as a **shareholder's rights plan**. Many companies have this defense in place on an ongoing basis, but even those that do not can adopt one at any time without delay and without shareholder approval.[34] When triggered, poison pills have the potential to grant holders of the company's shares the right to acquire additional shares at a deep discount to fair market value (such as $0.01 per share). The poison pill is triggered if a shareholder or shareholder group accumulates an ownership position above a threshold level (typically 15 to 20 percent of shares outstanding). Once this threshold is exceeded, the market is flooded with new shares that dilute the would-be acquirer's shareholdings and make it prohibitively expensive for the acquirer to take control of the firm through open market purchases or a tender offer. The effect is so severe that no acquirer will trigger the pill—instead, it will pressure the target board to disable the pill and allow the acquisition to go forward. At the same time, the acquirer will launch a proxy contest to replace the incumbent board with a board that is friendly to the deal and will disable the pill.[35]

A second layer of antitakeover defenses include those that prevent a hostile acquirer from replacing the incumbent board. The strongest protection is dual-class stock, which gives a controlling shareholder or management enough votes to control board elections. As explained in Chapter 3, a company with **dual-class shares** has more than one class of common stock. Each class is afforded a different set of voting rights even though they are otherwise economically equivalent. For example, Class A shareholders might have 10 times as many votes per share as Class B shareholders. The class of shares with more generous voting rights typically is not publicly traded, but is held by an insider, the founding family, or another shareholder that is friendly to management. A dual-class share structure means that a corporate raider can accumulate a majority economic stake in a company but still not have majority voting control to replace the board.

A company might also restrict the ability of shareholders to replace the incumbent board by adopting a **staggered board**, or **classified board**. As discussed in Chapter 3, in a staggered board, directors typically are grouped into three classes, each of which is elected to a three-year term. Only one class of directors stands for reelection in a given year. A staggered board structure prevents a corporate raider from gaining majority control of a board in a single year. Any proxy contest to have board members removed must be waged over at least a two-year period. The coupling of a poison pill with a staggered board is a very formidable antitakeover defense.

A company with an annually elected board might protect itself by restricting the ability of shareholders to replace the incumbent board between annual meetings. This is achieved through charter provisions that both restrict shareholder rights to call a special meeting (in which the vote would occur) and prohibit shareholders from voting by written consent (in which shareholders who are unable to meet physically can still vote on a matter). If either of these avenues is available to the target's shareholders, it can be used to hold an election in which the incumbent board is replaced. Still, these defenses are weaker than those described earlier because they only protect the incumbent board until the next annual meeting.

Finally, the state of a target's incorporation might provide takeover defenses by statute. However, as discussed in Chapter 3, expanded constituency provisions are limited in the protections they afford.

The vast majority of U.S. corporations have adopted some level of protection. Among a sample of roughly 4,000 companies, 50 percent have a staggered board, 28 percent have a poison pill protection in place, and 8 percent have multiple classes of shares with unequal voting rights. Seventy percent do not allow shareholder action by written consent and 47 percent have limited shareholder rights to call a special meeting (see Table 11.1).[36]

The question for the board is, should the company implement antitakeover protections? In the following sections, we examine the research on four common defense mechanisms: poison pills, staggered boards, state of incorporation, and dual-class shares. We consider whether these protections are successful in deterring takeovers and what impact they have on governance quality.

Table 11.1 Antitakeover Protections

Poison Pill	Companies (#)	Companies (%)
Expired	675	17.4%
In force	1,073	27.7%
None adopted	2,029	52.4%
Redeemed	58	1.5%
Terminated before expiration	40	1.0%
Dual-Class Shares		
No	3,566	92.0%
Yes	309	8.0%
Staggered Board		
No	1,948	50.3%
Yes	1,927	49.7%
Shareholder Limited Right to Call Special Meeting		
No	2,073	53.5%
Yes	1,802	46.5%
Shareholders Allowed to Vote by Written Consent		
No	2,701	69.7%
Yes	1,174	30.3%

Source: Computed using 2009 data for 3,875 companies covered by SharkRepellent, FactSet Research Systems, Inc.

Poison Pills

As explained before, poison pills are very effective in stopping a hostile takeover (particularly when they are combined with a staggered board). The poison pill defense was first used in 1982 by General American Oil to prevent a hostile takeover by T. Boone Pickens. The defense was ruled legal in 1985 by the Delaware Supreme Court and subsequently has been imitated by numerous other firms.[37] A poison pill might also be adopted to delay a takeover bid and give additional companies time to come forward with a competing bid.

In recent years, many companies in the United States have dropped their poison pills. According to Georgeson, the number of companies that had a poison pill fell by half between 2002 and 2007.[38] But as explained earlier in this chapter, a firm can adopt a poison pill quickly after a takeover attempt has become known. To this end, some companies that have eliminated their poison pills have expressly reserved the right to adopt a plan in the future. Some shareholder groups, however, have moved to limit this right by requiring that any new plan be subject to shareholder approval.[39]

Institutional investors take a mixed view on poison pills. The AFL-CIO supports "the legitimate use of shareholder plans," with the stipulation that its support applies only as long as "shareholders [are] given the opportunity to vote on these plans."[40] Morgan Stanley Investment Management votes "case-by-case on whether the company has demonstrated a need for the defense in the context of promoting long-term shareholder value; whether provisions of defense are in line with generally accepted governance principles; and specific context if the proposal is made in the midst of a takeover bid or contest for control."[41] By renewing poison pills with a periodic vote, shareholders are able to cast their opinion on whether the provision provides legitimate economic protection or acts as management entrenchment.

Brickley, Coles, and Terry (1994) found that the market reacts positively to the adoption of a poison pill if the company's board has a majority of outside directors and negatively if the board does not have a majority of outside directors. They concluded that shareholders view poison pills as protecting their economic interests if the board is independent, and that they view poison pills as entrenching management when insiders control the board.[42] Ryngaert (1988) reached a similar conclusion. He found no statistically significant reaction to the adoption of a poison pill across a broad sample of firms. However, among firms perceived to be takeover targets, he found a significant negative reaction. He also found that stock prices fall an average 2.2 percent when the plan is upheld in court and rise 3.4 percent when the plan is ruled invalid.[43]

In addition, research shows that poison pills are generally effective in preventing unsolicited takeovers. Ryngaert (1988) found that companies that implement a poison pill are twice as likely to defeat an unsolicited offer as companies without a poison pill. Furthermore, companies with a poison pill in place ultimately agree to takeover premiums that are roughly 5 to 10 percent higher.[44] These statistics are somewhat misleading, however, because they fail to take into account the decline in stock price that takes place when a company successfully uses a poison pill to defeat an unsolicited takeover. Ryngaert (1988) found that companies that defeat an offer experience market-adjusted declines of 14 percent.[45] That is, poison pills tend to reward shareholders if the bid is successful, but not if it fails.

Poison pills have extensive history in the United States but are less common in other countries. For example, in Japan unsolicited takeovers have generally not occurred, and so Japanese companies have not had to adopt poison pills. In recent years, however, with the growth of global capital markets, international investors have pressured Japanese managers to take aggressive actions to improve performance. This has encouraged the adoption of poison pills among Japanese companies to preserve their autonomy. It also reflects the tensions that can occur when Western styles of capitalism are applied to countries with different societal values (see the following sidebar).

Poison Pills in Japan

Bull-Dog Sauce

In 2007, U.S.-based hedge fund Steel Partners made a tender offer to acquire Bull-Dog Sauce, a Japanese-based food manufacturer, for ¥1,700 per share. The price represented a 27 percent premium over the company's 30-day average closing price. At the time, Steel Partners owned 10 percent of Bull-Dog's shares, which it had accumulated through open-market purchases. Steel Partners believed that the company's value could be improved through better management and more aggressive international distribution.

To block Steel Partners' efforts, Bull-Dog adopted a poison pill. The poison pill granted shareholders (including Steel Partners) three equity warrants for each Bull-Dog share. However, the plan barred Steel Partners from exercising its warrants for shares and instead required that they be converted into cash at ¥396 ($3.33) a share (¥2.3 billion, or $19.3 million total). The plan was approved by a shareholder vote, with 80 percent in favor.[46]

Steel Partners sued the company, alleging that the poison pill was discriminatory and violated Japanese law. A district court found in favor of Bull-Dog. It ruled that the plan was not discriminatory because shareholders had approved it. The Japanese Supreme Court upheld the decision, labeling Steel Partners "an abusive acquirer."[47]

Bull-Dog shareholders exercised their warrants and Steel Partners' ownership position was diluted to 3 percent (it did receive cash in compensation for its warrants). The hedge fund later sold its entire position.

Staggered Board

Staggered boards pose an obstacle to hostile takeover attempts, in that a corporate raider cannot gain control of the board in a single year through a proxy contest. Instead, the raider must win at least two elections, one year apart from each other, to gain majority representation. Although it is not impossible, winning two consecutive elections is significantly more costly and less likely to succeed (the corporation has the opportunity to quell shareholder dissatisfaction in the intervening year).[48]

Board classification seems to be a significant deterrent to unsolicited takeovers. Bebchuk, Coates, and Subramanian (2002) examined merger activity between 1996 and 2000 and found no instances of a corporate raider gaining control of a staggered board through a proxy contest. Furthermore, they found that companies with a staggered board are significantly more likely to defeat an unsolicited bid and remain independent (61 percent vs. 34 percent of companies with a single-class board). At the same time, companies with a staggered board that do get acquired receive a premium that is fairly similar to those with a single-class board (54 percent vs. 50 percent). The authors concluded that the staggered board structure does not "provide sufficiently large countervailing benefits to shareholders of hostile bid targets, in the form of higher deal premiums, to offset the substantially lower likelihood of being acquired."[49]

Pound (1987) reached similar conclusions. He examined a sample of 100 companies with staggered boards and supermajority provisions (companies with supermajority provisions require that mergers be approved by more than half of shareholders, typically 66 percent to 80 percent). He found that 28 percent of companies with these protections receive takeover bids, compared with 38 percent for a control sample without these protections. He also found that companies with these provisions that ultimately accept the bid do not receive a significantly higher premium to compensate for the lower likelihood of acquisition (51 percent vs. 49 percent). He, too, concluded that "these amendments increase the bargaining power of management ... to the detriment of shareholder wealth."[50]

Cases also arise in which companies decide to destagger their boards. Guo, Kruse, and Nohel (2008) found that the announcement to destagger is associated with about a 1 percent increase in stock price. They also found that firms that are considered to have good governance are more inclined to drop the staggered structure. These results are consistent with the view that forcing directors to face annual election is good for shareholders.[51]

Leaving takeovers aside, shareholders have potential benefits in owning a company with a staggered board. Staggered boards bring greater stability. They also afford greater independence to outside directors who can take a long-term perspective without pressure from management or shareholders.[52] At the same time, a clear risk exists that board classification insulates directors from shareholder pressure and reduces director accountability by reducing the frequency of elections. For this reason, many institutional shareholders oppose staggered boards. For example, in 2008, CalPERS sought to destagger the boards of Cheesecake Factory, Hilb, Rogal & Hobbs, La-Z-Boy, and Standard Pacific.[53]

State of Incorporation

More than half of all publicly traded companies in the United States are incorporated in the state of Delaware.[54] The rest are predominantly incorporated in the state in which they were founded or are headquartered. The state of incorporation is important because state law dictates most corporate governing rights. A company that faces the threat of a hostile bid can reincorporate in a state with more protective antitakeover laws. For example, Barzuza (2009) provided a review of state antitakeover laws and found that, whereas Delaware tends to have laws that protect shareholder value, at least some states have entered into a "race to the bottom" by allowing very restrictive protections.[55]

Most institutional investors oppose reincorporation for the purpose of protecting the firm from an unsolicited bid. They view this as an attempt to expand the powers of the board at the expense of shareholders, whose rights are curtailed. To this end, activist investor Carl Icahn has proposed that shareholders be given greater say over the matter with "a federal law that allows shareholders to vote by simple majority to move their company's incorporation to another state."[56]

State law can have an important impact on governance quality. Shareholders view restrictive state laws as negative. For example, Szewczyk and Tsetsekos (1992) measured the impact of the Pennsylvania Senate Bill (PA-SB 1310), which added significant new protections for Pennsylvania-based firms. Under PA-SB 1310, the following holds:

- Directors can consider the short-term and long-term impact *on all stakeholders* in their assessment of a takeover proposal. This provides considerably more flexibility than a focus on maximization of shareholder value, which is primarily achieved through takeover premium.
- Voting rights of shareholders who control 20 percent or more of the stock are removed until a majority of disinterested shareholders vote to restore their votes. As a result, a corporate raider who accumulates a significant position is not allowed to vote on his or her own takeover proposal unless other shareholders allow this.
- Profits realized by a control group from the disposition of equity within 18 months of obtaining control status are disgorged. This prohibits a raider from driving up the price of a stock and then dumping shares for a short-term gain.
- Severance (up to 26 weeks) must be provided to any employee terminated within 24 months after a change in control.
- An acquirer cannot terminate existing labor contracts after a change in control.
- However, firms can opt out of some or all of these provisions.

Clearly, the objective of PA-SB 1310 is to preserve the autonomy of Pennsylvania-based firms and maintain local employment. Companies are afforded considerable defenses for warding off unsolicited bidders, with shareholders bearing the cost of these defenses. What impact does this bill have on shareholder value? Szewczyk and Tsetsekos (1992) tracked the share price performance of a sample of Pennsylvania-based firms from the day PA-SB 1310 was first introduced in the state senate until it was signed into law six months later. They found that these firms performed significantly worse than a comparable sample of firms incorporated outside Pennsylvania. Based on the abnormal change in stock prices over the measurement period, the sample of Pennsylvania firms lost nearly $4 billion in market value through the enactment of the law. Furthermore, companies that subsequently chose to opt out of some or all of the provisions of PA-SB 1310 experienced significant positive stock price returns on the day of the announcement. The authors attributed "this favorable share price response to the firms' reaffirmation of the fiduciary responsibility of their directors to shareholders."[57]

Similarly, Subramanian (2003) examined whether companies are compensated for restrictive antitakeover laws through higher buyout premiums if the bid is ultimately successful. He found that companies incorporated in states with high takeover protections do not receive premiums that are significantly higher than companies incorporated in states with low takeover protections. He concluded that restrictive state laws do not increase the bargaining power of management relative to potential bidders.[58]

Dual-Class Shares

A company with dual-class shares has more than one class of common stock. In general, each class has proportional ownership interests in the company but disproportionate voting rights. The difference between the economic interest and voting interest of the classes is known as the **wedge** (for example, if Class A has 10 percent economic interest and 30 percent voting interest, the wedge is 20 percent). The class with favorable voting rights typically does not trade in the public market but is instead held by an insider, the founding family, or another shareholder that is friendly to management.

In a dual-class share structure, a corporate raider can accumulate a majority economic stake in a company but still not have majority voting control. For example, prior to its sale to News Corp., the Dow Jones Company had two classes of stock: Class A shares, which were publicly traded, and Class B shares, which were privately held by the Bancroft family. Shareholders of Class A and Class B were afforded equal ownership interests in terms of their rights to profits, dividends, and a claim on company assets. However, Class B shareholders were granted ten times as many votes per share as Class A shareholders. This meant that even though the Bancrofts had less than a 10 percent ownership interest, they still controlled 64 percent of the votes (a wedge of 54 percent). The only way for News Corp. to succeed with its unsolicited offer was to convince members of the Bancroft family to vote in favor of the deal.[59]

Most institutional investors oppose dual-class shares. Morgan Stanley Investment Management proxy guidelines state that it "generally supports management and shareholder proposals aimed at eliminating unequal voting rights, assuming fair economic treatment of classes of shares held."[60] Likewise, proxy advisory firm RiskMetrics/ISS votes "against proposals to create a new class of common stock with superior voting rights" and "votes against proposals at companies with dual-class capital structures to increase the number of authorized shares of the class of stock that has superior voting rights."[61] These positions are understandable, in light of the fact that institutional owners generally own the shares with inferior voting rights.

Circumstances exist under which it might make sense to create dual-class stock. For example, a high-growth firm might want to raise capital to pursue a promising new project but might not want to issue straight common stock for fear of giving up too much voting control (that is, the firm does not mind giving up a substantial economic interest to invest in the project but is concerned about losing control over the project to new investors). As a result, the company might decide to issue new stock in a separate class of shares with inferior voting rights.

The evidence, however, suggests that companies with dual-class shares tend to have lower governance quality. Masulis, Wang, and Xie (2009) examined the relationship between dual-class share structure and shareholder response to company behavior in terms of acquisitions, CEO compensation, cash levels, and capital expenditures. On average, insiders at the companies in the study held 67.4 percent of the voting rights, compared with only 40.8 percent of the economic rights (the wedge was 26.6 percent). The authors found that public shareholders respond negatively and are skeptical about the economic merits of an acquisition announcement. Furthermore, the authors found that as the size of the wedge increases, CEO compensation is higher, shareholders believe that large cash holdings are more likely to be put to uneconomic use, and shareholders place less value on large capital expenditures. The authors concluded that the evidence was "consistent with the hypothesis that insiders holding more voting rights relative to cash flow rights extract more private benefits at the expense of outside shareholders." That is, companies with dual-class shares are more likely to have agency problems than those with a single share class.[62] Other studies have replicated these findings.[63]

Warding Off Unwanted Acquirers

Research demonstrates that antitakeover protections generally reduce governance quality and shareholder value. They do so by increasing the transaction costs associated with a successful acquisition and by shielding management from the disciplining mechanism of otherwise efficient capital markets. However, as we have seen, some evidence also shows appropriate uses for antitakeover provisions.

Daines and Klausner (2001) provided a useful summary that ranks antitakeover protections by their level of protectiveness (from most difficult to least difficult to acquire):

1. Companies that have either dual-class shares or staggered boards and prohibitions on shareholder rights to call special meetings or act by written consent

2. Companies with staggered boards but no limitations on shareholder rights to call special meetings or act by written consent

3. Companies with annually elected boards but prohibitions on shareholder rights to call special meetings or act by written consent

4. Companies with annually elected boards and full shareholder rights to call a special meeting or act by written consent

5. Companies with no antitakeover provisions[64]

Perhaps the key issue for the board of a target company is to determine whether fighting a takeover attempt is in the best interest of shareholders. Bradley, Desai, and Kim (1983) found that companies that reject a takeover offer and are not subsequently taken over lose all the stock price gains earned prior to the announcement.[65] Similarly, Safieddine and Titman (1999) found that firms rejecting a takeover on the basis that the offer "is insufficient" experience a 3.4 percent stock price decline on the announcement date.[66] Nevertheless, if the target company is truly committed to increasing shareholder value, evidence shows that they can successfully do so. Safieddine and Titman (1999) find that target firms that increase their leverage after rejecting a bid outperform similar firms by about 40 percent over the following five years, whereas firms that do not increase their leverage underperform similar firms by about 25 percent over this time period. That is, the greater debt load gives management incentive (and demonstrates management's commitment) to increasing cash flow and shareholder value.[67] Thus, important contextual elements seem to contribute to whether stock prices rise or decline after a rejected takeover. Nevertheless, boards should consider the very real possibility that the stock price for their firm might never recover following a successful takeover defense (see the following sidebar).

Yahoo! vs. Microsoft

In January 2008, Microsoft made an unsolicited offer to acquire Yahoo! for $44.6 billion ($31 per share) in cash and stock. The bid represented a 62 percent premium over Yahoo!'s previous stock price of $19.[68] In pursuing Yahoo!, Microsoft sought to increase market share in online advertising and better position itself to compete against industry leader Google.

Yahoo! rejected the offer as "undervalued." In an effort to ward off Microsoft, the company pursued strategic alternatives with AOL, Google, and others. In a move that received less attention, Yahoo! implemented what is known as a **tin parachute**: a provision that allowed every employee in the company who was terminated without cause during the two years following a change in control to receive both their annual salary over a designated number of months and immediate vesting of all unvested stock options and restricted shares.[69] The move was designed to make a deal prohibitively expensive to Microsoft. Microsoft responded by withdrawing its bid. The stock price retreated to the mid-$20s, as some investors held out hope that some sort of deal would materialize.

In May, activist investor Carl Icahn purchased 50 million shares (through a combination of stock and options) and launched a proxy contest to replace Yahoo!'s ten-member board. In an interview, Icahn stated, "I am amazed at the lengths that [founder and CEO] Jerry Yang and the board went to entrench themselves in this situation." If the proxy contest was successful, Icahn would use the position to resume merger talks with Microsoft.[70]

At the company's annual meeting, Yahoo!'s directors were reelected, but with low support. CEO Jerry Yang received only 66 percent support, and Chairman Roy Bostock 60 percent.[71] Following the vote, Yang resigned and Yahoo! invited two Icahn nominees to the board. Still, Yahoo! and Microsoft could not agree to a merger, ultimately agreeing instead to a much smaller advertising deal. Yahoo!'s stock price fell into the low teens, where it remained for the next few years and performed significantly worse than the general market.

In evaluating antitakeover protections, shareholders and board members might consider the following set of issues. First, how important is the market for corporate control as a disciplining mechanism in the firm-specific governance structure? Perhaps other features of the corporate governance system are sufficient to mitigate agency problems. Second, what are the motives of potential acquirers? Are these motives consistent with the long-term shareholder or stakeholder objectives of the company? Finally, are the antitakeover provisions truly adopted to protect shareholder interests, or are they a manifestation of "entrenched management?"

Endnotes

1. For the economics of a merger to be attractive, the value of the target in the hands of the acquirer must be greater than the acquisition price plus the transactions costs. Transaction costs can be substantial. The various parties bidding for RJR Nabisco racked up $203 million in investment banking fees before KKR ultimately emerged as the winner, taking the firm private in 1988.

2. H. G. Manne, "Mergers and the Market for Corporate Control," *Journal of Political Economy* 73 (1965): 110–120.

3. On average, 60 proxy contests were initiated at U.S. public companies each year for the period 2001–2005, and 112 for the period 2006–2010. See Warren S. De Wied, "Proxy Contests," *Practical Law The Journal* (November 2010).

4. Note that this is not inconsistent with efficient markets. The market price of the firm can be correct as a free-standing entity, even though the sale of the firm to a different owner can still merit a substantial premium because it can more effectively use the assets.

5. Many researchers question the logic behind this argument. They argue that if shareholders value diversification, they can achieve it on their own through a diversified stock portfolio. To this end, the research literature has shown that companies organized in a conglomerate structure trade at a discount to a portfolio of similar monoline companies that exist as standalone entities.

6. One exception is Blackstone, which is publicly traded; its investments are still made through limited partnerships.

7. Steven N. Kaplan and Antoinette Schoar, "Private Equity Performance: Returns, Persistence, and Capital Flows," *Journal of Finance* 60 (2005): 1,791–1,823.

8. See Jeffrey Pfeffer, "Curbing the Urge to Merge. Why Do Companies Make Acquisitions? Ego Plays a Bigger Role Than CEOs Admit," *Business 2.0* (July 1, 2003). Accessed November 13, 2010. See http://money.cnn.com/magazines/business2/business2_archive/2003/07/01/345254/. Mark Hulbert, "Measuring CEOs on the Hubris Index," The New York Times online (May 22, 2005): Accessed October 15, 2010. See http://www.nytimes.com/2005/05/22/business/yourmoney/22stra.html.

9. Researchers have long noted that acquisitions occur in waves. See Michael Gort, "An Economic Disturbance Theory of Mergers," *Quarterly Journal of Economics* 83 (1969): 624–642.

10. As we saw in Chapter 8, "Executive Compensation and Incentives," the size of compensation packages tends to be correlated with company size. It is commonly alleged that this correlation encourages managers to seek growth via acquisitions. Lambert and Larcker (1987) and Avery, Chevalier, and Schaefer (1998) did not find this simple relationship to be true. See Richard A. Lambert and David F. Larcker, "Executive Compensation Effects of Large Corporate Acquisitions," *Journal of Accounting and Public Policy* 6 (1987): 231–243. Christopher Avery, Judith A. Chevalier, and Scott Schaefer, "Why Do

Managers Undertake Acquisitions? An Analysis of Internal and External Rewards for Acquisitiveness," *Journal of Law, Economics & Organization* 14 (1998): 24–43.

11. Equilar Insight, "Executive Compensation Trends—June: CEO Exit Packages, Fortune 200 CEO Severance & Change-in-Control Packages," Equilar (2007).

12. Carol Loomis, "Sandy Weill's Monster," *Fortune* (April 16, 2001).

13. "Mega-Merger Mania Strikes U.S. Banks," *The Banker* (May 1, 1998).

14. Janice Revell, "Should You Bet on the CEO?" *Fortune* 146, Issue 10 (November 18, 2002): 189—191.

15. Avery Johnson and Ron Winslow, "Drug Industry Shakeout Hits Small Firms Hard," *Wall Street Journal* (March 10, 2009, Eastern Edition): A.12.

16. Mark Maremont, "No Razor Here: Gillette Chief to Get a Giant Payday," *The Wall Street Journal* (January 31, 2005, Eastern Edition): A.1.

17. Michael A. Simkowitz and Robert J. Monroe, "A Discriminant Analysis Function for Conglomerate Targets," *Southern Journal of Business* (November 1971): 1–16. Donald L. Stevens, "Financial Characteristics of Merged Firms: A Multivariate Analysis," *Journal of Financial and Quantitative Analysis* 8 (1973): 149–158. A. D. Castagna and Z. P. Matolcsy, "Financial Ratios As Predictors of Company Acquisitions," *Journal of the Securities Institute of Australia* 6–10 (1976). Ahmed Belkaoui, "Financial Ratios As Predictors of Canadian Takeovers," *Journal of Business Finance and Accounting* 5 (1978): 93–108. J. Kimball Dietrich and Eric Sorensen, "An Application of Logit Analysis to Prediction of Merger Targets," *Journal of Business Research* 12: 393–402.

18. Krishna G. Palepu, "Predicting Takeover Targets: A Methodological and Empirical Analysis," *Journal of Accounting and Economics* 8 (1986): 3–35.

19. Paul Tracy, "How to Find Probable Takeover Targets," StreetAuthority Market Advisor (February 1, 2007). Accessed November 14, 2010. See http://web.streetauthority.com/cmnts/pt/2007/02-01-takeover-candidates.asp.

20. Richard A. Lambert and David F. Larcker, "Golden Parachutes, Executive Decision Making, and Shareholder Wealth," *Journal of Accounting and Economics* 7 (1985): 179–203.

21. Judith C. Machlin, Hyuk Choe, and James A. Miles, "The Effects of Golden Parachutes on Takeover Activity," *Journal of Law and Economics* 36 (1993): 861–876.

22. B. Espen Eckbo, "Bidding Strategies and Takeover Premiums: A Review," *Journal of Corporate Finance* 15 (2009): 149–178.

23. Michael C. Jensen and Richard S. Ruback, "The Market for Corporate Control: The Scientific Evidence," *Journal of Financial Economics* 11 (1983): 5–50.

24. Two explanations for this exist. In a hostile takeover, the acquirer is required to offer a more attractive price to overcome the target's objections to the merger and to persuade shareholders to accept the offer. Hostile bids are also likely to

trigger a bidding war if the target seeks a friendly merger partner or more attractive terms. See Henri Servaes, "Tobin's Q and Gains from Takeovers," *Journal of Finance* 46 (1991): 409–419.

25. Gregor Andrade, Mark Mitchell, and Erik Stafford, "New Evidence and Perspectives on Mergers," *Journal of Economic Perspectives* 15 (2001): 103–120.

26. Marina Martynova and Luc Renneboog, "A Century of Corporate Takeovers: What Have We Learned and Where Do We Stand?" *Journal of Banking and Finance* 32 (2008): 2,148–2,177.

27. Mark Goergen and Luc Renneboog, "Shareholder Wealth Effects of European Domestic and Cross-border Takeover Bids," *European Financial Management* 10 (2004): 9–45.

28. Marina Martynova and Luc Renneboog.

29. Ibid.

30. Aloke Ghosh, "Does Operating Performance Really Improve Following Corporate Acquisitions?" *Journal of Corporate Finance* 7 (2001): 151–178.

31. Anonymous, "BASF AG: Company Plans to Nominate Candidates to Engelhard Board," *Wall Street Journal* (January 30, 2006, Eastern edition): 1.

32. Jeffrey A. Krug and Walt Shill, "The Big Exit: Executive Churn in the Wake of M&As," *Journal of Business Strategy* 29 (2008): 15–21.

33. "Executive Agenda: Not So Fast," *A.T. Kearney*, 8 (2005): 1–13. Accessed March 3, 2009. See www.atkearney.com/shared_res/pdf/Not_So_Fast.pdf.

34. It is easiest for a company to adopt a poison pill if their charter authorizes **blank check preferred stock**. Preferred stock is a class of stock that is senior to common stock shareholders in terms of credit and capital. A target can protect itself from a corporate raider by issuing preferred stock with special voting rights to a friendly company or investor (**white knight**). The authorization of preferred stock has a similar effect as issuing dual class shares. Blank check preferred stock is a class of unissued preferred stock that is provided for in the articles of incorporation and that the company can issue when threatened by a corporate raider.

35. Cross-holdings can also be an effective deterrent to a takeover. Cross-holdings generally occur between companies that have close interrelation along the supply chain. This practice protects firms by having a friendly, passive shareholder that is sympathetic to present management. Cross-holdings are prevalent in several countries, such as the *keiretsu* of Japan (see Chapter 2, "International Corporate Governance").

36. Computed using 2009 data for 3,875 companies covered by SharkRepellent, FactSet Research Systems, Inc.

37. Money-Zine, "Poison Pill Defense" (2009). Accessed November 14, 2010. See www.money-zine.com/Investing/Stocks/Poison-Pill-Defense/.

38. Georgeson, "2007 Annual Corporate Governance Review: Annual Meetings, Shareholder Initiatives and Proxy Contests" (2007). Accessed November 14, 2010. See www.georgeson.com/usa/download/acgr/acgr2007.pdf.

39. Robert Schreck and Bryan Steil, "Inside M&A: Poison Pill Redux—Now More Than Ever," McDermott Will & Emery (May/June 2008). Accessed November 14, 2010. See www.mwe.com/info/news/insidem&a0608.pdf.

40. AFL-CIO, "Proxy Voting Guidelines: Exercising Authority, Restoring Account-ability" (2003). Accessed April 6, 2009. See www.afl-cio.org/corporatewatch/capital/upload/proxy_voting_guidelines.pdf.

41. Morgan Stanley Investment Management, "Proxy Voting: Policy Statement." Accessed June 9, 2010. See www.morganstanley.com/im/legal/proxy.html?page=legal#Voting.

42. James A. Brickley, Jeffrey L. Coles, and Rory L. Terry, "Outside Directors and the Adoption of Poison Pills," *Journal of Financial Economics* 35 (1994): 371–390.

43. Michael Ryngaert, "The Effect of Poison Pill Securities on Shareholder Wealth," *Journal of Financial Economics* 20 (1988): 377–417.

44. John Laide, "Poison Pill M&A Premiums," SharkRepellent, FactSet Research Systems., Inc. (2005). Accessed March 21, 2009. See www.sharkrepellent.net/pub/rs_20050830.html.

45. Michael Ryngaert.

46. Hiroyuki Kachi and Jamie Miyazaki, "In Japan, Activists May Find Poison," *Wall Street Journal* (August 8, 2007, Eastern edition): C.2.

47. Andrew Morse and Sebastian Moffett, "Japan's Companies Gird for Attack; Fearing Takeovers, They Rebuild Walls; Rise of Poison Pills," *Wall Street Journal* (April 30, 2008, Eastern edition): A.1.

48. Air Products and Chemicals attempted to circumvent this obstacle in its pur-chase attempt of competitor Airgas. In 2010, Air Products made an unsolicited offer to purchase Airgas for $5.5 billion. Airgas rejected the offer. Air Products waged a proxy contest and successfully gained three board seats on Airgas's board at the annual meeting held September 2010. At that same meeting, shareholders approved a bylaw amendment that brought forward the next annual meeting to January 2011, thereby allowing Air Products to run three more board candidates just four months later. Airgas sued, claiming that a 12-month wait was required between meetings. While a Delaware Chancery Courts upheld the bylaw amendment, the Delaware Supreme Court reversed the lower court's decision, ruling instead that directors had been elected under the company's charter to serve three-year terms and that changing the meeting date improperly shortened their terms. When a separate challenge to the com-pany's poison pill was rejected by the courts, Air Products gave up its attempt to acquire Airgas. See Jef Feeley, "Airgas Trial on Air Products Bid to Focus on Meeting," Bloomberg (October 1, 2010). Accessed November 14, 2010. See www.bloomberglaw.com/link/load/document/L9MGL50D9L35. Davis Polk,

"Delaware Court Permits Stockholders to Shorten Term of Airgas Staggered Board," Client Newsflash (October 11, 2010). Accessed November 14, 2010. See www.davispolk.com/files/Publication/c1bd17f7-3675-4e26-a8ac-5cfadedaece4/Presentation/PublicationAttachment/1226d660-fd07-40a9-8464-5d91d23be4de/101110_Airgas.html. Jef Feeley and Sophia Pearson, "Airgas Wins Ruling Invalidating Annual-Meeting Bylaw," Bloomberg Businessweek (November 23, 2010). Accessed February 2, 2011. See http://www.business-week.com/news/2010-11-23/airgas-wins-ruling-invalidating-annual-meeting-bylaw.html.

49. Lucian Arye Bebchuk, John C. Coates IV, and Guhan Subramanian, "The Powerful Antitakeover Force of Staggered Boards: Theory, Evidence, and Policy," *Stanford Law Review* 54 (2002): 887–951.

50. John Pound, "The Effects of Antitakeover Amendments on Takeover Activity: Some Direct Evidence," *Journal of Law and Economics* 30 (1987): 353–367.

51. Re-Jin Guo, Timothy A. Kruse, and Tom Nohel, "Undoing the Powerful Antitakeover Force of Staggered Boards," *Journal of Corporate Finance* 14 (2008): 274–288.

52. Gregory T. Carrott, "The Case For and Against Staggered Boards," NACD Directorship (September 22, 2009). Accessed November 14, 2010. See www.directorship.com/against-staggered-boards/.

53. "CalPERS Targets Five Companies on 2008 Focus List of Underperformers," CalPERS press release (March 25, 2008). Accessed November 14, 2010. See www.calpers.ca.gov/index.jsp?bc=/about/press/pr-2008/mar/focus-list-under-performers.xml.

54. SharkRepellent (2009). A total of 63.1 percent are incorporated in Delaware, 2.1 percent in Pennsylvania, and 4.6 percent in Maryland (states with anti-takeover provisions).

55 Michal Barzuza, "The State of State Antitakeover Law," *Virginia Law Review* 95 (2009): 1,973–2,052.

56. Carl C. Icahn, "Capitalism Should Return to Its Roots," Wall Street Journal Online (February 7, 2009). Accessed November 14, 2010. See http://online.wsj.com/article/SB123396742337359087.html.

57. Samuel H. Szewczyk and George P. Tsetsekos, "State Intervention in the Market for Corporate Control: The Case of Pennsylvania Senate Bill 1310," *Journal of Financial Economics* 31 (1992): 3–23.

58. Guhan Subramanian, "Bargaining in the Shadow of Takeover Defenses," *Yale Law Journal* 113 (2003): 621–686.

59. The Bancroft family held 83 percent of Class B shares. See Matthew Karnitschnig, "News Corp., Dow Jones Talks Move Forward," *Wall Street Journal* (June 27, 2007, Eastern edition): A.3.

60. Morgan Stanley Investment Management, "Proxy Voting: Policy Statement," Accessed June 9, 2010. See www.morganstanley.com/im/legal/proxy. html?page= legal#Voting.

61. RiskMetrics Policy Exchange, "RiskMetrics Group U.S. Policy." Accessed November 14, 2010. See www.riskmetrics.com/policy_exchange.

62. Ronald W. Masulis, Cong Wang, and Fei Xie, "Agency Problems at Dual-Class Companies," *Journal of Finance* 64 (2009): 1,697–1,727.

63. Paul A. Gompers, Joy Ishii, and Andrew Metrick, "Extreme Governance: An Analysis of Dual-Class Firms in the United States," *Review of Financial Studies* 23 (2010): 1,051–1,088.

64. Robert Daines and Michael Klausner, "Do IPO Charters Maximize Firm Value? Antitakeover Protection in IPOs," *Journal of Law Economics & Organization* 17 (2001): 83–120.

65. Michael Bradley, Anand Desai, and E. Han Kim, "The Rationale Behind Interfirm Tender Offers: Information or Synergy?" *Journal of Financial Economics* 11 (1983): 183–206.

66. Assem Safieddine and Sheridan Titman, "Leverage and Corporate Performance: Evidence from Unsuccessful Takeovers," *Journal of Finance* 54 (1999): 547–580.

67. This is consistent with target management committing itself to value-enhancing investments (similar to the disciplining role of debt suggested by Jensen [1986]). See Michael Jensen, "Agency Costs of Free Cash Flow, Corporate Finance, and Takeover," *American Economic Review* 76 (1986): 323–339.

68. Kevin J. Delaney, Robert A. Guth, and Matthew Karnitschnig, "Microsoft Makes Grab for Yahoo!," *Wall Street Journal* (February 2, 2008, Eastern Edition): A.1.

69. Steven M. Davidoff, "Dealbook Extra," *The New York Times* (June 6, 2008): 6.

70. Gregory Zuckerman and Jessica E. Vascellaro, "Corporate News: Icahn Aims to Oust Yahoo! CEO Yang If Bid for Board Control Succeeds," *Wall Street Journal* (June 4, 2008, Eastern Edition): B.3.

71. Jessica E. Vascellaro, "Yahoo! Vote-Counting Error Overstated Support for Yang," *Wall Street Journal* (August 6, 2008, Eastern Edition): B.6.

12

Institutional Shareholders and Activist Investors

Despite their ownership positions, institutional investors have only indirect influence on company affairs. The majority of their influence must be exerted through the board of directors, whom they elect to govern on their behalf. However, institutional shareholders can still be powerful: They can communicate their opinions directly to management and the board. If the response they receive is not satisfactory, they can seek to have directors removed, vote against proxy proposals sponsored by management, put forth their own proxy measures, or express their dissatisfaction by selling their shares ("voting with their feet").

In this chapter, we review these points in detail. We examine the broad universe of institutional investors to understand their objectives and the methods they use to gain influence. We consider the role that proxy advisory firms play in influencing the annual voting process. In addition, we consider the impact of potential regulatory changes, including a recent trend toward "shareholder democracy."

The Role of Shareholders

As discussed in Chapter 1, "Introduction to Corporate Governance," the **shareholder perspective** of the corporation states that the primary purpose of the corporation is to maximize wealth for owners. This implies that the question of effective governance, from the standpoint of shareholders, is quite simple: Governance practices should seek to create better alignment between management and shareholder interests, thereby reducing agency costs and increasing shareholder value. Therefore, effective governance focuses on the best way to create this alignment and increase shareholder value.

However, this is an oversimplification of the problem. Disagreements arise among shareholders about the best way to structure a firm's governance because shareholders themselves are not a homogeneous group.[1] They differ in terms of several important attributes. For example, shareholders do not have a single, common *investment horizon*. Long-term investors might tolerate significant swings in quarterly earnings and share price if they believe that the decisions management is making will ultimately yield a higher level of profitability. Investors with a shorter investment horizon might prefer that management focus on maximizing near-term earnings and stock price.[2]

Shareholders also have different *objectives*. A large mutual fund institution might only care about the economic results of the corporation. An institutional investor that represents a specific constituent— such as a union pension fund or socially responsible investment fund—might focus on how economic results are achieved and the impact on various stakeholders.

Furthermore, not all shareholders exhibit the same *activity level*. On one end of the spectrum are **passive investors**, such as index funds.[3] These investors attempt to generate returns that mirror the returns of a predetermined market index. They might be less attentive to firm-specific performance and governance matters. On the other end of the spectrum are **active investors**. These investors are active in the trading of company securities and care greatly about individual firm outcomes. They might also try to influence corporate affairs (by meeting with management, lobbying to have board members removed, voicing concern over compensation practices, and advancing policy measures through the company proxy).[4] Investors who try to influence governance-related matters within the corporation are referred to as **activist investors**.

Finally, shareholders vary by *size*. In contrast to small funds, large institutional investors tend to have significant financial resources that they can dedicate to governance matters. For example, BlackRock, with $3.3 trillion in assets under management, has 18 people in a group that directs proxy voting. These individuals—based in the

United States, Europe, Japan, Hong Kong, and Australia—coordinate voting policies and activities across 75 national markets and the 14,000 companies in which BlackRock invests.[5]

The heterogeneity of shareholder groups creates a coordination problem. Differences in investment horizon, investment objective, activity level, and size make it difficult for shareholders to coordinate efforts to influence management and the board toward a common goal. In some cases, shareholders can work at cross-purposes to one another, even though they share an objective of improving corporate performance.

Coordination is further complicated by the well-known **freerider problem**. Shareholder actions—such as proxy contests and shareholder-sponsored proxy proposals—require the expenditure of resources. While one institutional investor bears the cost of these efforts, the benefits are enjoyed broadly by all shareholders (who are said to enjoy a "free ride"). For example, an activist institutional fund might lead a successful campaign to destagger a company board or remove economically harmful antitakeover protections. Although all shareholders enjoy the outcome of this effort, the activist investor alone incurs the costs. The asymmetry of cost and payout creates a disincentive for any one firm to take action and can result in underinvestment by institutional investors to improve corporate governance.

Shareholders suffer from having only **indirect influence** over the corporation. They must rely principally on the board of directors to exert direct influence. The board hires and fires the CEO, sets compensation, oversees firm strategy and risk management, oversees the work of the external auditor, writes company bylaws, and negotiates for a change of control. If shareholders do not believe that the board is sufficiently representing their interests in these matters, they must either persuade them to change policies or seek to have them removed. As we saw in Chapter 11, "The Market for Corporate Control," removing the board is a cumbersome and costly process.

Blockholders

A **blockholder** is an investor with a significant ownership position in a company's common stock. No regulatory statute classifies an investor as a blockholder, although researchers generally define a blockholder as any shareholder with at least a 1 to 5 percent stake. A blockholder can be an executive, a director, an individual shareholder, another corporation, or an institutional investor. For the purposes of this chapter, we limit our discussion to nonexecutive blockholders. (Chapter 9, "Executive Equity Ownership," discusses executive blockholders.)

U.S. regulations require that corporations disclose major shareholders to the public. According to Thomson Reuters, 90 percent of publicly listed companies have an institutional shareholder with at least a 1 percent ownership position, 79 percent with at least a 3 percent position, and 68 percent with at least a 5 percent position. Three and a half percent of public companies do not have an institutional investor—at least, not one that is required to declare its holdings to the SEC[6] (see Table 12.1). Furthermore, the data suggests that blockholders tend to retain their ownership position over time. Barclay and Holderness (1989) found that firms that have a blockholder at one point in time are likely to continue to have a blockholder five years later. They also found that the ownership position of the largest blockholder tends to increase over time.[7]

Table 12.1 Blockholders among U.S. Corporations

	Market Value ($ Millions)	Average Number of Institutional Holders	Average Number of Holders		
			1%	3%	5%
Quintile 1	$2,936.5	223.0	16.0	6.0	2.0
Quintile 2	$550.4	103.0	14.0	5.0	2.0
Quintile 3	$181.6	49.0	9.0	4.0	2.0
Quintile 4	$57.6	20.0	5.0	2.0	1.0
Quintile 5	$12.4	10.0	2.0	1.0	1.0
All Firms	**$181.5**	**48.0**	**8.0**	**3.0**	**1.0**

Median values. Sample includes 5,857 firms during 2008.

Source: Thomson Reuters Institutional Holdings (13F) Database.

Blockholders are predominantly institutions rather than individuals. Among a sample of randomly selected manufacturing firms with blockholders, Mehran (1995) found that 23 percent are individuals, and 77 percent are corporate and institutional blockholders.[8]

If they decide to act, blockholders are in a position to impose governance reforms on corporations. Their significant voting stakes can determine the outcome of a contested director election or proxy proposal. They can change the outcome of a heated takeover battle or prod a company to put itself up for sale or change strategy. If they hold a large enough position, they can gain board representation and directly influence strategy, risk management, executive compensation, and succession planning.

However, the blockholders' influence likely depends on the nature of the investment, the nature of the investor, and the relationship between the investor and the corporation. For example, Toyota likely has a different relationship with the auto suppliers it invests in than does a large institutional owner or activist hedge fund. As we saw in Chapter 9 when we examined managerial equity ownership, block ownership has the potential to either improve or impair firm performance, depending on whether the blockholder treats ownership as an incentive to better the business or uses the position of influence for private gain.

The research literature has examined the impact of block ownership on firm performance. Barclay and Holderness (1989) found that large blocks of shares (at least 5 percent of a company's stock) trade at a 16 percent premium to open-market prices.[9] This indicates that block ownership is perceived to have value either because the acquirer believes it will give them the influence needed either to monitor and improve firm outcomes or to extract some type of private gain from the corporation. The research does not, however, demonstrate that block ownership actually translates to superior performance. McConnell and Servaes (1990) found no relationship between block ownership by an outside investor and a company's market-to-book value.[10] Mehran (1995) also did not find a relationship between block ownership and market value or between block ownership and firm performance.[11] This suggests that the presence of outside blockholders is not associated with improvements in firm performance. In aggregate, however, the research is inconclusive on this point.[12]

Researchers have also studied the relationship between block ownership and governance quality. Core, Holthausen, and Larcker (1999) found that CEO compensation is lower among firms in which an external shareholder owns as least 5 percent of the company shares.[13] Similarly, Bertrand and Mullainathan (2000) examined the relationship between representation by a blockholder on the board of directors and so-called "pay for luck." They found that companies with blockholder directors are less likely to give pay increases for profit improvements that result from industry conditions outside the executive's control (such as changes in commodity prices).[14] This suggests that external blockholders might be better monitors of managerial performance and compensation.

Furthermore, Mikkelson and Partch (1989) found that companies with an external blockholder on the board of directors are more likely to be the target of a successful acquisition.[15] At the same time, they found that if the external blockholder is not on the board, the company is no more likely to receive an acquisition offer or to accept the offer. This suggests that a *combination* of concentrated ownership and board representation might be effective in decreasing management entrenchment.

Founders and Families

Approximately one-third of the Standard & Poor's 500 have a founder or member of the founding family in senior management or on the board of directors.[16] Significant ownership by a founder or founding family might be beneficial because these parties tend to have a personal as well as financial stake in the success of the firm. As such, we might expect them to exert more vigilant oversight, design more rational compensation packages, and encourage a focus on long-term performance. However, influence by the founder can be negative if they view the corporation as their private property, extract private benefits, or otherwise seek to influence outcomes beyond their legal voting rights. Concentration of the family's wealth in one company might also make executives or the board risk averse and therefore less willing to pursue promising but risky new projects that can contribute to long-term value creation.

Some evidence shows that family-controlled firms exhibit fewer agency problems. Ali, Chen, and Radhakrishnan (2007) found that family-controlled firms report higher-quality earnings and are more likely to warn about an earnings downturn. They concluded that this is "consistent with the notion that, compared to nonfamily firms, family firms face less severe agency problems, leading to less opportunistic behavior in terms of withholding bad news."[17] However, it is not clear that family-controlled firms uniformly perform better than non-family-controlled firms. Villalonga and Amit (2006) found that the presence of the founding family has a positive impact on firm value when the *founder* serves as chairman or CEO, but a negative impact when a *descendent* of the founder serves in one of these roles. That is, the nature of the agency problem likely depends on the relationship between the family member and the firm.[18]

Institutional Investors and Proxy Voting

We have seen tremendous growth in institutional ownership of publicly traded companies in the United States during the last 50 years. In 1950, institutional owners held less than 10 percent of publicly traded shares. By 2005, this percentage had risen to more than 70 percent.[19] Institutional investors include mutual funds, pension funds, endowments, hedge funds, and other investment groups. Shares held by the institution are ultimately managed on behalf of individual owners.

Because of their size, institutional investors are in a better position than individuals to impose governance changes. They might exercise this influence by voting against management recommendations on company-sponsored proxy matters, such as director elections, auditor ratification, equity-based compensation plans, and proposed bylaw amendments. Casting votes on the company proxy is a fiduciary responsibility of the institution and required by SEC regulation.

According to data from RiskMetrics/ISS, institutional investors vote in line with management recommendations about 90 percent of the time when management is seeking a vote "for" a proposal and 62 percent of the time when management is seeking a vote "against" a proposal. Among the 10 institutional investors with the largest number of votes, Rydex votes with management the most (99 percent when management recommends "for" an issue and 95 percent when management recommends "against" an issue), and Dimensional votes with management the least (85 percent and 24 percent, respectively).[20] (See Table 12.2.)

Table 12.2   Institutional Investor Voting Record (Voting with Management)

Institution	Number of Votes	With Management "For"	With Management "Against"
Vanguard Group	237,170	94%	88%
Fidelity Management & Research	233,485	76%	71%
Barclays Global Investors	208,576	93%	80%
Rydex Investments	153,766	99%	95%
TIAA-CREF Asset Management	137,221	91%	50%
Dimensional Fund Advisors, Inc.	136,765	85%	24%
MassMutual Financial Group	113,365	90%	48%
State Street Global Advisors	108,932	91%	77%
EQ Advisors Trust	103,664	91%	63%
ProFund Advisors	98,573	88%	24%

Includes the 10 institutional investors with the largest number of votes based on Form N-PX 2009 filings.

Source: Data from ISS Voting Analytics (2009). Calculation by the authors.

Are these appropriate levels of support, or do they represent a breakdown in fiduciary oversight by fund managers? On one hand, many proxy proposals are routine, including ratification of the external auditor and the approval of various noncontroversial bylaw amendments. In these cases, no significant governance impact might occur from regularly voting in favor of these matters. On the other hand, it is plausible that routinely voting in accordance with management recommendations is not consistent with fiduciary oversight on behalf of institutional shareholders.

The SEC adopted Form N-PX partly to provide greater incentive to institutional investors to exercise judgment in voting corporate proxies. Form N-PX requires institutional investors to disclose how they voted on each item on the proxy.[21] Before Form N-PX, an individual investor could see the aggregated results of a proxy vote, but not a breakdown on a firm-by-firm basis. If shareholders believe the institution is overly supportive of management, they can put pressure on it to take a tougher stance or shift their investment to another fund.

It is important to point out that an institution's voting record might not fully capture the relationship between itself and the corporation. The institution might communicate its concerns behind the scenes in ways that are not visible to the individual shareholder. According to a governance official at Vanguard, "We can be more nuanced in these discussions [with the board] than we can in actual voting. While it's important, voting only represents one piece of governance."[22]

Proxy Advisory Firms

Many institutional investors rely on a **proxy advisory firm** to assist them in voting the company proxy and fulfilling the fiduciary responsibility to vote the shares held in a fund in the interests of shareholders. The largest proxy advisory firms are RiskMetrics/ISS and Glass Lewis (see Table 12.3).[23]

Table 12.3 Proxy Advisory Firms

Firm	Founded	Employees (Estimated)	Clients (Estimated)	Client Equity $ (Estimated)
RiskMetrics Group/ISS	1985	630	1,700	$25.5 trillion
Glass Lewis & Company	2003	70	300	$15 trillion
Egan-Jones Proxy Services	2001	—	400	—

Source: U.S. Government Accountability Office, "Report to Congressional Requesters."

An institutional investor can gain potential benefits from using the services of an advisory firm. These firms provide a detailed examination of corporate governance issues that might be beyond the expertise of certain institutional investors. This is particularly true for small institutions that cannot afford to dedicate staff resources to reviewing the proxies of all the companies they invest in. As such, proxy advisory firms can provide a careful review of items put before shareholders, including director elections, equity compensation plans, structural changes to the board, and bylaw amendments.

However, several potential drawbacks can occur from relying on the advice of a proxy advisory firm. First, proxy advisory firms take a somewhat inflexible approach toward certain governance matters and do not always properly consider the unique company situation (see the following sidebar). As a result, the recommendations of these firms might reflect a one-size-fits-all approach to governance and the propagation of "best practices" that the research literature has not supported. Second, these firms might not have sufficient staff or adequate expertise to evaluate the items subject to shareholder approval, particularly complicated issues such as the approval of equity-based compensation plans or proposed acquisitions.[24] Third, some of these firms have potential conflicts of interest because they provide consulting services to the companies whose proxies they evaluate (see Chapter 13, "Corporate Governance Ratings," for a discussion). Finally, the complete reliance on proxy advisory firms might constitute an abdication of fiduciary responsibility. Institutional investors are ultimately responsible for ensuring that their votes are in the best interest of their shareholders.[25]

The Reelection of Warren Buffett

The Coca-Cola Company

In 2004, RiskMetrics/ISS opposed the reelection of Warren Buffett to the board of the Coca-Cola Company. At the time, Buffett served on Coke's audit committee. RiskMetrics/ISS recommended that shareholders withhold their vote for his re-election because Buffett's company, Berkshire Hathaway, distributed Coca-Cola products in two of its subsidiaries. The proxy advisory firm believed this business relationship compromised his independence. It did not make an exception for the fact that Berkshire was the largest shareholder in the company or that Coca-Cola was Berkshire's largest equity investment, valued at $10 billion.[26]

RiskMetrics/ISS explained its opposition by stating: "It's not that we distrust Buffett. We want him on the board. But when you're talking about the external market in the current environment, we think it's the best thing for the company to literally have a zero tolerance policy when it comes to directors having ties and serving on the audit committee." It also stated, "It's a very slippery slope you start down when you start making exceptions for individuals."

The Coca-Cola Company responded to this position by stating, "Mr. Buffett's independence is consistent with the standards set by the New York Stock Exchange (NYSE) .... Mr. Buffett is a man with an eminent reputation for integrity and his effectiveness as an audit committee member is widely regarded. Given his substantial ownership in our Company, there are few people more closely aligned with the interests of our shareowners."

Buffett was ultimately reelected to the board with 84 percent of the vote. He commented, "I think it's absolutely silly .... Checklists are no substitute for thinking. We've encouraged the idea of shareholders behaving like owners. The question is: Can they behave like intelligent owners?"[27]

The largest institutional investors vote in accordance with the RiskMetrics/ISS recommendation 94 percent of the time when the proxy advisory firm recommends a vote "for" a proxy item and 57 percent when it recommends "against" (or "withhold"—see Table 12.4).[28]

There is little research evidence to support the suitability of proxy advisory recommendations. In a recent study, Larcker, McCall, and Ormazabal (2011) examined the impact of RiskMetrics/ISS voting policies on exchange offers during 2004 to 2009. They found that 42 percent of plans that are submitted to shareholders are compliant with RiskMetrics/ISS guidelines. When the sample is expanded to include plans that do not require shareholder approval, only 22 percent are compliant. The discrepancy suggests that companies alter the terms of a plan to gain RiskMetrics/ISS approval when a shareholder vote is required. Although there is positive stock price reaction to exchange offers in general, the stock price reaction is less positive when the exchange offer is constrained to meet RiskMetrics/ISS guidelines. Firms that do so exhibit statistically lower excess stock price returns following announcement of the offer, lower future operating performance, and higher executive turnover. This suggests that RiskMetrics/ISS recommendations might not enhance, and instead might actually decrease, shareholder value.[29] Similarly, anecdotal evidence from corporate directors suggests that RiskMetrics/ISS recommendations are perceived to be arbitrary and not necessarily in the interest of shareholders (see the following sidebar).

Table 12.4 Institutional Investor Voting Record (Voting with RiskMetrics/ISS)

Institution	Number of Votes	With RiskMetrics/ISS "For"	With RiskMetrics/ISS "Against"
Vanguard Group	237,170	93%	35%
Fidelity Management & Research	233,485	79%	64%
Barclays Global Investors	208,576	94%	39%
Rydex Investments	153,766	96%	12%
TIAA-CREF Asset Management	137,221	96%	54%
Dimensional Fund Advisors	136,765	100%	99%
MassMutual Financial Group	113,365	96%	76%
State Street Global Advisors	108,932	91%	37%
EQ Advisors Trust	103,664	95%	56%
ProFund Advisors	98,573	100%	98%

Includes the 10 institutional investors with the largest number of votes based on Form N-PX filings.

Source: Data from ISS Voting Analytics (2009). Calculation by the authors.

RiskMetrics/ISS and Equity-Based Compensation Plans

RiskMetrics/ISS recommendations regarding equity-based compensation plans are among the most controversial of its recommendations.[30] Although shareholders do not have a binding vote on the total compensation paid to executives, they do have the right to approve or reject equity-based plans. This is because granting equity to employees dilutes the ownership interest of shareholders, which cannot be done without their consent. Shareholders might vote to approve such plans when the cost of dilution is more than offset by the positive effects on corporate value that are expected to occur when executives have appropriate economic incentives. Unfortunately, it is quite difficult to quantify either the costs or benefits of these types of equity-based plans.

RiskMetrics/ISS uses four tests to inform its recommendations on equity-based compensation:

1. **Burn rate**—A calculation of how many shares have been granted through equity-based plans annually during the previous three years, as a percentage of average shares outstanding. A company fails this test if its burn rate is one standard deviation higher than the industry average, as computed by RiskMetrics/ISS.

2. **Pay for performance**—A determination of whether the company has generated positive total shareholder return during the previous one-year period or three-year period and whether it has increased the total direct compensation of the CEO in the previous year. A company fails this test if total shareholder return is negative during both of these periods and the company has raised CEO compensation.

3. **Shareholder value transfer (SVT)**—A calculation of the value of equity that has been paid to all company employees and still stands to be paid to employees (and directors) under both existing and proposed equity plans as a percentage of the total market capitalization of the company. A company fails this test if SVT exceeds an industry-specific cap that is determined by a proprietary calculation of SVT among companies

in the same industry and at the top quartile of the industry in terms of shareholder returns.

4. **Poor pay practices**—A company fails this test if it engages in compensation practices that RiskMetrics/ISS generally deems to be "poor," such as option repricing, high concentration of grants to senior executives, egregious employment contracts, excessive benefits and perquisites, poor pay disclosure, internal pay inequity, and other practices.[31]

RiskMetrics/ISS recommends a vote in favor of the company's plan only if it passes all four of these tests.[32] Studies indicate that the firm supports only 70 to 75 percent of plans.[33]

To gain approval, some companies explicitly adjust their plans to conform to the firm's models. For example, the 2010 proxy of Chesapeake Energy states, "In connection with our seeking shareholder approval ..., the Board of Directors' stated intent is to limit the Company's average annual burn rate ... to not more than 2.62%. 2.62% is RiskMetrics' average allowable burn rate cap over 2009 and 2010 for our industry." That same year, United Online stated, "Our Board of Directors and the Compensation Committee of our Board commit to our stockholders that for the next three fiscal years ..., the 'burn rate' will not exceed 6.11% per year on average, which is the average of the 2009 and 2010 'burn rate' limits published by RiskMetrics."[34]

It is clear that companies are restricting their compensation plans to comply with RiskMetrics/ISS models. However, it is not clear whether these models are consistent with increased shareholder value. The limits established by the firm might actually destroy value by arbitrarily limiting equity incentives to key employees. To our knowledge, this question has not yet been rigorously tested.

Activist Investors

Loosely speaking, an **activist investor** is a shareholder who uses an ownership position to actively pursue governance changes at a corporation. Examples of activist investors might include the following:

- Pension funds that manage assets on behalf of union employees
- Institutional funds with a social mission, such as environmental, religious, or humanitarian causes
- Hedge fund managers driven by a desire for short-term gain
- Individual investors with outspoken personal beliefs

Although activists might have a stated objective of improving shareholder value, they also might have secondary motives, such as advocating on behalf of a chosen constituency or stakeholder, or promoting a political or social agenda. The pursuit of these objectives may not be value enhancing for shareholders over the long term. Through lobbying efforts, activists may have an outsized influence on corporate governance outcomes in relation to their ownership position.

Activists have widely varying levels of economic stake in their targets. For example, Calvert Funds and People for the Ethical Treatment of Animals used positions of 803 and 110 shares of common stock, respectively, to sponsor a proxy initiative that would require restaurant operator Brinker International to publish a report on the slaughter methods used by its food suppliers.[35] As such, an activist investor with a very small position must work in coordination with other funds to gain greater leverage in achieving its objectives. In other instances, the activist owns a significant economic stake. For example, the Children's Investment Fund, a London-based hedge fund, acquired a 4.6 percent stake to lodge a proxy battle with U.S. railroad company CSX in 2007. However, even funds with a material ownership position need to secure the cooperation of other institutional owners to gain majority influence.

Activists use two main tools to influence corporate policy: shareholder-sponsored proxy proposals and proxy contests (threatened or actual). Under SEC Rule 14a-8, a shareholder owning at least $2,000 or 1 percent in market value of a company's securities for at least one year is eligible to submit a **shareholder proposal**. The shareholder must continue to hold the shares through the annual meeting and present the proposal in person at the meeting. Shareholders are limited to submitting one proposal at a time, which is due by a company-specified deadline, generally 120 days before the annual meeting.[36]

The company is entitled to exclude shareholder proposals that violate certain restrictions. These include proposals that would violate federal or state law or that deal with functions under the purview of management, the election of directors, the payment of dividends, or other substantive matters. (The Dodd–Frank Financial Reform Act expanded shareholder rights to nominate directors. These changes are discussed in more detail in the later section "Shareholder Democracy.") Furthermore, the company can reject a proposal if it relates to a "personal grievance [or] special interest ... which is not shared by the other shareholders at large." Also the company is entitled to exclude proposals that deal with "substantially the same subject matter" as another proposal on the proxy in the preceding five calendar years that received only nominal support.

In recent years, shareholder proposals have focused primarily on executive compensation reform, board-related matters (such as requiring the appointment of an independent chairman), anti-takeover protections (such as the removal of poison pills or declassifying the board), or procedural changes to governance matters (such as cumulative voting or supermajority provisions). See Figure 12.1.[37]

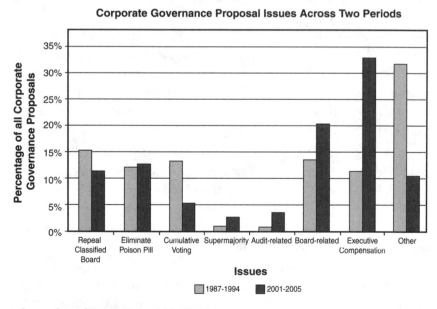

Corporate Governance Proposal Issues Across Two Periods

Source: Stuart Gillan and Laura Starks (2007).

Figure 12.1   Shareholder-sponsored proxy proposals, by topic.

Union-backed funds and individual activists are the most active sponsors, initiating more than 80 percent of shareholder-sponsored proxy proposals. For example, union funds have sponsored a series of initiatives in recent years in an attempt to reform executive compensation practices at Nabors Industries. In 2009, the Massachusetts Laborers' Pension Fund (6,691 shares) proposed that the company adopt a "pay for superior performance" plan that more clearly tied CEO compensation to long-term operating and share-price performance. In 2008, the AFL-CIO (2,030 shares) proposed that the company no longer guarantee the payment of tax gross-ups on behalf of the CEO in the event of a severance payment resulting from a change in control. In 2007, the AFL-CIO (200 shares) proposed that the company adopt a say-on-pay policy in which shareholders would be given an advisory vote on executive compensation. All three of these initiatives failed to receive majority support.[38]

Shareholders have mixed results gaining majority approval for shareholder-sponsored proxy proposals. According to RiskMetrics/ISS, shareholder-sponsored proposals for antitakeover protections gained the most support in 2009 (70 percent average approval for proposals to end or reduce supermajority requirements, 66 percent approval to repeal classified boards, and 51 percent approval for rights to call special meetings). Support is lower for general governance changes (58 percent average support for majority voting in director elections, 37 percent for requiring an independent chairman, and 34 percent for cumulative voting). Shareholders usually do not receive majority support for compensation-related proposals (46 percent requiring say-on-pay, 40 percent for requiring a vote on executive death benefits, 33 percent for requiring a vote on golden parachutes, and 26 percent support for adding retention periods to stock awards).[39] However, shareholder initiatives can be an effective tool for influencing governance outcomes. Even when a shareholder proposal is rejected, the company might voluntarily adopt a related policy change as a compromising gesture (see the following sidebar).[40]

Shareholder Influence Outside the Proxy Voting Process

Nike

In 1996, the General Board of Pension and Health Benefits of the United Methodist Church (61,700 Class B shares) submitted a proposal that would require Nike to perform a summary review of labor conditions in the factories of certain suppliers in Indonesia. Among other things, Nike would be required to work with Indonesian-based nongovernmental organizations to "establish independent monitoring and enforcement mechanisms," "strengthen internal monitoring procedures," and "utilize positive influence to encourage suppliers to adhere to Nike standards of conduct."[41] The proxy proposal was just one tactic that activists employed to coerce Nike to improve labor conditions in supplier factories. Even though the proxy proposal was rejected by a wide margin (3.6 million votes in favor, 111.2 million opposed, 5.8 million abstained), the company ultimately enacted a series of reforms consistent with the spirit of the proposal, including establishing a minimum age for employment, stricter clean air regulations in supplier factories, and training and monitoring programs.[42]

Shareholders can also influence corporate policy through a proxy contest. In a proxy contest, an activist shareholder nominates its own slate of directors to the company's board (known as a dissident slate). The proxy contest represents a direct attempt to gain control of the board and alter corporate policy, and it is usually attempted in conjunction with a hostile takeover. As we discussed in Chapter 11, proxy contests require significant out-of-pocket expense by the activist shareholder, including purchasing the list of shareholders, preparing and distributing proxy materials, and soliciting a favorable response from key institutional investors. The cost and high risk of failure substantially limit the frequency of proxy contests.[43]

Pension Funds

Public pension funds manage retirement assets on behalf of state, county, and municipal governments. Beneficiaries primarily include public employees who are covered by a collective bargaining agreement. The largest public pension funds include the following:

- California Public Employees' Retirement System (CalPERS), $220 billion in assets under management
- New York State and Local Retirement System, $134 billion
- California State Teachers' Retirement System (CalSTRS), $118 billion
- Florida State Board of Administration (Florida SBA), $112 billion
- Ontario Teachers' Pension Plan, $96 billion[44]

Private pension funds manage retirement assets on behalf of trade union members. The largest trade union is the American Federation of Labor and Congress of Industrial Organizations (AFL-CIO), comprising more than 50 national unions and 12 million workers. Affiliates of the AFL-CIO include the Airline Pilots Association (ALPA), the Associated Actors and Artists Association (AAAA), the International Brotherhood of Electrical Workers (IBEW), and the United Auto Workers (UAW). Other trade unions include the International Brotherhood of Teamsters, the Service Employees International Union, and the United Brotherhood of Carpenters and Joiners of America.

The assets of private pension funds are managed either by a single employer (such as the Boeing Company Employee Retirement Plan) or by multiple employers in the same industry (such as the Western Conference of Teamsters Pension Plan). Pension assets are held in trust, and the management of these funds is overseen by a board of trustees whose sole purpose is to meet the financial obligations to trust beneficiaries.

Pension fund administrators are active participants in the proxy voting process. As noted earlier, more than 40 percent of shareholder proxy proposals are sponsored by a union-backed or public pension fund. However, pension activism is not limited to proxy items that the organization has sponsored. Funds also take vocal positions on proposals that other institutions have sponsored. For example, the AFL-CIO keeps a scorecard of what it considers "key votes." The 2008 scorecard recommended an affirmative vote on 25 proxy measures, including the adoption of lead directorships, cumulative voting, declassification, and compensation reform (see Figure 12.2).

2008 AFL-CIO Key Votes Survey Preliminary Scorecard
March 26, 2008

Shareholder Proposals:

Votes "FOR" these proposals are consistent with the AFL-CIO Proxy Voting Guidelines:

Company	Proposal Subject
Chevron	Report on Country Selection Standards
Citigroup	Advisory Vote on Compensation
Coca Cola Enterprises	Vote on Future Golden Parachutes
Comcast	Cumulative Voting
Dollar Tree	Vote on Future Golden Parachutes
ExxonMobil	Lead Director
General Electric	Advisory Vote on Compensation
General Motors	Principles for Health Care Reform
Hershey	Child Labor/Human Rights
JP Morgan Chase	Advisory Vote on Compensation
Lennar Corporation	Establishment of Compliance Committee
Marsh & McLennan	De-Classify Board
Morgan Stanley	Advisory Vote on Compensation
Nabors Industries	Bans on Gross-Ups
Occidental Petroleum	Disclose Compensation Consultants
Pulte	Advisory Vote on Compensation
Raytheon	Supplemental Executive Retirement Plan
RR Donnelly	Disclose Compensation Consultants
Tenet Healthcare	Eliminate Super-Majority Voting Requirements
United Technologies	Adopt Principles for Healthcare Reform
UnitedHealth Group	Adopt Principles for Healthcare Reform
Wal-Mart	Advisory Vote on Compensation
Wendy's	Principles for Healthcare Reform
Xcel Energy	Principles for Healthcare Reform
Yahoo!	Internet Censorship

Source: AFL-CIO.

Figure 12.2   AFL-CIO key vote scorecard (2008)

Some research suggests that union pension funds might not place a priority on maximizing financial returns for their beneficiaries but instead use their ownership position to support labor-related causes. In a highly controversial study, Agrawal (2010) examined the voting record of the AFL-CIO between 2003 and 2006. He found that the AFL-CIO is significantly more likely to vote against directors at companies that are in the middle of a labor dispute, particularly when the AFL-CIO represents the workers. He concluded that the union does not make voting decisions from a purely shareholder-centric perspective, but instead "oppose[s] directors partly as a means of supporting union workers who face opposition from management during collective bargaining and union recruiting effort."[45]

Despite the size of pension funds, the evidence suggests that their activism has only moderate impact on long-term corporate performance. For example, before 2010, CalPERS published an annual "focus list" of a handful of companies that it believed exhibited both poor corporate performance and poor governance quality. According to CalPERS, "We're shining the light on lackluster portfolio companies over serious governance and financial performance issues. Besides having subpar stock performance, these companies refused to address corporate governance issues that have a bearing on how they perform in the market" (see Figure 12.3).[46]

Market Capitalization: $1.5 Billion

CalPERS' Holdings: $6.0 Million

Total Return Returns Ending 02/29/2008

TSR Ending 2/29/2008	Cheesecake Factory Inc (CAKE)	Russell 3000 Index	*Relative Return Russell 3000 Index*	Restaurants Russell Industry Peer Index	*Relative Return Russell Peer Index*
5 years	6.00%	79.70%	*-73.70%*	146.62%	*-140.5%*
3 years	-38.55%	18.13%	*-56.69%*	25.51%	*-64.06%*
1 year	-23.38%	-4.52%	*-18.86%*	-2.19%	*-21.19%*

CalPERS' Concerns:

- Cheesecake Factory's stock has severely underperformed relative to the Russell 3000 index and its industry peer index over the 1, 3, and 5 year time periods ending February 29th.

- Deterioration in annual business fundamentals such as same store sales, operating margin, return on assets, and return on equity.

- Lack of board accountability—The company would not agree to seek shareowner approval to remove the company's 80% supermajority voting requirements in the articles and bylaws. Only a small minority of companies in the Russell 3000 have voting thresholds of this magnitude.

- Concern over shareowner rights—The company would not agree to grant shareowners the right to act by written consent.

- Board Entrenchment Concern—Uncontested director elections are currently conducted using a plurality vote standard.

- The company does not currently disclose a policy for recapturing executive compensation ("Clawback Policy") in the event of executive fraud or misconduct.

Source: CalPERS.

Figure 12.3 CalPERS 2008 focus list company at-a-glance: Cheesecake Factory.

Barber (2007) examined whether CalPERS activism increased shareholder value. His sample included all companies that made the "focus list" from 1992 to 2005. He found only marginal increases in shareholder value on the day CalPERS announced that a company was on the list, indicating that the market expected only a moderate impact from CalPERS intervention. Over the long term, Barber (2007) found practically no excess positive returns. He commented that "long-run returns are simply too volatile to conclude that the long-run performance of focus-list firms is unusual." This suggests either that CalPERS did not select the right targets for its activism (although, in some cases, they certainly targeted egregious behavior), that it did not have the ability to influence the governance choices at these firms, or that CalPERS' alternative governance features were no better than the existing governance structure.[47] As a result, the influence of public pension funds, although visible, is not well established. (In 2010, CalPERS discontinued the practice of a public focus list, choosing instead to pursue direct communication with companies.)[48]

Social Responsibility and Other Stakeholder Funds

Social responsibility and other stakeholder funds cater to investors who value specific social objectives and want to invest only in companies whose practices are consistent with those objectives. For example, an individual investor who values humanitarianism and fair labor practices might invest in companies that meet acceptable labor standards. Examples of social responsibility include fair labor practices, environmental sustainability, and the promotion of religious or moral values.

By one estimate, more than 150 socially responsible mutual funds exist, totaling more than $300 billion in assets.[49] Examples include the following:

- Calvert Funds, which "examines corporate performance in seven broad areas," including governance and ethics, workplace, environment, product safety and impact, international operations and human rights, indigenous peoples' rights, and community relations.[50]

- Walden Asset Management, which engages in "five broad areas of analysis [that] encompass clients' concerns: products and services, environmental impact, workplace conditions, community relations, and corporate governance."[51]

- Ave Maria Catholic Values Fund, which takes "a pro-life and pro-family approach to investing, with a proprietary moral screening process that examines corporate compliance with Catholic teaching regarding abortion, pornography, and policies that undermine the sacrament of marriage. Investments are made only in companies whose operations do not violate core teachings of the Roman Catholic Church as determined by the Funds' Catholic Advisory Board."[52]

- Amana Funds, which "invest according to Islamic principles, or sharia. Generally, these principles require that investors avoid interest ("riba") and investments in businesses such as liquor, pornography, gambling, and banks."[53]

Socially responsible funds vary in the extent to which they engage in activism to achieve their objectives. Some funds limit their activism to abstaining from investments in companies that violate their social values. Other funds actively attempt to change corporate practices. For example, Walden Asset Management claims on its Web site, "We do not subscribe to the simplistic view that some companies are 'socially responsible' while others are not. Instead, Walden seeks to identify and invest in companies that are responsive to the concerns of our clients. We strive to build portfolios by investing in companies that best reflect their financial and social priorities, while engaging in shareholder advocacy on behalf of our clients to strengthen corporate responsibility and accountability."[54]

Fund managers such as these are actively involved in the proxy-voting process, which they use to advocate their positions. In 2005, the Catholic Funds (2,900 shares) sponsored a shareholder proposal on the proxy of Morgan Stanley to require the company to "limit the compensation paid to the CEO in any fiscal year to no more than 100 times the average Compensation paid to the company's nonmanagerial workers in the prior fiscal year."[55] The proposal failed with a vote of 114 million in favor and 658 million against.[56]

According to RiskMetrics/ISS, shareholders submitted 410 resolutions relating to social and environmental objectives in 2008. Of these, 202 came to a vote.[57] On average, social and environmental proposals receive fairly low levels of support (ranging from 5 percent to 10 percent).[58]

The low approval rate of resolutions relating to social causes suggests that these investors do not hold considerable influence over the proxy voting process. However, some funds treat the annual proxy as one tool to gain leverage with the corporation. For example, Walden Asset Management claims to have influenced the policies of numerous companies regarding sustainability, nondiscrimination, and fair treatment of labor by suppliers.[59] Whether or not these funds are successful through the proxy voting process, they often engage in multiyear initiatives to meet their broad objectives. As such, companies should consider them a permanent feature of the governance system.

The research literature is inconclusive regarding whether socially responsible investment funds achieve their dual objectives of advocating a social mission and generating financial returns on behalf of shareholders. Geczy, Stambaugh, and Levin (2005) found that socially responsible mutual funds significantly underperform comparable indices. However, the authors acknowledged that their model did not take into account the "nonfinancial utility of 'doing good.'" That is, the social benefit that restricting investment might have on corporate behavior was not included.[60] Similarly, Renneboog, Ter Horst, and Zhang (2008) found that socially responsible mutual funds in the United States, the United Kingdom, and many European and Asian countries underperform their respective benchmarks by 2.2 percent to 6.6 percent per year. However, they found that risk-adjusted returns are not significantly different from comparable mutual funds (that is, the difference in performance might be driven by the cost of active management instead of the social constraints).[61]

Activist Hedge Funds

Hedge funds are private pools of capital that engage in a variety of strategies—long–short, global macro, merger arbitrage, distressed debt, and so on—in an attempt to earn above-average returns in the capital markets. More than 1,000 hedge funds exist in the United States, managing between $2 trillion and $2.5 trillion in assets.[62] Because they limit their investor pool to **accredited investors** (those with at least $1 million in investable assets or $200,000 in annual income), many hedge funds are exempt from the Investment Company Act of 1940. Following the Dodd–Frank Act, hedge funds with more than $150 million in assets under management are required to register with the SEC.

Hedge funds are notable among institutional investors in the fee structure that they charge clients. The typical hedge fund charges both a management fee, which is a fixed percentage of assets (typically 1 to 2 percent) and a performance-based fee (typically 20 percent) known as the **carry**, which is a percentage of the annual return or increase in the value of the investor's portfolio. In some cases, the management fee covers administrative expenses; in other cases, expenses are passed through separately to the client.

The fee structure charged by the industry necessitates superior financial performance. The magnitude of the fees is a considerable hurdle for the fund manager to overcome to simply match an index return. For example, in a year when the S&P 500 Index returns 8 percent, the fund manager needs to return 12 percent before fees for the investor to match the index return. This is not an insignificant challenge. (Perhaps for this reason, management fees have declined in recent years. According to research by Preqin, the median management fee in 2009 declined to 1.5 percent and the median performance fee declined to 18.9 percent.)[63]

Failing to exceed market returns has two repercussions. First, the fund is likely to lose client money. Even a hedge fund client with a long-term horizon, such as a pension fund, tends to evaluate hedge fund managers over shorter periods because of the fees involved. (Because hedge fund clients are more likely to redeem their investment following poor short-term performance, they are sometimes referred to as "hot money.") Second, underperformance can lead to turnover among the analysts, traders, and portfolio managers who work for the hedge fund. These individuals are compensated based on the size of the carry, and poor performance directly translates into lower compensation. **High water marks** exacerbate this problem.[64] In many cases, an underperforming hedge fund manager will prefer to close shop and open a new fund instead of attempting to "earn back" any relative underperformance.

Pressure to perform might shorten the investment time horizon of hedge funds. The importance of short-term performance presents a challenge because the prices of common stocks are subject to market forces that are outside the control of any one investor. Even a security that is deemed to be "undervalued" does not necessarily revert to "fair value" simply because it has been identified as such. As a result, some hedge funds decide to engage in activism to compel the price of the stock to converge upon its estimated fair value. Notable activist hedge funds include Pirate Capital, Steel Partners, Carl Icahn & Co., Highfield Capital, and Relational Investors.

Brav, Jiang, Thomas, and Partnoy (2008) provided a detailed analysis of hedge fund activism. They found that activist hedge funds resemble value investors. Target companies have relatively high profitability in terms of return on assets and cash flow (relative to matched peers) but sell in the market at lower price-to-book ratios. They tend to have underperformed the market in the period preceding the hedge fund's investment. They have more leverage and a lower dividend payout ratio, and are slightly more diversified in terms of operating businesses. Finally, they tend to be small in terms of market valuation, although their shares trade with more liquidity and are followed by a higher number of investment analysts.[65] Of note, they do not tend to suffer from noticeable firm-specific operating deficiencies.[66]

On average, activist hedge funds accumulate an initial position representing 6.3 percent of the company's shares (median average). In 16 percent of the cases, the funds also disclose derivative positions or securities with embedded options, such as convertible debt or convertible preferred stock (this figure likely understates the true derivative exposure because disclosure of derivative investments is not required under SEC regulations). Hedge funds are likely to coordinate their efforts with other funds to gain leverage. The study found that, in 22 percent of the cases, multiple hedge funds reported as one group in their regulatory filings with the SEC (this figure likely understates coordination because funds employing a **wolf pack strategy** and those that "pile on" are not required to report a coordinated relationship).[67] Multiple hedge funds reporting as a single group take a 14 percent position, on average.

Institutional investors that acquire material ownership in a company are required to disclose the nature of their investment with the

SEC.[68] Approximately half of the funds in this study cited "undervaluation" as the reason for their investment. The rest stated that they intended to compel the company to make some sort of business or structural change—such as a change in strategy, capital structure, or governance system—or to pursue a sale of the company. These funds also used aggressive tactics to achieve their objectives, including regular and direct communication with the board or management (48 percent), shareholder-sponsored proposals and public criticism (32 percent), and full-fledged proxy contests to seize control of the board (13 percent).

The market reacts positively to news of initial investment by an activist hedge fund. On the announcement day, target stock prices generate abnormal returns of approximately 2.0 percent. During the next 20 days, the stock price continues to trend higher, with cumulative abnormal returns of 7.2 percent. However, the extent to which piling on by other hedge funds and institutional investors contributes to these short-term abnormal returns is unclear.

Klein and Zur (2009) studied the long-term success of activist hedge funds. Using a sample of 151 funds between 2003 and 2005, they found that hedge funds achieved a 60 percent success rate in meeting their stated objectives. Almost three-quarters (73 percent) of the funds that pursued board representation were successful. All hedge funds (100 percent) that wanted the target company to repurchase stock, replace the CEO, or initiate a cash dividend were successful. And half (50 percent) were able to compel the company to alter its strategy, terminate a pending acquisition, or agree to a proposed merger. These findings indicate that activist hedge funds are influential as a disciplining mechanism on the corporation.[69]

However, the evidence for their impact on long-term financial performance is mixed. Klein and Zur (2009) found that target companies exhibit abnormal returns around the announcement day of the investment but no subsequent improvement in operating performance. Instead, they reported a modest decline in return on assets and cash from operations. They also reported a decline in cash levels (consistent with increased stock buybacks and dividend payouts) and an increase in long-term debt. Bratton (2006) found some evidence that hedge funds are able to beat a benchmark portfolio in terms of shareholder value creation. However, these computations are quite sensitive to assumptions regarding risk adjustment and choice of the firms selected for the benchmark portfolio.

Shareholder Democracy

In recent years, we have seen a considerable push by Congress, the SEC, and governance experts to increase the influence that shareholders have over corporate governance systems. These efforts are broadly labeled **shareholder democracy** because they are intended to give shareholders a greater say in corporate matters. Advocates of shareholder democracy believe that it will make board members more accountable to shareholder (and possibly stakeholder) objectives.

Elements of shareholder democracy include majority voting in uncontested director elections, the treatment of broker nonvotes, proxy access, say-on-pay, and other voting-related issues.

Majority Voting in Uncontested Director Elections

As we discussed in Chapter 3, "Board of Directors: Duties and Liability," companies have a choice of method for conducting director elections. Under plurality voting, directors who receive the most votes are elected, regardless of whether they receive a majority of votes. In an uncontested election, a director is elected as long as he or she receives at least one vote.

Many shareholder advocates believe that plurality voting reduces governance quality by insulating directors from shareholder pressure. As such, they recommend that companies adopt majority voting procedures, in which a director must receive at least 50 percent of the votes (even in an uncontested election) to be elected. A director who receives less than a majority must tender a resignation to the board. The board can either accept the resignation or, upon unanimous consent, reject the resignation and provide an explanation for its conclusion. (Mandatory resignation and acceptance by the board if a director running unopposed fails to get a majority of votes was part of the original Dodd–Frank Financial Reform Act but was ultimately dropped from the final version of the legislation). More than 80 percent of the 100 largest companies in the United States have adopted some variant of majority voting.[70] However, majority voting in director elections is less common in smaller companies. A broad survey by the NACD found that only 46 percent of companies have adopted some form of majority voting.[71]

It is not clear whether majority voting would improve governance quality. Dissenting votes are often issue-driven and not personal to the director. For example, an institutional investor might withhold votes to reelect members of the compensation committee if they believe the company's compensation practices are excessive. This might inadvertently work to remove a director who brings important strategic, operational, or risk-management qualifications to the board.

Broker Nonvotes

Shares held at a brokerage firm are registered under the name of the brokerage ("street name"), even though they are beneficially owned by the individual. Brokers are required to forward the company proxy for shares held in street name to the beneficial owner and vote according to owner instructions. If the broker does not receive instructions within 10 days of the vote date, a **broker nonvote** is said to occur.

Under New York Stock Exchange Rule 452, a broker who has not received shareholder instructions can vote these shares for routine matters but not for nonroutine matters (with "routine" and "nonroutine" being defined terms by the NYSE). Brokers tend to vote with management recommendations on routine matters. Historically, routine matters have included uncontested director elections and the ratification of the external auditor. Nonroutine matters have included mergers or consolidations, alterations to the terms or conditions of existing stock or indebtedness, shareholder proposals that management opposes, and the issuance of 5 percent or more of the company's outstanding shares as part of equity-based employee compensation plans.[72]

In 2009, Rule 452 was amended to prohibit brokers from voting in uncontested elections (that is, director elections were reclassified as nonroutine). An estimated 20 percent of the votes will be affected by these changes. Furthermore, if a significant number of shares are unvoted, companies might not have sufficient shares to constitute a quorum. As such, this technical change might profoundly affect the dynamics of director elections (see the following sidebar).

The New Math of Director Elections

Assume that a director requires a majority of votes for reelection and that 100 share votes are outstanding. Assume also that 20 percent of the votes are broker nonvotes and that an additional 20 percent are heavily influenced by the recommendation of Risk-Metrics/ISS.[73]

Historically, the 20 broker nonvotes are cast for the incumbent director. Therefore, the director needs 30 of the 80 unallocated votes (37.5 percent) to achieve a majority.

Under the new rules, the 20 broker nonvotes are not counted. Therefore, the director needs 40 of the 80 votes (50 percent) to achieve a majority.

Assume now that RiskMetrics/ISS sides with an activist investor who opposes the director's reelection, and 20 votes are cast in line with the firm's recommendation. The director needs 40 of the 60 (66.7 percent) available uncommitted votes.

The new voting rule has the potential to compound the challenges facing incumbent boards and might increase the influence of activists and proxy advisory firms over director elections.

Proxy Access

Historically, the board of directors has had sole authority to nominate candidates whose names appear on the company proxy. Current SEC proposals (facilitated by Dodd–Frank) would amend Rule 14a-8 to allow shareholder-designated nominees to be included on the proxy, alongside the nominations set forth by the company. Shareholders or coalitions of shareholders who hold 3 percent or more of the company's shares and who have held their positions continuously for at least three years would be eligible to nominate up to 25 percent of the board. Shareholders would have the right to adopt proxy access rules that are more lenient than these but not more strict (see the following sidebar).[74]

Proxy Access

In September 2010, Discovery Equity Partners issued a letter to the management of Tier Technologies expressing its intent to nominate up to two candidates for election to the board at the company's 2011 annual meeting. Discovery Equity Partners and its affiliates together beneficially owned 13.5 percent of the company's common stock.[75] It was one of the first actions taken by shareholders under proxy access rules proposed by the SEC.

The extent to which proxy access rules will be effective in driving change, particularly at small companies, is unclear. For example, Tier Technologies had a market capitalization of $90 million when Discovery Equity Partners approached it. This makes it relatively easy for a fund to accumulate a stake higher than the minimum ownership threshold or to coordinate with others to do so. By contrast, the largest ten public pension funds combined did not own the more than 3 percent required as a threshold position of large-capitalization companies such as Bank of America, IBM, or ExxonMobil.[76]

Furthermore, critics of proxy access have raised legal objections to the rules. In September 2010, the Chamber of Commerce and Business Roundtable filed suit against the SEC, claiming that "the rule is arbitrary and capricious [and] violates the Administrative Procedure Act, and ... the SEC failed to properly assess the rule's effects on 'efficiency, competition, and capital formation' as required by law."[77] In response, the SEC agreed to delay implementation of proxy access until the courts have had a chance to review.

It is not yet known what impact proxy access will have on director elections or governance quality. Few, if any, traditional, "long only" institutional investors (such as index funds and mutual funds) that own block positions are likely to run a dissident slate of directors. Instead, activist hedge funds and pension funds likely will wage contested elections. It is also not clear whether dissident directors will be more qualified than existing directors, or how their presence on the board will change boardroom dynamics. Still, the threat of a contested election might be sufficient to improve the leverage of activists and wrest concessions from the company to meet their demands. This is particularly true if the company wants to avoid the media coverage that a contested election would likely bring.

Recent research suggests that shareholder democracy initiatives reduce shareholder value. A forthcoming study by Larcker, Ormazabal, and Taylor found that the market reacts negatively to potential say-on-pay regulation and proxy access, and that the reaction is more negative among companies that are most likely to be affected. They concluded that "the market perceives that the regulation of executive compensation will ultimately result in less efficient contracts and potentially decrease the supply of high-quality executives to public firms." They also concluded that "blockholders ... may use the new privileges afforded them by proxy access regulation to manipulate the governance process to make themselves better off at the expense of other shareholders."[78]

Survey data suggests that directors do not view provisions for shareholders democracy favorably. At a 2010 conference, directors were asked whether say-on-pay, proxy access, compensation clawbacks, or whistleblower provisions (all approved as part of Dodd–Frank) were most likely to improve corporate governance. Fifty-nine percent responded with "none of the above," 18 percent clawbacks, 11 percent say-on-pay, 11 percent proxy access, and only 1 percent whistleblowers.[79] These results suggest that legislative changes to governance might increase tensions between shareholders and the board. (We discussed say-on-pay in greater detail in Chapter 8, "Executive Compensation and Incentives.")

Proxy Voting

Finally, the SEC has been examining the proxy voting process to determine whether rules should be implemented to increase efficiency and transparency. At issue is whether third-party agents have an inappropriate influence on the voting process to the detriment of shareholder value. One such party is broker-dealers who act as a fiduciary for beneficial shareholders. Another is vote tabulators (such as Broadridge), intermediaries, and proxy service providers who have access to vote data and might influence votes. A third is institutional investors who lend their securities and might not recall their shares in time to vote on certain matters. The SEC is examining whether the voting process should be changed or disclosure increased to improve decision making. The SEC is also examining ways to increase voting participation by individual shareholders.[80] As Figure 12.4 illustrates, the proxy voting process is extremely complicated and, in some cases, not well understood.

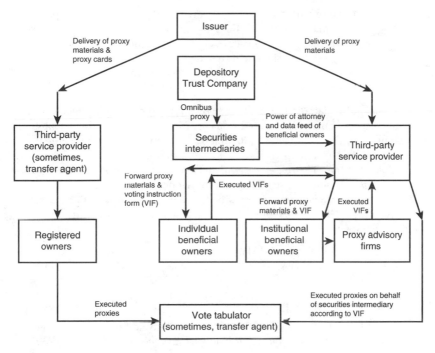

Source: Securities and Exchange Commission: Concept Release on the U.S. Proxy System. July 14, 2010.

Figure 12.4   Proxy voting procedures: a complex process.

Endnotes

1. The industry of investor relations consulting attempts to understand the various roles played by different types of institutional investors and to move the shareholder base to investor types that are perceived as more desirable by management. See David F. Larcker and Brian Tayan, "Sharks in the Water: Battling an Activist Investor for Corporate Control," Stanford GSB Case No. CG–20 (February 2, 2010).

2.   Bushee (2001) classified institutional investors as transient (short-term invest-
      ors interested in short-term stock price movements), dedicated (long-term
      investors with a concentrated portfolio), or quasi-indexers (passive, long-term
      investors with a diversified portfolio). He found that companies with high
      concentration of transient investors overemphasize short-term earnings. He
      concluded that "this evidence supports the concerns that many money man-
      agers have about the potentially adverse effects of an ownership base domi-
      nated by short-term focused institutional investors." See Brian J. Bushee, "Do
      Institutional Investors Prefer Near-Term Earnings over Long-Run Value?"
      Contemporary Accounting Research 18 (2001): 207–246.

3.   The role of passive index funds in the governance debate is somewhat prob-
      lematic. If the fund holds roughly the same stocks as the index, it is not clear
      whether passive funds will be an active change agent for better corporate gov-
      ernance. Still, given their sizeable ownership position, many people believe
      that index funds should use their position to advocate responsible governance
      reforms when appropriate.

4.   Regulation FD (fair disclosure) has greatly limited the extent to which com-
      pany management meets with individual investor groups. The SEC adopted
      Regulation FD in October 2000 to limit the selective disclosure of material
      nonpublic information to investors who might gain an advantage by trading on
      such information. The rule provides that when an issuer, or person acting on its
      behalf, unintentionally discloses such information, it has an obligation to
      promptly disclose the same information to the public. Following the adoption
      of Regulation FD, companies have been less likely to meet with individual
      investor groups.

5.   BlackRock, "Proxy Voting and Shareholder Engagement." Accessed November
      14, 2010. See www2.blackrock.com/global/home/AboutUs/ProxyVoting/index.
      htm.

6.   Thomson Reuters on WRDS, 13f Institutional Holdings (CDA/Spectrum).

7.   Michael J. Barclay and Clifford G. Holderness, "Private Benefits from Control
      of Public Corporations," *Journal of Financial Economics* 25 (1989): 371–395.

8.   Hamid Mehran, "Executive Compensation Structure, Ownership, and Firm
      Performance," *Journal of Financial Economics* 38 (1995): 163–184.

9.   Michael J. Barclay and Clifford G. Holderness.

10.   John L. McConnell and Henri Servaes, "Additional Evidence on Equity
      Ownership and Corporate Value," *Journal of Financial Economics* 27 (1990):
      595–612.

11.   Hamid Mehran.

12.   Clifford G. Holderness, "A Survey of Blockholders and Corporate Control,"
      Economic Policy Review—Federal Reserve Bank of New York 9 (2003): 51–63.

13.   John E. Core, Robert W. Holthausen, and David F. Larcker, "Corporate
      Governance, Chief Executive Officer Compensation, and Firm Performance,"
      Journal of Financial Economics 51 (1999): 371–406.

14. Marianne Bertrand and Sendhil Mullainathan, "Do CEOs Set Their Own Pay? The Ones without Principals Do," NBER working paper Series w7604, *Social Science Research Network* (2000). See http://ssrn.com/abstract=228095.

15. Wayne H. Mikkelson and Megan Partch, "Managers' Voting Rights and Corporate Control," *Journal of Financial Economics* 25 (1989): 263–290.

16. Ashiq Ali, Tai-Yuan Chen, and Suresh Radhakrishnan, "Corporate Disclosures by Family Firms," *Journal of Accounting and Economics* 44 (2007): 238–286.

17. Ibid.

18. Belen Villalonga and Raphael Amit, "How Do Family Ownership, Control, and Management Affect Firm Value?" *Journal of Financial Economics* 80 (2006): 385–417.

19. Stuart Gillan and Laura Starks, "The Evolution of Shareholder Activism in the United States," *Journal of Applied Corporate Finance* 19 (2007): 55–73.

20. Data from ISS Voting Analytics (2009). Calculation by the authors.

21. Release no. 33-8188, "Disclosure of Proxy Voting Policies and Proxy Voting Records by Registered Management Investment Companies," Securities and Exchange Commission. See www.sec.gov/rules/final/33-8188.htm.

22. Sam Mamudi, "In Penney Proxy Vote, It's Fund vs. Fund; Board Re-Election Shows How Firms Differ over the Issues," *Wall Street Journal* (September 11, 2008, Eastern edition): C.13.

23. RiskMetrics Group is owned by MSCI, a publicly traded company that purchased the firm in 2010 for $1.4 billion. Glass Lewis is a private company, purchased by Canada's Ontario Teachers' Pension Plan in 2007 for $46 million. See Aaron Lucchetti, "MSCI Seizes RiskMetrics in Union of Niche Firms," *Wall Street Journal* (March 2, 2010, Eastern edition): C.3. Joann S. Lublin and David Reilly, "Glass Lewis: New Owner, Conflict?" *Wall Street Journal* (October 6, 2007, Eastern edition): B.3.

24. RiskMetrics Group has approximately 600 employees. Not all 600 employees are "governance analysts." Some of these employees are involved in tedious data collection and other administrative tasks.

25. The Department of Labor has proposed broadening the definition of a fiduciary to any entity that provides investment advice to employee benefit plans. If enacted, this would include proxy advisory firms. Marc Hogan, "DOL Proposal Could Threaten ISS," *Agenda* (November 8, 2010). Accessed November 8, 2010. See www.agendaweek.com/articles/20101108/proposal_could_threaten.

26. Berkshire Hathaway, "2003 Annual Report." Accessed August 27, 2007. See www.berkshirehathaway.com/2003ar/2003ar.pdf.

27. Philip Klein, "Reformers' Proxy Votes Polarize Governance Debate," Reuters News (April 18, 2004). Andrew Countryman, "Coke Can Go Better with Icon Buffett," *Courier-Mail* (April 12, 2004): 18. The Coca-Cola Company, Form DEFA 14-A filed with the Securities and Exchange Commission April 9, 2004. Margery Beck, "Buffett Calls Effort to Make Him Leave Coca-Cola Board 'Absolutely Silly,'" Associated Press Newswires (May 2, 2004).

28. Data from ISS Voting Analytics (2009). Calculation by the authors.

29. David F. Larcker, Allan McCall, and Gaizka Ormazabal, "The Role of Proxy Advisory Firms in Stock Option Exchanges," Rock Center for Corporate Governance at Stanford University, working paper (2011).

30. An example of the RiskMetrics Group analysis in report form can be found at www.calstrs.com/Newsroom/What's%20New/OKE_RMG_Report.pdf. Accessed June 4, 2010.

31. RiskMetrics Policy Exchange, "RiskMetrics Group U.S. Policy." Accessed November 14, 2010. See www.riskmetrics.com/policy_exchange.

32. Christopher Armstrong, Ian Gow, and David F. Larcker, "Consequences of Shareholder Rejection of Equity Compensation Plans." This unpublished working paper found that RiskMetrics Group has a substantial impact on shareholder votes. The "for" vote is 86 percent for plans when RiskMetrics Group recommends a "for" vote, but only 70 percent "for" votes when Risk-Metrics Group recommends something other than "for."

33. Ed Hauder and Reid Pearson, "Equity Plan Proposal Failures: 2007–2009: Lessons to Consider When Requesting Shares," Exequity and The Altman Group (June 2010). Accessed November 14, 2010. See http://edwardhauder.com/reference-materials/special-reports/. During 2001–2010, Armstrong, Gow, and Larcker (2010) found that RiskMetrics Group recommends a "for" vote for 77 percent of equity plans voted on by shareholders. See Christopher Armstrong, Ian Gow, and David F. Larcker.

34. Chesapeake Energy Corp, Form DEF-14A, filed with the Securities and Exchange Commission April 30, 2010. United Online, Form DEF-14A, filed with the Securities and Exchange Commission April 14, 2010.

35. Brinker International, Form DEF-14A, filed with the Securities and Exchange Commission September 8, 2006.

36. University of Cincinnati College of Law, "Securities Lawyer's Deskbook. General Rules and Regulations Promulgated under the Securities Exchange Act of 1934: Rule 14a8—Proposals of Security Holders," Accessed November 15, 2010. See www.law.uc.edu/CCL/34ActRls/rule14a--8.html.

37. Stuart Gillan and Laura Starks.

38. Nabors Industries, Form DEF-14A, filed with the Securities and Exchange Commission April 30, 2009. Nabors Industries, Form DEF-14A, filed with the Securities and Exchange Commission April 29, 2008. Nabors Industries, Form DEF-14A, filed with the Securities and Exchange Commission April 29, 2007. Nabors Industries, Form DEF-14A, filed with the Securities and Exchange Commission April 29, 2007. See also David F. Larcker and Brian Tayan. "Executive Compensation at Nabors Industries: Too Much, Too Little, or Just Right?" Stanford GSB Case No. CG-5 (February 2, 2007).

39. RiskMetrics Group-ISS Governance Services, "2009 Proxy Season Scorecard As of December 15, 2009." Accessed November 15, 2010. See www.riskmetrics.com/knowledge/proxy_season_watchlist_2009.

40. Some evidence confirms that this occurs. See Jie Cai, Jacqueline L. Garner, and Ralph A. Walkling, "Electing Directors," *Journal of Finance* 64 (2009): 2,389–2,421. Paul E. Fischer, Jeffrey D. Gramlich, Brian P. Miller, and Hal D. White, "Investor Perceptions of Board Performance: Evidence from Uncontested Director Elections." *Journal of Accounting & Economics* 48 (2009): 172–189. However, Armstrong, Gow, and Larcker (2010) found little evidence for this type of effect. See Christopher Armstrong, Ian Gow, and David F. Larcker.

41. Nike Corp., Form DEF-14A, filed with the Securities and Exchange Commission August 12, 1996.

42. Voting results from Nike Corp., Form 10-Q for the quarter ending August 31, 1996, filed with the Securities and Exchange Commission October 15, 1996. Corporate reforms from Debora L. Spar and Lane T. La Mure, "The Power of Activism: Assessing the Impact of NGOs on Global Business," *California Management Review* 45 (2003): 78–101.

43. See Chapter 11, endnote 3. Warren S. De Wied, "Proxy Contests," *Practical Law The Journal* (November 2010). Accessed November 13, 2010. See http://us.practicallaw.com/.

44. CalPERS, "Current Investment Values. Reflects market value as of market close November 11, 2010." See www.calpers.ca.gov/index.jsp?bc=/investments/assets/mvs.xml. New York Retirement System, "About Us. Values as of March 31, 2010." See www.osc.state.ny.us/retire/about_us/index.htm. CalSTRS, Fast Facts. "Values As of June 30, 2009." See www.calstrs.com/About%20CalSTRS/fastfacts.aspx. State Board of Administration, "Values As of August 31, 2010." See www.sbafla.com/fsb/. Ontario Teachers' Pension Plan, "Values As of April 2010." See www.otpp.com/wps/wcm/connect/otpp_en/Home/Corporate+Info/About+Us/.

45. Ashwini K. Agrawal, "Governance Objectives of Labor Union Shareholders: Evidence from Proxy Voting," NYU Stern working paper series no. Fin-08-006, *Social Science Research Network* (July 2010). See http://ssrn.com/abstract=1285084.

46. CalPERS press release, "CalPERS Targets Five Companies on 2008 Focus List of Underperformers" (March 25, 2008). Accessed November 14, 2010. See www.calpers.ca.gov/index.jsp?bc=/about/press/pr-2008/mar/focus-list-under-performers.xml.

47. Brad Barber, "Monitoring the Monitor: Evaluating CalPERS' Activism," *Journal of Investing* 16 (2007): 66–80.

48. Marc Lifsher, "CalPERS Changes Tactics on Poor Performers," The Los Angeles Times blogs online (November 15, 2010). Accessed November 25, 2010. See http://latimesblogs.latimes.com/money_co/2010/11/calpers-company-focus-list.html.

49. Social Investment Forum, "Socially Responsible Mutual Funds Chart: Financial Performance. Information Current As of September 30, 2010." Accessed November 15, 2010. See www.socialinvest.org/resources/mfpc/.

50. Calvert Investments, "Sustainable & Responsible Investing Signature Criteria" (April 2009). Accessed November 15, 2010. See www.calvertgroup.com/sri-signature-criteria.html.

51. Walden Asset Management, "Social Change Strategies: Social Research & Portfolio Screening" (2010). Accessed November 15, 2010. See www.waldenassetmgmt.com/social/strategies/research.html.

52. Ave Maria Mutual Funds, "About Us" (2010). Accessed November 15, 2010. See http://avemariafunds.com/aboutUs.php.

53. Amana Mutual Funds Trust, "Sharia Compliant Investment Solutions" (2010). Accessed November 15, 2010. See www.amanafunds.com/.

54. Walden Asset Management, "Advocating for Social Change" (2010). Accessed November 15, 2010. See www.waldenassetmgmt.com/social.html.

55. Morgan Stanley, Form DEF-14A, filed with the Securities and Exchange Commission February 15, 2005.

56. Morgan Stanley, Form 10-Q, filed with the Securities and Exchange Commission April 6, 2005.

57. Carolyn Mathiasen and Heidi Welsh, "2009 Proxy Season Preview: Environmental and Social Issues," RiskMetrics Group. Accessed April 2, 2009. See www.riskmetrics.com/print/136296.

58. RiskMetrics Group, "2010 Proxy Season Preview: Environmental & Social Resolutions." See www.riskmetrics.com/docs/esg-proxy-preview.

59. Walden Asset Management, "Leading Social Investor Announces Shareholder Advocacy Program for 2007." Released January 3, 2007. See www.waldenassctmgmt.com/social/action/library/press07.html.

60. Christopher Charles Geczy, Robert F. Stambaugh, and David Levin, "Investing in Socially Responsible Mutual Funds," *Social Science Research Network* (October 2005).

61. Luc Renneboog, Jenke Ter Horst, and Chendi Zhang, "The Price of Ethics and Stakeholder Governance: The Performance of Socially Responsible Mutual Funds," *Journal of Corporate Finance* 14 (2008): 302–322.

62. Wikipedia, "Hedge Funds." Accessed November 15, 2010. See http://en.wikipedia.org/wiki/Hedge_fund.

63. Preqin, "Hedge Funds: The Fee Debate—An End to '2 & 20'?" Preqin Research Report (April 2010). Accessed October 16, 2010. See www.preqin.com/docs/newsletters/HF/HF_Spotlight_April_2010.pdf.

64. High water marks are clauses that disallow the hedge fund from assessing the carry unless the client's account value is at its largest levels.

65. Small, liquid targets enable the activist hedge fund to accumulate a sizeable position with relative speed and without running up the price of the stock. Presumably, it also enables the firm to eventually exit the position quickly and without depressing the stock.

66. Alon Brav, Wei Jiang, Frank Partnoy, and Randall Thomas, "Hedge Fund Activism, Corporate Governance, and Firm Performance," *Journal of Finance* 63 (2008): 1,729–1,775.

67. In a **wolf pack strategy**, multiple hedge funds work together to force change on a target company. Piling on refers to unaffiliated hedge funds accumulating a position in a stock when they learn that an activist has taken a significant position. Hedge funds that pile on to a target are not activists themselves. However, these hedge funds are likely to support the recommendations of the activist.

68. SEC rules require that an investor who holds more than 5 percent of a company's stock disclose its position. Disclosure on Form 13G indicates that the investor intends to hold the position as a passive investment (that is, the investor does not intend to become active with management or to seek a change in control). Disclosure on Form 13D indicates a possible active holding.

69. April Klein, and Emanuel Zur, "Entrepreneurial Shareholder Activism: Hedge Funds and Other Private Investors," *Journal of Finance* 64 (2009): 187–229.

70. Sterling Shearman, "Eighth Annual Corporate Governance Surveys of the Largest U.S. Public Companies," Corporate Governance Practice (2010). Accessed September 2, 2010. See www.shearman.com/Practices/Detail.aspx?practiceID=9d34e2ef-d21f-45ee-8ce0-7601b9c190c9.

71. National Association of Corporate Directors, "2009 NACD Public Company Governance Survey," Washington, D.C.: National Association of Corporate Directors (2009).

72. NYSE Rules (October 15, 2007). See http://rules.nyse.com/NYSE/NYSE%5FRules/.

73. Adapted from Professor Joseph A. Grundfest, Rock Center for Corporate Governance at Stanford University, "Corporate Governance and the Politicization of the Corporation," Rock Center Program for Journalists: A Primer in Corporate Governance. New York City (June 22, 2010).

74. In October 2010, the SEC decided to delay finalization of proxy access rules, pending the decision of a lawsuit brought by the Business Roundtable and Chamber of Commerce, which alleged that the law is "arbitrary and capricious" and "exceeds the Commission's authority." See Kristin Gribben, "SEC Agrees to Put Proxy Access on Hold," *Agenda* (October 4, 2010). See www.agendaweek.com/. See also The Business Roundtable and U.S. Chamber of Commerce Petition for Review filed in the United States Court of Appeals for the District of Columbia Circuit (September 29, 2010): See www.uschamber.com/sites/default/files/files/1009uscc_sec.pdf.

75. Tier Technologies, Schedule 13D/A, filed with the Securities and Exchange Commission September 8, 2010.

76. Jesse Westbrook and Michael B. Marois, "CalPERS Urges Obama to Oppose Higher Threshold for Proxy Access," Bloomberg (June 17, 2010).

77. U.S. Chamber of Commerce press release, "U.S. Chamber Joins Business Roundtable in Lawsuit Challenging Securities and Exchange Commission" (September 29, 2010). The Business Roundtable and U.S. Chamber of Commerce Petition for Review filed in the United States Court of Appeals for the District of Columbia Circuit (September 29, 2010): See www.uschamber.com/sites/default/files/files/1009uscc_sec.pdf.

78. David F. Larcker, Gaizka Ormazabal, and Daniel J. Taylor, "The Market Reaction to Corporate Governance Regulation," *Journal of Financial Economics* (forthcoming).

79. Full survey results are available here: Laura J. Finn, "Directors Vote Best and Worst of Dodd–Frank Act," Boardmember.com (2010). Accessed November 18, 2010. See www.boardmember.com/Article_Details.aspx?id=5433.

80. For more on this issue, see Securities and Exchange Commission: Concept Release on the U.S. Proxy System. Dated: July 14, 2010. http://www.sec.gov/rules/concept/2010/34-62495.pdf.

13

Corporate Governance Ratings

Governance ratings are a relatively new industry in which consulting companies develop quantitative metrics that claim to measure the effectiveness of a company's governance system. The inputs in these models are based on governance attributes that we have discussed throughout this book, including the structure of the board, elements of the executive compensation plan, antitakeover provisions, and similar features. Interviews with firms suggest that both executives and board members feel pressured to change their policies to increase their governance ratings. However, the question remains whether this industry improves governance outcomes or creates value for shareholders.

In this chapter, we discuss the methodology used to develop governance ratings and evaluate the ability of these ratings to identify firms with good or bad governance. We begin by reviewing the ratings developed by RiskMetrics/ISS, GovernanceMetrics International, and The Corporate Library. We then examine the models of governance quality that have been developed by researchers.

Third-Party Ratings

Ratings by knowledgeable independent third parties are common and can be useful to consumers in assessing the quality of products or services. Ratings are particularly important in markets where consumers do not have complete information about the items they are evaluating or when product or service quality is not easily observable. For example, restaurant customers can rely on Michelin Guide or Zagat ratings to select a restaurant in a new city, auto customers can review J.D. Power and Associates or Consumer Reports rankings to assess customer satisfaction with various models, and prospective under-graduate and graduate students can read the rankings of *U.S. News & World Report* to determine the prestige of a particular educational institution.

For ratings to be useful, they must provide credible information. Three factors are particularly critical in establishing credibility. First, ratings must be objective, in that they are based on data that an outside observer would similarly evaluate. Second, the ratings provider must be free from conflicts of interest that would compromise the judgment of the provider. Third, the ratings provider must be able to demonstrate the **predictive ability** of its ratings. That is, the ratings must not simply describe past outcomes, but must be correlated with future outcomes of interest to the users. This last point is critical. For example, if a traveler finds that the ratings of Zagat are not consistent with her own experience at the same restaurants, she will cease to rely on them when making decisions about where to eat. The Zagat system then would lose its relevance. Another way to state this is that market pressure creates an incentive for Zagat to maintain the integrity of its ratings system.

Finally, ratings are important not only for their role in shaping consumer behavior, but also for their impact on the company whose products and services are being rated. The very presence of J.D. Power in the market puts pressure on car manufacturers to maintain and improve the quality standards of each successive model. Because of their perceived expertise, ratings firms can serve as a disciplining mechanism on product or service providers. Given this position of influence, it is particularly important that the ratings system maintain integrity. The ratings industry can provide important information to consumers and firms that ultimately leads to more efficient decision making and resource allocation.

Credit Ratings

Perhaps the most prominent providers of financial ratings in the marketplace are **credit-rating agencies**. The largest three credit-rating agencies are Moody's Investor Services, Standard & Poor's, and Fitch Ratings. These institutions provide ratings on corporations based on their expected ability to repay debt obligations, or their **creditworthiness**. Creditworthiness is determined based on a combination of quantitative and qualitative factors, including availability of collateral, leverage ratios, interest coverage, and diversity and stability of revenue streams, among other factors. Institutional investors that invest in corporate debt use credit ratings to determine the likelihood that they will be paid the full principal and interest owed to them over the life of the bond. In some cases, investors such as money market funds are only allowed to invest in debt with a sufficiently high rating. Companies with higher credit ratings are generally rewarded in the market with lower interest rates on their borrowings, while companies with lower credit ratings are generally charged higher interest rates in an effort to compensate for the inherent risk.

The relative success of the credit rating system can be demonstrated by its predictive ability over time. For example, Moody's keeps detailed statistics on default frequency by ratings category. Through this data, they can demonstrate that higher-rated institutions have a lower likelihood of default than lower-rated institutions. For example, corporations that received Moody's highest rating (Aaa) between 1970 and 2009 defaulted at a rate of less than 1 percent over the ten years following the receipt of that rating. By contrast, corporations that received a speculative grade rating (Ba or lower) defaulted on their debt obligations almost 20 percent of the time during the ten years following that rating.[1] As a result, Moody's can point to historical correlations, supported by a deep sample of data, to demonstrate that its corporate credit ratings are predictive in nature (see Figure 13.1).

As with other ratings systems, credit ratings fail when they are based on faulty assumptions or omit critical input data. For example, in 2001, Moody's came under considerable criticism for maintaining an investment-grade rating on Enron (Baa1) just weeks before the company collapsed into bankruptcy. Although the default of an investment-grade rated company is not a failure in a statistical sense, in the case of Enron, it was a failure in a methodological sense. Moody's rating model failed to incorporate significant off-balance-sheet obligations that Enron had committed to through special-purpose vehicles. By failing to count these toward the total indebtedness of the company, Moody's did not properly measure the riskiness of Enron's capital structure. As a result, Enron's creditworthiness was not consistent with the Baa1 rating assigned to it by Moody's.

Figure 13.1   Cumulative default rates by ratings categories.

A similar methodological breakdown occurred in the rating of various asset-backed securities backed by U.S. subprime residential home mortgages between 2006 and 2008. Moody's—and the other two major rating agencies—made assumptions about future home price appreciation, default frequency at the individual borrower level, and the correlation of default across geographical markets that proved to be highly erroneous. As a result, there was a systemic failure in securities backed by these mortgages, which spread to affect derivative investments that were tied to those securities as well. This failure contributed to the collapse of the credit markets in 2008.

The success and failure of credit ratings can serve as an example as we turn to the topic of corporate governance ratings. As we examine models developed by commercial providers and academics, we ask first and foremost whether they pass the test of predictive ability. Are positive corporate governance ratings correlated with positive corporate outcomes? Are the relative ratings assigned by each provider consistent with the relative outcomes of the entities being rated? Are methodological shortcomings compromising the integrity of these ratings systems? After all, if market participants are expected to make investment and financial decisions in part based on corporate governance ratings, they should have some assurance that these ratings are accurate. To make that assessment, the ratings must stand up to rigorous, objective testing.

Finally, because of their importance to securities markets, credit-rating agencies are subject to regulation both in the United States and in foreign markets. For example, the Dodd–Frank Financial Reform Act creates an Office of Credit Ratings within the SEC to oversee credit rating compliance with rules and regulations. It also requires rating agencies to enhance their internal controls and disclose material changes to rating procedures and methodologies. These requirements are intended to improve transparency and decrease potential conflicts of interest that might impair the objectivity of ratings. The act also lowers the threshold for lawsuits to be brought against the rating agencies, by subjecting them to "expert liability." Lawmakers hope that increased legal exposure will give the credit-rating agencies greater incentive to ensure that their methodologies and processes are sound.

Commercial Corporate Governance Ratings

Three prominent corporate governance ratings firms exist: RiskMetrics/ISS, GovernanceMetrics International (GMI), and The Corporate Library (TCL). Governance ratings firms rate companies on the overall quality of their governance system, taking into account important structural factors. In many cases, governance ratings firms assign subratings on specific areas, such as audit quality, compensation, and antitakeover protections.

RiskMetrics/ISS: Corporate Governance Quotient

Historically, RiskMetrics/ISS assigned a rating called the Corporate Governance Quotient (CGQ) to publicly traded U.S. corporations.[2] The methodology underlying the CGQ evolved over time. A recent iteration was based on 65 variables in eight broad categories: the board of directors, audit, charter and bylaw provisions, state of incorporation, executive and director compensation, qualitative factors, equity ownership by board members and executives, and director education (see Table 13.1).[3]

Table 13.1 Selected RiskMetrics/ISS: Corporate Governance Quotient Variables (2007)

Ratings Factors	
Board	Written consent
Board composition	State of incorporation
Board size	Special meetings
Cumulative voting	Capital structure, dual class
Boards served on	**Executive and Director Compensation**
Former CEOs	Cost of option plans
Chairman/CEO separation	Option repricing permitted in plan
Board attendance	Director compensation
Related party transactions	Option burn rate
Majority voting	Performance-based compensation
Audit	**Qualitative Factors**
Audit committee	Board performance reviews
Audit committee, financial experts	Individual director performance reviews
Audit fees	CEO succession plan
Auditor ratification	Directors resign upon job change
Restatements	**Ownership**
Charter/Bylaws	Executive stock ownership guidelines
Poison pill adoption	Director stock ownership guidelines
Vote requirements, charter/bylaw amendments	Mandatory holding period for equity grants
Vote requirements, approval of mergers	**Director Education**
	Director education

Source: Institutional Shareholder Services, "U.S. Corporate Governance Quotient Criteria."

Companies were ultimately assigned a numeric score on a scale of 0 (unfavorable) to 100 (favorable). Rankings were distributed along a forced curve and were not an absolute measure of corporate governance risk. Each company received two CGQ scores: The first measured its governance quality relative to its index and the second relative to its industry. RiskMetrics/ISS claimed that CGQ was "a reliable tool for 1) identifying portfolio risk related to governance and 2) leveraging governance to drive increased shareholder value."[4] In its marketing materials, the company stated, "There is no doubt that CGQ ratings could have helped some investment manager avoid the gigantic losses experienced during the corporate scandal era defined by the melt-downs at Enron, Global Crossing, and WorldCom."[5] In addition to providing governance ratings, RiskMetrics/ISS is the largest proxy advisory company in the world, with more than 1,700 institutional clients managing an estimated $25 trillion in equity securities. (See Chapter 12, "Institutional Shareholders and Activist Investors," for a discussion of proxy advisory firms.)

On its website, RiskMetrics/ISS explained that it developed the CGQ using a three-step process.[6] First, it made a comprehensive review of best practices in governance, based on academic research and consultation with industry professionals and institutional money managers. From this, key input variables were identified. Second, the firm performed statistical modeling to determine the correlation of each with company performance. RiskMetrics/ISS used the results of this analysis to assign weightings to each input variable. Third, the weighted variables were aggregated to create the CGQ model.

RiskMetrics/ISS: Governance Risk Indicators

In 2010, RiskMetrics/ISS introduced a new system of governance rat-ings known as Governance Risk Indicators (GRId), to replace CGQ.[7] GRId is based on a maximum of 166 data inputs in four broad areas (or "subsections"): audit, board structure, shareholder rights, and com-pensation. Selected inputs include these:

- The percentage of non-audit fees as a percentage of total fees
- The company has been subjected to an enforcement action in the previous two years
- The percentage of independent directors
- Independent or dual chairman/CEO
- Single or dual class of shares
- Poison pill that shareholders did not approve
- The percentage of the chairman's compensation that is performance-based

The number of variables included in the company's rating varies based on the country of origin. For example, the rating of a U.S. company is based on 63 variables. Variables that are mandated by law (such as independence standards of the compensation committee) and variables based on governance features that are not applicable (such as composition of the supervisory board) are not included. Each variable is then weighted. The weightings themselves also vary based on country of origin. For example, annual director elections are more heavily weighted in Canada than they are in the U.S. "to reflect geographical differences."[8]

Companies receive a composite GRId score for their overall governance quality and GRId scores for each subsection. Scores are distributed across a 10-point scale, +5 to –5, with zero representing neutral. Positive scores indicate "low concern" for a company's governance and are awarded to companies that "exceed local best practice guidelines." Neutral scores indicate "medium concern," and negative scores indicate "high concern." Unlike CGQ, GRId scores are on an absolute scale, and are not relative to the company's industry or index.

RiskMetrics/ISS notes that GRId ratings are not intended to predict future operating performance or shareholder returns. Instead, the firm states that GRId can "help institutions and other financial market participants measure and flag investment risk."[9] It can also "spur discussions on how best to improve corporate governance practices globally."

RiskMetrics/ISS also notes that GRId does not reflect a "uniform approach," but instead factors in local nuances that impact firms of different national origin. Still, company-specific circumstances and qualitative factors are not included in the computation. After adjusting for national differences, each company is subjected to a uniform set of standards.

Despite the expanded list of variables and use of an absolute (rather than relative) scale, it is not clear that GRId is materially different than CGQ. Both ratings are based on a composite score of structural and procedural governance features. RiskMetrics/ISS has not disclosed its methodology for determining weightings. No qualitative overlay or adjustment is made based on the company's circumstances, business model, or culture.

GovernanceMetrics International

GovernanceMetrics International (GMI) evaluates companies on 600 discrete variables that are assigned a value of either "yes," "no," or "not disclosed."[10] These variables are grouped into six broad categories: board accountability, financial disclosure and internal controls, shareholder rights, remuneration, market for corporate control, and corporate behavior. Each is ultimately given a score on a scale of 1 (unfavorable) to 10 (favorable), with scores calculated on a relative basis. The company is then assigned an overall score of 1 to 10. GMI states that by measuring companies according to discrete variables and summarizing algorithms that it "eliminate[s] a large degree of subjectivity" with its ratings.[11]

> In its marketing materials, GMI implies that its ratings are predictive of future operating and stock price performance: "[The] GovernanceMetrics International premise is straightforward: companies that emphasize corporate governance and transparency will, over time, generate superior returns and economic performance and lower their cost of capital. The opposite is also true: companies weak in corporate governance and transparency represent increased investment risk and result in a higher cost of capital."[12] Finally, the company states that its "scoring algorithm has also been tested and validated by outside statistical experts and is patent pending."[13]

The Corporate Library

The Corporate Library (TCL) uses a "grade" scale of A to F to indicate governance risk. Each rating is based on an assessment of four components: the company's board and succession planning, CEO compensation practices, takeover defenses, and board-level accounting concerns. A- and B-rated companies do not exhibit significant risk in any of these categories. C-rated companies exhibit risk in no more than one category; D-rated companies in two or more categories; and F-rated companies are either bankrupt, delisted from an exchange, or described as companies in which "management has achieved effective control over the company ... and conducts its business with disregard for the interests of any minority public shareholders."[14] According to Nell Minow, editor and cofounder of TCL, "Everything that we look at is designed to answer one question—can the board say no to the CEO? You can have corporate governance policies that are so beautiful they should be in an illuminated manuscript, but it doesn't mean that you are following them."[15]

Of the three rating agencies, TCL discloses the least information about its methodology. The use of a grading scale suggests that the company uses more discretion in arriving at an ultimate rating than RiskMetrics/ISS and GMI, which both emphasize the statistical underpinnings of their calculations. TCL says, "We have identified a small number of proven dynamic indicators of special interest to shareholders and other stakeholders in an effort to determine which boards are most likely to enhance and preserve shareholder value, and which boards actually increase risk."[16]

Testing the Predictability of Corporate Governance Ratings

The three governance ratings agencies employ different methodologies, but all three suggest that their ratings have predictive power. For example, TCL points to the fact that it warned of troubles at American International Group, Global Crossing, Sprint, and Tyco in advance of their occurrences. GMI assigned low ratings to Interstate Bakeries and Krispy Kreme before they collapsed. RiskMetrics/ISS gave low ratings to Adelphia, Hollinger, Parmalat, and Worldcom.[17]

This raises some questions. If all three agencies purport to rate the same thing (governance quality), why are their methodologies so different? After all, the major credit-rating agencies—Moody's, Standard & Poor's, and Fitch—employ similar models to rate corporate credit quality. Credit ratings are based on leverage ratios, cash flow coverage, and other quantitative and qualitative factors that have been shown to be correlated with the probability of default. If corporate governance quality is likewise driven by proven correlation to structural features, shouldn't we expect governance ratings models to share common methodologies?

Asked another way, can vastly different models of corporate governance produce reliable ratings? It seems unlikely. Our first clue comes from the fact that surprisingly little correlation occurs among the outputs. For example, in 2007, pharmaceutical company Pfizer received an industry rating of 100 from RiskMetrics/ISS, a 9 from

GMI, and a D from TCL. Likewise, The Home Depot received an industry rating of 100 from RiskMetrics/ISS, a 10 from GMI, and an F from TCL (see Table 13.2). What conclusions should a shareholder draw from these conflicting assessments of governance quality? (See the next sidebar.)

Table 13.2 Comparison of Corporate Governance Rating Results (2007)

Company	RiskMetrics/ISS	The Corporate Library	GMI
Aetna	99.3	C	9
Black & Decker	99.2	D	7.5
General Electric	99.2	D	9
General Motors	100	D	9
Home Depot	100	F	10
Lockheed Martin	69.8	F	9.5
Medtronic	64.9	B	8
Pfizer	100	D	9
Safeway	100	D	7.5
Xerox	100	F	10

Source: Corporate Board Member, "ISS Gave Your Board a Lousy Rating. Should You Care?" (First Quarter, 2009).

Differing Assessments of Governance Quality

Maytag

In 2004, CalPERS added appliance maker Maytag to its "focus list" of poorly governed companies. The pension fund called Maytag a "model of an entrenched board" and criticized the company for refusing to implement two proposals that shareholders had approved in previous years. One aimed to eliminate the company's staggered board, and the other would put the company's poison pill provision up for shareholder vote. CalPERS also criticized Maytag for poor financial performance, which stemmed largely from significant international competition.

Ric Marshall, an analyst at TCL, was quoted in the *Wall Street Journal* as saying, "We were not surprised at all that CalPERS ended up with Maytag on their focus list—they have been one of our lowest-rated companies for a long time." The other two ratings firms, however, had much more positive assessments. GMI rated the company an 8, and RiskMetrics/ISS gave it an index rating of 75.7 and an industry rating of 95.3. RiskMetrics/ISS indicated that the heavy concentration of outside directors on the board, a dedicated board committee for governance issues, and a mandatory retirement age for directors were just a few of the many positive factors in Maytag's governance system.[18]

Ultimately, the usefulness of a governance rating is contingent upon its predictive nature. It is not sufficient for a governance ratings firm to articulate and defend the rationale behind its methodology. It needs to demonstrate that its ratings are correlated with outcomes that investors care about, such as operating performance, stock price performance, or the avoidance of bankruptcy, accounting restatements, and litigation (see the following sidebar). Recently, a developing body of work has been examining these questions.

Ratings Miss: One-Time Error or Methodological Flaw?

American International Group (AIG)

In 2004, RiskMetrics/ISS assigned AIG an index rating of 88.3 and an industry rating of 92. Among the positive attributes supporting the rating were the facts that the full board was elected annually, the company had a board-approved CEO succession plan in place, all directors with more than one year of service owned stock, and fees paid to the company's accounting firm for nonaudit services were less than those paid for audit services. Among the negative attributes were lack of disclosure about a mandatory retirement age or term limits for directors, lack of disclosure about equity ownership guidelines for executives or directors, and the fact that no directors had participated in an "ISS accredited" director education program.[19]

At the time, Hank Greenberg was chairman and CEO of the company. Less than six months later, the New York State Attorney General and the Department of Justice launched inquiries into certain business practices of the company, including allegations that it had participated in "bid rigging" (issuing false and artificially high insurance bids to create the appearance of a competitive bidding process) and had used retroactive insurance policies to smooth earnings.[20] Greenberg was forced to step down from the company he had led for more than 40 years.

Three years later, the company again ran into trouble, this time following disclosure that it had suffered severe financial losses from derivative contracts tied to the value of mortgage securities. After a series of CEO resignations, the company sought a bailout from the U.S. government. Its collapse, along with that of Lehman Brothers, was widely seen as triggering the financial crisis of 2008.[21]

A RiskMetrics/ISS executive admitted that the company's ratings were not foolproof: "If we had a perfect solution, I'd be a billionaire running a hedge fund. And I would be pretty quiet about it."[22]

Spellman and Watson (2009) examined the relationship between GMI scores and long-term stock performance. The study found that a portfolio of firms with high and medium GMI scores outperforms a portfolio of firms with low GMI scores over a five-year period. Unfortunately, a number of statistical and methodological limitations to this research call its findings into question.[23]

Quantitative Services Group (QSG) (2010) evaluated the link between TCL grades and future stock price performance, using as a sample the companies in the Russell 1000 index between July 2003 and February 2010. QSG found that a "long-only" portfolio that includes all firms rated A, B, or C by TCL (and excludes firms rated D or F) outperformed the market over the measurement period. A close examination of the results, however, reveals that more than half of the excess returns came from risk adjustments made by the researchers and far less from firm-specific ratings.[24] Moreover, virtually all the excess return was produced in a single year, 2009. (TCL's ratings did not outperform during the financial crisis of 2008). Thus, the economic returns associated with TCL ratings are modest and appear to be specific to the time period.

A study of governance ratings conducted by Daines, Gow, and Larcker (2010) found little predictive ability among the ratings of any of these three firms. First, the authors examined the correlation of ratings across firms. They found that the ratings of RiskMetrics/ISS (CGQ) and GMI have moderate correlation (0.5), but there is almost no correlation between CGQ and TCL ratings or between GMI and TCL ratings. These results are unexpected. As discussed earlier, we would expect governance ratings to be more highly correlated if they seek to measure the same thing (governance quality). The study offered two explanations for these results: "Either the ratings are measuring very different corporate governance constructs and/or there is a high degree of measurement error (i.e., the scores are not reliable) in the rating processes across firms."[25]

Next, the authors measured the predictive ability of ratings by examining their association with future outcomes across five metrics: accounting restatements, class-action lawsuits, accounting operating performance (return on assets), market-to-book ratio, and stock price performance. They found little evidence that the ratings predicted or were correlated with any of these outcomes. They noted that "there seems to be a serious disconnect between the rankings' actual predictive validity and the frequent claims [that the firms themselves make] about their accuracy and significance."

Finally, the study examined the relationship between the ratings provided by RiskMetrics/ISS and the proxy voting recommendations made by the same firm. This analysis tests the hypothesis that a strong correlation should exist between the two (even if the activities are housed in different areas of the firm) because it is reasonable that RiskMetrics/ISS would apply common principles in deciding both its ratings and its proxy recommendations. (That is, one would presume that RiskMetrics/ISS would tend to support the governance proposals put forth by companies with high CGQ scores and oppose proposals of companies with low CGQ scores.) Surprisingly, the study finds little correlation between CGQ scores and proxy voting recommendations.

In summary, the study found low correlation among the ratings of the three firms, low correlation between the ratings of each firm and future performance, and low correlation between the ratings of Risk-Metrics/ISS and the proxy recommendations of RiskMetrics/ISS. The authors concluded that "these governance ratings have either limited or no success in predicting firm performance or other outcomes of interest to shareholders. ... Our view is that ... the commercial ratings contain a large amount of measurement error. ... These results suggest that boards of directors should not implement governance changes solely for the purpose of increasing their ranking."[26]

Despite the shortcomings, many companies show an interest in improving their ratings. For example, in 2003, Aetna received a CGQ rating of 30 from RiskMetrics/ISS. The company paid RiskMetrics/ISS to learn how its score was tabulated and what steps it could take to improve. Upon receiving access to RiskMetrics/ISS's database, Aetna discovered a mistake in the calculation. The Risk-Metrics/ISS database showed that 11 of Aetna's directors were independent, when 13 actually were. The correction boosted Aetna's CGQ score to 50. Aetna then entered hypothetical governance changes to measure their impact on its score. It discovered that by making several changes, it could improve its score dramatically. Those changes included removing a poison pill provision, publicly disclosing governance policies and procedures, making selected changes to the company's bylaws, reducing the shareholder approval threshold for mergers from two-thirds to simple majority, and others. Aetna implemented these changes, and as a result, its industry CGQ increased to 99.7 (see Table 13.3).[27]

After boosting its rating, Aetna issued a press release with the title "Aetna Earns High Ranking on Corporate Governance." Aetna Chairman and CEO John W. Rowe stated, "We are gratified to have earned this recognition. It reinforces the importance that Aetna places on sound corporate governance and emphasizes our efforts to properly align our corporate governance practices with shareholder interests."[28] The company did not mention that it had worked with RiskMetrics/ISS to determine how to improve its score.

The potential for this practice to take hold in the marketplace is troubling. Without a demonstrated link between a change in governance score (regardless of the provider) and shareholder or stakeholder value, it does not make economic sense for an organization to make structural changes to improve its rating. To this end, we believe that corporate participants would benefit from greater disclosure about the methodologies that underlie these ratings so that investors, researchers, and other professionals can better assess their reliability and ability to predict outcomes of interest to shareholders. Market participants should not rely on ratings to make decisions if their reliability cannot be established.

Table 13.3   Changes in Aetna's Corporate Governance Quotient

Corporate Governance Factor	Impact on CGQ
Aetna CGQ, before hiring RiskMetrics/ISS	30
Has 13 independent directors (error correction)	+ 20
Has supermajority of directors be outsiders	+ 15
Has fully independent key board committees	+ 6
Shows strength of audit committee practices	+ 7
Sends board to director training	+ 2
Removes "poison pill" takeover defense	+ 10
Has a mandatory retirement age for directors	+ 1
Discloses governance documents	+ 3
Other/combinatory effects	+ 5
Aetna CGQ, after hiring RiskMetrics/ISS and making changes	99

Point values vary by company, industry, date, and other factors.

Source: Adapted from Monica Langley (2003).

Governance Rating Systems by Academic Researchers

Academic researchers have also put considerable effort toward the development of models to measure governance quality. The typical model takes the form of a **corporate governance index** that aggregates several input variables into a single metric. To construct an index, the researcher selects governance features that are deemed to be important, such as board structure, antitakeover provisions, and bylaw restrictions. These variables are quantified (usually through the assignment of binary numerical values, 0 or 1) and compiled into a single figure that is said to reflect overall governance quality. A company's governance score can be readily compared against those of others to gauge its relative effectiveness.

Gompers, Ishii, and Metrick (2003) developed one of the first firm-specific corporate governance indices.[29] They included in their study 1,000 publicly traded U.S. corporations (primarily those in the S&P 500 Index and other major indices) between 1990 and 1999. To construct the index, they relied upon corporate governance features tracked by the Investor Responsibility Research Center (IRRC). IRRC collects data on 28 variables, 22 relating to governing documents and 6 relating to antitakeover protections (reduced by the authors to 24 after taking into account overlaps—see Figure 13.2).

	Percentage of firms with governance provisions in			
	1990	1993	1995	1998
Delay				
Blank Check	76.4	80.0	85.7	87.9
Classified Board	59.0	60.4	61.7	59.4
Special Meeting	24.5	29.9	31.9	34.5
Written Consent	24.4	29.2	32.0	33.1
Protection				
Compensation Plans	44.7	65.8	72.5	62.4
Contracts	16.4	15.2	12.7	11.7
Golden Parachutes	53.1	55.5	55.1	56.6
Indemnification	40.9	39.6	38.7	24.4
Liability	72.3	69.1	65.6	46.8
Severance	13.4	5.5	10.3	11.7
Voting				
Bylaws	14.4	16.1	16.0	18.1
Charter	3.2	3.4	3.1	3.0
Cumulative Voting	18.5	16.5	14.9	12.2
Secret Ballot	2.9	9.5	12.2	9.4
Supermajority	38.8	39.6	38.5	34.1
Unequal Voting	2.4	2.0	1.9	1.9
Other				
Antigreenmail	6.1	6.9	6.4	5.6
Directors' Duties	6.5	7.4	7.2	6.7
Fair Price	33.5	35.2	33.6	27.8
Pension Parachutes	3.9	5.2	3.9	2.2
Poison Pill	53.9	57.4	56.6	55.3
Silver Parachutes	4.1	4.8	3.5	2.3
State				
Antigreenmail Law	17.2	17.6	17.0	14.1
Business Combination Law	84.3	88.5	88.9	89.9
CashOut Law	4.2	3.9	3.9	3.5
Directors' Duties Law	5.2	5.0	5.0	4.4
Fair Price Law	35.7	36.9	35.9	31.6
Control Share Acquisition Law	29.6	29.9	29.4	26.4
Number of Firms	1357	1343	1373	1708

Source: Gompers, Ishii, and Metrick (2003).

Figure 13.2   Governance features included in G-Index.

As we can see from the list, the input variables are heavily weighted toward antitakeover measures, which was the main focus of IRRC during this time. Each company was assigned one point for each provision that is viewed as negatively impacting shareholder rights and a zero for each provision that favors shareholder rights. These values were then totaled to create a governance index (or G-Index), which, according to the authors, served as a "proxy for the balance of power between shareholders and managers."

To test their model, the authors grouped companies with similar G-Index scores into buckets. Those with a low G-Index score (less than or equal to five) were deemed to be shareholder friendly. These companies were given the label "democratic" companies. Those with a high G-Index (greater than or equal to 14) were deemed to restrict shareholder rights and were labeled "dictator" companies. The results of the study are striking. An investment strategy that involves simultaneously buying the democratic portfolio and shorting the dictator portfolio earned abnormal returns of 0.71 percent per month (8.5 percent annually) over the measurement period (September 1, 1990, to December 31, 1999). Furthermore, the authors found that a one-point increase in the G-Index was correlated with an 11.4 percent reduction in market-to-book value over the measurement period. That is, the companies with more favorable shareholder rights exhibited higher stock price returns and higher market valuations than companies with worse shareholder protections.

These returns are extremely impressive. In fact, they are so impressive that they merit closer scrutiny. Is it possible for a collection of publicly available, plain-vanilla governance features to produce this level of excess stock returns? Is the stock market this inefficient in processing information on corporate governance?

Several researchers have re-examined the findings. Core, Guay, and Rusticus (2006) found that the G-Index investment strategy lost the ability to generate substantial excess returns when the time period in the analysis was extended to include 2000–2003.[30] Whereas the democratic portfolio of Gompers, Ishii, and Metrick (2003) outperformed the dictatorship portfolio between 1990 and 1999 (23.3 percent versus 14.1 percent), it substantially underperformed between 2000 and 2003 (–5.8 percent versus 4.3 percent). That is, after the crash of the technology sector, there were no statistical differences between the returns to dictator and democracy firms (see Figure 13.3).

Does Weak Governance Cause Weak Stock Returns?

— Democracy
—• Dictatorship
— Hedge

Source: Core, Guay, and Rusticus (2006).

Figure 13.3   Performance of G-Index before and after 2000.

More recently, Bebchuk, Cohen, and Ferrell (2009) attempted to refine the G-Index to improve its predictive ability. The authors posited that one of the shortcomings of the G-Index could be that its inputs were not selected based on a pre-existing and proven correlation to corporate performance. Instead, they were chosen on the simple fact that IRRC tracked them. Potentially, several could be irrelevant or redundant. The authors therefore selected a subset of the IRRC inputs that they believed had the strongest relationship to corporate performance. These included staggered boards, limitations on shareholder ability to amend the company bylaws, limitations on shareholder ability to amend the company charter, the requirement of a supermajority to approve a merger, the use of golden parachutes, and the use of a poison pill. The authors explained that they selected the first four of these because they limited "the extent to which a majority of shareholders can impose their will on management." The last two were selected because they are "the most well-known and salient measures taken in preparation for a hostile offer."[31]

Companies were assigned a 1 for the enactment of each provision that restricted shareholder rights and a 0 for the absence of such provisions. Total values therefore ranged from 6 to 0, with a 6 indicating poor corporate governance and a 0 indicating good corporate governance. The authors named their index the E-Index because it was intended to measure management entrenchment. Most firms scored between 1 and 4, indicating moderately low levels of management entrenchment. The measurement period included 1990–2003, thereby taking into account both favorable and adverse stock market conditions.

The authors then applied a similar "long–short" strategy, whereby companies with low E-Index scores were purchased and companies with high E-Index scores were shorted. They found that such a strategy would have yielded average abnormal returns of nearly 7 percent per year over the measurement period. Furthermore, they found that a long–short strategy that pitted the very best E-Index companies (long = 0) against the very worst (short = 5–6) was superior to one that pitted several rankings of the best scores (long = 0–2) against several rankings of the worst (short 3–6) (see Figure 13.4).

The results of Bebchuk, Cohen, and Ferrell (2009) are also striking. However, Johnson, Moorman, and Sorescu (2009) argued that excess returns in the portfolio were driven by different industry composition in the long and short portfolios and not by differences in governance features.[32] Using better-specified tests for computing excess returns that adjust for industry differences, Johnson, Moorman, and Sorescu (2009) concluded that neither the Gompers, Ishii, and Metrick (2003) trading strategy nor Bebchuk, Cohen, and Ferrell (2009) trading strategy produced excess returns. If these results are correct, little empirical evidence indicates that a governance index (measured by antitakeover provisions) is able to predict long-run shareholder value.

In more recent research, Cremers and Ferrell (2010) found mixed evidence that the G-Index and E-Index are associated with future abnormal stock returns.[33] Their results varied depending on time period considered and the specific computation used to calculate returns.

Monthly abnormal returns: baseline model, equally weighted portfolios.

Monthly abnormal returns: baseline model, value-weighted portfolios.

Source: Bebchuk, Cohen, and Ferrell (2009).

Figure 13.4   E-Index.

Taken as a whole, definitive conclusions have not been reached about the predictive ability of an index composed of mostly anti-takeover provisions on future firm performance.

The Viability of Governance Ratings

Holding aside the mixed empirical research described in this chapter, a fundamental conceptual flaw arises with the idea of developing governance indices and ratings. Throughout this book, we have seen that although elements such as board independence, compensation structure, audit quality, and antitakeover provisions are important to governance quality, few obvious and uniform standards exist to aid in measuring these elements. In certain corporate situations, one structure might be effective in decreasing agency costs, while in other situations, that same structure might impose inefficient costs that actually impair corporate performance. A ratings model built on the assumption that a single governance structure can be built as a "best practice" and then uniformly applied across firms seems likely to fail.

Instead, governance quality should be assessed on a case-by-case basis, using independent judgment and a critical understanding of how various governance structures interact to improve or detract from corporate performance. One example of how this might work is seen in the method by which Fitch Ratings incorporates governance data into its credit analysis. The firm is cognizant of the fact that corporate governance can have an important influence on the likelihood of corporate default, so it incorporates an assessment of governance quality into its credit ratings. Although the firm reviews statistical data to uncover differences between companies and flags those with potentially outsized risk, Fitch makes its ultimate evaluation using what it calls a "contextual review." This includes a "review [of] governance practices that require more qualitative analysis and cannot be readily measured in a data set (including the interplay of different practices)." Areas of particular focus are "board quality (independence and effectiveness), related party transactions, reasonableness of management compensation, integrity of audit process, executive and director stock ownership, and shareholder rights/takeover defenses." Companies with "exceptionally weak or deficient governance practices" face the risk of downgrade.[34]

That is, Fitch aims to evaluate many of the governance functions that we have discussed throughout this book, but it does so through independent analysis, not under a check-the-box methodology. The firm clearly believes that this leads to richer, more thoughtful conclusions. Investors, regulators, and other constituents with a vested interest in corporate success might benefit by adopting a similar approach.

Endnotes

1. Kenneth Emery and Sharon Ou, "Corporate Default and Recovery Rates, 1920-2009." Moody's Investors Service (February 2010). Accessed November 22, 2010. See www.moodys.com/cust/content/Content.ashx?source=StaticContent/Free%20Pages/Regulatory%20Affairs/Documents/corporate_default_and_recovery_rates_02_10.pdf.

2. RiskMetrics was spun off from J. P. Morgan in 1998. In 2007, RiskMetrics purchased Institutional Shareholder Services (ISS). In 2010, RMG was acquired by MSCI. For simplicity, we refer to legacy ISS as RiskMetrics/ISS.

3.   Adapted from David F. Larcker and Brian Tayan, "Corporate Governance Ratings: Got the Grade ... What Was the Test?" Stanford GSB Case No. CG-08 (October 15, 2007). Copyright © 2007 by the Board of Trustees of the Leland Stanford Junior University. All rights reserved. Used with permission from the Stanford University Graduate School of Business.

4.   Institutional Shareholder Services, "Corporate Governance Quotient." Accessed August 27, 2007. See www.issproxy.com/esg/cgq.

5.   As cited in Robert Daines, Ian D. Gow, and David F. Larcker, "Rating the Ratings: How Good Are Commercial Governance Ratings?" *Journal of Financial Economics* 98 (2010): 439–461.

6.   Institutional Shareholder Services, "U.S. Corporate Governance Quotient Criteria." Accessed August 27, 2007. See www.issproxy.com/esg/uscgqcriteria. html.

7.   Full documentation is available from Subodh Mishra, "Governance Risk Indicators: A New Measure of Governance-Related Risk," Governance Institute ISS Governance Services (March 10, 2010). Accessed October 18, 2010. See www.riskmetrics.com/sites/default/files/ISS_GRId_Tech_Doc_20100310.pdf.

8.   RiskMetrics/ISS explains: "[T]he weighting is higher in Canada (50 percent, compared with 33.3 percent for U.S. companies, of the takeover defenses subsection), reflecting the sharpened focus on Canadian issuers who elect their board through bundled or slated elections."

9.   These claims are self-contradictory. Risk and performance are related. If you can predict "investment risk," this necessarily translates into better risk-adjusted performance.

10. In 2010, The Corporate Library (TCL) purchased GMI. GMI and TCL continue to operate as standalone entities, and each maintains its separate ratings systems. Also in 2010, Audit Integrity merged with the combined TCL and GMI.

11. GovernanceMetrics International, "About GMI: Overview and Methodology." Accessed November 16, 2010. See www.gmiratings.com/about.aspx.

12. As cited in Robert Daines, Ian D. Gow, and David F. Larcker.

13. GovernanceMetrics International, "GMI Governance and Performance Studies." Accessed November 16, 2010. See www.gmiratings.com/(ocxm4dnvzqdbqoyoyj40 zdeg)/Performance.aspx.

14. The Corporate Library, "Governance Risk Rating System Tested Against Investment Returns." Accessed November 16, 2010. See www.thecorporatelibrary. com/info.php?id=53.

15. Martha Graybow, "Lifting the Lid: Governance Report Cards Prove Tricky," Reuters News (November 24, 2006).

16. The Corporate Library.

17. Marc Gunther, "Forecasting the Next Big Blowup." *Fortune* 152 (2005): 46–48.

18. "For Investors, Is Glass Half Full or Half Empty?: As Maytag's Feud with CalPERS Shows, There's Little Consistency in Corporate-Governance Ratings," *Wall Street Journal* (June 17, 2004, Eastern edition): C.1.

19. Institutional Shareholder Services, American International Group, Inc. CGQ Governance Profile, shareholder meeting date May 19, 2004; most recent CGQ profile update April 30, 2004.

20. Ian McDonald and John Hechinger, "Uneasy Sits the Greenbergs' Insurance Crown: Marsh Faces Hurdles to Regain Investor Trust As It Confronts Yet Another Batch of Allegations," *Wall Street Journal* (October 18, 2004, Eastern edition): C1. Theo Francis and Jonathan Weil, "AIG Could Face Criminal Charges," *Wall Street Journal* (October 22, 2004, Eastern edition): C.1.

21. Matthew Karnitschnig, Deborah Solomon, Liam Pleven, and Jon E. Hilsenrath, "U.S. to Take Over AIG in $85 Billion Bailout: Central Banks Inject Cash as Credit Dries Up; Emergency Loan Effectively Gives Government Control of Insurer; Historic Move Would Cap 10 Days That Reshaped U.S. Finance," *Wall Street Journal* (September 17, 2008, Eastern edition): A.1.

22. Stephen Taub, "Did Governance Raters Foresee Marsh, AIG?" *Compliance Week* (October 26, 2004). Accessed November 12, 2010. See www.compliance-week.com/article/1268/did-governance-raters-foresee-marsh-aig-.

23. The sample is subject to survivorship bias. Only firms that exist for five years are included, so it fails to take into account the ratings of the many companies that failed, declared bankruptcy, or merged during the period. Also, the risk adjustments used in the paper are not consistent with contemporary methods used in finance, making it unclear whether the results reflect true risk-adjusted returns. These shortcomings compromise the rigor of this report. See G. Kevin Spellman and Robert Watson, "Corporate Governance Ratings and Corporate Performance: An Analysis of GovernanceMetrics International (GMI) Ratings of U.S. Firms, 2003 to 2008," *Social Science Research Network* (January 1, 2009). See http://ssrn.com/abstract=1392313.

24. More specifically, these results are for a long-only strategy that excludes all firms with a TCL rating of D or F for either the composite, board only, or compensation rating. See Quantitative Services Group (QSG), "Finding Value in Corporate Governance: Does It Impact Equity Returns?" QSG Equity Research (March 2010).

25. The sample included 5,059 company ratings by RiskMetrics/ISS (CGQ ratings), 1,565 ratings by GMI, and 1,906 ratings by TCL. All ratings are as of 2005. Robert Daines, Ian D. Gow, and David F. Larcker.

26. Ibid.

27. Monica Langley, "Making the Grade: Want to Lift Your Firm's Rating on Governance? Buy the Test—ISS Ranks Corporations—and Sells a Road Map for Improving Their Score—Drop the Poison Pill: 10 Points," *Wall Street Journal* (June 6, 2003, Eastern edition): A.1.

28. Aetna, Inc., "Aetna Earns High Ranking on Corporate Governance," AETNA news release (April 7, 2007). Accessed November 16, 2010. See http://investor.aetna.com/phoenix.zhtml?c=110617&p=irol-newsArticle&ID =398587&highlight=.

29. Paul Gompers, Joy Ishii, and Andrew Metrick, "Corporate Governance and Equity Prices," *Quarterly Journal of Economics* 118 (2003): 107–155. © 2003 by the President and Fellows of Harvard College and the Massachusetts Institute of Technology.

30. John E. Core, Wayne R. Guay, and Tjomme O. Rusticus, "Does Weak Governance Cause Weak Stock Returns? An Examination of Firm Operating Performance and Investors' Expectations," *Journal of Finance* 61 (2006): 655–687.

31. Lucian Bebchuk, Alma Cohen, and Allen Ferrell, "What Matters in Corporate Governance?" *Review of Financial Studies* 22 (2009): 783–827.

32. Shane A. Johnson, Theodore C. Moorman, and Sorin Sorescu, "A Reexamination of Corporate Governance and Equity Prices," *Review of Financial Studies* 22 (2009): 4,753–4,786.

33. Martijn Cremers and Allen Ferrell, "Thirty Years of Shareholder Rights and Firm Valuation," CELS 2009 4th Annual Conference on Empirical Legal Studies paper, *Social Science Research Network* (February 1, 2010). See http://ssrn. com/abstract=1413133.

34. Kim Olson, "Corporate Governance from the Bondholder's Perspective: Measurement and Analytical Considerations," Fitch Ratings (February 9, 2005).

14

Summary and Conclusions

In this book, we have taken a thorough and critical look at corporate governance from an organizational perspective. We started by reviewing the environment in which the organization competes to understand how legal, social, and market forces influence the control mechanisms it adopts to prevent or discourage self-interested behavior by management. Next, we introduced the board of directors and examined the structure, processes, and operations of the board. We emphasized that the qualifications and engagement of these individuals are likely the most important determinants of their ability to advise and monitor the organization.

We then explored the functional responsibilities of the board, including strategic oversight and risk management, CEO succession planning, executive compensation, accounting quality and audit, and the consideration of mergers and acquisitions. In later chapters, we examined the role of the institutional investor to understand how diverse shareholder groups and third-party proxy advisory firms influence governance choices. We ended with an assessment of commercial and academic governance ratings systems.

Throughout this book, we have attempted to discuss each topic through the lens of rigorous statistical and research analysis, supplemented by real-life examples, to arrive at informed conclusions. We hope that we have met this objective. Furthermore, we hope that, in reading this book, you have a more thorough understanding of the governance choices an organization has and the consequences of those choices for future performance and oversight.

Many of the conclusions of this book are phrased in the negative. For example, we have seen that most structural features of the board have little or no relation to governance quality. We have seen that most auditor restrictions have no impact on financial statement quality, that commercial and academic governance ratings systems largely lack predictive ability, and that regulatory requirements for many mandated governance practices have neutral or negative impacts on corporate outcomes and shareholder value.

While the lack of positive correlations may disappoint you, this has important implications for the current debate on governance and your evaluation of the types of governance systems that organizations might require. The central lessons of the book follow.

Testing Remains Insufficient

First, the lack of positive correlations suggests that most of the best practices—either those recommended by blue-ribbon commissions and high-profile experts or those required by regulators—have likely not been tested, or important influencers have not properly understood the results of those tests. We saw this clearly in the passage of both Sarbanes–Oxley and the Dodd–Frank Act, in which considerable disconfirming evidence was not considered when restrictions were placed on nonaudit services provided by the auditor (see Chapter 10, "Financial Reporting and External Audit") and greater shareholder democracy was required (see Chapter 12, "Institutional Shareholders and Activist Investors").

Instead, we share the sentiments of Myron Steel, Chief Justice of the Delaware Supreme Court, who recently wrote:

> Until I personally see empirical data that supports in a particular business sector, or for a particular corporation, that separating the chairman and CEO, majority voting, elimination of staggered boards, proxy access with limits, holding periods, and percentage of shares—until something demonstrates that one or more of those will effectively alter the quality of corporate governance in a given situation, then it's difficult to say that all, much less each, of these proposed changes are truly reform. Reform implies to me something better than you have now. Prove it, establish it, and then it may well be accepted by all of us.[1]

This standard should be a precondition to all governance changes, both those mandated by law and those voluntarily adopted. Governance changes are costly, and failed governance changes even more so. They are costly to the firm in terms of reduced decision-making quality and inefficient capital allocation, and they are costly to society in terms of reduced economic growth and value destruction for both shareholders and stakeholders. We believe that careful theoretical and empirical work can go a long way toward better understanding what works and does not work so that changes can be made in a cost-effective manner. There is no question to us that "governance matters." The fundamental challenge is to understand *when* and *how* it matters.

The Current Focus Is Misdirected

Second, the lack of positive correlation signals that much of the discussion focuses on the wrong issues, such as independent chairman, staggered boards, risk committees, and director stock ownership guidelines. As such, efforts to improve governance systems (and the regulations that tend to come with them) are likely misdirected. Instead of focusing on *features* of governance, more attention should be paid to the *functions* of governance, such as the process for identifying qualified directors and executives, strategy development, business model analysis and testing, and risk management. To illustrate this point, consider the following sets of questions:

CEO Succession

1. Does the company have a CEO succession plan in place?
2. Is the CEO succession plan operational? Have qualified internal and external candidates been identified? Does the company engage in ongoing talent development to support long-term succession needs?

Risk Management

1. Is risk management a responsibility of the full board of directors, the audit committee, or a dedicated risk committee?

2. Do the board and management understand how the various operational and financial activities of the firm work together to achieve the corporate strategy? Have they determined what events might cause one or more of these activities to fail? Have these risks been properly mitigated?

Executive Compensation

1. What is the total compensation paid to the CEO? How does this compare to the compensation paid to other named executive officers?

2. How is the compensation package expected to attract, retain, and motivate qualified executive talent? Does it provide appropriate incentive to achieve the goals set forth in the business model? What is the relationship between large changes in the company stock price and the overall wealth of the CEO? Does this properly encourage short- and long-term performance without excessive risk?

In each of these, the first question asks about a governance feature, the second about a governance function. A focus on the latter will almost certainly yield significantly more benefit to the organization and its stakeholders.

A mistake that many experts make is to assume that the presence of the feature necessarily implies that the function is performed properly. That is, if a succession plan is in place, the assumption is that it is a good one; if there is a risk committee, the company takes risk management seriously; if compensation is not excessive, it encourages performance. Throughout this book, we have seen clear evidence that this is not always the case. If experts and proxy advisory firms are to add any value, they should shift from a service that verifies that features are in place, to one that evaluates the success of various functions. This no doubt would require a substantial increase in analytical skills and processes, but it is a shift that markets would likely value.

Important Variables Are Clearly Missing

Third, the lack of positive correlation suggests that important variables that impact governance quality have been inappropriately omitted or underemphasized in the discipline. After all, governance is an *organizational* discipline. As such, the analysis should incorporate organizational issues—such as personal and interpersonal dynamics, and models of behavior, leadership, cooperation, and decision making. Without offering a comprehensive list, we believe the following elements are central to understanding how a governance system should be structured and when and where it is likely to fail:

- **Organizational design**—Is the company decentralized or centralized in structure? Have internal processes been rigorously developed, or did they evolve from historical practice?

- **Organizational culture**—Does the culture encourage individual performance, or cooperation? How are successes and failures treated? Is risk-taking encouraged, tolerated, or discouraged?

- **The personality of the CEO**—Who is the CEO, and what motivates this individual? What is his or her leadership style? What are the individual's ethical standards?

- **The quality of the board**—What are the qualifications of these individuals? Why and how were they selected? Are they engaged in their responsibility, or do they approach it with a compliance-based mindset? What is their character?

As evidence, we saw throughout this book that some of these aspects appear in the literature but often peripherally and without thorough consideration. For example, an analysis of the linguistic patterns of the CEO and CFO is shown to have some relation to the probability that the company will have to restate earnings in the future (see Chapter 10). Strong leadership, clear access to information, and parameters around corporate risk taking are important in ensuring that the company develops an appropriate risk culture (see Chapter 6, "Organizational Strategy, Business Models, and Risk Management"). Directors with extensive personal and professional networks facilitate the flow of information between companies. This can lead to improved decision making by both allowing for the transfer of best practices and acting as a source of important business relationships (see Chapter 5, "Board of Directors: Structure and Consequences").

We believe that these types of analyses should be pursued further and with greater rigor. Doing so will require tools and techniques across disciplines. It is a mistake to think that corporate governance can be adequately understood from a strict economic, legal, or behavioral (psychological and sociological) perspective. All of these views are necessary to understanding complex organizational systems.

Furthermore, this necessarily implies that the optimal governance system of an organization will be firm-specific and take into account its unique culture and attributes. Adopting "best practices" will likely fail because that approach attempts to reduce a complex human system into a standardized framework that does not do justice to the factors that make it successful in the first place. This explains why two companies can both succeed under very different governance structures.

Context Is Important

Finally, governance systems cannot be completely standardized because their design depends on the setting. For example, governance systems differ depending on whether you take a shareholder perspective or a stakeholder perspective of the firm, as well as the efficiency of local capital markets and labor markets. They also differ depending on your view of the prevalence of self-interest among executives.

Consider, for example, John Bogle, founder of Vanguard, who has written about self-interested behavior among executives:

> Self-interest got out of hand. It created a bottom-line society in which success is measured in monetary terms. Dollars became the coin of the new realm. Unchecked market forces overwhelmed traditional standards of professional conduct, developed over centuries. The result is a shift from moral absolutism to moral relativism. We've moved from a society in which "there are some things that one simply does not do" to one in which "if everyone else is doing it, I can, too."[2]

The extent to which you believe this is the norm in society will have a direct impact on the extent to which you believe control mechanisms should be in place to prevent the occurrence of self-interested behavior and the rigor of those controls. Nevertheless, in the end, a balance must be struck. Excessive controls will lead to economic loss by retarding the rate of corporate activity and decision making. Lenient controls will lead to economic loss through agency costs and managerial rent extraction.

As this book demonstrates, context is critical to designing an effective corporate governance system.

Endnotes

1. Myron Steele, "Verbatim: 'Common Law Should Shape Governance,'" *NACD Directorship*, February 15, 2010. Accessed November 16, 2010. See www.directorship.com/verbatim-myron-steele/.

2. John C. Bogle, "A Crisis of Ethic Proportions," *Wall Street Journal* (April 21, 2009, Eastern Edition): A.19.

INDEX

F

Q–R